Introducing Aviary

Mike Peutz

friendsof

DESIGNER TO DESIGNER™

an Apress® company

Introducing Aviary

Copyright © 2009 by Mike Peutz

ISBN-13 (pbk): 978-1-4302-7201-4

ISBN-13 (electronic): 978-1-4302-7200-7

Printed and bound in the United States of America 9 8 7 6 5 4 3 2 1

Trademarked names may appear in this book. Rather than use a trademark symbol with every occurrence of a trademarked name, we use the names only in an editorial fashion and to the benefit of the trademark owner, with no intention of infringement of the trademark.

Distributed to the book trade worldwide by Springer-Verlag New York, Inc., 233 Spring Street, 6th Floor, New York, NY 10013. Phone 1-800-SPRINGER, fax 201-348-4505, e-mail orders-ny@springer-sbm.com, or visit www.springeronline.com.

For information on translations, please e-mail info@apress.com, or visit www.apress.com.

Apress and friends of ED books may be purchased in bulk for academic, corporate, or promotional use. eBook versions and licenses are also available for most titles. For more information, reference our Special Bulk Sales—eBook Licensing web page at http://www.apress.com/info/bulksales.

The information in this book is distributed on an "as is" basis, without warranty. Although every precaution has been taken in the preparation of this work, neither the author(s) nor Apress shall have any liability to any person or entity with respect to any loss or damage caused or alleged to be caused directly or indirectly by the information contained in this work.

The source code for this book is freely available to readers at www.friendsofed.com in the Downloads section.

Credits

President and Publisher:
Paul Manning

Lead Editor:
Ben Renow-Clarke

Technical Reviewer:
Meowza Katz

Editorial Board:
Clay Andres, Steve Anglin, Mark Beckner,
Ewan Buckingham, Gary Cornell, Jonathan Gennick,
Jonathan Hassell, Michelle Lowman, Matthew Moodie,
Duncan Parkes, Jeffrey Pepper, Frank Pohlmann,
Douglas Pundick, Ben Renow-Clarke,
Dominic Shakeshaft, Matt Wade, Tom Welsh

Copy Editor:
Kelly Moritz

Copy Editor:
Ginny Munroe

Indexer:
BIM Indexing & Proofreading Services

Artist:
April Milne

Cover Designer:
Kurt Krames

This book is dedicated to my ever patient and loving wife, Beth.

Contents at a Glance

Contents

About the Author

Mike Peutz is a graphic designer who has worked in the printing industries for several years. He recieved a bachelor of fine arts degree in 2001 and has since taught himself digital image editing. For the past year and a half, he has helped moderate the Aviary.com site to assist users, study the applications, and write tutorials for the site. Along with other users, Mike has written commprehensive documentation for the Aviary.com application suite. You can see his work by visiting his Aviary profile Aviary.com/artists/mpeutz.

About the Technical Reviewer

 **Meowza Katz** is a self-taught graphic artist and illustrator from Vancouver, BC, Canada, who has been a full-time freelance artist since 2004. His work has been seen in media all over the world and includes logo design, graphics, and branding for Aviary.com. He has had work featured in and he has written image-editing tutorials for various publications including *ImagineFX, Advanced Photoshop, Mac|Life*, and *.PSD Magazine*. He authored Aviary's first image-editing tutorial book *More Than One Way to Skin a Cat.* His personal work can be found on his website www.meowza.org. Meowza also likes colorful pants.

Acknowledgments

I want to thank the creative and supportive staff at Aviary for making such an incredible service. Thanks to Avi for giving me this opportunity. The dedication and passion of the people of Avi are evident in their work, and they make it possible for everyone to tap into the creative side.

Huge thanks goes to the helpful community of artists at Aviary. They are always eager to ask and answer any question that arises. A special thanks to Redstar, Bassp, Cobra405, Lynx, Stevek, and Meowza who helped with advice, support, and patience.

Introduction

Aviary is an incredible service. I was hooked as soon as I started using it. It wasn't nessisarilly the applications that impressed me at first; it was the idea that anyone who had a computer could create and edit images. It was a game-changing idea. No longer did you have to buy expensive desktop applications. Oh sure, there are great open source alternatives, but the learning curve of those application is steep. Aviary's applications, which have to run in a user's browser, are pared down to the base features that a graphic editor needs. This has wonderful side effects: The applications are straight forward, and the tools are easy to use. These simple applications are perfect for users who are just learning digital graphics and they are great tools for teachers.

Aviary draws many who want desperately to learn; however, with the staff busy building and maintaining the applications, there is little documentation about the tools. Meowza Katz wrote a book of Phoenix tutorials that was a huge success and helped the growing community of artists. His book addresses only one application; there is demand for documentation of the other applications. Last year, Lyxs approached me about creating unofficial user documentation about Peacock, Aviary's most complex application. We collaborated, and with the help of Copper, we created the Peacock wiki, a comprehensive overview of the application. It was well recived and was added to the Aviary site. This led to Raven, Toucan, Talon, and Falcon documentations with more comming. Because of this documentation, I was given the opportunity to write this book and jumped at the chance. The community asked for a just this type of documentation. I hope that it helps Aviary users understand the suite of tools, enabling them to tap into their creativity.

Layout Conventions

To keep this book as clear and easy to follow as possible, the following text conventions are used throughout.

Important words or concepts are normally highlighted on the first appearance in **bold type**.

Code is presented in `fixed-width font`.

New or changed code is normally presented in **`bold fixed-width font`**.

Pseudo-code and variable input are written in *`italic fixed-width font`*.

Menu commands are written in the form **Menu ➤ Submenu ➤ Submenu**.

Where I want to draw your attention to something, I've highlighted it like this:

Ahem, don't say I didn't warn you.

Sometimes code won't fit on a single line in a book. Where this happens, I use an arrow like this: ➥.

This is a very, very long section of code that should be written all on the same ➥

line without a break.

Chapter 1

Welcome to the Aviary

Have you ever wanted to create stunning images on your computer to discover that the preinstalled programs lack key features or are too clumsy to be efficient? On the other hand, a full-fledged desktop graphic-editing program costs thousands of dollars and has hundreds of features that you will never use. There is a solution. It is a computer graphic revolution called Aviary. Aviary is an online service that enables you to upload, edit, create, and manage images. You no longer have to install large programs or be tied down to a single computer. All of Aviary's applications are hosted online and you can access them and your Images on any computer or mobile device that has Internet access and the Flash Player plug-in. The applications run on most browsers; they also work on most operating systems, including Linux. Aviary and its suite of creation applications set you free, enabling you to make creations on the fly.

You might ask what exactly Aviary applications do. The Aviary tools give you the power to create and manipulate images without the need to purchase and maintain software on your computer. Furthermore, all of your images can be stored on Aviary's servers, so you can keep precious hard drive space for other things. Because these creations are stored on the servers, you can access them from any computer connected to the Internet. This is a revolutionary idea that gives you the ability to create images no matter where you are. It is creation "on the fly."

Aviary's six graphic applications

Currently, Aviary's suite of tools consists of six tools. The true power of these tools becomes apparent when they are used together. Aviary also has a seventh application, the audio editor Myna; however it is not discussed in this book.

Phoenix is Aviary's image editor. Phoenix enables you to create, manipulate, and combine bitmap images. It uses industry standard applications that enable you to alter tones, colors, and contrast in images. Its many selection tools make it easy to isolate, copy, paste, and transform areas in a bitmap. Phoenix also has a powerful painting system that lets you paint with shape brushes, erase, clone, and liquefy. Arguably the most important feature of Phoenix is the layer system that lets you stack and merge images in editable layers, which can be saved and edited in different sessions.

Raven is Aviary's vector image editor. Vectors are the heart and soul of logo design, print graphics, and digital illustrations. Raven has a robust path system that makes it easy to construct detailed and intricate shapes. Geometric objects can be created directly on the canvas or set with predefined parameters. Layers and blend modes let you take these created shapes and paths and merge them in interesting and complex ways. Raven also has the capability to import bitmaps for textures or to use as an image that you can manually trace. The cherry on top of this application is the built-in bitmap-to-vector trace function that enables you to automatically change a bitmap image, such as a photograph that you change into a vector image. Finally, these Raven creations can be taken with you anywhere with an SVG export system, making it an indispensable tool for any designer.

Peacock is Aviary's effects editor that enables you to construct mind-boggling graphical effects. Its hub system uses a visual, intuitive method to create effects, and you can chain over 60 different hubs to build advanced effects. These effects are a great way to open new avenues of creation possibilities. It is also exciting to connect and adjust parameters to make compelling effects. It is possible to create unique, evocative images from the great diversity of the hubs—it just takes is a little experimentation. With UI Element hubs, Peacock gives you the ability to create what Aviary calls Blackboxes, which are reusable custom effect modules. These Blackboxes can be imported into Phoenix as custom filters, making it easy to add complex effects to your images. The Peacock effects rival those in expensive desktop programs.

  Toucan, Falcon, and **Talon** are specialized applications at Aviary. They help the other applications and can take your creativity to the next level. Toucan is Aviary's swatch editor that enables you to create color palettes using different color harmony formulas. You can alter, arrange, and sample colors from various sources to build colors to use in all of Aviary's applications. Falcon is Aviary's lightweight image markup editor. With it, you can crop, resize, and add graphics to any of your images or captures. Talon is Aviary's Firefox® add-on that enables you to take screen shots of anything you might stumble upon while exploring the Web. It is tightly integrated into the rest of the applications, so you can quickly edit captures with any of Aviary's applications.

Application switching lets you tap into all of Aviary's applications and features. At first glance, many might think that the applications are underpowered compared with the big desktop rivals. When treated as standalone applications, there is some weight to that argument; however, with application switching, the smaller parts come together to make a graphics program that equals the professional desktop graphic editors. Jump from Phoenix's image-editing tools to Raven's vector paths, tie them together with Peacock's effects, and then sprinkle in screenshots from Talon, make adjustments with Falcon, and unify the colors with Toucan.

Aviary has three subscription levels: Fledgling, Pro, and Student. Everyone who signs up for Aviary is started at the free Fledgling level. As a Fledgling, you are given access to the applications and the rest of the Aviary site. You are able to comment on other posts or write your own in the forum, and you have access to basic tutorials. It is a great level to test the power that Aviary has to offer at no cost to you. For a small, yearly fee, you can upgrade to a Pro subscription. The bargain price gets you the added benefit of access to unreleased alpha prototype applications. It also lets you set the viewing permission on your creations, so that you can control who sees your images. It is a great way to hide an image before you are ready for the community to gush at the creativity. With a Pro subscription, you can create and administer user groups that enable you to have private collaborations with other users. Finally if you are currently in school or an educator, you can get a Student subscription at a reduced price. The Student level gets you unlimited creations and access to private groups.

Cloud computing and Aviary

Aviary is a cloud computing service. In cloud computing, resources are provided as a service over the Internet. Like a real cloud, the internal workings of cloud computing are obscured from the average user. You send information to the cloud; it is processed and then returned to your computer (see Figure 1-1). You do not have to know how to install, set up, and maintain software other than an Internet connection and a web browser. It works immediately. Furthermore, because the service is hosted in the cloud, you have access to the same service from any computer. Your creations are stored in the cloud, too. The entire Aviary library can be accessed while you are on the move. It is immediate, user friendly, and decentralized.

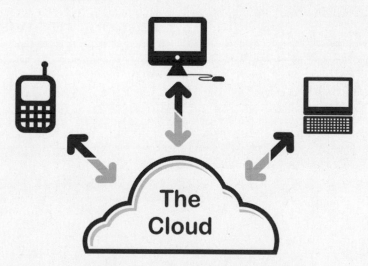

Figure 1-1. Aviary is a service that performs image manipulation in the cloud.

Another advantage to hosting your Aviary creations in the cloud is that all of your images are stored there and do not take up space on your hard drive. They are secure and backed up. If your computer hard drive fails or your laptop is lost, all your Aviary images are safe and accessible to you on the server. You also never have to worry about transferring them to a new computer when you change or upgrade hardware. The cloud computing model that Aviary uses takes the worry out of managing images and files and lets you focus on creating stunning images.

Project 1.1—Signing Up for Your Aviary Account

You can use some of Aviary's features without an account, but the features are limited and to access all the awesome features of Aviary, it is highly recommended that you sign up for an account. It is easy to sign up for an account and doing so gives you access to Aviary's site and applications from any computer.

1. First, point your browser to `http://aviary.com/` to see the Welcome screen (see Figure 1-2). Here, you can learn about the applications, watch videos, and even launch example files. However, the first thing that you should do if you haven't visited Aviary before is set up an account. You can sign up for an account by either clicking the `Sign up!` link at the top, right of the screen or by clicking `Create your account` in the lower, right of the screen.

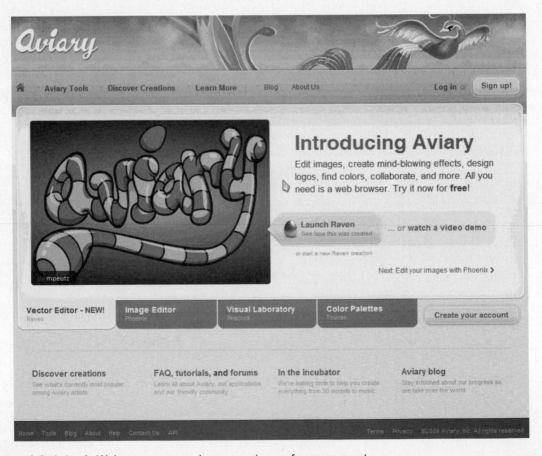

Figure 1-2. Aviary's Welcome screen where you sign up for an account

2. You are presented with the Account Creation page. This is where you set a username and password that identify you on the site, and this is where you agree to the `Terms of Use`. You need to fill out a few things to create an account (see Figure 1-3). These are self-explanatory, so you shouldn't have any problems. They are as follows:

> `Username`: This is where you choose and enter your nickname to identify you on the site. It must be more than three characters long, and consist of letters and numbers only. It cannot contain spaces, symbols, or already be in use by another member.
>
> `Email address`: Your email is used to contact you if you forget your password, to set up email notifications, or to opt you into the newsletter.
>
> `Password/Confirm it`: Sets the password to access your Aviary account.
>
> `Human check`: This ensures you are a human.
>
> `Email opt-in`: Check this box if you want to receive a periodic newsletter from the Aviary staff.
>
> `The legit bit`: You must read and agree to the `Terms of Use` before you can create your account.

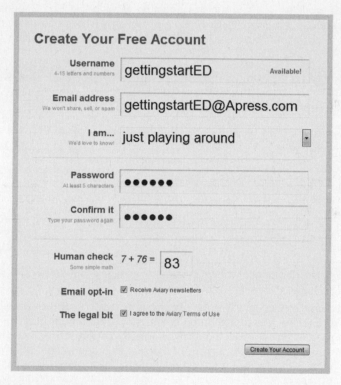

Figure 1-3. The Create Your Free Account form

*The **Terms of Use** is an explanation of the service provided by Aviary. This contains a list of exclusions and cases where Aviary disclaims liability, alters service, discontinues service, uses artists' work, and more. It is highly recommended that you take time to look at the **Terms of Use**. The staff at Aviary has written an entertaining and easy-to-understand summary. This is the way Terms of Services should be explained. You should also read and understand the **Privacy Policy** and the **Copyright Policy**. You can find a link to all three documents at the bottom of every page on Aviary: **terms**, **privacy**, and ©2009 Aviary, Inc.***

3. After you sign up for an account, you are presented with the **Find Your Friends on Aviary** option to search various email contact lists where you can find your friends (see Figure 1-4). If someone in your email contact list has signed up for an account on Aviary, his or her name is displayed with an option to add them as a contact. You can have Aviary pull contacts from your various email services by clicking on the appropriate button. This is a great way to get connected with your friends. If you want to wait and have Aviary find your friends later, or, if you get a different email provider, you can run this again by clicking the Find Friends button 🔍 Find friends on **Your Dashboard's** sidebar. Click the **You** option in the green navigation bar at the top of each page to access your Dashboard (see Chapter 10 for more information on your Dashboard).

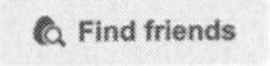

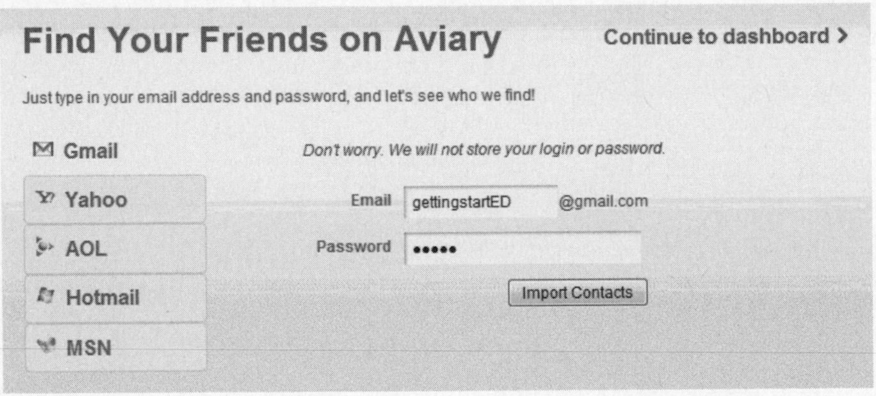

Figure 1-4. Have Aviary look for friends who might already be signed up on the site

4. Now, you just need to sign in with your **Username** and **Password** to access the site (see Figure 1-5). Aviary also allows you to sign in once and stay logged in on that computer even after you have left the site. To do this, click the **Stay logged in on this computer?** option; you will stay logged in until you manually log out of the site. You can log out at any time by pressing the Logout button that is located at the upper, right of any Aviary page. Use this option only if you are on your own secure computer. If you forget your password, you can have Aviary email it to you using the **Forgot your password?** option located directly under the **Password** label.

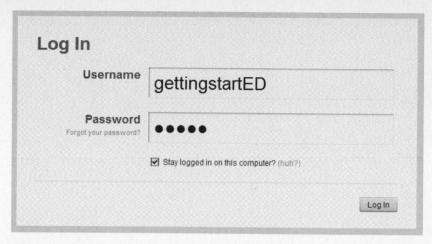

Figure 1-5. The Log In screen

Chapter Review

The Aviary application's name implies that it is a place where birds congregate, mingle, and roost. All of the applications are names of birds. Phoenix, the mythical bird of rebirth, is the image editor application. The grandly ornate Peacock is an effects editor. The brooding Raven is a vector editor. The colorful Toucan creates color palettes. There is the fast and nimble Falcon image markup application, and Talon is the dexterous screen capture extension that rounds out the flock. Aviary hosts the applications and all your images in the cloud, so you do not have to manage, transfer, or worry about losing your images. It is quick and easy to sign up for an account to get access to these free and powerful tools and to engage with a large, active community of fellow artists. In this book, you learn how to use these applications to create images that rival the ones made with professional desktop programs. Next, you jump right into the wonderful world of creativity with Aviary.

Chapter 2

Creating Images with Phoenix

Phoenix is a full-featured image editor that is similar to many of the desktop image editors you might have seen or used. Many of the tools are located in the same vicinity and act similarly. Aviary is designed this way to make it easy for people who have used other applications to learn Aviary. Phoenix enables you to manipulate images in various ways, build files in layers, and save files to keep objects separated for easy editing. You can adjust the color, brightness, and contrast of images. A versatile selection system enables you to isolate and alter intricate and complex areas of images. With the Clone and Liquefy tools, you can push, pull, and relocate pixels. Phoenix might at first look like a simple image editor, but as you will see in this chapter, it is sophisticated and enables you to create incredible images.

Launching Aviary's tools

Aviary gives you several ways to launch Phoenix from different locations around the site, and if you have the Talon Firefox® or Chrome extension, you can launch an application any time your web browser is open.

You can launch Phoenix or any of the other tools from your Aviary Dashboard page. The Dashboard is your start page when you sign into Aviary, so it is an ideal place to display the launch button. On the right side of the page are launch buttons for all the Aviary tools, as shown in Figure 2-1.

9

Figure 2-1. The Phoenix launch button on your Dashboard page

You can also launch any of the tools from the green menu bar that is at the top of each page on the site. Hovering the mouse over the **Create** menu opens a launch dropdown menu. In this menu, you can launch a tool, upload an image, or even find more information about the various tools by clicking the buttons (see Figure 2-2).

Figure 2-2. The **Create** menu lets you launch all of Aviary's tools.

You can also launch a creation (a file that is created using Aviary) in various tools from its creation page. Each creation has a page with information, comments, and more specific options related to that image. Above each one is a launch button; when you click this button, it launches the image in the tool it was created in. Furthermore, if you hover the mouse over this button (see Figure 2-3), a dropdown menu displays that lets you launch a different tool and automatically import the creation. This is a great way to explore images Aviary users create to see how they are made.

Figure 2-3. Launch a tool and automatically import a creation from the launcher on a creation page.

Finally, if you use Firefox® or Chrome as your web browser, you can download Aviary's Talon extension. It gives you the ability to take screen shots or launch any of the Aviary tools. After you install Talon, an extra Aviary button on the browser's menu bar becomes available. Clicking this button gives you a dropdown menu that has commands to launch all of Aviary's tools (see Figure 2-4). If you get an idea for a creation while surfing the Web, you can launch a tool immediately from the menu instead of going to the Aviary site.

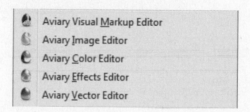

Figure 2-4. Talon's tool launcher menu

Phoenix basics

Let's take a quick look at Phoenix. First, launch Phoenix by opening your web browser and going to www.aviary.com. Sign in to your account, and the Dashboard page will display. On the right side of the page is a sidebar with the launch buttons. Click the `Image Editor` button to launch Phoenix. The application opens with a splash screen and two options: `Start from Scratch` and `Load existing file`. `Start from Scratch` takes you to the `New File` screen that enables you to set your file's dimensions. The default size is 625 by 625 pixels. `Load existing file` takes you to the Load File screen where you can import an image from your computer or from an Internet URL address into your new file. Choose the `Start from Scratch` option and accept the default canvas size by clicking the `Create` button. When you first open the application, you can see the tool icons on the left side of the workspace and a color selector under them. To the right is the Layer and History panel, and at the top is the HTML Save bar and the `File` menu bar.

Phoenix has a robust set of tools. Each icon has a specific function and just needs to be clicked to activate it. Some of the tools are stacked in the same icon. To access these, click the icon; a fly-out with the extra tool opens. As you progress through each project, a more thorough explanation of each tool is presented. For now, following is a brief overview of each of the tools and its function.

 The Move tool is used to quickly move objects and layers without confirmation.

 The Transformation tool is used to move, skew, rotate, and scale an object.

 The Distortion tool is used to stretch an object like a sheet of rubber.

 The Rectangular Selection tool is used to select a square section of an object.

 The Circular Selection tool is used to select a circular section of an object.

 The Freeform Selection tool is used to draw a selection of an object.

 The Polygonal Selection tool is used to select an irregular section of an object.

 The Magic Wand tool is used to select a certain color range.

 The Paintbrush tool is used to paint on a layer.

 The Shape Brush tool is used to paint shaped brushes.

 The Eraser tool erases areas on a layer.

 The Color Replacement tool replaces the color of a painted area.

 The Paint Bucket tool fills a color range with a flat color.

 The Gradient Fill tool fills an area with color gradients.

 The Eye Dropper tool changes the current color to the one that has been sampled by the tool.

The Shape tool draws geometric shapes. There are six basic shapes.

 The Text tool adds text to a layer.

 The Smudge tool is used to move and blend pixels.

 The Dodge/Burn tool is used to increase lightness or darkness that is painted.

 The Blur tool blurs the area that is painted.

 The Sharpen tool sharpens an area that is painted.

 The Liquefy tool pushes, pulls, and blends pixels as if they were liquid.

 The Clone Stamp tool enables you to clone parts of an image to a painted area.

On the opposite side of the tools, on the right side of the application and above it is the **Layers** panel (see Figure 2-5); below it is the **History** panel. The **Layers** panel shows each individual layer in a file. A **layer** is a group of pixels that acts as a distinct image and is isolated from other layers. You can think of a layer as a sheet of clear acetate that you can draw on and add more layers above and below to build an image while keeping the parts separate. Layers have effects, transformations, and Blend Modes that are applied to all the pixels currently on the layer. The editing power of Phoenix is in its layer-based file system. You can manipulate, layer, and merge individual layers while keeping other layers unaltered. The Layers panel also contains many layer-specific commands such as **Duplications**, **Alpha**, **Blend Modes**, **Layer Filters**, and more.

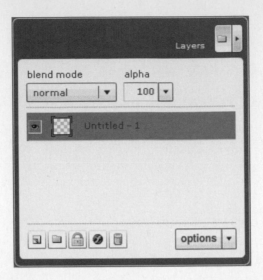

Figure 2-5. The Layers panel is where you can organize all the layers in your file.

Below the **Layers** panel is the **History** panel (see Figure 2-6). The **History** panel displays the past 15 commands you used. This enables you to go back to a previous state in your file. If you find that you made a mistake several steps back, you can find it in the step you want to backtrack to by using the **History** panel. It also has a preview, so you can visually identify the step you want to find.

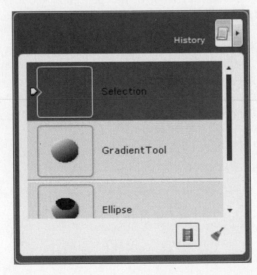

Figure 2-6. The History panel shows the previous 15 actions you took, so you can go back to a previous step to fix a mistake.

At the top of the application is the HTML bar and the menu bar (see Figure 2-7). The blue HTML bar shows the title of the current file, when it was last saved, and the **Save** button that enables you to save the file. The **Save as** command opens the **HTML Save** dialog box where you can name your file, add tags, and set permissions for your file. Directly below this is the menu bar, which includes the commands for Phoenix. Here, you have specific commands for the file grouped in eight dropdown menus: **File**, **Edit**, **Image**, **Layer**, **Select**, **Filters**, **Feedback**, and **Help**.

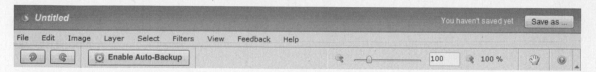

Figure 2-7. The menu bar gives you access to most of the Phoenix commands.

Under the tool icons is the color selector (see Figure 2-8). This is where you can select the overall colors that are used with the tools and functions in Phoenix. Two colors can be selected at one time: the foreground color represented in the upper left box and the background color in the lower right box. To change the colors, double-click either box to display the color selector. The foreground color sets the fill of the shapes, the color of lines, and the color of the paint bucket fill. The background color sets the outline color of shapes. The black and white icon at the lower left resets the colors to black foreground and white background. The arrow icon in the upper right side will reverse the foreground and background colors.

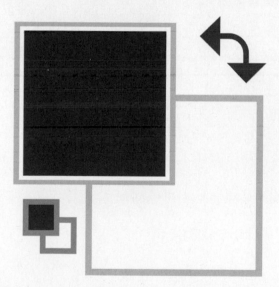

Figure 2-8. The color selector shows the currently selected foreground and background colors.

Project 2.1—Create a Simple Depth of Field Image from Scratch

Phoenix has several tools that let you create images from scratch. In this first project, you are introduced to the basics of Phoenix and you create an image without outside resources. You explore the functions of selections, gradient fills, and layers. You create two spheres and simulate depth by adding shadows and highlights to those objects. We also discuss how to achieve this depth using different effects, sizing, and placement of objects. Figure 2-9 shows what you will create in this project.

Figure 2-9. This is the image you will make in this project.

Key features used in this project

- Layers
- Layer filters
- Gradients
- Circular selections

Find this file online at
http://aviary.com/artists/gettingstartED/creations/chapter_2_project_1.

1. Launch Phoenix if it isn't already open, and then click the **Start from Scratch** option. On the **New File** menu, switch the Background Color from transparent to white (see Figure 2-10). Leave the default width and height so that your canvas is square. Click the **create** button to initialize the new file. A white square fills the workspace. This is your canvas. Like Phoenix, Raven and Peacock also have a canvas. Your final image displays only what is inside of the canvas.

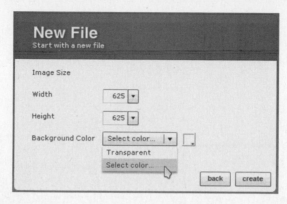

Figure 2-10. **New File** dialog

2. Add a new layer to the file by clicking the icon in the Layers panel. It is good practice to name your layers so that it is easy to identify them as your file grows in complexity. Layers are assigned the name **Untitled**, which is followed by a number when they are created. To change this, double-click the default title to edit the layer's name. Name the initial layer Background and the newly created one Shadow (see Figure 2-11).

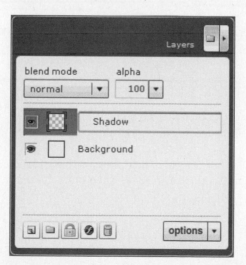

Figure 2-11. Naming layers in the Layers panel

The **Layers** panel displays all the layers in a file and is located at the upper right of the application (see Figure 2-12). Phoenix files use layers to organize elements in a file. Just think of layers as transparent pieces of glass stacked up on top of each other (see Figure 2-13). When drawing on or altering one of these layers, the other layers are unaffected. This is a great way of grouping or isolating specific elements in a file. Furthermore, these layers can be blended together in different ways, giving you ultimate control over your image. See Appendix A for an explanation of Blend Modes.

Figure 2-12. The Layers panel

Figure 2-13. Think of layers as stacked pieces of glass. Here are three objects on three layers tilted to demonstrate the stack.

3. To begin the image, first, you create the shadow for the spheres. Start by selecting the Elliptical Shape tool from the Rectangular Shape tool's fly-out. However, before you draw on the canvas, you need to change the **Alpha** of the shadow's shape. Click the black box in the Shape tool fly-out. These are the fill and stroke color indicators, and by clicking on either one, you can open the Color Picker to change the color or **Alpha**. Keep the color black, but set the **Alpha** to 55 (see Figure 2-14).

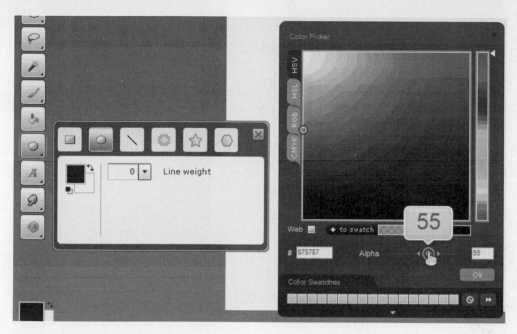

Figure 2-14. Use the Color Picker to set color and Alpha fill.

4. Next, draw two ellipses on the canvas with the Ellipse tool . Do this by clicking where you want the one corner of the ellipse to start and dragging diagonally. The ellipse is drawn between the start point and the mouse cursor. Make the ellipses wider than tall to simulate a shadow on a horizontal surface by drawing the ellipse further horizontally and then vertically to achieve this (see Figure 2-15). Because you are trying to create a sense of depth, make the back ellipse smaller than the front. Notice that these ellipses look gray because of the 55% **Alpha**. Shadows are rarely completely black.

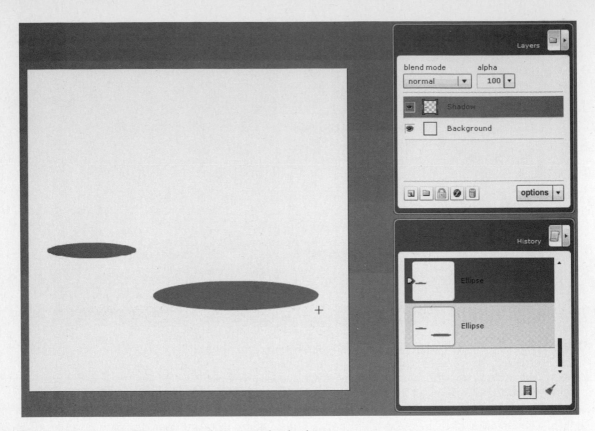

Figure 2-15. Use the Ellipse tool to draw some basic shapes.

5. Next, you need to blur the edges of the ellipses to make the shadow more believable. To do this, you use a Layer Filter. Open the Layer Filters panel by clicking the `Layer Filter` button in the Layers panel. Because you want to soften the edges of the shadows, check the box next to the `Blur` option in the Layer Filters panel. Now, change the settings to 40 for `Blur x` and 10 for `Blur y`. This softens the edge of the shapes by 40 pixels horizontally and 10 pixels vertically (see Figure 2-16). The reason you are not using the same settings for the x and y blurs is because they are simulating depth. If the shadow had a uniformed blur, it would flatten it. However, if you give them a stronger horizontal blur, it looks as if the object is laying on a horizontal surface because the leading and trailing edges are foreshortened. See Figure 2-17 for an example of the difference between uniform blur and stretched blur.

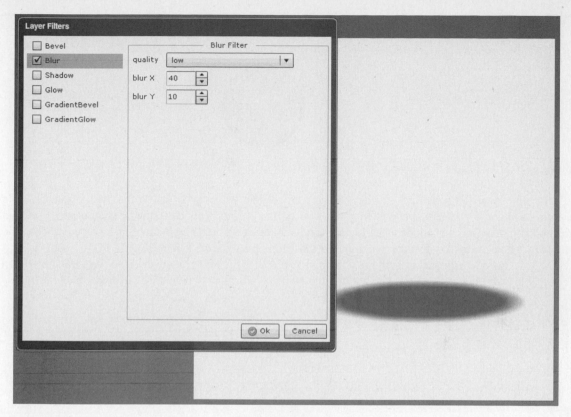

Figure 2-16. Layer Filters are a nondestructive way to add effects to objects.

Figure 2-17. You can see the difference between the left image with a uniform blur as opposed to the right image, which has a different Blur x and Blur y radii. The right image gives a stronger sense of perspective than the left.

Layer Filters are effects that can be applied to any layer. You can activate the function with the **Layers Filters** button at the bottom of the Layers panel (see Figure 2-18).

Figure 2-18. The **Layer Filters** button can be found at the bottom of the Layers panel.

These effects are nondestructive, which means they retain the original still in the file, enabling you to return to them if you are unhappy with the effects you create. You can alter a layer's pixels without committing permanent changes to the original pixels. At any time in the creation process, you can open the **Layer Filters** dialog to adjust or remove the filter. Because the original pixels in the layer are still there, you always have access to them. It is advisable you use a Layer Filter whenever you want to add an effect to a layer, because an effect might need to be adjusted later when you are building a file.

There are six distinct Layer Filters:
Bevel Layer Filter: Creates a highlight and shadow to simulate a raised, three-dimensional (3D) effect (see Figure 2-19).

Figure 2-19. The Bevel Layer Filter

Blur Layer Filter: Creates a blurring effect (see Figure 2-20).

Figure 2-20. The Blur Layer Filter

Shadow Layer Filter: Creates a shadow under or inside an object (see Figure 2-21).

Figure 2-21. The Shadow Layer Filter

Glow Layer Filter: Creates a colored halo around or inside an object (see Figure 2-22).

Figure 2-22. The Glow Layer Filter

Gradient Bevel Layer Filter: Creates a bevel effect with multiple colors (see Figure 2-23).

Figure 2-23. The Gradient Bevel Layer Filter

Gradient Glow Layer Filter: Creates a glow effect with multiple colors (see Figure 2-24).

Figure 2-24. The Gradient Glow Layer Filter

6. Now, create a new layer using the same method you used in Step 2 and name it Red Sphere. Lay out the first sphere by making a circular selection on the canvas using the Elliptical Selection tool 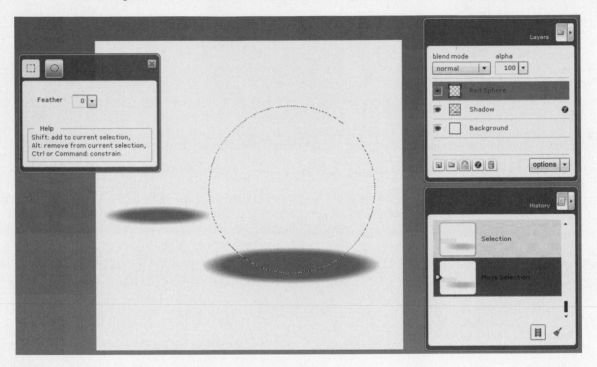. However, this time, while holding down the Ctrl key (or the Command key ⌘ on Apple keyboards), click and drag as you did for the shadow ellipses. Holding the Ctrl key down while drawing a selection can constrain the height and the width to the same dimension and make the selection a perfect circle. Make this selection about as wide as the biggest shadow shape. After you release the mouse button, you will see moving dotted outline of a circle. Finally, with the Select tool still active, click inside the selection area of the circle and position it so that the bottom center is aligned with the center of the shadow (see Figure 2-25).

Figure 2-25. Use selections to isolate an area on the layer.

The Elliptical Selection tool is used to isolate portions of an image (see Figure 2-26). This is useful for making changes selectively without affecting the entire image.

Figure 2-26. The Elliptical Selection tool lets you make a circular selection.

To create an elliptical selection, click to set the start point and drag while holding down the mouse button. This draws the elliptical selection in between these two points. After the mouse button is released, the size and shape of the elliptical selection is set. Click inside this selection to move its location. The `feather` parameter sets how much blur, in pixels, is applied to the edge of the selection. A setting of 0 produces a hard-edged selection and is the default setting. By using the Ctrl+C and Ctrl+V functions, selections can be copied and pasted to a new layer.

7. Now, select the **Gradient Fill** tool. It is located in the `Paint Bucket` fly-out menu. Click the Paint Bucket tool icon to activate the fly-out, and then select the **Gradient Fill** tool . The Gradient colorbar displays. This is where you set the colors for your gradient. The default setting is white fading to black. Every new gradient has two color stops; this one has a starting white one and an ending black one. A color stop is a defined color inside a gradient and is represented by a triangle control under the colorbar. These color stops can be move to different positions along the colorbar by dragging the triangle controls. To add additional colors to your gradient, click anywhere on the colorbar to add a new color stop set to black. Add a new color stop in between the two default color stops. Change this color stop's color to red by clicking on the triangle Icon to open the Color Picker, choosing a bright red color, and clicking OK (see Figure 2–27 and Figure 2–28). Now you have a gradient that starts white, fades to red, and then ends with black. Finally, to give the sphere a round appearance, set the `Gradient type` to Radial.

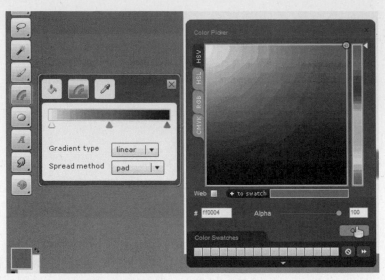

Figure 2-27. The Gradient tool and color selector

 The Gradient Fill tool is used to add blended color fills and can either be linear or radial (see Figure 2-28).

Figure 2-28. The Gradient Fill tool

A **linear** gradient's colors blend from a start point and travel in a straight line to an end point. These points are set by first clicking on the canvas to set the start, holding the mouse button down while dragging and releasing to set the end point. **Radial** gradient colors blend outward in all directions from the start to the end point. **Radial** gradients are set the same way as the linear gradients.

These gradients can consist of any two or more colors. The gradient setting colorbar in the fly-out parameter box is the area where colors are set in the gradient. The triangle icons are called color stops and can be dragged along the colorbar to set a gradient. There can be up to ten different color stops. Add a color stop by clicking on an area under the colorbar, set the color and Alpha by double-clicking a color stop, and delete a color stop by dragging it away from the colorbar. Finally, the **Spread method** sets how the gradient is drawn past the original area. With **Pad**, the end color is extended in the extended region; with **Reflect**, the gradient is reversed in the extended region; and with **Repeat**, the gradient is repeated in the extended region (see Figure 2-29).

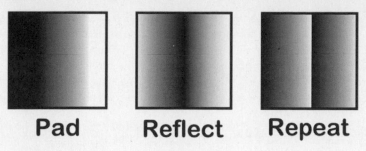

Figure 2-29. The Spread method defines how the gradient reacts in the extended regions.

8. Now, with the **Gradient Fill** tool still selected, go to the selected circle area that you created in Step 6. Starting just a little above and to the left of the selections center, click and drag in a 45-degree angle down, and then release the mouse just below the bottom of the selection, as in Figure 2-30. The gradient fills the selected area. If you don't like the results, you can fill until you get the gradient the way you want it. You can also move the red color stop in the gradient to change the amount of white or black in the gradient fill. Because the circular selection was used, this fill affects only the area inside. Using selections to section off areas in your images is a forgiving method to construct objects in your images. When you are satisfied with the sphere, use the `Selection ➤ Select None` command in the main menu. Alternatively, you can use the keyboard shortcut to cancel the selection; the shortcut is Ctrl+D or Command+D on the Mac.

Figure 2-30. The selection contains the gradient.

9. To create the second circle, repeat the steps used to create the first circle. First, create a new layer and name it Green Sphere. Then, use the Elliptical Selection tool while remembering to press the Ctrl key to keep it round. Be sure to create this circle smaller than the first one. Because you are simulating depth, this circle is going to be further behind the red sphere, and objects that are smaller appear further away. Finally, while the Elliptical Selection tool is still selected, you can move it so that it is centered above the second shadow (see Figure 2-31).

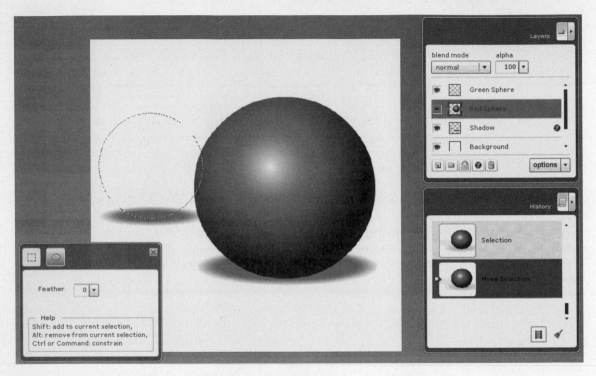

Figure 2-31. Move selections with the Elliptical Selection tool.

10. This time, change the sphere color by switching the red color to green in the gradient. This is done by double-clicking the color stop in the colorbar. Fill the selection with the new gradient (see Figure 2-32). Try to match the position and angle of the first sphere. Again, when you are satisfied, clear the selection with the **Select** ➤ **Select None** command or the Ctrl+D keyboard shortcut.

Figure 2-32. Fill the selection with the second gradient.

11. The green sphere, the smaller one, is positioned on top of the larger, red sphere, which is not how it should be. To give the illusion of the smaller sphere being further away, it needs to be behind the larger one. This is easy to do because you kept each object on its own layer. You can change which object is above another by arranging them in the **Layers** panel and by dragging them to change their order. Click and hold the green sphere layer and drag it directly under the red one. A black line shows where the layer is positioned when you release the mouse button. When this black line is in between the Red Sphere layer and the Shadow layer, release the mouse button to set the new layer order. In the image, notice that the spheres have changed their stacking order and the green is now behind the red sphere (see Figure 2-33 and Figure 2-34).

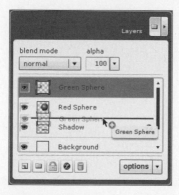

Figure 2-33. Drag layers to change the stacking order.

Figure 2-34. The stacking order is changed.

The image is almost done, but there is not quite enough depth to the image yet. This is because both spheres are in focus. When objects are further away, they lose focus and become blurry. You need to add blur to the green, smaller sphere using Layer Filters. Make sure the green sphere's layer is selected, and then open the Layer Filters panel by clicking the `Layer Filter` button. Activate the `Blur` effect and change the `Blur x` and `Blur y` settings to 8. This added blur gives these spheres a sense of depth (see Figure 2-35).

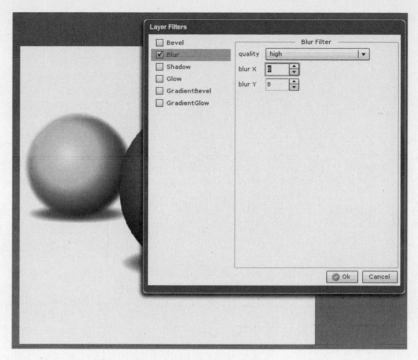

Figure 2-35. Using Layer Filters to blur the green, smaller sphere.

12. The background needs some depth, too. In the final step, you need to add a subtle gradient (see Figure 2-36). First, add a new layer and name it Background 2. Drag it to the position below the Shadow layer. Next, select the Gradient Fill tool and set the gradient white to light gray. To get back to only two color stops in this gradient, take the green stop and drag it away from the colorbar. This deletes that stop. Make sure there are only two stops and set them as white and light gray. Change the Gradient type back to Linear. Now, fill the new layer with the gradient by starting near the center of the image, clicking, and dragging upward. Play with the gradient until you get it the way you want it.

Figure 2-36. Add a background with a gradient.

13. Now that this image is finished, you need to save your creation. In the blue file management bar at the top of the application, click the `Save as` button (see Figure 2-37). This opens the save parameters. Set your Creation's title and add a Description, Tags, and Permissions. Then, click the `Save as a new creation` button. Your file shows up in the gallery for everyone to see.

Figure 2-37. The Save toolbar

Project review

In this project, you learned how to construct a layered file in Phoenix from scratch. Layers can be arranged and ordered by dragging them in the Layers panel. Naming layers is important to help organize a file for later and to let others easily navigate your files. You learned how to use Selection tools to isolate areas on layers and you learned how to set Gradient fill color to fill these selections. Layer Filters are useful for adding nondestructive effects to a layer. In the next project, you explore `Blend Modes` of layers used to combine layers. You also work with imported Resources to add text elements as graphics.

Project 2.2—Create a Grunge Style Collage Image

Grunge and dirty images are a popular graphic style. Many top designers have used these techniques to distress an image, imparting extra emotions to a standard stock image. In this project, you delve deeper into the Phoenix functions. In the first project, you were introduced to layers and you created objects. In this project, you take the power of layers to the next level using Blend Modes to combine imported resources. Blending layers is key to composing objects. Finally, you see how to use Phoenix's Text tool to add graphic elements to your file. See Figure 2–38 for the final image you will create in this project.

Figure 2-38. The final image created in this project.

Key features used in this project

- Layer Blend Modes
- Importing resources
- Color overlay
- Text tool

> *Find this file online at*
> *http://aviary.com/artists/gettingstartED/creations/chapter_2_project_2.*

1. Start this file with an image from your computer. Any photographic image will work. We used a portrait here. You also need a texture file to "distress" the portrait. You can use any texture you like here. We use a photograph of a wall with some cracked plaster. At the start screen, instead of selecting the **Starting from Scratch** option, use the **Load existing file** option to load your texture image. From the **Load File** screen, locate the texture you want to use either by browsing your computer or from an online location with a URL address (see Figure 2-39). Clicking the **Upload** button creates a new Phoenix file and imports the image you just selected, placing it on a new layer. Name this layer Crack Texture and name the lower layer Background (see Figure 2-40). Starting a file this way speeds up the creation process if you already know the texture of the image that you want to use in your file. Many sites offer textures for use in projects. The images that were used in this example are from `http://cgtextures.com`, a great royalty-free site.

Figure 2-39. Images can be started with an imported resource, such as a photograph.

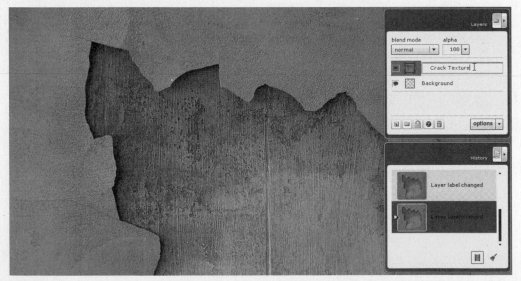

Figure 2-40. When an image is loaded from the start screen, the canvas is automatically sized to fit that resource.

2. Import the image of your main subject. This can be a portrait, an image of an object, or even a landscape. In this example, a portrait is used. Images that are imported into Phoenix are referred to on the site as resources. To import a resource, use the `Import File` function on the `File` menu (see Figure 2-41). This opens the `Resource Browser` window, which is different than initiating a file with an image as in Step 1. This window lets you import from many different sources, even from some online image sites, and it is standard for all applications. Navigate to and select the image to be imported, click on it, and then click `Upload File` (see Figure 2-42).

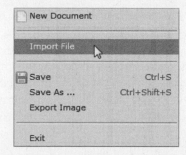

Figure 2-41. Use the `File` ➤ `Import File` command to add additional resources to a project.

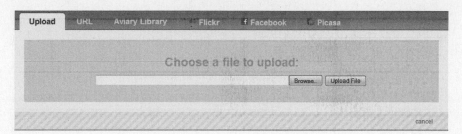

Figure 2-42. The Resource Browser window facilitates importing resources from many different sources.

3. On the chance your imported resource is bigger than the current canvas dimension, Phoenix prompts you to choose how it should handle the resource (see Figure 2-43). `Resize image` scales the resource to fit to the canvas, `Resize canvas` scales the canvas to match the resource, and `Crop image` crops the extra area from the resource so it will fit onto the canvas. For this image, choose `Resize image`. Phoenix creates a new layer and places the imported resource on it. As before, name this layer Portrait to keep your file organized.

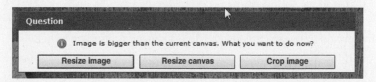

Figure 2-43. If the imported image is larger than the current canvas, you need to choose how Phoenix will handle the size differences.

4. The image of the main subject is too clean for the final result and needs some processing to make it suitable for a grunge style. Because you will color the image in later steps, we do not need any color in the portrait resource. Use the `Desaturate` feature located at `Image ➤ Desaturate` to remove the color from it (see Figure 2-44). Next, add a little noise distortion to the resource by using the `Jitter` filter. The `Jitter` filter is located in the main menu under the `Filters` tab. The `Jitter` filter does just that—it randomly shifts pixels around giving the image a rougher look. It depends on the size of image you are working with, but in this example, a Jitter setting of 6 gives you a nice amount of distortion without over powering (see Figure 2-45). Finally, adjust the `Levels` to add some extreme contrast to the subject (see Figure 2-46). `Levels` let you set the range of lightness and darkness in an image. This process uses more than the normal amount of your computer's processing, so it has its own preview window. Move the end controls on the slider under the graph or histogram to narrow the dark and light range. Next, move the center control to set the median gray in the image. For a grunge style, you want strong values and need to narrow the tonal range. Move the left minimum value control value to 75, the right maximum value to 157, and the middle midrange value to 102.

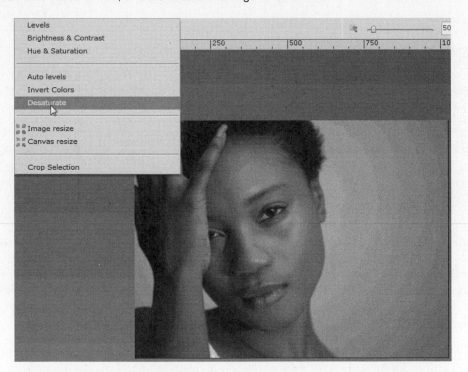

Figure 2-44. Use the Image ➤ Desaturate function to remove color from an image.

Figure 2-45. The Filters ➤ Jitter function adds some roughness to the image.

Filters are more powerful than Layer filters because they alter the actual pixels of an object. This makes them destructive; they permanently change the pixels in a layer. You can always use the Undo or History feature to remove a filter. However, only a set amount of history is saved, and if you surpass that amount, you cannot go back and remove the effect.

You can construct custom filters with Peacock using the Blackbox feature. See chapter 9 for information about Blackboxes and custom filters.

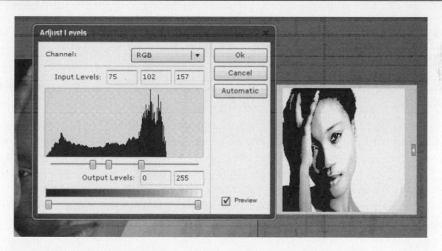

Figure 2-46. Control the tonal values in an image with Levels.

5. The portrait image looks good now, but it covers up the cracked texture underneath it. You want to blend these two resources together. This is easy to do with layer **Blend Modes**. **Blend Modes** combine the pixels in two layers together. You can achieve many different effects with the different **Blend Modes**. With the portrait layer selected, click the **Blend Mode** command to display a dropdown menu with the different modes. Because the grunge style is usually dark, pick **Multiply** from the menu (see Figure 2-47). This **Blend Mode** makes the light colored pixels in the Portrait layer transparent so that only the dark areas are left. This lets the underlying Crack Texture layer show. For more information about what each **Blend Mode** does, see Appendix A.

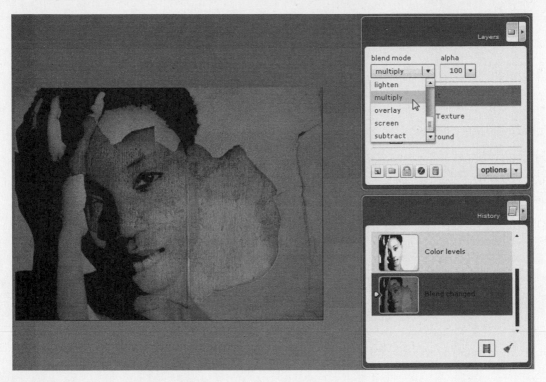

Figure 2-47. Use the multiply Blend Mode to combine the layers together.

6. Import another texture that is rough, but not too distracting because it gets layered over the subject. Here we've used a paint texture, again from www.cgtextures.com. Import this as you did in Step 2 to add it as a new layer above the others. Name this new layer **Texture Overlay**. Change the Blend Mode from normal to **Overlay** (see Figure 2-48). Overlay Blend Mode makes the mid value pixels transparent so only the darkest and lightest areas show up. This blends the layer with everything underneath it.

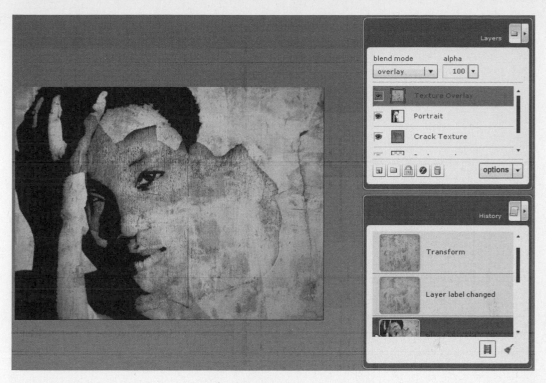

Figure 2-48. Add more texture to the image with another resource and set its **Blend Mode** to **Overlay**.

7. Create a new layer and name it Color. You use the Paint Bucket tool to fill an area with color. Before you fill the new layer, you need to set the fill color. Notice that in the lower right corner of Phoenix, under the tool icons, is the color selector. The two boxes represent the foreground and background colors. The box that is on top is the foreground color selector, and the covered square is the background color selector. Select the Paint Bucket tool. The Paint Bucket tool fills an area with the foreground color, so you just need to change the foreground color to brown. Click the foreground color to open the Color Picker. After the color is set, make sure the Color layer is still selected and click the canvas to fill it with the color. The layer **Blend Mode** needs to be changed to **Overlay,** letting the underlying elements show through it (see Figure 2-49). The advantage of doing a color overlay is that you can change the overall color in an image just by changing the color of the fill layer.

Figure 2-49. Use the Paint Bucket tool on a new layer to fill the whole layer with a color.

 The Paint Bucket Tool is used to fill areas with a single color (see Figure 2-50).

Figure 2-50. The Paint Bucket tool fills an area with a color.

To use this tool, select a color from the Color Picker, and then click the canvas to fill an area. The Paint Bucket tool fills all like-colored pixels that surround the initial click point. If the layer is empty, it fills the entire space. Clicking with this tool inside a selection isolates the fill operation to that area.

8. Text is a quick way to add graphics to your image without the need to import a resource. Many fonts contain graphics instead of letters; these fonts are called dingbats. Many dingbat fonts are

available for free on various sites. The ones used in this project can be found at www.DaFont.com.

Select the Text tool 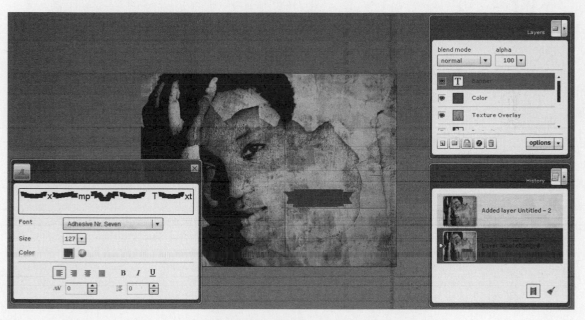 to open the Text tool's menu. Set the font to the dingbat font you are going to use. This project uses the font Adhesive Nr. Seven. Set the `Size` to 288 and the color to a dark red. Now, click in the area where you want your text to start. The Text tool sets a gray line on the canvas, and the text you type displays above it. In this case, the letter H gives a grungy banner shape (see Figure 2-51). To alter this graphic, you need to convert it from a text element to a bitmap. Phoenix keeps text elements editable so that you can change the text or the font in them. However, you are not allowed to rotate, scale, or skew the text while it is still an editable text element. You need to convert the text element to a bitmap to scale and rotate the dingbat. With the text layer selected, open the `Options` menu in the Layers panel and select the `Convert Layers to Bitmap` command.

Figure 2-51. Keep adding layers and setting Blend Modes to build the collage effect.

9. After the text element is converted into a bitmap, you can manipulate it. Select the Transform tool , which draws a box around the graphic. This box has eight control handles, one in each corner and one on each side. Clicking and dragging a control handle resizes the graphic, whereas clicking and dragging just outside of the corner controls rotate it. Rotate and scale the graphic so it fills the area on the right side of the image (see Figure 2-52). Press the Enter key to commit the transformation. Finally, rename this layer Banner so the conversion process erases any layer names.

Figure 2-52. Use the Paint Bucket tool to fill in open areas.

10. Use Text tool with a distressed font this time. Add a title to the image using the same process as in Step 8. Change the color and make sure the size is set to 288 (see Figure 2-53). Again, use the `Convert Layers to Bitmap` command in the Layer panel's `Option` menu so you can use the Transform tool on this element. Position this element so that it lies on top of the banner graphic, and then press Enter to commit the transformation (see Figure 2-54). Name the layer AVIARY to make it easy to identify layers later.

 When using the Transformation tool, you will see a gray rectangle with eight small square controls at each corner and at the midpoints of the sides.

Figure 2-53. The Transformation tool is used to position, rotate, scale, and skew objects.

Different transform operations are done depending on where the cursor is relative to this rectangle and the controls. Clicking and holding inside the large rectangle or bounding box moves the object. Dragging on a corner control scales the object. Holding down the Ctrl key while scaling keeps the proportions of the original object. Dragging on a midpoint control scales the object constrained horizontally or vertically. Clicking anywhere on the edge of the bounding box other than the controls skews the object. Finally, dragging just outside of the corner controls enables you to rotate the object. You can see the cursor change to a circular arrow when you can rotate. The rotation center can be changed by dragging the small target icon in the center of the bounding box (see Figure 2-55).

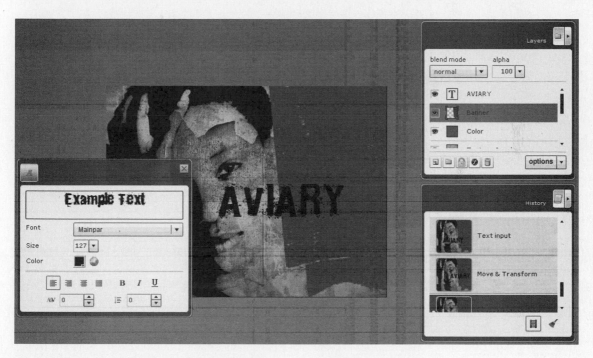

Figure 2-54. Add a distress title with the Text tool.

Figure 2-55. Finish the image by positioning the text.

Project review

In this project, you learned how to import Resources into Phoenix and how to layer their pixels with **Blend Modes**. These **Blend Modes** use different formulas to mix the pixels of two separate layers. With **Blend Modes** ranging from **Multiply,** which makes light pixels transparent, to **Overlay,** which covers only the lightest and darkest pixels, they are diverse and powerful. You also learned that destructive Filters are different than **Layer Filters** because they permanently alter the pixels with the effect. Finally, some fonts can give you quick access to graphics without having to import an image. In the next project, you explore more advanced selection techniques. You learn how to use and control the Clone Stamp tool, which is indispensable for separating objects. You will see how to remove pixels with the Eraser tool while painting shadows and highlights with a soft Paintbrush.

Project 2.3—Create a Hybrid Image Worthy of Worth1000

Your friends might have sent you some funny images of a horse driving a car or an alien dressed in a suit and tie. These images and thousands like them have one key technique in common. That is the separation of foreground and background so they can be juxtaposed with other elements. Many examples of this can be found at www.Wortht000.com. This project shows you how to use the Clone Stamp tool to paint a foreground object. You then edit and replace a new object in its place. Figure 2–56 shows the final image you will create with this project.

Figure 2-56. The final image for this project.

Key features used in this project

- Transformation tool
- Eraser tool
- Clone Stamp tool
- Freeform/Polygonal Selection tool
- Paintbrush tool

> *Find this file online at*
> `http://aviary.com/artists/gettingstartED/creations/chapter_2_project_3`.

1. Start the file by importing your background resource. For this project, we used an image of a couple out walking their dog. On the start screen, choose the `Load existing file` option. Then, locate and upload your image (see Figure 2-57). This is a useful way of starting files because the canvas is automatically scaled to match the imported resource. Name the bottom layer Background and the layer with the couple Walkers.

Figure 2-57. Start the creation with an image.

2. First, you need to remove the element that you are going to replace. In this case, it is the fluffy white dog. You could just use the Eraser tool to remove the dog, but you would be left with a hole in your image. If the object that is to replace it isn't big enough to cover that hole, a problem results. In this case, you need to remove a foreground element while leaving the background.

    This can be achieved with the Clone Stamp tool (see Figure 2-58). The Clone Stamp tool samples pixels from one area of a layer and copies them to another. To use the tool you must first establish a sample point. Find an area that you want to clone; in this case, you clone the road texture over the white doge. While the Clone Stamp tool is selected, hold the Shift key and click a part of the road area to set the sample point. Now, everywhere you paint with the Clone Stamp tool, the pixels from the sample area will be copied.

Figure 2-58. The Clone Stamp tool enables you to sample areas of an image and paint portions in different locations.

The Clone Stamp tool copies a portion of an image and paints it to another location (see Figure 2-59). This tool takes a little practice, but is a powerful technique to know. To use the Clone Stamp tool, first you have to tell Phoenix which pixels to sample. To set the sample point, hold down the Shift key (the Opt key on Mac) while clicking on the area with the Clone Stamp tool. A small gray cross displays and identifies the center of the sampled area. After setting the sample point, you can paint with the Clone Stamp tool as you would with the Paintbrush tool to draw the sampled area pixels anywhere on your canvas. The sample point moves in unison with the painted clone (see Figure 2-60). Like the other brush tools, you can set the edge **Hardness**, **Size** and **Alpha**. Adjusting these parameters helps to blend the cloned pixels with the background.

Figure 2-59. The Clone Stamp tool is stacked with the Liquify tool.

47

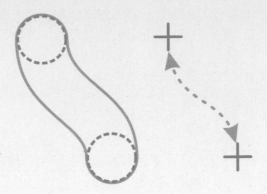

Figure 2-60. The sample point moves in unison with the Clone brush.

3. You need to move and reset the sampled area several times. The goal is to paint over the dog with the cloned road texture (see Figure 2-61). This requires that you resize the bush and the Hardness to blend the clone textures with the background. It helps to make the final image more believable if you can also clone the shadows of the walking couple. It doesn't have to be perfect, but any added detail now will help later in the image. Finally, you need to leave the leash element so you can attach it to the rhino later.

Figure 2-61. Paint over the object with the Clone Stamp tool to remove it from the background.

4. Expert Clone Stamp tool users can make an element entirely disappear from an image. As a beginner, you should not worry if you have trouble getting a perfect result. It takes practice. It isn't as important to have the area where you removed the dog to be extremely clean because the replaced element will cover much of it (see Figure 2-62).

Figure 2-62. The dog has been removed from the image. It is a little rough, but do not worry because much of this is covered later.

5. Import the image of the element that will replace the dog. We are going to use an image of a rhino in this project. Open the Resource Browser by using the `Import File` command from the File tab on the main menu. Navigate to the file on your computer, Aviary library, or one of several photo sites (see Figure 2-63). Load the photo into the file by clicking the `Import File` button. Name this layer Rhino.

Figure 2-63. Import the replacement object with the `File ➤ Import File` command.

6. Now that you have your replacement image imported into the file, you need to clean it up. In this case, you have to remove the white background from around the rhino. To make this process a little easier, create a new layer and fill it with a contrasting color. Put this layer directly below the Rhino layer, and name this layer Temp (see Figure 2-64).

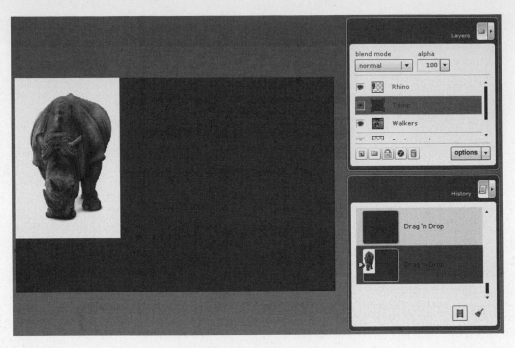

Figure 2-64. Adding a contrasting fill behind objects is helpful to see the process of background removal.

7. There are several different ways to separate foregrounds from backgrounds. This method is the one you will probably use most of the time. First, remove the bulk of the background using the Freeform Selection tool [image]. With the Freeform Selection tool, drag just outside the figure (see Figure 2-65). Hold down the mouse button while you draw the selection ending at the start point. Currently, the area inside the selection is active. If you press the Delete key at this time, the rhino would be erased; however, you want the background removed instead. To change the area of the selection that is active, use the **Selection ➤ Invert Selection** command from the main menu. Now, when you press Delete, the outside area is removed.

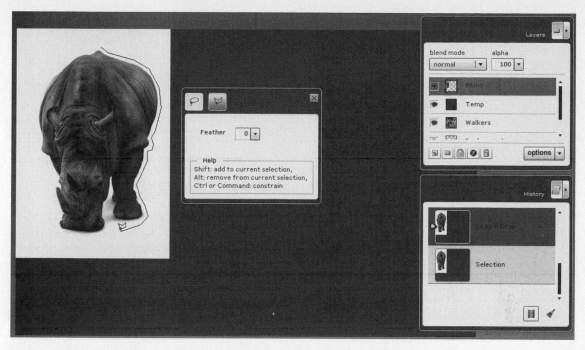

Figure 2-65. Use the Freeform Selection tool to roughly remove a bulk of the extra background.

8. Alternatively, you can use the Magic Wand tool to make automatic selections. The tool selects like-colored pixels, so in an image like this where there is a high contrasting background, you get a decent selection (see Figure 2-66). You can select how much difference you want between the selected and unselected pixels by using the `Tolerance` setting. A higher setting selects a larger range of pixels. The `Contiguous` setting when enabled picks all the like-colored pixels in the image, and when disabled, it picks only like-colored pixels that are touching.

Figure 2-66. The Magic Wand tool can make automatic selections, but it can give undesired results.

 Both the Freeform and Polygonal Selection tools enable you to select irregular areas of a layer (see Figure 2-67 and Figure 2-68). To use the Freeform Selection tool, click and hold down the mouse button while drawing a freeform selection. Releasing the button closes the selection with a straight line from the ending point to the start point. To use the Polygonal Selection tool, click and release the mouse button. This draws a straight line between these points. Continue to set points to define the selection area. To close the selection with the Polygonal Selection tool, either double-click the mouse or click the start point. Like other selections, it can be modified in the main menu selection command.

Figure 2-67. The Freeform tool is used to draw a selection.

Figure 2-68. The Polygonal Selection tool is used to draw straight-edged selections.

9. Now, use the Eraser tool to remove the remaining background. Change the Size and Hardness of the tool depending on the need. These parameters are located in the fly-out menu for the tool (see Figure 2-69). The Hardness sets how sharp the edge of the Eraser is. In this case, a setting of 80–90 gives a good mix of control and softness. After you have removed the background, delete the Temp layer with contrasting color as it is no longer needed.

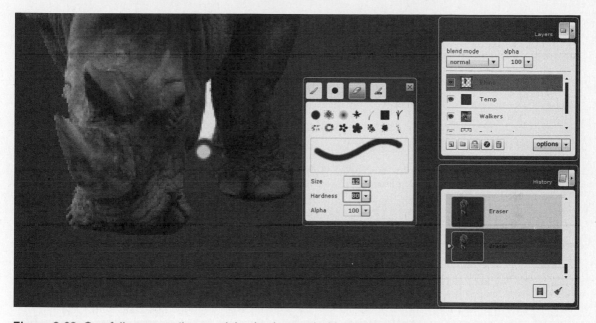

Figure 2-69. Carefully remove the remaining background with the Eraser tool.

The Eraser tool is found under the Paintbrush tool and is used to remove pixels from a layer (see Figure 2-70).

Figure 2-70. The Eraser tool removes pixels.

The Eraser has many different shaped brushes and settings. The Size setting scales the Eraser in pixels from 1–255.The Hardness sets the edge blending. A setting of 100 produces a hard-edged eraser, whereas a 0 produces a soft, feathered edge to the Eraser (see Figure 2-71). Finally, Alpha sets the transparency of the eraser. A setting of 1 removes almost no pixels and 100 removes all pixels that are erased.

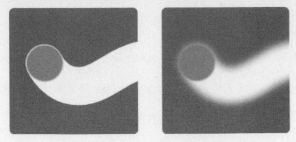

Figure 2-71. The left image has an eraser with a Hardness setting of 100, and the image on the right has a setting of 0.

10. Use the Transformation tool  to scale, rotate, and position the rhino. You need it to be similarly sized to the white dog that was removed in Step 2 and in the same location. You also need the end of the leash to be in approximately the same location as where a collar would be on the rhino's neck (see Figure 2-72). This is hard to see because the rhino covers up the leash, so you need to set the `Alpha` on this layer to about 60, which lets you see both the rhino and the leash making it easier to line up. After you are satisfied with the placement, turn the `Alpha` back to 100.

Figure 2-72. Position the rhino in the image.

11. You need to make the leash to be on top of the rhino, and the easiest way to do this is to make a copy and put it on a new layer above the rhino. Temporarily hide the rhino by clicking on eye icon

on the layer. This is a great way to temporarily hide objects so you can work on other layers without having it interfere. Now, use the **Polygonal Selection** tool to select a portion of the leash that will be on top of the rhino. The Polygonal Selection tool is like the **Freeform Selection** tool, but allows only straight-edged selections. It is useful for geometrical selections like the straight edges of the leash. Click points around the leash, making sure to follow the edges as closely as possible (see Figure 2-73). With the leash selected, use the `Copy` command and then the `Paste` command located in the Edit tab on the main menu. This copies the selected area. Create a new layer and insert the copied object on that layer. Alternatively, you can use keyboard shortcuts: Ctrl+C (Command+C on Mac) to copy and Ctrl+V (Command+V on Mac) to paste. Click the Eye icon to display the rhino, and name this new layer Leash. Now, the leash overlaps the rhino.

Figure 2-73. Use the Selection tools to make room for the leash.

12. The rhino is a different shape than the dog, so the existing shadow doesn't quite fit. Create a new layer and name it Cast Shadow. Then, using either Freeform or Polygonal Selection tool, draw a rough area for a new shadow (see Figure 2-74). Try to follow natural edges in an image, for example the selection ends at the edge of the road. This way you are not adding an additional edge into the image, which can make an image like this become less believable. Fill that selection with a standard white to black gradient. Make sure that the black side of the gradient is at the rhino's feet while the white extends away. Shadows are always darker closer to their source. In

55

this case, the source is the rhino's feet. Change the Blend Mode of this layer to multiply, which means that the light-colored pixels turn transparent, leaving only the darker ones. Finally, drag this Cast Shadow Layer under the rhino layer.

Figure 2-74. Use the Polygonal Selection and Gradient tools to add a shadow to the rhino.

13. The rhino needs a little shading to make it fit into the scene. To do this, create a new layer above the Rhino layer, and name it Shading. Select the Paintbrush tool to open the fly-out parameter panel. The shading should be subtle, so set the color to black, the **Hardness** to 0, and the **Alpha** to 25. This brush produces a soft, light shade wherever you paint and it creates a convincing shadow. Looking at the image, you can see that the light appears to be coming from the upper left, so the shadows should be painted on the right side of the rhino. Paint in shadows and don't worry about painting outside the rhino; you will remove that later (see Figure 2-75). After you are satisfied with the results, you can remove the shading that fell outside of the rhino. In the Layers panel, while holding down the Shift key, click the preview image of the Rhino layer. This selects all the pixels of that layer. You will see that the selection border is drawn around the rhino (see Figure 2-76). Use the **Select ➤ Invert Selection** command from the main menu to reverse the selection. Then, use the **Selection ➤ Modify ➤ Feather** and set the feather to 2. The **Feather** command softens the edge of a selection. In this case, the selection is feathered by 2 pixels. Select the layer with the shading and press the Delete key. All the extraneous shading is removed.

Figure 2-75. Use the Paintbrush tool set to 0 `Hardness` to add shading to the rhino.

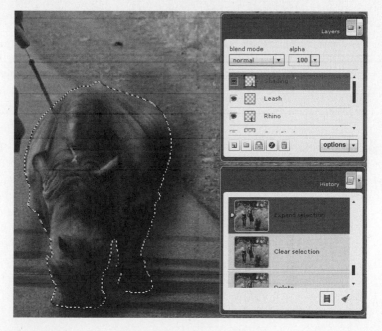

Figure 2-76. Select the rhino.

14. Create another layer above the shading and name it Highlights. Change the Paintbrush color to white and start painting the light on the left side of the rhino. Then, using the same process as in step 13, select the rhino's pixels, invert the selection, and feather it by 2 (see Figure 2-77). Making sure that the Highlights layer is selected, press Delete to remove the extraneous highlight that falls outside of the rhino. Set this layer's **Blend Mode** to **Add**. The **Add** Blend Mode intensifies light-colored pixels and brightens up the highlights you just painted. Finally, set this layer's **Alpha** to 40, decreasing the harsh highlights.

Figure 2-77. Add highlights to the left side of the rhino.

The Paintbrush tool is used to paint colors directly on an image (see Figure 2-78). Set the color and Alpha with the Color Picker in the tools parameter fly-out. Alternatively, you can set the Paintbrush's Alpha using the `Alpha` setting directly on the fly-out. The `Size` parameter scales the brush from one pixel to 300 in diameter. Like other brush tools, the `Hardness` parameter sets how the edge is feathered. A setting of 100 produces a hard-edged brush, whereas 0 produces a soft, feathered edge brush. `Flow` controls how fast the color "flows" from the brush.

Figure 2-78. The Paintbrush tool lets you add colored pixels to a file.

Project review

In this project, you learned to use the Clone Stamp tool. This tool takes some practice, but it is indispensable because of its versatility and power. Cloning textures is a great way to remove objects from their backgrounds. You also looked at ways to remove backgrounds, from erasing the background pixels to using the automatic Wand tool. Finally, you experimented with the Paintbrush tool to create light and shadows. You saw the need to change the parameters of tools periodically to suit your needs. In the next project, you learn about using text elements and dynamic angles to create a billboard advertisement. You use more compound Layer effects to enhance graphic elements.

Project 2.4—Creating an Advertisement in Phoenix

Text can add focus, give extra meaning to an image, or change the context of an image. Advertising companies have been using text to advance their product, inspire patriotism, and inform the public. In this project, you construct a simple ad for Aviary by embellishing a standard text element with shading and textures. You then wrap this ad on to a billboard. See Figure 2-79 for the results of this project.

Figure 2-79. The image you will create for this project.

Key features used in this project

- Text tool
- Transformation tool
- Shape tools
- Polygonal Selection tool
- Gradient Fill tool

Find this file online at
http://aviary.com/artists/gettingstartED/creations/chapter_2_project_4.

1. Create a new file using the `Start from Scratch` option and the default dimensions. Now add the title text; in this case, you are making an Aviary ad. To do this, select the Text tool 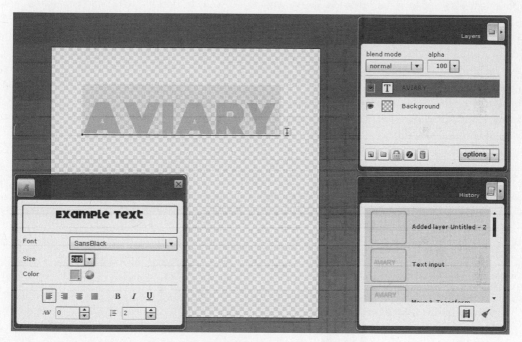 by opening the fly-out panel. Phoenix gives you access to all the fonts that are installed on your computer. From the `Font` menu, choose a heavy typeface so you can add embellishments to it in the next step. Set the `Size` to the maximum 288 and set the color to a light gray, so you can see it. Click the canvas to set the start point for the text. The tool draws a gray horizontal line where you clicked, and the text you type with your keyboard is placed on that line. Type the word AVIARY (see Figure 2-80).

Figure 2-80. Use the Text tool to add a bold text element.

The Text tool is used to add text to a file (see Figure 2-81).

Figure 2-81. Add words and letters to your file with the Text tool.

To add a text element to a file, click the image where you want to add the text. You will see a gray line extended to the right; your text is added above this line. Set the Font from the Font Parameters fly-out. `Size` sets how large the font is. `Color` sets the color of the font. Click the square for a simple Color Picker of Web-safe colors, or use the circle icon to open the advanced Color Picker. Use any of the four align buttons to set the alignment of the text to Left, Right, Centered, or Justified. Add styling to your text with the `Bold`, `Italic`, and `Underline` buttons. To fine-tune the spacing of the letters, use the kerning or `A/V` setting. Negative numbers tighten the characters, whereas positive numbers spread out the characters. Finally, use the `Line Spacing` setting to adjust the space between multiple lines of text. Negative numbers reduce the line spacing, whereas positive numbers increase the line spacing. Aviary's Text tool can use any of the fonts currently installed on your computer. However, if you open a file that has editable text but do not have the font installed on your computer, you are prompted to rasterize or switch to an installed font. Rasterized fonts are fonts that have been converted from an editable text element to a bitmap. After a text element is rasterized, you cannot change any of the lettering with the Text tool.

2. The Aviary text is editable, which means you can change the text by clicking it with the Text tool and making whatever changes you want. However, due to current limitations in Phoenix, you cannot scale, rotate, or skew with the Transformation tool. So you need to convert the text to a bitmap, making it a regular image instead of just text. After your text is converted, you can no long change the words, font, or spacing of the text. From the **Option** menu in the **Layers** panel, use the **Convert Layer to Bitmap** option (see Figure 2-82). This enables you to alter the text like any other bitmap resource instead of a text element.

Figure 2-82. Convert the text to a bitmap.

3. Add some subtle shading to create a 3D effect on the text. The font used in this example lends itself to this kind of effect. Create a new layer above the Aviary layer and name it Shading. Use the Polygonal Selection tool ![] to section off a portion of one of the letters. The idea is to follow the direction of the edges to create a folded paper look to the font (see Figure 2-83).

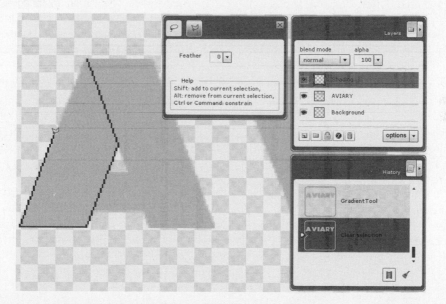

Figure 2-83. Use the Polygonal Selection tool to isolate sections of the text.

4. Now, select the Gradient Fill tool 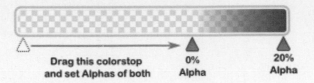 and set both color stops to black. Then, set the **Alpha** of the right color stop to 20. Set the left color stop's **Alpha** to 0% and drag it to the center of the color bar (see Figure 2-84).

Drag this colorstop and set Alphas of both   **0% Alpha**   **20% Alpha**

Figure 2-84. The setting of the color stops in the Gradient tool

5. Now use the Gradient Fill tool 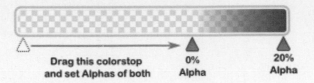 to fill in the selection. The goal of this is to simulate a shadow and impart a 3D effect to the text (see Figure 2-85). Continue this process until all the letters have been decorated the same way, following the edge.

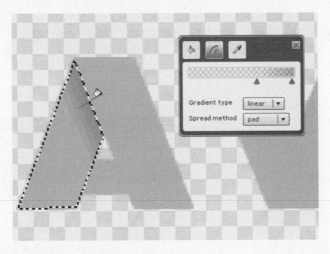

Figure 2-85. Use the Gradient Fill tool to add depth.

6. Now that you have added the embellishments to the text, you can change the font color to white. An easy way to do that is to use the Brightness & Contrast adjustments. With the AVIARY text layer selected, open the Brightness and Contrast adjustment under the Image menu. Set the **Brightness** to 50 (see Figure 2-86). This increases the overall lightness in the layer and turns the light gray text to white. Click **OK** to commit the brightness adjustment.

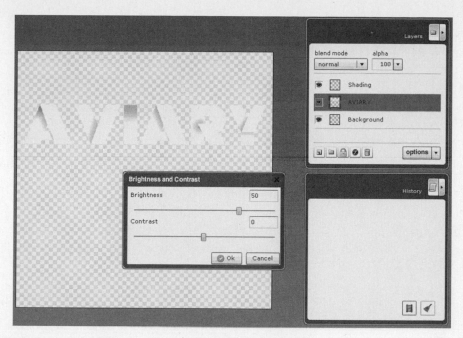

Figure 2-86. Increase the brightness of the text to make it white.

7. Adjust the Shading layer's Alpha until you are satisfied with how it looks with the font. This effect looks best when the shading is light. Next, hold down the Ctrl key (Command on Mac) and select both the Shading and the AVIARY layer. They should both be highlighted in blue when they are selected. Be sure they are both highlighted and choose the `Merge Layers` option from the `Options` dropdown in the Layers panel (see Figure 2-87). This permanently combines both layers. If there are any Blend Modes that are applied to any of the layers, they are thrown out, and the layers are combined normally. This behavior changes in the future, and then the merged layers inherit their `Blend Modes.`

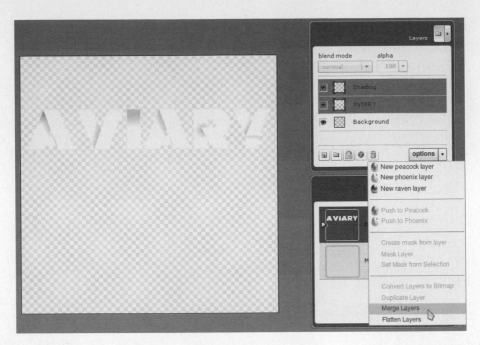

Figure 2-87. Merge the Text and Shadow layers into a single layer.

8. Add the smaller Motto under the Title. Select the Text tool again and select the same text as the first. Set the size to 40 and set the color to white. Click the area under the AVIARY to set your text start point and type in the motto "Creation on the Fly," Aviary's motto (see Figure 2-88). If you need to position the text so that it is centered under the other, you should use the Move tool. The advantage to using the Move tool instead of the Transformation tool is that you do not need to convert the text to a bitmap when positioning it. This works only when positioning a text element; you have to convert it to a bitmap if you plan on sizing, rotating, or skewing it. When you are satisfied with the position of the motto, select the AVIARY and the Motto layer and combine them with the **Merge Layer** command following the same procedure as in Step 7. Finally, name this newly merged layer Text.

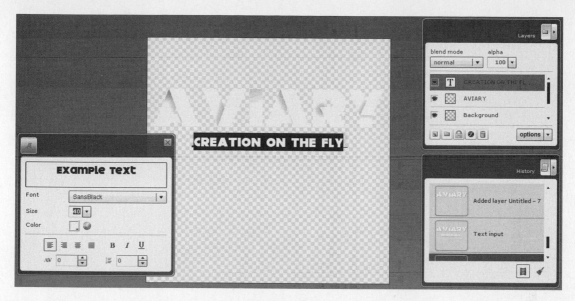

Figure 2-88. Add a smaller motto under the first text element.

9. With the text elements combined into a single Text layer, add a dark glow around it with a `Layer Filters`. With the Text layer selected, click the `Layer Filter` button in the Layers Panel to open the `Layer Filters` dialog. Click the Glow effect and set the color to black to create a black halo around the text. Next, set the `Blur x` and `Blur y` setting to 4 to tone down the glow. Then, set the `Alpha` to 0.5, which reduces the glow intensity even more (see Figure 2-89). Make it fit well with the subtle shading on the text. You can set the `Quality` to high if you like, but it takes a little more processing power from your computer. Usually, you won't be able to tell the difference.

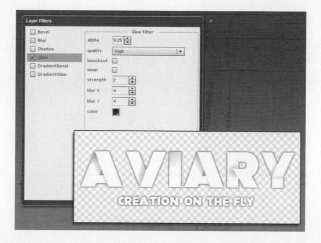

Figure 2-89. Add a dark glow around the text to set it off from the background.

10. Now import a backdrop. Use the `File` ➤ `Import File` command from the main menu and locate an image to use as a backdrop. We use a simple texture image here. Size the backdrop with the Transformation tool and move the layer to the bottom of the layer stack (see Figure 2-90). Name this layer Background.

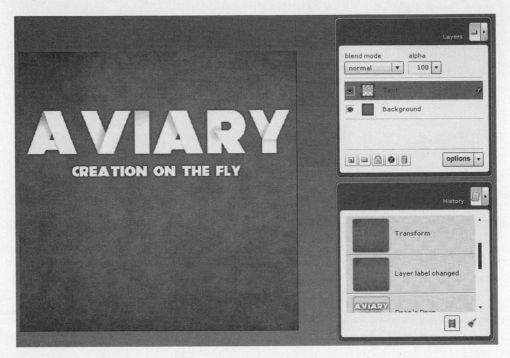

Figure 2-90. Add a texture to use as a background for the text.

11. To add some drama to the text, use the Transformation tool and rotate it to a 45-degree angle. With the Text layer selected, hold down the Shift key while rotating the text object. The text constrains the rotation to 45-degree increments. Then, center it in the middle of the canvas, pressing the Enter button to commit the rotation and position changes (see Figure 2-91).

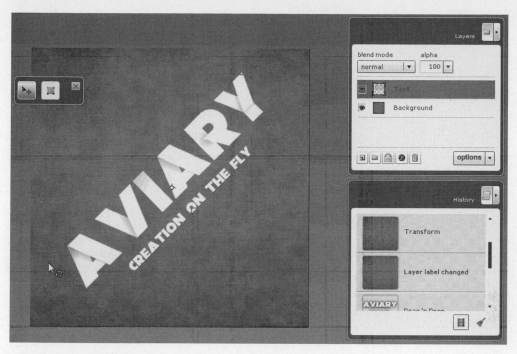

Figure 2-91. Rotate the text element.

12. Add graphic elements. Shapes are predefined geometric objects. These objects can quickly add elements to a file without having to build them from scratch. Furthermore, they give you access to regular geometric shapes, which would be extremely tedious to lay out by hand. Here, you add a few colored stripes. Start by creating a new layer and name it Stripes. Next, select the Rectangular Shape tool ⬜. This opens the parameters fly-out. Be sure the `Corner Radius` and `Line weight` are set to 0. Now, set the foreground color by clicking on the top square in the color indicator, just below the tools. Draw a tall, skinny rectangle in the center of the canvas by clicking and dragging diagonally. The rectangle is drawn in between these two points. Try to make this shape fill as much of the vertical space as possible (see Figure 2-92). Repeat this process to create two more rectangles for a total of three. Change the color of each and draw them off to the side of the first. Leave a little space between them because you will use Layer Filters to fill that space.

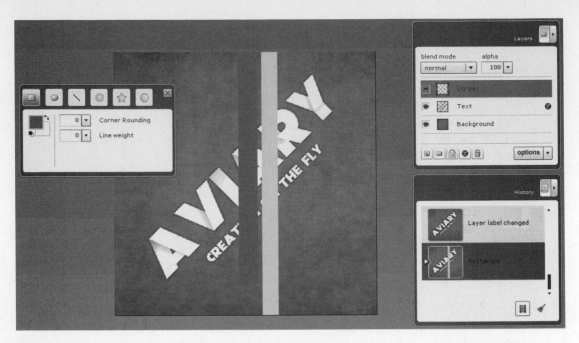

Figure 2-92. Use the Shape tool to add some graphic elements.

 The Shape tools are used to add predefined geometric shapes to a layer (see Figure 2-93). There are six different shapes that can be used and each has its own settings.

Figure 2–93. The Shape tools enable you to add geometric objects to your file.

A shape's color is set with the Color Selector in the Parameters fly-out panel. The foreground color sets the fill color and the background sets the stroke color of the shape. Every shape also has a line weight parameter. This sets how wide the stroke is drawn around the shape in pixels. A `line weight` setting of 0 produces a shape with no stroke. All the shapes are added in the same way. First, click the canvas at the start point location. While continuing to hold down the mouse button, drag and release the button at the end point location. The shape is drawn in between these two points. Finally, hold down the Shift key while drawing a shape to constrain its proportions, making the height and width equal. The exception is the Line Shape where the Shift key constrains the angle to 45-degree increments. Following are descriptions of the six shapes and their parameter settings:

1. **Rectangular Shape**: This draws a rectangle or square. The corner rounding parameter sets how round the corners are drawn. A setting of 0 produces sharp corners.
2. **Elliptical Shape**: This draws an ellipse or circle.
3. **Line**: This draws a straight line.
4. **Gear Shape**: This draws a round gear shape including the teeth. Inner radius sets how far from the center of the shape that the teeth start. Sides set how many teeth are drawn on the gear. The Hole option enables or disables a hole to be drawn in the center of the shape.
5. **Star Shape**: This draws a star shape. Inner radius sets how far from the center of the shape that the arms of the star will start. Sides set how many arms are drawn on the star.
6. **Polygon Shape**: This draws a straight-sided geometric shape. Sides set how many sides are drawn on the polygon.

13. Use the Transformation tool to skew, position, and scale the stripes. To balance the stripes with the text elements, position them at a perpendicular angle. This can be achieved by skewing them. Skewing is a tilting type of distortion. To skew with the Transformation tool, hover the mouse over one side of the large rectangle around the transform object. The cursor switches to a double arrow, and the tool is set to skew. Transform the stripes until they are perpendicular to the text (see Figure 2-94). When you are satisfied with how these look, move the Stripe layer under the two text elements in the Layers panel.

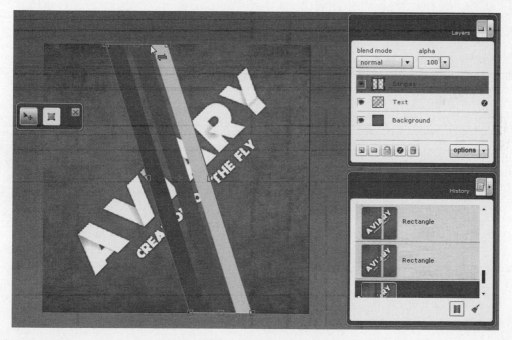

Figure 2-94. Transform the rectangles to add a dramatic effect to the image.

14. Add `Layer Filters` to the Stripe layer to make them more dynamic. Open the `Layer Filters` while the Stripe layer is selected. Add a white stroke around the shapes. As you can see, there is no stroke effect. You can create a stroke with the Glow filter. Select Glow, and in the parameters, change the color to white. Then, set the `Strength` to 100. `Strength` sets how quickly the Glow effect fades out, so the higher the setting, the quicker the glow goes from opaque to transparent. Finally, set the `Blur x` and `Blur y` to 7, making them a little thicker (see Figure 2-95).

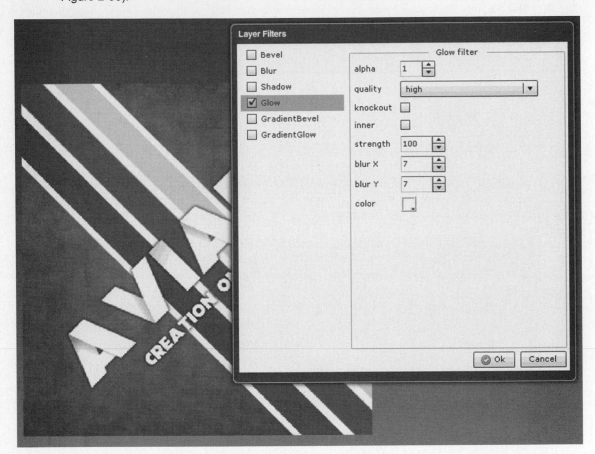

Figure 2-95. Use the Glow Layer filters to add a stroke around the stripes.

15. With the `Layer Filters` panel still open, add a Shadow effect and set the `Blur x` and `Blur y` to 8. This gives the stripes more dimension (see Figure 2-96). Finally, commit the effect to the layer by clicking `OK`.

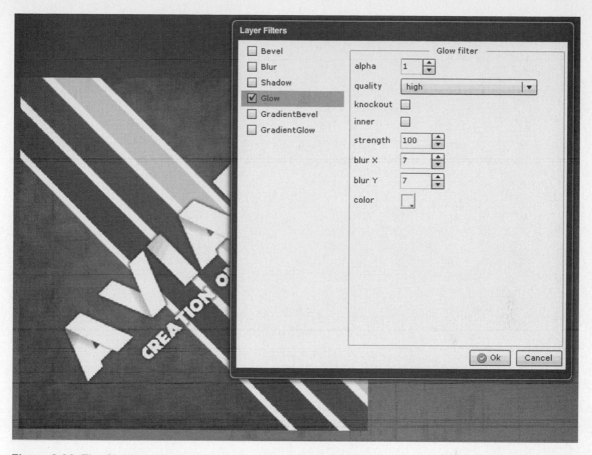

Figure 2-96. The Shadow effect gives depth to the graphic elements.

16. To get some of that great texture of the background resource to show through the stripes, set the **Blend Mode** of the stripe elements to **Overlay**. This alters the color a little, but it also ties the image together. Finally, and most important, use the **Flatten Layers** command from the **Layers** panel's **Options** dropdown menu (see Figure 2-97). This permanently merges all of the layers into one single layer. Normally, you should keep all of the layers separate so that you can edit individual elements as the need arises. However, in this case, we need to deform the current image and to make it a single layer. If we did not, we would have to deform each layer separately and it would never line up quite right. Finally, name this layer Sign.

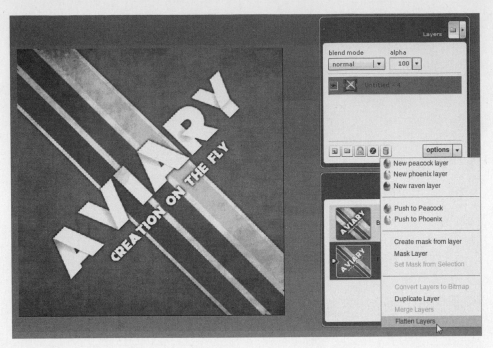

Figure 2-97. Change the Blending Mode of the Stripe layer, and then merge all the layers with the **Flatten Layers** command.

17. Now that you have the basic ad, place it in a location to help visualize what it might look like as a real-world billboard advertisement (see Figure 2-98). Import a backdrop, and this time, if Phoenix prompts you, choose the **Resize canvas** option. This makes the canvas the same size as the imported resource (see Figure 2-99). Finally, name this layer Backdrop and drag this layer to the bottom of the layer stack.

Figure 2-98. Use the resource browser to import the background image.

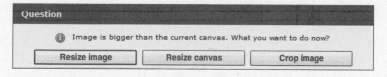

Figure 2-99. Use the Resize canvas option for easy image sizing.

18. With the ad layer on top of the layer stack and selected, choose the Distortion tool ⬚. This tool is located in the Transformation tool's fly-out panel. Four control boxes at each corner of the object can be dragged around. This stretches and pulls the object in line with these controls, like a sheet (see Figure 2-100). Distort the ad until it lines up with the edge of the sign backdrop. Finally, set the `Blend Mode` of the Sign layer to `Multiply` and adjust the `Alpha` until it blends with the backdrop.

Figure 2-100. Stretch and manipulate objects with the Distortion tool.

 The Distortion tool enables you to stretch, twist, and manipulate an object. To use this tool, just enable the tool while the object that you want to distort is selected. Four control handles show up in the four corners of the object (see Figure 2-101).

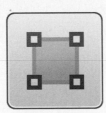

Figure 2-101. Stretch the pixels in a layer with the Deform tool.

Clicking and dragging these handles enables you to manipulate the object. The object is stretched between the four controls like a sheet of rubber. The control handles are drawn on the very edge of the object's area, so they might be far away from it if there is a lot of empty space in the object.

Project review

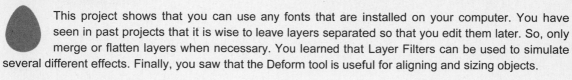

This project shows that you can use any fonts that are installed on your computer. You have seen in past projects that it is wise to leave layers separated so that you edit them later. So, only merge or flatten layers when necessary. You learned that Layer Filters can be used to simulate several different effects. Finally, you saw that the Deform tool is useful for aligning and sizing objects.

Chapter review

From the outset, Phoenix might look as if it lacks in features, but as you have seen in this chapter, that is not the case. Compared with an expensive desktop image editor, it has all the features you would regularly use with those programs. There are many advantages to using Phoenix from images hosted online or opening other files to see how they are made. Phoenix is a great learning tool for the beginner and has enough features for the advanced user. In this chapter, you learned the basic tools in Phoenix. You explored selection techniques, painted and erased pixels, added text elements, and transformed objects. You saw the importance and power of Phoenix's layer-based system. Objects can be kept separated for complex editing and construction of images. As you worked through these projects, the importance of Blend Modes became evident, and allowed you to created interesting combinations of layers. Finally, Layer Effects added depth to your images.

In the next chapter, you use more advanced techniques to manipulate images. You learn to enhance the color and tone of you images and how to fix many different problems that can ruin a photo. Finally, you will see how custom filters can be used to your advantage and much more.

Chapter 3

Image Manipulation with Phoenix

Digital and cell phone cameras changed the face of photography forever. Developing photos from film used to be expensive and time-consuming, and photo correction was basic. Many of the tools in digital editing programs come from this early photo manipulation. Dodge and burn meant cutting stencils from paper and manually over and under exposing sections of film, which was a tedious and imprecise process. Colored-glass filters were used to adjust the hue and saturation in a photo; to remove an object from a photo literally took a brush to manually paint it out. It has gotten much easier in the computer age. Photos are digitized, turned into discrete points of color and value. These digital pixels are much easier to manipulate than film and negatives. Photo manipulation has become cheaper and more accessible. Furthermore, with the advent of the digital camera, cheap memory, and photo-hosting sites, digital photography is in reach of the average person. No longer do we carry around huge SLR cameras and canisters of film; we can now pull out our cell phones and snap a picture. Our world is instantly saved. The only downside to this accessible and immediate medium is that it sacrifices quality. The average point-and-shoot digital camera does not take images of quality on par with film cameras. This is where Phoenix can give you the power to fix the quality and enhance details.

Along with Phoenix's selection and painting tools, it has powerful commands to adjust the color, contrast, and value. Phoenix lets you take command of the tone of an image. Increasing contrast, boosting color, and altering the brightness can be done online without having to open a cumbersome desktop application. Phoenix can also access the power of Peacock, Aviary's effects editor. You can import `custom filters` to use on you image, from `Blackbox` files created in Peacock. These custom filters with the native features of Phoenix give you the power to manipulate photos like a professional.

In this chapter, you explore the different methods used to manipulate an image's colors. You are introduced to custom filters and the role that Peacock can play in creating advanced effects. You also learn how to repair different problems in photos from fixing colors or even repairing physical damage. Finally, you explore some more advanced techniques to enhance your photos.

Project 3.1—Age an Image and Make a Photograph Pinup

We all have a pile of poor photographs, such as subjects that are cropped, people with red eye, blurry images, and more. These images might live in a shoe box or drawer or are buried in a folder on your hard drive, and you have no intention of letting them see the light of day. Do not delete or hide those images because they can be saved. In this project, you see how to push the color range of a photo to simulate vintage photography, change the composition, or emphasize a good aspect in the photo. Something nostalgic about old photographs makes a viewer overlook slight imperfections in a photo. In this project, you learn how you can use the color commands along with the tools you have been acquainted with in the previous chapter to mask a poor quality image and turn it into an aged photo pinup.

The Polaroid™ film that you reproduce in this project has a slightly desaturated, blue tint (see Figure 3-1). You can always use the `Hue & Saturation` command to attempt to reproduce this effect. However, the hue shift alters all the colors of an image, and it won't produce a believable color adjustment. For this effect, you want to use the `Levels` function. `Levels` stretch the brightness range and shift the midpoint of the value in an image or individual channels. In this instance, you adjust each of the three channels to produce the effect. (See the sidebar for an explanation of channels.)

Figure 3-1. This is the image you will create in this project.

Key features used in this project

- Color operations
- Levels
- Brightness &Contrast
- Hue & Saturation
- Layer filters

> *Find this file online at*
> *http://aviary.com/artists/gettingstartED/creations/final_chapter_3_project_1.*
>
> *The source image for this project can be found at*
> *http://aviary.com/artists/gettingstartED/creations/start_chapter_3_project_1.*

1. Launch Phoenix and use the `Load an Existing File` command from the splash screen. Use the `Browse` button to locate the image you want to manipulate, or insert the HTML link (URL) to an image. Click the `Create` button to open the application and import the image. For this project, we use a photograph of a pet dog. Start by naming your layers—Background for the bottom empty layer and Image for the imported image layer. It is a good practice to name your layers in Phoenix, so you are able to find objects in a file. Next, open the `Levels` dialog by selecting `Image ➤ Levels`. The `Level` function uses more than normal processing power, thus the `Adjust Levels` dialog has a built-in preview window. The `Levels` dialog has a Channel selector to perform actions on individual channels, a histogram graph that displays the amount of pixels, and a given value. Finally, there are several sliders used to control the values. Start by selecting the `Red channel` from the `Channels` dropdown menu (see Figure 3-2). Under the histogram is a slider with three controls. The two controls on each end control the black and white start points, respectively, whereas the middle one controls the midpoint of the brightness. Adjust the center slider under the histogram graph. Moving it to the left increases the brightness in the channel, thus increasing the amount of red in the image. Be careful not to move the slider too far, as it is easy to overdo this effect. Do this with the `Green` and `Blue channels` (see Figure 3-3 and Figure 3-4). However, to give the final result a blue tint, move the `Blue channel's` midslider a little more to the left than the `Red` and `Green`. In this example, the `Red channel's` midpoint is set to 120, the `Green` is set to 120, and the `Blue` is set to 105.

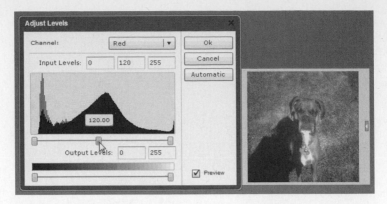

Figure 3-2. Adjust the levels in the Red Channel.

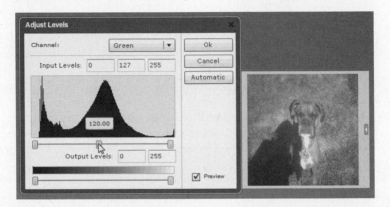

Figure 3-3. Adjust the levels in the Green Channel.

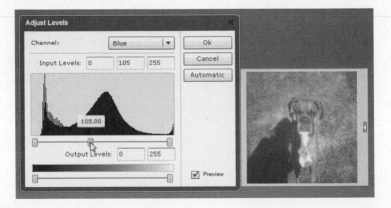

Figure 3-4. Adjust the levels in the Blue Channel.

Computer monitors combine red, green, and blue light to generate their images. This is an additive coloring method or RGB, which is an acronym for the three channels: `Red`, `Green`, and `Blue`. By varying the different amounts of each of these three colors, a computer can recreate a wide range of other colors (see Figure 3-5).

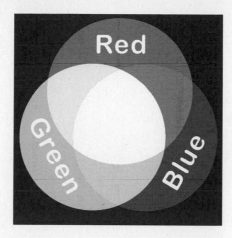

Figure 3-5. How the Red, Green, and Blue Channels mix to create colors

Every image on Aviary consists of these three colors channels, and you can access them separately with various tools. There are advantages to altering individual channels as opposed to luminosity, which is the combination of the three. You can make corrections to a color channel by changing brightness without altering other channel levels. You can see how the color is distributed in an image by looking at individual channels. You can create interesting effects by filtering individual channels.

2. Use the Rectangular Selection tool to reduce some of the ugly, excess background. Start by selecting the Rectangle Selection tool and drag a square selection around the area you want to save. The actual picture part of a Polaroid™ is square, so to make this selection square. Hold down the Shift key while selecting the area. This constrains the width and height, which makes the selection a perfect square. You can move the selection area by clicking and dragging inside it. Position it so your subject is in the center (see Figure 3-6). Then, modify the selected with the `Selection ➤ Invert Selection` function. This reverses the selection so that the areas that were previously deselected are now the active selected areas. Click the Delete button to remove the area around the subject.

Figure 3–6. Remove the extra background to focus on the subject.

3. Insert ch3rectangleshape.png inline after the words Rectangular Shape tool. Use the Transformation tool to size the image area. You want to make it about two-thirds the height of the canvas and center it. Now, create a new layer, name it Frame, and drag it under the Image layer.

Select the Rectangular Shape tool ▢. Make sure the `Corner Rounding` and `Line Weight` are both set to 0. Set the foreground color to a light gray color (#ebebeb). Proceed to draw a rectangle around the image. To achieve that Polaroid™ shape, it should be equal distance on the top and two sides while extending down three times that distance at the bottom (see Figure 3-7). The reason you use a light gray instead of white is that it enables you room in the value to add a highlight. A white highlight doesn't show up on a white background.

Figure 3-7. Use a rectangle to build the photo frame background.

4. To make the frame around the image appear like a three-dimensional (3D) object, you need to add a subtle bevel to the rectangle. To add the bevel to the light gray rectangle, double-click the Layer Filters icon ⓕ in the Layers panel to open the **Layer Filters** dialog, and click the check box next to the **Bevel** option. For a convincing bevel, you need to reduce the intensity of the default effect. Set the **Blur x** and **Blur y** values to 2 and the **distance** to 2. Next, set the **shadow's Alpha** to 0.15, which reduces the intensity of the shadow. You don't have to change the **highlight Alpha** because the frame is light; you need as much of a highlight as possible (see Figure 3-8). Click **OK** to apply the effect. Next, select the Image layer, and from the Layers panel, bring up the Layer Filters. Use the **Bevel** effect for this layer. This inserts a bevel around the outside of the image. However, this pushes the Image layer up off the Frame when it should be inset. To achieve that, select the **Outer** option from the **type** menu. This places the bevel to the outside of the object, which gives you the desired effect of the image being inset into the background. Next, set the **angle** to 225 so that the shadow part of the bevel emanates from the top left corner, reduce the **shadow Alpha** to 0.4, reduce the **distance** to 2, and then click **OK** to apply the effect (see Figure 3-9).

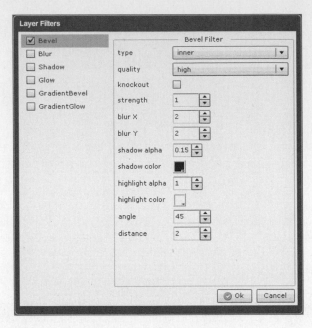

Figure 3-8. Settings of the Bevel Layer Filter for the Frame layer.

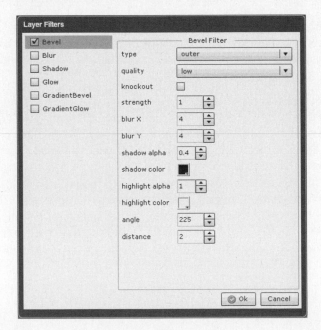

Figure 3–9. Settings of the Bevel Layer Filter for the Image layer.

5. Add a caption to the image using the Text tool . When you select the Text tool, it opens the fly-out panel. The **Font** menu shows you all the fonts on your computer that you have access to in Phoenix. Select the font you want to use for the caption from the **Font** menu. In this case, look for one that resembles handwriting, because many people like to write directly on their photos. Next, set the **size** of the text to something a bit larger, somewhere around 80–100; it depends on the font you have chosen and the size of your image (see Figure 3-10). You can always size the text element later, but you will get a better quality if you keep the amount of scaling later to a minimum. Then, click the canvas where you want the text to be placed. The tool draws a gray line on the canvas where you clicked; this is where the text is placed. Type in your caption for the picture. If you find that you don't like the font you've chosen, you can always select the text with the Text tool and chose a new font. Use the Move tool to position the text at the large section at the bottom of the photo frame if needed. Finally, if you want to make the handwriting text more convincing, you can use the **Convert Layer to Bitmap** from the Layers panel **Option** menu. Then, use the Transformation tool to rotate the text slightly, which gives it a more handwritten feel.

Figure 3–10. Add a caption that resembles handwriting.

6. After the photo is the way you want it, use the **Flatten Layers** command from the Layer panel's **Option** menu to combine all the layers (see Figure 3-11). The **Flatten Layers** command automatically merges all the visible layers and discards the hidden ones in a file. This makes it so you can alter them as one unit. Name this newly fattened layer Picture.

Figure 3–11. Merge the layers to make the image easy to manipulate.

7. Import a background into the image. For this image, we used a cork texture to simulate the photo pinned to a corkboard. Several free textures are available from www.CGtextures.com, which is where we got this example. This cork texture is a small, seamless pattern intended to be used as a tile. **Tiling** is a method of repeating an image horizontally and vertically to cover an area that is larger than the original. In cases like this, where an image is smaller than the canvas, you can use the **Define Pattern** function to quickly create a texture fill pattern. This works well with all seamless patterns. Start by selecting the area you want to use as the pattern. In this case, it is the entire cork pattern. Because the pattern was imported into the file on a new layer, you can select it by holding down the Shift key and clicking the layer preview image in the **Layers** panel. This selects all the pixels in the layer, which happens to be the entire cork pattern. Use the **Select ➤ Define Pattern** function to load the selection as a pattern (see Figure 3-12). After the pattern is defined, it becomes your active foreground color, and you are able to use the Paint Bucket tool to fill an area with the pattern. Furthermore, you can paint with this texture using the Paintbrush or Shape Brush tools. Click the **Delete** button to clear the current cork texture because it is still selected. Then, use the Paint Bucket tool to fill this layer with the pattern texture (see Figure 3-13). Finally, name this layer Cork. Move this layer under the Picture layer in the Layers panel.

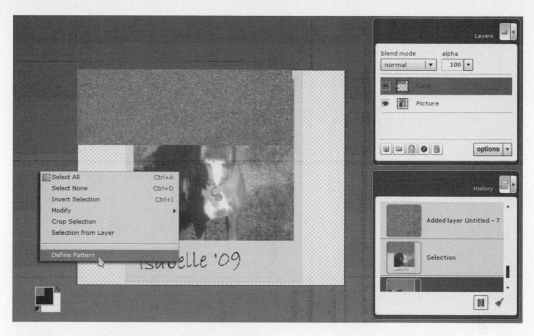

Figure 3–12. Define the cork texture as a pattern fill.

Figure 3–13. Fill a new layer with this pattern texture.

8. With the Transformation tool , select the merged Picture layer and rotate it about 15–30 degrees. Move the cursor near one of the controls in the corner of the transform box. You see that the cursor changes to a looped arrow, which means the Transformation tool rotates the object when you click and hold the mouse button (see Figure 3-14).

Figure 3-14. Rotate the photo image with the Transformation tool.

9. You can use **Layer Filters** to create a quick drop shadow for the photo, but it is limited in how much control you have over it. You can create a shadow on its own layer to make it more customizable. Start by holding down the Shift key and clicking the layer preview image of your merged photo layer in the **Layers** panel. This selects all the pixels in a layer. Alternatively, you can use the **Select ➤ Selection from Layer** to do the same. Next, create a new layer naming it Shadow, and fill it with black using the Paint Bucket tool (see Figure 3-15). You have to reset the color from the pattern fill to a regular fill. You can do this in one step by clicking the small black and white icon under the color selector (see Figure 3-16).

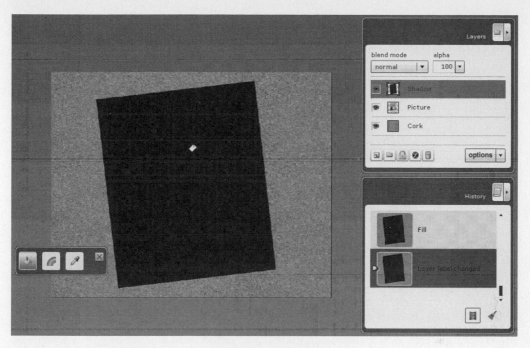

Figure 3–15. Create a base shape to be turned into a drop shadow under the picture.

Figure 3-16. Restore the default colors in the color selector.

10. With the new black rectangle layer on top, use the Distortion tool to drag the bottom, left corner down slightly. This distortion makes the corner of the photo appear to lift farther than the rest off of the surface (see Figure 3-17). If you left the shadow uniform, it would make the object appear parallel to the surface. Next, open the `Layer Filters` dialog, and add `Blur` to this layer. This is a big object, so you have to increase the `Blur x` and `Blur y` values to 10, and then click `OK` to apply the blur. Finally, drag this shadow layer under the photo layer and above the cork texture layer on the `Layers` panel. If the shadow is too dark, you can always reduce its opacity by lowering the `Alpha` setting for the layer.

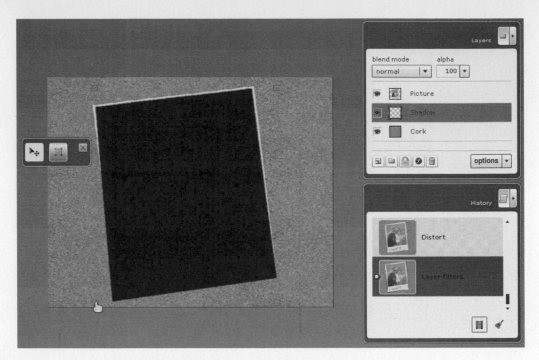

Figure 3–17. Use the Distortion tool to deform the shadow.

11. The photo needs something to hold it on the corkboard. In this example, there is an imported pushpin image that was made in Raven, Aviary's vector editor (see Chapter 4 for information on Raven). Because this image was made in Raven, it is imported into the Phoenix file with all transparencies intact. After importing the pushpin resource, which can be found on the gettingstartED user account, use the Transformation tool to scale the pin and place it in position at the top and center of the photo (see Figure 3-18).

Figure 3-18. Add a pushpin graphic to the image.

12. The image is close to being finished and many would stop here. However, adding a final layer can tie the elements in an image together. You need to create a cast shadow across the image as if light from a window was falling on the corkboard that the photo is pinned to. Start by setting the Gradient Fill tool's colors to opaque black fading to transparent yellow (see Chapter 2 for information about the Gradient Fill tool). Next, create a new layer and name it Light. Then, start adding gradients to the image. With the light coming from the top and right, apply the gradient in the opposite corners: the bottom left and the top right. Click in the corners and drag toward the center of the image (see Figure 3-19). After you have placed a few gradients, set the layer's **Blend Mode** to **Hardlight**, and set the **Alpha** to 50. The **Hardlight Blend Mode** intensifies the light pixels in the layer, but keeps the dark pixels intact. This makes these gradients blend over the image, and the low **Alpha** tones down the blackest parts of this layer. Look at the image and add any extra gradients as needed.

Figure 3-19. Tie it all together with a gradient overlay.

Projects 3.1b—Other Methods to Simulate Photographic Effects and Adjusting Colors

Phoenix is well equipped to handle color, tonal, and luminosity adjustments in images. With its tools, you have quite a bit of control over the colors in your images, as you saw in the Project 3.1. In the next section, you will see other basic ways to control the tonal and luminosity using the image from the 3.1 project (see Figure 3-20).

Figure 3–20. The original image. It has several good things going for it, but we have to remove emphasis from the undesired elements to make it usable.

Contrast and brightness

In the image that was used in Project 3.1, you can see that it has several undesirable elements. First, the person taking the photo has his shadow is in the photo and that shadow covers a section of the subject. Second, the background blends in with the subject and is not nice to look at. Finally, the colors are washed out.

To correct this photo, first, you need to explore what kind of tonal corrections can be done. Start by looking at Brightness and Contrast.

Start with the original image imported into Phoenix. Click **Image ➤ Brightness & Contrast** to bring up the dialog box to adjust the lighting values of an image. **Brightness** sets the overall lightness or darkness of the image. **Contrast** is the difference in brightness between two different pixels. For example, turn on a flashlight on a sunny day. The light it produces does not seem very bright. This is considered low contrast because the flashlight also produces light. If you turn on the same flashlight at night, it lights up a large area. This is considered high contrast because the flashlight is producing substantially more light than is available at night. In this example, you decrease the **Brightness** setting it to –30. This makes the colors appear more intense because you reduce the effect of the light that is washing out the colors. Next, increase the **Contrast** to 25 (see Figure 3-21). This further intensifies the colors because the difference in brightness between the pixels increases. This is a good technique to enhance dull, dark, or overexposed photos. For this example it intensifies the cast shadow of the photographer, which you don't want. Cancel the **Brightness & Contrast** dialog, and let's try a different effect.

Figure 3-21. Enhance lightness and darkness with the Brightness & Contrast operation.

Adding film grain

An easy and quick way to make a digital image look old is to add film grain. **Film grain** is random texture that shows up in some film processing. This is due to small grains of metallic silver depositing on the photograph during development. You apply a `custom filter` to achieve the film grain effect. Phoenix uses `custom filters` that are actually made in Peacock, which is Aviary's effects editor. These custom filters are special files known as Blackboxes in Peacock and can be as simple as changing colors to as complex as generating three-dimensional filters. Next, you are introduced to custom filters and learn how to find and use them in your creations.

1. Start with the original image imported into Phoenix. With the image layer selected, use the **Filters ➤ Import Custom Filter** command to open the **Blackbox Browser**. The Blackbox browser enables you to find all the available filters on Aviary. To find the **Film Grain Blackbox**, type the word **Grain** in the search field in this browser. This filters only the Blackboxes that have **Grain** in the name or tags that are keywords associated with the file. If this filter process produces more than one file, you can click the display detail button on the blue bar ▤ (see Figure 3-22). This lists the files with their names so that they are easy to find. Locate the file titled **Film Grain Blackbox**, and click the **OK** button to import it into the current Phoenix file.

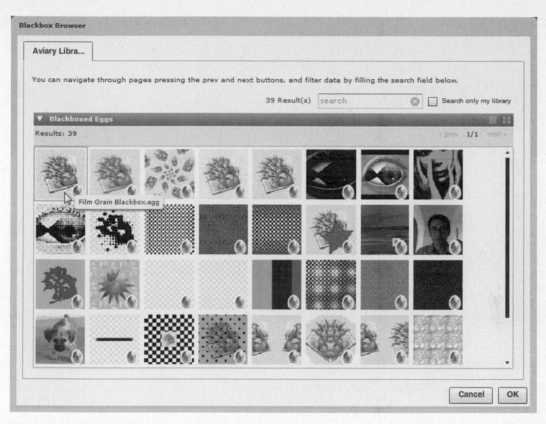

Figure 3-22. Import a custom filter to add film grain to an image.

2. When you load a `custom filter` into Phoenix, it launches and opens a dialog window. This window has an effect preview window, a progress bar, and properties for the filter. The Film Grain filter is relatively small so it renders the effect quickly in the preview window, but as the filters get more complex, you might have to wait for an effect to render. The filter has three properties. `Film Grain` amount controls the amount of noise that is applied to the image simulating the film grain. A `Randomize` button that renders the effect with a new random pattern. Finally, the `Grayscale` parameter toggles between a colored and monochrome grain. Set the `Film Grain` amount to 50 and make sure the `Grayscale` option is unchecked (see Figure 3-23). Click **OK** to commit the filter effect to the file. Your image is duplicated and put on a new layer with the effect added. For more information and how to make a Blackbox or custom filter, see Chapter 9.

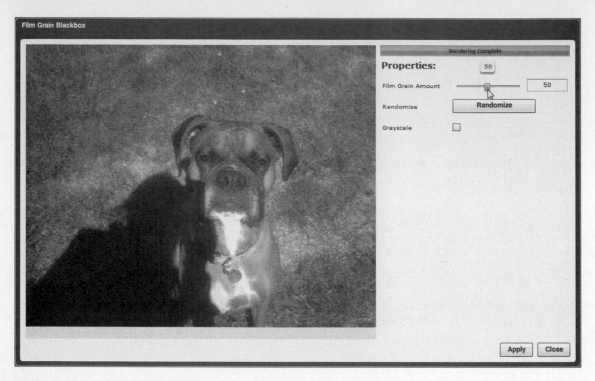

Figure 3-23. Set the parameters of your custom filter.

Create a sepia tone effect

You can age the photo even more by making it black and white or simulating a sepia tone effect. **Sepia toning** is a process used to develop film. It was used in older photographs because it made a more durable photo. Some say that is why many old photographs survived longer than others did. Next, you see how to use Blending Modes and a color over layer to give a Sepia tone look to an image.

   1. Start with the original image in Phoenix. Click the `Image` ➤ `Hue & Saturation` function. The `Hue and Saturation` dialog displays; it is where you can control the overall tone of an image. Use the `Saturation` slider to decrease the amount of color in the image. Set the `Saturation` slider to –60 to significantly reduce the color in the image because color shows through the final overlay, and alter the sepia toning effect. Then use the `Hue` slider to shift the overall colors in the image to an orange/yellow tint; for this image, it is a setting of 30 (see Figure 3-24). Click `OK` to commit the new color settings.

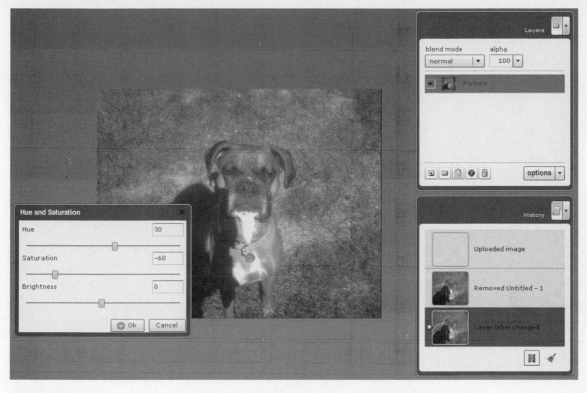

Figure 3-24. Use the Hue & Saturation operation to control the overall tone of the image.

 Hue is the main property of a color. It Is what you think of as a base color, such red or blue-green. However, it doesn't describe the lightness or how much color is present. The `Hue` slider in the `Hue & Saturation` command offsets the colors in an image (see Figure 3-25).

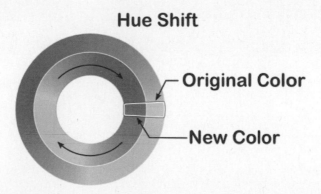

Figure 3-25. Hue color wheel

Basically, it shifts all of the colors around the color wheel.

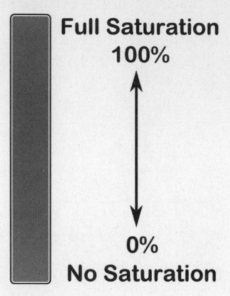

Figure 3-26. Saturation levels of a color

Saturation is the amount of hue or color that is in an image. Neon colors have high saturation, and pastels have low saturation (see Figure 3-26). Setting this to 0 turns off all the color information and produces a black and white image.

2. Create a new layer, and name this layer color. Next, set the current color to brown by clicking the foreground color box in the color selector. Select the Paint Bucket tool , and click the canvas to fill it with the brown color (see Figure 3-27).

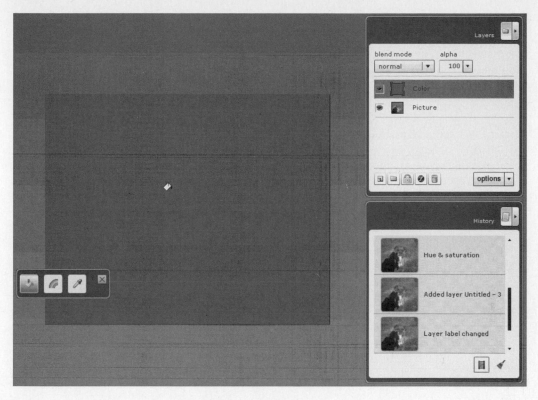

Figure 3–27. Create a new layer and fill it with a brown color.

 The Foreground/Background color selector shows the current selected colors and sets colors (see Figure 3-28).

Figure 3–28. The color selector

The two large squares represent the foreground and background colors, or the fill and strokes of shapes added with the Shape tool. Double-clicking either square brings up the Color Picker window to set the color. The small black and white squares icon in the lower left restores the colors to the default black foreground and white background. The double arrow icon in the upper right reverses the foreground and background colors.

3. Finally, set the `Layer Blend Mode` to `Overlay`. This gives the whole image a brown tone, and this can be decreased by reducing the `Alpha`. In this example, an `Alpha` setting of 60 produces the effect you want (see Figure 3-29).

Figure 3-29. Set the brown layer to `Overlay` to complete the sepia tone effect.

Project review

In this project, you saw how altering the color can drastically change the mood of an image. Levels and adjustment of individual channels give you better control over an image's values and color. Several tools can be used to adjust the colors, values, and saturation of images. You also learned that you can colorize an image by covering it with color and setting the **Blend Mode** to **Overlay**. Custom filters are imported effects that can save time and extend Phoenix's power. **Define Pattern** is an underused feature that enables you to quickly and easily fill areas and even paint with patterns. Finally, you made a complete scene to display your image to disguising poor quality and imperfections. In the next project, you explore the use of selections to cut a photo into parts and recombined them into a more interesting and dynamic composition. You see how you can extend an object outside of your image. This changes an average image into something more. Finally, you also explore the use of Blend Modes further by creating a simulated lighting effect.

Project 3.2—Enhancing Photographs

Phoenix contains many tools that enable you to manipulate photos directly. With robust color correction and powerful selection tools, you can turn a regular photo into an exciting image. This can be used to create a digital scrapbook page or a dynamic flier. By selectively cutting parts of a photograph and putting them together as you would in a collage, you can create a more interesting composition. In this project, you take a photo and use various selection techniques and blending modes to turn it into a postcard-inspired image. See Figure 3-30 for an image of what you will make in this project.

Figure 3–30. This is the final image you make in this project.

103

Key features used in this project

- Modifying selections
- Fills
- Blend Modes
- Custom filters

> *Find this file online at*
> *http://aviary.com/artists/gettingstartED/creations/chapter_3_project_2.*

1. Import the image into Phoenix from the start screen by selecting the `Load existing file` option. This lets you load the image that you are working on and simultaneously size the canvas to match it. If you already have Phoenix open, you can use the `File > Import file` command and then choose the `Resize canvas` option. Name this layer Lighthouse and the bottom layer Background. This is a large image and there is too much space to the left. You need to crop some of this space out of the image. Start by selecting the area that you want to keep by dragging the Rectangular Selection tool ⬚ around the desired portion (see Figure 3-31). After you have the selection the way you want it, use the `Image > Crop Selection` function to remove the area that is not selected. Cropping removes this area from all layers and resizes the canvas to fit.

Figure 3–31. Crop the image.

2. In this file, you want the lighthouse tower extended outside of the picture frame. To do this, you need a copy of the tower. Start by duplicating the Lighthouse layer so you have exactly the same two layers. Do this by selecting **Layer ➤ Duplicate Layer**. This copies the selected layer onto a new layer and appends the name with suffix "– Copy." It is handy to duplicate a layer to test destructive filters on so that you always have a copy to return to if you do not like the results.

Because this image has mostly straight lines, use the Polygonal Selection tool and carefully select points around the shape. The Polygonal Selection tool draws a straight-edged selection between each point you set with the mouse. To complete or close the selection, click the same point you where you started the selection. The more precise you create your selection, the less clean up time needed later in the process. Also, if you close a selection and you want to add to it, hold down the Shift key and select the area you want to add. This new selected area is merged with the existing area. If you want to subtract from the selection, hold down the Alt key and select the portion that you want to remove. Remember to use the zoom slider to get a closer look at your file and make the selection process easier (see Figure 3-32).

Figure 3–32. Select the area to extend outside of the frame.

3. Choose **Select ➤ Invert Selection** to reverse the area that is selected. You can always use the keyboard shortcut of Ctrl+I (Command ⌘+I on the Mac) to do the same (see Figure 3-33). Next, press the Delete key to remove the area selected around the lighthouse tower. Because you have the original layer underneath this copied layer, you won't see an apparent change in the file. To check the results of the deletion, you can temporarily turn off the visibility of the original Lighthouse layer by clicking the Show/Hide button 👁 on the layer. Hide the original layer and check to see if the Lighthouse – copy layer just contains the tower. Finally, rename the Lighthouse – copy layer to Tower reflecting the object on the layer.

Figure 3–33. Invert the selection and delete the area around the tower.

4. We want to remove a section of the background. Start by selecting the Lighthouse layer in the **Layers** panel. Use the Rectangular Selection tool ⬚ to select an area that allows the tower of the lighthouse to extend out of it. This is when you need to think of composition, where you want the subject positioned in the final image, what the overall scale of the objects is, and what objects should be removed. Most of these can be influenced by how this selection is sized and located. In this example, you want most of the rocks and ocean and some of the sky. You also want to have the tower of the lighthouse off center to give more visual interest to a static picture (see Figure 3-

34). After you have the selection the way you want, use **Selection ➤ Invert Selection** or **Ctrl+I** and remove the area around the outside with the Delete key.

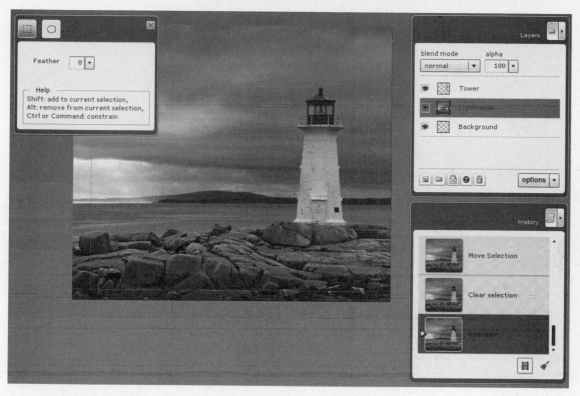

Figure 3–34. Select and remove some of the background.

5. To set this image off of the background, you need to fill it with a strong color. Select the empty Background layer, and use the default Paintbucket tool to fill this entire layer with Black (see Figure 3-35). Now you can see how the selection process from the earlier steps works with each other. The image covers much of the bottom half of the image, whereas the tower extends out of that image into the black background.

Figure 3–35. Fill the background with black.

6. Select the Lighthouse layer's pixels by holding down the Shift key and clicking the layer preview image in the Layers panel. You will make a white boarder around the square image of the Lighthouse; this simulates the border you can find around many picture postcards. To do this, you modify the selection. With the pixels in the Lighthouse layer selected, use the `Select ➤ Modify ➤ Expand` function. This command brings up the `Expand Selection` dialog where you set the amount in pixels to be added to the selection. Set this to 15 to expand this selection by 15 pixels and click `OK`. Notice that the selection area has grown and extends past the lighthouse layers image. Finally, use the Paint Bucket tool to fill the new selection with white, careful to click in the space where the selection expanded (see Figure 3-36). Then clear the selection with the `Select ➤ Select None` command or by pressing Ctrl+D on the keyboard (Command ⌘+D on the Mac).

Figure 3–36. Fill the selection to make a frame.

There are four modifiers that can be performed on a selection (see Figure 3-37).

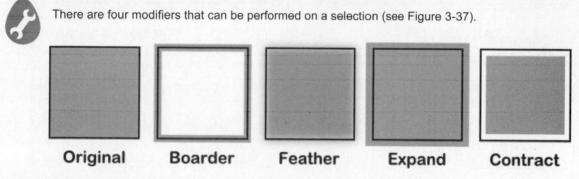

Original **Boarder** **Feather** **Expand** **Contract**

Figure 3–37. Examples of the four selection modifiers. The black rectangle is the original selection, and the blue area is the modified selection.

Any of these bring up a dialog box to set the amount of modification in pixel amounts.

• **Border**: This modification takes the current selection and creates a new selection that follows the edge of the original with the thickness of this new selection set in pixels.

- **Feather**: This modification softens the edges of the current selection. This softening extends both inside and outside of the original selection.
- **Expand**: This modification expands the current selection in all directions.
- **Contract**: This modification shrinks the current selection in all directions.

7. Now that you have a background behind the Lighthouse and Tower layers, you can see that the edge might need some cleanup. Select the Tower layer, and use the Eraser tool with the **Hardness** set to 80. The **Hardness** setting controls the blending at the edge of the Eraser. Setting of 100 produces a sharp-edged eraser, whereas a setting of 0 produces a soft blended edge. Carefully erase any rough areas around the object (see Figure 3-38). Remember to change the size of the Eraser tool and zoom into the image as needed to get into tight spaces.

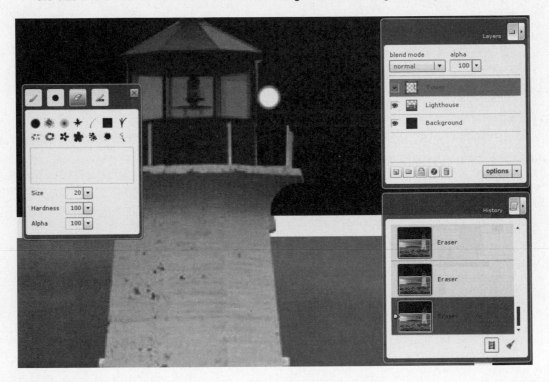

Figure 3-38. Clean up the edges.

8. Now that the Linage is cleaned up, you need to add light emanating from the lighthouse. The quickest way to do this is to use a **custom filter**. Again, a **custom filter** is an effects file that was constructed with Aviary's effects editor Peacock. For more information on Peacock, see Chapters 5 and 6. Use the **Filters ➤ Import Custom Filter** command to open the **Blackbox Browser**. Blackbox is the term for custom filter files in Aviary's effects editor Peacock. Type "Radiating" in the search box in the Browser to filter only Blackboxes that contain

the word radiating in their titles or tags. Locate and select the Radiating Light Blackbox file from the filter list, and click `OK` to load the Filter into the file. This automatically opens the Radiating Light Blackbox properties window. Set the `Width` and `Height` parameters to the same dimensions as the Phoenix file. This image is 1145 X 978; however, this setting is different for everyone and was set when you cropped the image in step 1. To find the current size of the file, cancel the `custom filter,` and then use the `Image ➤ Image resize` command to bring up the `Image resize` dialog. It has the current file dimensions in the width and height fields. Write these numbers down and cancel the resize dialog. Next, go back to the `Filters ➤ Custom Filter ➤ Radiating Light Blackbox` and set the height and width parameters accordingly. Finally, set the `Size` parameter to 50, which sets how big the radiating effect is, and click `Apply` to commit the effect to the file (see Figure 3-39).

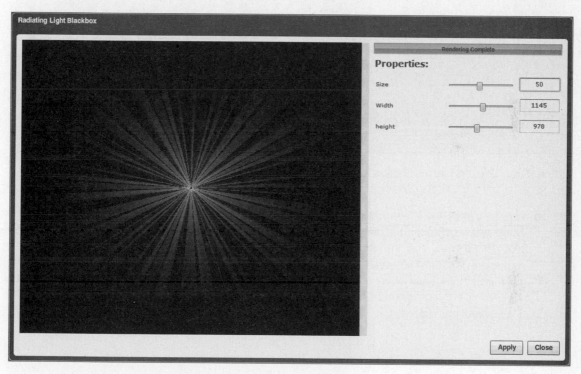

Figure 3-39. Adding light to the lighthouse using a custom filter.

9. The custom filter produced a new layer containing a radiating pattern. First, name this layer Light1, because there is a second light layer. Next, set the `Blend Mode` to Add. The `Add Blend Mode` makes all dark pixels transparent and greatly intensifies the light pixels. This makes the radiating pattern blend with the lighthouse image. The pattern is a bit too intense, so set the `Alpha` of the Light1 layer to 60. Next, select the Transformation tool and use it to position the radiating pattern so that the center is directly over the light of the tower (see Figure 3-40).

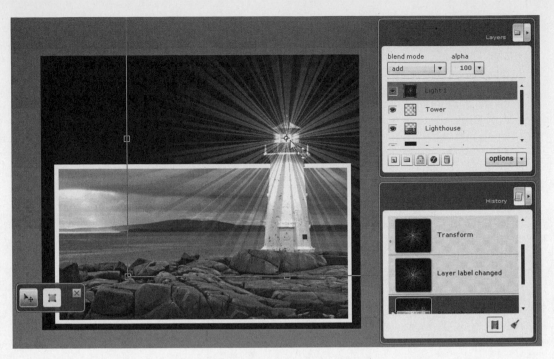

Figure 3–40. Use the Transformation tool to position the light and set the Blend Mode to add.

10. Create a new layer and name it Light2. Next, select the Gradient Fill tool, and set the colorstops to light yellow (#ffed8a) fading to a medium gray (#808080). Then, set the gradient type to **Radial** and the **spread method** to **Repeat** (see Figure 3-41). This produces a repeating gradient that radiates from the start point in concentric rings like a target. Start your gradient at the center of the light coming from the tower and drag out at a 45° angle; release the mouse to set the gradient. Finally, set the **Blend Mode** in this layer to **Overlay**, which makes the gray values transparent.

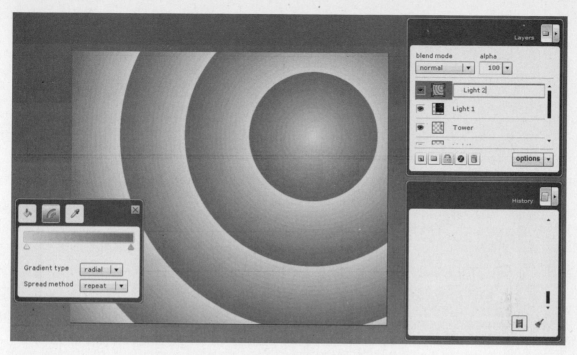

Figure 3-41. Fill a new layer with a repeating radial gradient and set the **Blend Mode** to **Overlay**.

11. You now delete the part of the radial gradient that is over the Lighthouse image. Start by selecting the pixels in the Lighthouse layer by holding down the Shift key and clicking the preview in the Layers panel (See Figure 3-42). Next, reselect the Light2 layer, make sure the selection around the Lighthouse image is still active, and then press the Delete button to clear the part of the gradient that is over the image.

Figure 3-42. Delete a portion of the radial gradient.

12. You can add a title to your image. Like many postcards, the title tells the people you are sending it to what you have been doing on your vacation. Select the Text tool [icon], and select a font that matches your image. In this image, use a serif font for a professional look. Then, set the `color` to white and the `size` to 80. Next, click the upper-left area of the image to set the text start point and type in your title (see Figure 3-43). In this case, it is a postcard of scenic Lighthouses.

Position the text element with the Move tool [icon]. Finally, use the `Convert layer to Bitmap` command in the `Options` menu of the Layers panel to convert the text to an image. Name this converted layer Text.

Figure 3–43. Set the light layer's Blend Mode to `Overlay`.

13. Add a Layer Filter effect to make the text standout. Open the `Layer Filters` dialog for the text layer by clicking the `Layer Filters` button 🔵. Select the `Layer Filter Glow`, and then set the `color` to a golden yellow and the `quality` to high (see Figure 3-44). This produces a glowing halo around the text, setting it off from the background.

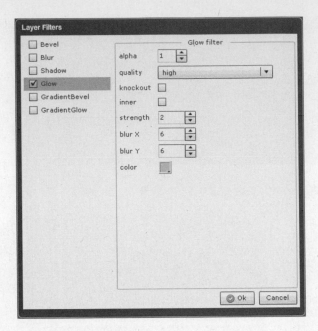

Figure 3-44. Add a Glow Layer Filter to the text.

Project review

In this project, you saw how you can change the composition of a photo by using the crop and selection tools. Selecting and cutting portions of an image and repositioning them enable you to create a new dynamic layout of image elements. You also learned about the Selection modification commands, which give you better control over your selections. Blend Modes are used to create simulated lighting effects. You saw how a text element can add another dimension to your image. In the next project, you learn about new methods for altering colors in images. You explore how to selectively desaturate an image to increase the focus on the subject and how to fix a color error in a photo due to camera flash. You also use Phoenix's Color replacement tool to quickly change the color of objects in an image. Finally, you see how to paint color onto an image to give a surreal effect.

Project 3.3—Manipulate Colors in Images

Readily accessible to most people and everywhere around us, modern digital cameras are great tools to catch immediate moments. However, they are usually not the best for recording accurate colors. Oversaturated colors, underexposed, and grainy images are the side effects of this. As you have seen in previous projects, these problems can easily be fixed. However, you can take color correction to the extreme and use it to make an image more dramatic. In these exercises, you learn various ways to colorize images. Along with the uses of selective desaturation (see Figure 3-45), you can turn an average photo into a work of art and cover up flaws in the image along the way.

Exercise 1—Selective desaturation

Figure 3-45. Extreme colorizing by selective desaturation

Key features used in this project

- Desaturate
- Eraser tool
- Levels
- Hue & Saturation
- Overlay Blend Mode

> *Find this file online at*
> *http://aviary.com/artists/gettingstartED/creations/chapter_3_project_3.*

117

1. This selective desaturation effect works best with bright and vibrantly colored images. The intent is to make the entire image black and white except for the subject that retains its color. Launch Phoenix and import your image; do this by using the **`Load existing file`** from the splash screen when launching the application or by using the **`File ➤ Import File`** command. Name the layer with the image Berries and the bottom layer Background. Duplicate the Berries layer by select **`Duplicate Layer`** command from the **`Options`** menu in the **`Layers`** panel, so there are two identical layers on top of each other (see Figure 3-46). This new layer is automatically named Berries – copy; this is a perfect name for it, so there is no need to rename that layer.

Figure 3-46. Duplicate the image.

2. Next, desaturate the Berries - copy layer using the **`Image ➤ Hue & Saturation`** command. In the **`Hue & Saturation`** dialog, set the **`Saturation`** level to -100. You can also adjust the value of the image with the **`Brightness`** control. In this example, the **`Brightness`** was set to -8 (see Figure 3-47). Alternatively, you can remove all the color from an image in one step by using the **`Image ➤ Desaturate`** command. This method does not let you adjust the brightness of the image, it removes only the color. Finally, use the **`Image ➤ Auto Levels`** command to stretch the value range of the image. **`Auto levels`** automatically analyze the values in an image, and if the lightest and the darkest areas are not pure white or pure black, it stretches the values until

they span the entire value range from black to white. This makes your images as rich as they can be without manual adjustments.

Figure 3-47. Desaturate the duplicated top layer.

3. Erasing part of the top desaturated layer lets the full color layer underneath show through. Select the Eraser tool, set the **Hardness** to 80, and start erasing the area where you want to have color (see Figure 3-48). Note that everywhere you erase, the color starts showing up as though you are painting with color. Carefully erase the top layer to reveal the color underneath. Adjust the size of the Eraser tool and the **Hardness** as necessary. You usually cannot use the same size eraser to do the entire job.

Figure 3-48. Use the Eraser tool to uncover the color form from the lower layer.

4. You have to zoom in to the image to erase as close as possible to the edge. Use the `Zoom Level` slider at the top, right of the application to zoom into the image up to 400% of the original (see Figure 3-49). After you zoom in, a quick way to navigate around the canvas is to use the Pan tool . You can temporarily enable the Pan tool by holding down the Space bar. When you see the cursor turn into the hand icon, you are in Pan Mode. Clicking on the canvas and dragging moves the image around the workspace. After the Space bar is released, the cursor reverts back to the last used tool. This is a great shortcut and speeds up your work flow when zoomed in.

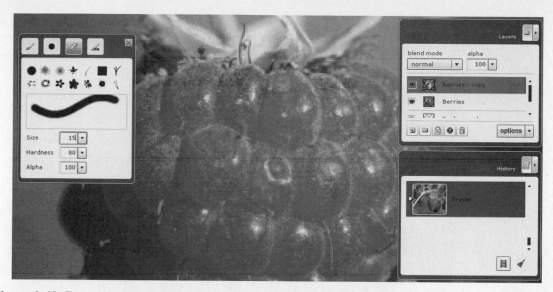

Figure 3-49. Zoom into your image to erase as close to the edges as possible.

5. As a last step, you want to enhance the subjects color. The color of the object is quite bright against the desaturated background but it could be even more dramatic. Select the colored Berries layer and bring up the **Image ➤ Hue & Saturation** function to enhance the layer. Set the **saturation** level to 22; this increases the color in the underlying layer but doesn't overpower it or produce garish colors (see Figure 3-50).

Figure 3–50. Increase the saturation of the underlying layer to make the image pop.

6. For fun, you can even change the color of the saturated part of the image. Open the `Hue & Saturation` function again, but this time, cycle through the colors of the `Hue` slider. For this example, turn the berry bright blue by setting the `Hue` to -115 the `Saturation` to 7 and decrease the `Brightness` by -40 (see Figure 3-51).

Figure 3-51. Adjust the hue to create a whimsical image.

Exercise 2—Red eye fix

> *Find this file online at*
> *http://aviary.com/artists/gettingstartED/creations/start_chapter_3_project_3_2.*

Have you ever gotten film back from the developer only to find that all the people have menacing red eyes? This is called red eye and is a problem that happens when the strong light of a camera's flash reflects off the back of an eye. Many digital cameras have ways to minimize this effect, but it can still happen in certain lighting conditions. This can be disturbing and ruin a photo, but with a few quick steps, you can rid your photo of these picture-wrecking problems. See Figure 3-52 for the final results of this process.

Figure 3-52. Fix red-eye problems in your images.

1. Start by loading your image that has a problem with red eye into Phoenix. The easiest way is to import the image directly from the start menu using the Load existing file from the splash screen. This automatically resizes the canvas to the dimensions of the imported image. At this point, it is useful to zoom into the problem area. The Zoom Level slider in the top, right zooms in and out of the image. Use the Elliptical Selection tool to select only the red area of the eye (see Figure 3-53). You can always fine-tune this selection by clicking inside the selected area with the tool to move it.

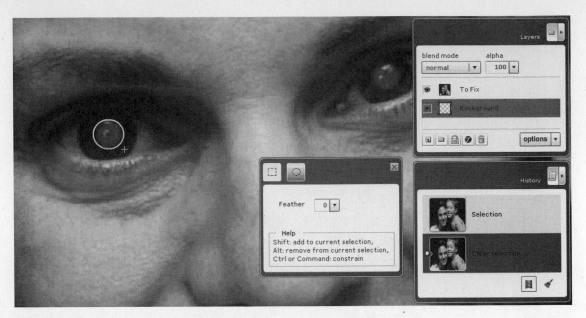

Figure 3-53. Red eye is one of the common problems of flash photography.

 The zoom control sets the magnification level of the image in the workspace area; 100% sets the image to be 1:1 pixel ratio to the screen (see Figure 3-54).

Figure 3-54. This slider controls the zoom level in a file.

Sliding the control lets you set the zoom to 400% or all the way out to 10%. Alternatively, by clicking the plus or minus magnifying icon on either side of the control zooms in and out of the image in 50% increments. Finally, you can type in the desired zoom level in the box to go directly to a specific view.

2. Open the `Hue & Saturation` dialog, and reduce the `Saturation` of the red-eye area. This reduces the color in that area. Next, decrease the `Brightness` setting. You usually do not want to reduce it all the way to -100, because that would wash out any of the highlights. Reduce the `Brightness` just enough to make the pupil dark without losing the highlights (see Figure 3-55).

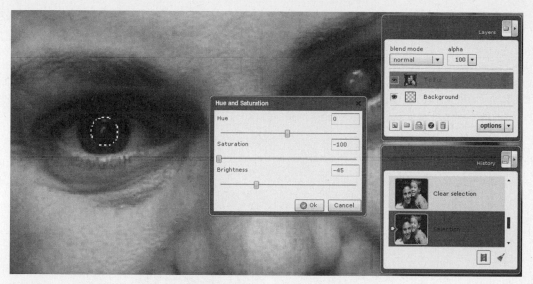

Figure 3-55. Darken the red eye with the Hue & Saturation controls.

3. The edge around the repaired area will be rough; you want to use the Blur tool 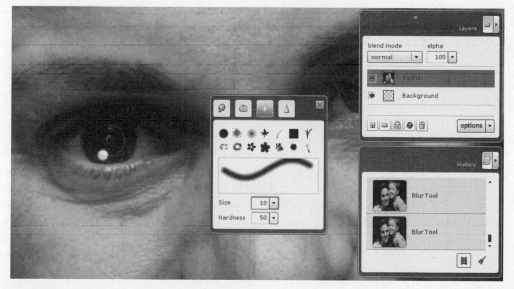 to smooth out some of the edges. Set the Blur tool `Size` and the `Hardness` fairly small, depending on your image, and blur away any edges that look unnatural (see Figure 3-56). This example uses size 10 with a hardness of 50 to achieve the results. You don't want to blur out too much detail, so carefully soften the edges of the fixed red-eye area with the rest of the eye by just following the rough edge.

Figure 3-56. Cleaning up the edges with the Blur tool.

Exercise 3—Color replacement tool

Aviary comes with a convenient tool that enables you to change a color in an image. You only have to select the replacement color and the color to be replaced. However, like many automated tools, it does take some fine-tuning to get a good result, and it usually works only with certain images. When all the conditions are right, you can experience a truly amazing tool. See Figure 3-57 for the results of this project.

> *Find this file online at*
> *http://aviary.com/artists/gettingstartED/creations/chapter_3_project_3_3.*

Figure 3-57. It is easy to replace color in certain images.

1. On occasion, you might want to change the color of an object in a photo. This can be done quickly with the Color Replacement tool. A word of caution about the Color Replacement tool

   . It isn't perfect and does take some practice to get good results. Furthermore, it works best when the image has high contrast and strong, dissimilar colors. Start by duplicating the layer using the `Layer ➤ Duplicate Layer` command; this makes an exact copy of the image on a new layer. You use this later when you need to clean up the image. Next, select the Color Replacement tool in the tool's fly-out menu. The parameters for this tool are similar to the other brush tools with the exception of a Foreground/Background color selector. The color set in the background color box is the color that is replaced with the color set in the foreground color box. To start, double-click the background color box to bring up the `Color Picker` window. However, instead of trying to set the right color manually, click the image to sample the color you want to replace. A useful feature of the `Color Picker` window is the ability to sample colors directly from the image. Any time the cursor is outside of the `Color Picker` window, it turns into a sample tool represented by the Eye Dropper cursor. The Color Picker sets itself to any color clicked on in the image. Click the color you want to replace. Don't pick the lightest or darkest version of the color, but instead try to find a middle range (see Figure 3-58). This gives you a better result. Next, double-click the foreground color box and select the color you want to replace it with. In this example, purple was used.

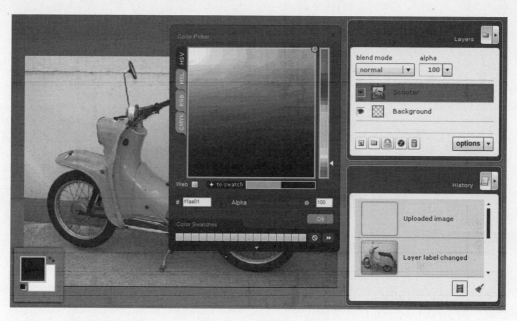

Figure 3-58. Easily replace colors in an image with the Color Replacement tool.

2. This is the fun part. Paint over the area of the image where you want the color replaced. If you find that not as much of the color is getting replaced as desired, try increasing the Tolerance setting. This setting controls how much difference there is between the color from the background color selected in the tool parameter and the one in the image being replaced (see Figure 3-59). A higher setting replaces a greater range of colors than a smaller setting.

Figure 3-59. Apply the new color.

3. In this example, the wall behind the scooter is similar in color to the one I was replacing. Consequently, there was some bleeding of the purple color onto the wall. This is where the duplicated layer from the first step comes in handy. Use the Eraser tool with a **Hardness** setting of 80 to carefully erase any color that bleeds outside of the scooter (see Figure 3-60). With the original layer underneath the color-replaced layer, any erasing enables the original layer to show through.

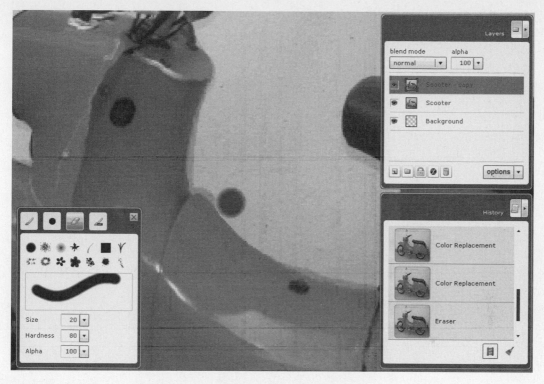

Figure 3-60. Use the Eraser tool to clean up the overflow of color.

Exercise 4—Quick colorizing

You used this overlay coloring technique in other projects like the sepia toning project. You can color an entire image this way. Before you used color overlays to tone and change the color of an entire image. In this exercise, you see how you can use blend modes to color individual elements in an image. See Figure 3-61 for the results from this project.

Find this file online at
http://aviary.com/artists/gettingstartED/creations/chapter_3_project_3_4.

Figure 3-61. Color an image using a layer set to `Overlay`.

1. Launch Phoenix and import your image either via the **`Load existing file`** from the splash screen of the **`File` ➤ `Import File`** command. Don't forget to name the layers. If your image is in color, you need to desaturate it. Use the **`Image` ➤ `Desaturate`** command to rid the image of its color, making it black and white. Next, create a new layer and name it Color. Set its **`Blend Mode`** to **`Overlay`**; by doing this, you are able to see how the coloring process is going and select the area that you want to colorize. In this example, using the Freeform Selection tool gives us the best and easiest selection. Draw a selection around the head of the flower (see Figure 3-62). Try to follow just outside the edge. You usually need to zoom into the image to make following the edge easier. This Selection does not have to be perfect because you clean up the edges later.

Figure 3-62. Select the area that you want colored with the Freeform Selection tool.

2. Use the Paint Bucket tool to fill the selection with the desired color. In this example, color the flower pink (see Figure 3-63). Clear the selection with the Ctrl+D command.

Figure 3-63. Fill the selection with color.

3. The selection might have some rough edges that need to be fixed. Select the Paintbrush tool with the pink color, and then clean up the edges (see Figure 3-64). Paint in color where the selection might have missed covering the object. You also need use the Eraser tool with the **Hardness** set to 80 to clean up the edges wherever the color extends outside the object. Remember that you need to adjust the size of the brushes to enable you to paint in small areas.

Figure 3-64. Clean up the edges with the Eraser tool.

4. Next, add some color to the stem of the flower. Select the Paintbrush tool again and change its color to a bright green (see Figure 3-65). Using this color, paint over the area of the stem on the Color layer. This method of colorizing an image does not produce a realistic coloring of the object, but instead produces a stylized coloring.

Figure 3-65. Use the method to color areas in the image.

Project review

With the exercises in this project, you learned several different ways to add, modify, and change colors using Phoenix. First, you saw that altering the color of a duplicated layer and using the eraser to uncover the underlying color lets you selectively desaturate areas of an image. You also learned how to quickly salvage a ruined photo with red-eye problems. The Color Replacement tool can completely swap out the colors in an image, but some touchup is necessary. Finally, you saw how you can paint color directly onto an image using a layer set to `Overlay`. In the next project, you learn how to repair physical damage and imperfections in photos. You see how to cover large areas of damage, strengthen your use of the Clone tool, and use previous color manipulation techniques to unify the color in the photo.

Project 3.4—Repairing Images

Fixing images is sometimes more than color corrections. Old family photos that have had a hard life, including dog-eared edges, water stains, tears, and more, can be repaired. You can breathe new life into these images using the tools in Phoenix. In this project, you learn how to copy and paste textures to cover large areas of damage. You have the opportunity to build more skills with the Clone tool. Finally, you utilize the techniques you learned in the last project to unify the color of the photo. After learning these techniques, you can dust off the old photos and display them again. See Figure 3-66 for the final results of this project.

Figure 3-66. After this project, you can fix damaged images.

Key features used in this project

- Copy command and Paste command
- Merge Layers
- Clone Stamp tool
- Hue & Saturation
- Blur tool

> *Find this file online at*
> *http://aviary.com/artists/gettingstartED/creations/chapter_3_project_4.*

1. Start by launching Phoenix and importing the image that you want to repair. You can do this by using the **Load Existing File** from the splash screen of use the **Image ➤ Import File**. Do not worry about naming layers in this file until the end because you merge layers often and that resets any naming of the layers. Next, remove all the color using the **Image ➤ Desaturate** command (see Figure 3-67). Only do this step if you are working on a black and white image like this example or if you want it to be black and white in the end.

Figure 3-67. Use the Desaturate function to remove the splotchy color in the image.

2. When fixing large areas with little detail in them, it is easiest to copy and paste textures from different areas of the image. Start by identifying the area that you want to fix. In this example, it is tears around the picture. This area needs a texture pasted over it. Next, look for an area that is clean or has no damage and has similar textures and values. This is the area you copy to the paste area. After you have the two areas chosen, select the Freeform Selection tool and set the **Feather** setting in the parameter fly-out panel to 15 (see Figure 3-68). The feathering softens the edges of the selection. This can also be done after selecting a portion of the image with the **Select ➤ Modify ➤ Feather** function. Next, draw a freehand selection around the area that you want to copy. After it is selected, press Ctrl+C (Command+C on the Mac) to copy that selection. Next, press Ctrl+V to paste the copied selection to a new layer. When you paste any object in Phoenix, it automatically creates a new layer with your copied object placed in.

Figure 3-68. Use the Freeform Selection tool to copy clean textures.

3. Select the new layer that contains the pasted object. Next, using the Transformation tool , position this object over the damaged area (see Figure 3-69). You can rotate this, but try to keep the stretching and skewing to a minimum because it distorts the texture. After you have the object the way you want it, press the Enter key to confirm the transformation.

Figure 3-69. Use the Transformation tool to position the new texture.

4. While the pasted object is still selected, adjust the color with the `Hue & Saturation` command to match the color and brightness with the rest of the image. You can see that any changes you make with the sliders are updated in the image, which makes it easier to match values (see Figure 3-70). Also, do not worry about the ragged boarder around the photo, which is cropped out later.

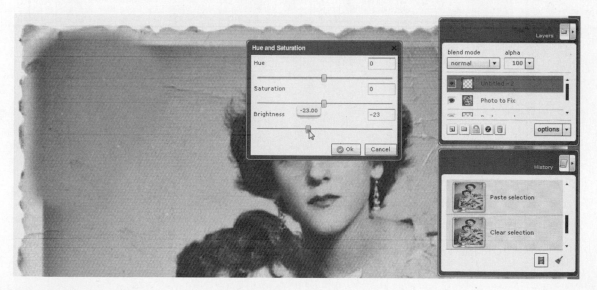

Figure 3-70. Match the value of the pasted texture.

5. After you have the pasted texture in place and its color adjusted to match the rest of the image, remove the selection by selecting **Select** ➤ **Select None**, or use the Ctrl+I keyboard shortcut. Next, select the pasted object layer and the image layer while holding down the Ctrl key. This selects both layers at the same time. Finally, use the **Merge Layers** in the **Layers** panel **options** dropdown menu to combine the two layers (see Figure 3-71). Note that you cannot select multiple layers if you have the Move tool , Transformation tool , or the Distortion tool active.

Figure 3-71. Merge layers.

6. Repeat these Steps 1–4 in any areas of large flat textures. This technique usually works best for backgrounds. You can also shape any of these pasted textures with the Eraser tool . Set the **Hardness** to 0 to keep the edges of the pasted texture soft as you remove any areas that are covering details (see Figure 3-72). Continue until you have all the large areas repaired.

Figure 3-72. Continue the previous steps and shape the pasted texture with the Eraser tool. You can see the texture being erased to let the lady's hair show.

7. The Clone Stamp tool is well suited for touching up images. This tool samples an area of an image and lets you paste it to another area (see the Clone Stamp tool sidebar in Chapter 2, Project 3 for more information). Start by selecting the Clone Stamp tool, and set the `Alpha` to around 30 or 40. Next, click the area you want to sample from while holding down the Shift key. You see a small gray cross-hair icon; this is the sample point. Now wherever you paint on the image with the Clone tool, it copies the area at the sample point and pastes it there (see Figure 3-73). The clone and the sample move in unison. Use the Clone Stamp tool to sample clean areas and the Clone tool to cover any damaged areas or blemishes.

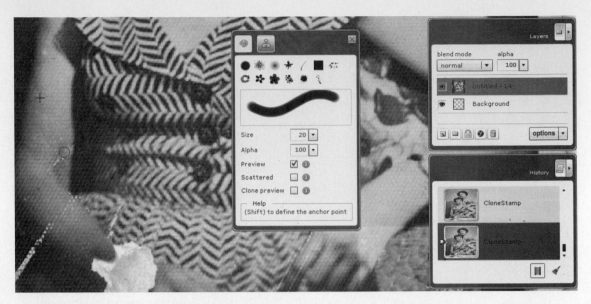

Figure 3-73. It is hard to see in this example, but use the Clone Stamp tool to cover more damage.

8. Carefully use the Clone Stamp tool to cover and blend the damaged areas. Keep resetting the sample point as needed. Adjust the `Size` and `Alpha` periodically so that you can blend the cloned areas in with the original. Depending on how much damage an image has, this process can take a long time (see Figure 3-74). Cloning is not the easiest skill to pick-up and takes some practice. If you are using the Clone Stamp tool for the first time, don't get frustrated. Remember, you can always undo a previous action by using the `Edit` ➤ `Undo` command or by using the keyboard shortcut Ctrl+Z (Command+Z on the Mac).

Figure 3-74. Change the size and Alpha of the Clone Stamp tool to suit your needs.

9. Next, select **Image ➤ Levels** to open the **Adjust Levels** window. Use the slider controls under the histogram graph to adjust the brightness levels. The left sets the black level, the right sets the white level, and the middle sets the midpoint value. The histogram graph in Figure 3-74 shows the current amount of brightness in the image. Start by moving the two end controllers so that they are positioned where each end of the graph starts. This ensures that the darkest areas in the image are black and the lightest are white. Then, move the middle slider to enhance the mid-range value in the image (see Figure 3-75). After you are satisfied with the result in the preview, click **OK**. In this example, the settings of 25, 155, and 250 strengthen the values of the image.

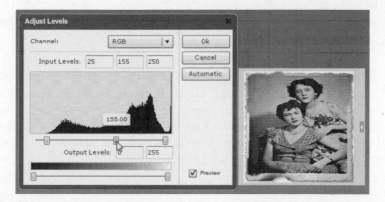

Figure 3-75. Adjust the values in the image with the Level Function.

10. You can now crop out the ragged boarder that surrounds the photo. The reason you left this until the end is so you can use that space to extend the textures and cloning area, and you are not confined by the smaller canvas size. Select the Rectangular Selection tool , and draw a selection just to the inside of the boarder around the photo. Then, use the **Image ➤ Crop Selection** command to crop out the boarder, which cleans up the image even more (see Figure 3-76).

Figure 3-76. Crop the ragged border out of the image.

11. Next, duplicate the image layer using the **Duplicate Layer** command from the **Options** menu of the Layers panel. Then, use the **Filters ➤ Sharpen** command on the duplicated layer to enhance the detail in the image (see Figure 3-77). This effect can do too much sharpening and create jarring highlights. Performing the sharpening on a duplicated layer enables you to decrease the **Alpha** level to fade the effect and blend it with the unaltered layer. Set the **Alpha** level of this layer to 60 to tone down the sharpening effect.

Figure 3-77. Sharpen the image on a Duplicated layer so you can fade the effect.

12. To add color back to this image, you need to first add a new layer. Next, using the Paint Bucket
tool , fill this new layer with an orange-brown color. Finally, set the **Blend Mode** to
Overlay, and reduce the **Alpha** to approximately 50 to achieve a subtle sepia tone to the entire
image (see Figure 3-78). Finally, name the layers accordingly—Color for the color overlay,
Sharpen for the sharpened layer, Picture for the fixed image, and Background for the bottom
layer.

Figure 3-78. Us a color overlay with Blend Mode set to `Overlay` to add color toning to the image.

Project 3.4a—Enhancing a Portrait

In this project, you learn how to simulate a high dynamic range (HDR) photo. An HDR image usually takes several separate exposures of the same picture that are layered and combined to create a dramatic effect. Unfortunately, a true HDR image has more information per pixel than a normal digital image, and Phoenix cannot handle that much information. The effect can, however, be simulated using filters and Blend Modes. By creatively layering and enhancing layers, you can make an image look like HDR. You can see the results of this in the final image from this project in Figure 3-79.

Figure 3-79. Enhanced portrait

Find this file online at
http://aviary.com/artists/gettingstartED/creations/chapter_3_project_4a.

1. Launch Phoenix and import your image by using the `Load Existing File` from the splash screen or the `Image` ➤ `Import File` command. You need to clean up any imperfections in your subject because this technique enhances everything, including imperfections. Start by cleaning up small blemishes or drastic irregularities in the skin with the Clone Stamp tool 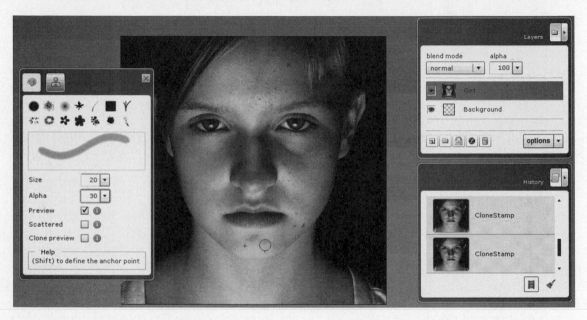. Set the `Alpha` to 40–50 and the `size` according to that area you are cloning, and then cover blemishes or imperfections on your subject (see Figure 3-80).

Figure 3-80. Clean up blemishes and imperfections.

2. Duplicate the image. Then, use the `Filters` ➤ `Blur` function to add a blur to the duplicated layer. The reason for using the filter instead of the layer filter is that it saves you a couple of steps because you don't have to convert the layer effect to bitmap (see Figure 3-81). This is the first step to enhance the edges of the subject.

Figure 3-81. Use filters to enhance the highlights.

3. Next, use the `Filters` ➤ `Find Edges` command on the duplicated layer. This turns the layer black, except where there are areas of high contrast. This is usually at the edges of shapes and roughly follows the outline of objects. This is done so that you can create an enhancement with Blend Modes at the edges of the subject. Next, use the `Image` ➤ `Auto levels` to extend the brightness range and strengthen the effect (see Figure 3-82). You now see the edges of the subject appear out of the initial black that the `Find Edges` filter created.

Figure 3-82. Use a filter to enhance the edges in the image.

4. Change the `Blend Mode` of the layer to `Add` (see Figure 3-83). This mode ignores the black areas of the layer and brightens the lighter pixels. This creates harsh and rough highlights on the portrait.

Figure 3-83. Change the Blend Mode.

5. To soften the effect, add a moderate blur to the layer; this time, use the Blur Layer filter (see Figure 3-84). Set the **Blur x** and **Blur y** values to 10–12 on the layer filter. Duplicate this layer using the **Duplicate Layer** function in the **Options** menu in the Layers panel. This intensifies the highlights.

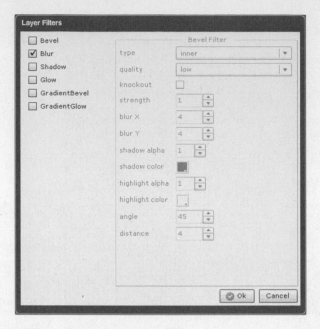

Figure 3-84. Soften the highlights with the Layer Filter Blur.

6. Duplicate the original image layer and move it to the top of the layer stack. Open the `Levels` window by selecting `Image ➤ Levels`. Reduce the light end of the level and increase the midpoint. (see Figure 3-85). This creates a harsh contrast in the image, washing out the lighter areas and strengthening the blacks. In this example, the settings were 0, 40, and 50. Set the `Blend Mode` for this layer to `Multiply`. `Multiply` ignores all the lighter areas of a layer and just blends the darker tones. Reduce the `Alpha` of this layer to 65.

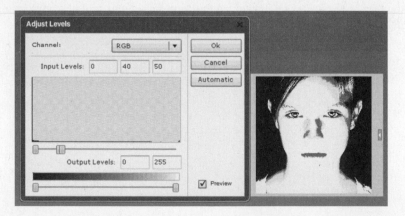

Figure 3-85. Adjust the black levels.

Project review

In this project, you saw how to use the **Copy** and **Paste** commands to quickly transfer textures to cover damaged areas. You also learned the importance of feathering selections to blend these textures together. You had to master the Clone Stamp tool to convincingly repair flaws in your image. Duplicating layers, adding filters, and then reducing Alpha levels enable you to fade these effects. You also saw how the mix of filters and Blend Modes can be used to create a dynamic image. Finally, duplicating layers with **Add Blend Mode** is an easy way to intensify them.

Chapter review

In this chapter, you learned how to manipulate photographs. The first project showed you how to simulate vintage photography styles. You also saw that making a scene for your photo can mask poor quality and undesirable elements. Then, you learned how to use the selection tools to cut up an image and reassemble it into a more dynamic composition. Further, you learned how Blend Modes can be used to create simulated light in your images. You went through four colorizing exercises, learning different methods used to manipulate the color and the tone of your images. You then honed your Clone Stamp skills by using it to repair damaged images. Finally, you saw how to simulate High Dynamic images by mixing filters and Blend Modes. In the next chapter, you use Raven, Aviary's vector editing applications. Vectors are different from the bitmap images you have been using so far. Unlike bitmaps that are made up of pixels, vectors are defined by vertexes and lines. Vectors are used by illustrators and designers because they can be scaled to any level, which means a vector design looks the same at one centimeter as it does at a kilometer.

Chapter 4

Raven—Vector Editing

Raven is used to create fully scalable vector art appropriate for logos or t-shirt designs. Unlike the bitmaps you have used in previous chapters, Raven uses vectors. A **vector** is an object defined by points in space, lines connecting those points together, and color that fills the shape in between those lines. Vectors are defined mathematically and are drawn in real time so they are always drawn at the optimum resolution for the display. Thus, it is a great format for printers, illustrators, and logo designers. You won't find another tool quite like Raven on the Web.

Bitmaps and vectors explained

Two-dimensional (2D) digital images can be constructed basically in two different ways: raster images, commonly referred to as bitmaps, or vector images. Photos and realistic images usually work best as raster images because there is a lot of different color and variations in them. Vectors work well for logos, text, and printed graphics. These two formats can be mixed together with incredible results. In fact, many advertisements you see have a raster image with vector text and logs incorporated into them

Raster images are defined by rows and columns of individual dots (pixels); each has its own color and Alpha. This is a versatile and easily manipulated format. Unfortunately, it does not scale up easily. As shown in Figure 4-1, when a bitmap is scaled up or zoomed in, the pixels become apparent. For normal use, the advantages of bitmaps outweigh the scaling issues. Pixels can be painted into a bitmap; this painting can be blended with the surrounding pixels. Advanced effects can be applied, and interactions with the pixels can be complex. However, when it comes to outputting raster images to a printer, there can be significant problems. If the image needs to be scaled up for print, you start seeing jagged edges and the individual pixels that create a bitmap image. Bitmap images that are designed for print output need to be constructed with size and resolutions that fit the final dimensions. If there are several different print sizes required, there has to be a specific file for each.

Vector images are defined by lines connected between vertices (nodes or points) and a color. For instance, a straight line is defined by a start point and an end point. Because a vector is just an instruction for the computer to draw a line rather than a defined map of every pixel, it maintains crisp, smooth edges at any resolution and zoom level. This format is ideal for printing because it can be scaled to fit any media. As you can see in Figure 4-1, when viewed at screen resolutions, both raster and vector look good. However, when you have to zoom in, scale up, or set to print, the pixels that makes up the raster image start to become apparent, whereas the vector still looks crisp. Another advantage of vector graphics is the size of the files. For example, to define a one-meter circle as a raster image, it would have to define the color and locations of millions of pixels, making an enormous file. On the contrary, to define the one-meter circle as a vector, it needs only the definition of a circle, the radius length, and the color. This is quite a huge difference.

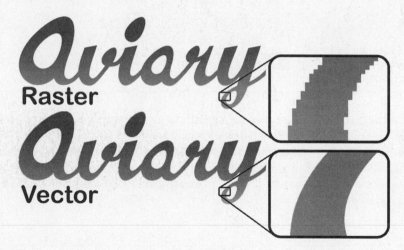

Figure 4–1. The differences between bitmaps and vectors

Vector objects are constructed using paths. A **path** is a line that is defined by discrete points. These points are called vertices, nodes, or anchor points. There has to be a minimum of two to define a path. The start point and end point are located using x and y coordinates. A line segment is drawn between these points or as they are referred to in Raven, vertices, as shown in Figure 4-2. The process is similar to a "connect-the-dots "puzzle.

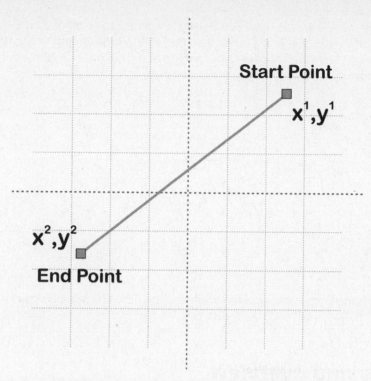

Figure 4–2. A line is defined by two points located by x and a y coordinates.

These lines can be curved or straight. The curved segments, or Bézier curves as they are more properly known, are set using control handles. The segments curve toward the control handles. The line always goes from a start point to an end point, but the position of the control handles influence how it curves on its way between the points (see Figure 4-3). Imagine the control handles are magnets that attract the line. The farther the control handle is moved from the vertices, the more the connecting line segment bends.

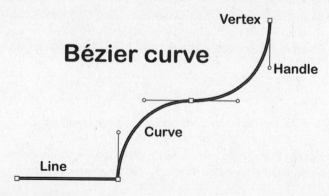

Figure 4–3. Anatomy of a vector path

Paths can either be open or closed. An **open path** is where the ends are not connected. To end open paths, double-click the vertex that you want as the end point. A **closed path** is one where the ends are connected; for example, a circle is a closed path (see Figure 4-4). To close a path, click on the start point. The end and start points connect, resulting in the closed path.

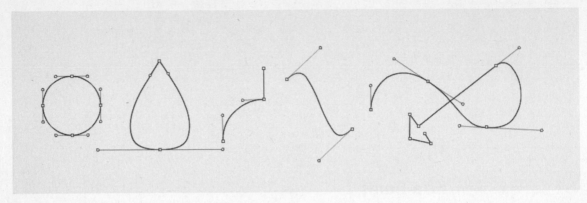

Figure 4–4. Bézier curves can make simple to complex paths. The first two are closed paths; the last three are open paths.

Raven tools and overview

The layout of Raven is similar to Phoenix and other desktop vector editors. At the top is a Main menu that contains `File`, `Edit`, `Rulers`, `Path`, `Object`, `Feedback`, and `Help` menu commands (see Figure 4-5). From the `File` commands, you can save the file, edit the document size, and import resources. The `Edit` menu has the `Undo/Redo` function along with `Copy` and `Paste` commands. `Rulers` let you set the rulers that boarder the workspace. The `Path` menu give you access to advanced path modifiers. The `Object` menu has commands for aligning, distributing, and arranging layers. The Object menu also includes the trace functions. `Feedback` lets you send a bug report directly to the developers. `Help` gives you access to information about the current version of Raven. Under the menu commands, there are dedicated buttons for `Undo` and `Redo` functions. To the right is the Zoom Level slide that enables you to zoom in and out of the workspace. Finally, there is the dedicated Pan feature that enables you to pan around the workspace.

Figure 4-5. The menu bar has the file commands and many advanced functions.

On the left are the tool icons. Each gives you access to a specific function. Some tools have nested-tools or properties that can be selected or adjusted from a fly-out parameter dialog.

The Select and Move Objects tool is used to select or move objects and paths.

 The Quick Edit tool is used to manipulate path segments.

 The Transform tool is used to position, scale, rotate, and skew objects and paths.

The Edit Paths by Nodes tool is used to modify the vertices in paths.

 The Convert Anchor Point tool is used to toggle between straight and smooth vertices.

 The Create Bézier and Lines tool is used to create paths

 The Draw Freehand Lines tool is used to create free form paths.

 The Text tool is used to add text objects using the fonts installed on your computer.

The Create Shapes tool is used to add geometric shapes.

 The Gradient Transform tool is used to edit and set gradient fills.

 The Edit Guides tool is used to modify guides.

You can see all of these tools in action and explore how they work as you make your way through all of the projects in this chapter.

Under the tools is the Fill and Stroke color selector (see Figure 4-6). This enables you to set the stroke, outline, and fill colors in a file. The black and white icon in the lower left is restore colors, which resets the colors to their default of white fill and black stroke. The double arrow icon in the upper right swaps the fill and stroke colors.

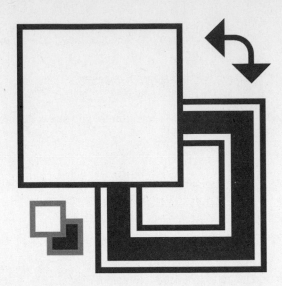

Figure 4-6. The Fill and Stroke color selector

The **Layers** panel is at the upper right of the workspace. This is similar to the Layers panel in Phoenix.

You should use these layers to group objects or paths. You can create **nested layers**, which are layers that are inside another layer (see Figure 4-7). You can also set **Blend Modes** and **Alphas** for entire layers, an object, or a path.

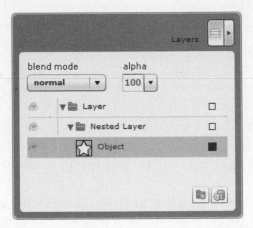

Figure 4-7. The Layers panel

The **Fill and Stroke** property panel consists of three tabs, **Fill**, **Stroke**, and **Stroke Style** (see Figure 4-8). The **Fill** tab lets you set the fill color, gradient color, and gradient type, and it saves color swatches. The **Stroke** tab is where you set the stroke color, stroke type, and save swatches. The **Stroke Style** tab is where you set the stroke weight, end caps, and miter. After a **Fill** and **Stroke** property is set, all newly draw objects or paths will have those properties. This is handy when you are drawing multiple objects that you want to have the same fill and `stroke`.

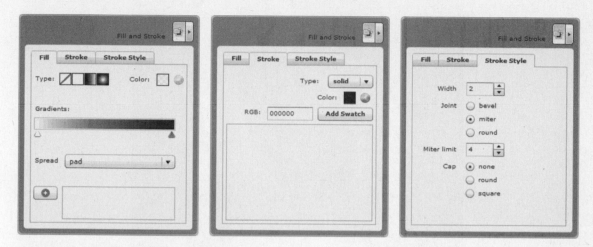

Figure 4-8. The `Fill and Stroke` panel tab.

Finally, the center of the application is the workspace, this is where you will do all of your work. The rectangle in the center of this workspace is the canvas. Any objects or paths that are inside the canvas area are included in the final image, and any that are outside of it are not included in the image.

Project 4.1—Getting Familiar with the Path Tools

In all vector-editing applications, there is a path tool. Most work the same way with slight variations, and Raven is no exception. Raven's Bézier and Line tool is arguably the most important and versatile tool in the application. You will undoubtedly need to use it to make the most of the application. However, it is not an intuitive tool to learn. In this first project, you will go through a guided tour of how to create an image with Raven's Create Bézier and Lines tool. This is a tracing exercise that will teach you how to use this versatile tool. See Figure 4-9 for the final result from this project.

Figure 4-9. This is the image you will create in this exercise.

Key concepts in this project

- Create Bézier and Lines tool
- Edit Paths by Nodes tool
- Convert Anchor Point tool

> *Find this file online at*
> `http://aviary.com/artists/gettingstartED/creations/chapter_4_project_1`.

1. Use the link for this project in the sidebar to open the exercise in Raven (see Figure 4-10). It takes time to load because of the large file size. You should review the instructions before starting because the instructions are on their own layer. You can toggle the visibility of this layer at any time to review the instructions. The white background has already been set so that you can focus on the paths. Your initial point is at the Start Here location and continues around the shape. The arrow directs you to the next point to set a vertex and to close or end a shape. Click the start point. On the red squares, you click and release the mouse button to set a straight vertex. On the blue circles, you click and drag to the darker blue circle following the dotted line and release the mouse button. This sets a curved vertex. You need to position the trailing edged control handles to the yellow circle icon. This is accomplished with the Edit Paths by Nodes tool, after you have completed a shape.

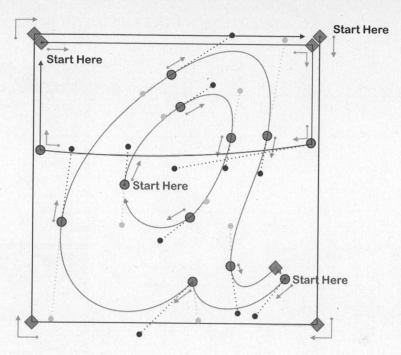

Figure 4-10. The path exercise guide

2. Set the start properties and make the outside square. Start by setting the default fills to **None** by clicking on the No-Fill icon ⬜ in the Fill and Stroke panel. This sets the starting properties of any new path that is created. You want to set these paths to have no-fill so you can see the guides underneath them. You can always add fills to these paths later. Then, hide the guides you won't use immediately. To toggle the visibility of a layer, click the Eye icon 👁 next to it in the Layers panel. Hide the layer for Shape 2, Shape 3, and Shape 4. Finally, click the layer titled Draw on this layer to activate it. With the purple guide showing, you are ready to create your first vector path. The Create Bézier and Lines tool ✒ is used to make lines, paths, and shapes. You make simple lines by first clicking on the lower circle to set the first vertex, which is an anchor point of this path. Next, while holding down the mouse button, drag upward. You can see a red line or control handle extending form that vertex to the cursor. This control handle affects the curve of the line that is being made. You can see what the line would look like by the blue preview line. After you are satisfied with the line, release the mouse. From here, you can continue setting points in this path if you want; however, you are done for now. To end the path, you have to double-click on the last vertex. The purple guide has red rectangles showing where you set straight vertices and blue circles for curved vertices. Notice that our first shape has only straight vertices. Start this shape by clicking on the red rectangle in the upper right to set your start point. Continue setting a straight vertex at each of the three other points indicated around the shape as red rectangles (see Figure 4-11). The connecting

161

lines will line up on the purple lines in the guide. To end the shape, click the first point you set. This is how you end a closed path.

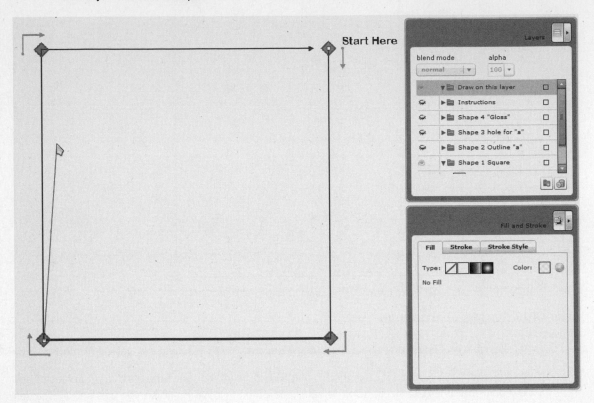

Figure 4-11. Create a straight-edged path.

Figure 4-12. The Create Bézier and Lines tool

The Create Bézier and Lines tool is the most versatile tool in Raven, but can be unwieldy at first (see Figure 4-12). This tool is used to create both lines and curves. The tool sets a vertex where ever you click in the workspace. After a vertex is set, there is a connector line from it to the mouse cursor showing a preview of the path. You can create both straight lines and Bézier curves. To create a straight vertex and line, click and release the mouse button where you want the vertex to be set. To create a curved vertex, click, and while holding the mouse button, drag out a control handle. This control handle influences the curve of the line connecting to the vertex. By moving these control handles before releasing the mouse button, you can see a preview of the curve. Releasing the mouse button sets the curve and you are ready to set the next vertex.

3. Create a path for the outside of the letter "a" Hide the layer with the purple guides containing the path you just created. Next unhide the layer titled Shape 2. Now, make sure you select the **Draw on this Layer** again so the object is placed on this layer. This guide has the blue circle indicators, which is where you set curved vertices. It also has smaller blue and yellow circles connected by dotted lines to show where to place the control handles when you drag them out from a vertex. For now, do not worry about the trailing edge control handles indicated by the yellow circles. You will set these later. Start the shape on the only red rectangle on the guide. Because this is a red indicator, click and release the mouse button to set this vertex. The next vertex is a blue circle, showing that the line is curved. To set this one, click in the blue circle and while continuing to hold the mouse button, drag the control handle so that the end is in the small blue circle connected to the larger one by a dotted line, and then release the mouse button (see Figure 4-13). Continue around the shape setting the curve's vertices and their control handles. End the path by clicking on the first vertex you set.

163

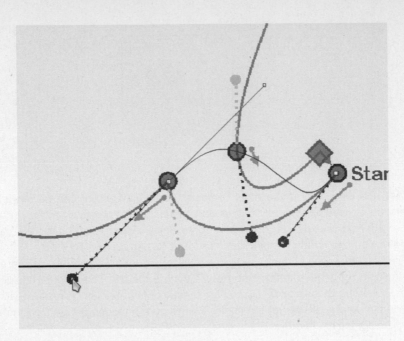

Figure 4-13. Set the control handles on curved vertices.

4. You can see that the path that you created doesn't quite follow the guide. You need to use the Edit Paths by Nodes tool to adjust the vertices and control handles. Select the Edit Paths by Nodes tool and start by clicking on the circle at the end of the control handle you want to adjust. You can move the control handle while holding the mouse button and it will stay when you release it (see Figure 4-14). Most of the control handles that are on the light blue indicators shouldn't need much adjusting; however, the opposite ones need to be placed on the yellow indicators. Continue around the shape adjusting the control handles and vertices so that they are in the right places (see Figure 4-15).

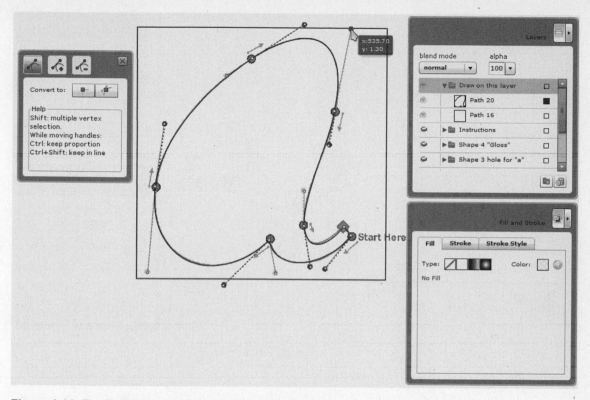

Figure 4-14. The Edit Paths by Nodes tool is used to modify the vertices and control handles.

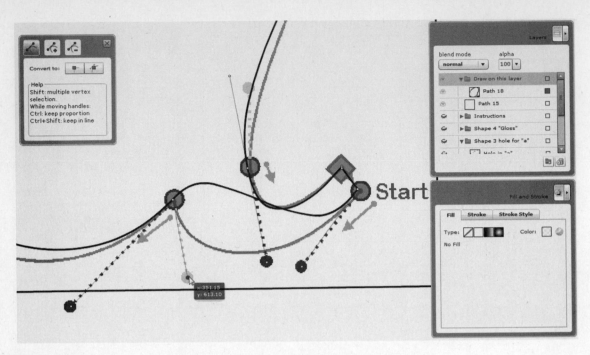

Figure 4-15. Set the trailing control handles with the Edit Paths by Nodes tool.

Figure 4-16. The Edit Paths by Nodes tool

The Edit Paths by Nodes tool is used to modify the Bézier curves and shapes (see Figure 4-16). With it, you can select a shape or path and edit its vertices individually, clicking and dragging on them to change their positions. You can modify the actions of this tool. You can move both control handles in unison if you hold down the Ctrl key (the Command key on Mac) when dragging one of them. You can make the control handles symmetrical if you hold down the Shift and Ctrl key while dragging the control handle. Set symmetrical control handles at 180° from each other and set them an equal distance from the vertex. This is good for creating a smooth curve across several vertices.

Figure 4-17. The Add Path's Vertex tool

With the Add Path's Vertex tool, you can click anywhere on the selected path and add a new vertex (see Figure 4-17). This new vertex has its control points automatically adjusted to match the current curve. When you have this tool active and hover over a path segment, the places where you are able to add a vertex turn red.

Figure 4-18. The Delete Path's Vertex tool

The Delete Path's Vertex tool deletes a path's vertex when you click on it (see Figure 4-18). Deleting a vertex changes the shape. The path will try to maintain its previous shape.

5. Next, you make the center hole in the letter "a." Hide the guide layer titled Shape 2 and unhide the layer titled Shape 3. Again, make sure you select the Draw on this layer before you draw any object or path, so that it is placed on this layer. Use the Create Bézier and Lines tool to set the curved vertices as in Step 4 (see Figure 4-19). All of the vertices will be curved, so you drag the control handles from each, including the end one that closes the path. When ending this path, instead of clicking and releasing, click and drag out the control handles. You reset the same control handle that you set on the start point. If you don't drag out this control handle like this on the last vertex, you won't have a complete set. Just clicking the start point when closing a path gives you only one control handle on that vertex. Consequently you have to use the Convert Anchor Point tool to add them, but doing that forces you to reset several control handle locations.

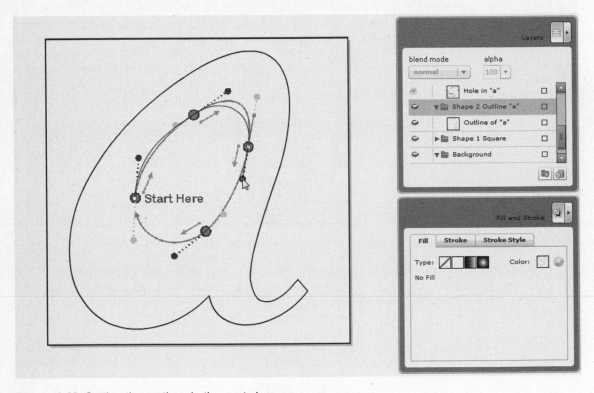

Figure 4-19. Setting the vertices in the next shape

6. Create a shape that is a glossy highlight. To do this, first hide the orange guides and unhide the layer titled Shape 4. Then make sure that the Draw on this Layer is selected so the shape is placed on it. This guide has a mix of straight and curved vertices. Set them as you did in the previous steps. Start your path at the location indicated by the Start Here label. Create a straight line across the top and left side. You set a curved vertex at the bottom, right corner of the shape, but this curves the straight, right side you just set. Don't worry; you can fix this after you finish the path. Both sides of this shape should bulge out after you finish the path. You can adjust the paths with the Edit Paths by Nodes tool, but it is easier to use the Convert Anchor Point tool. This tool can switch a curved

vertex to a straight one by clicking on it. Or, click and drag the control handles from a straight vertex to a curve. Click the top, right vertex to convert it to straight (see Figure 4-20). This sets the line that makes up the right side of the shape to straight. Finally, adjust the remaining control handles to fit the shape to the guide.

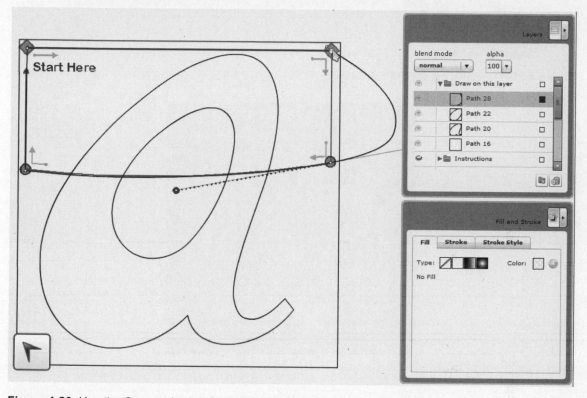

Figure 4-20. Use the Convert Anchor Point tool to switch from straight to curved vertices.

7. Color in the paths. Hide the remaining guides because you won't need them. Select the first shape you created, the square, by clicking it with the Edit Paths by Nodes tool. You can select paths with many different tools, but this one should be active. In the Fill and Stroke panel, click the **Radial Gradient Fill** button . Set this gradient to light blue fading to dark blue (see Figure 4-21). This is done by double-clicking the color stops under the gradient colorbar. This opens the Color Picker for that color stop so you can set the color. Do this for both color stops. This fills the square shape with the gradient. Next, use the Gradient Transform tool ; you will see an L-shaped control in the center of the shape. Click and drag the control handle in the center of this control and drag it to the bottom of the shape. This repositions the center of the gradient fill (see Figure 4-22). Finally, click the Add Swatch button to save this gradient for the hole in the "a."

Figure 4-21. The radial gradient fill color setting

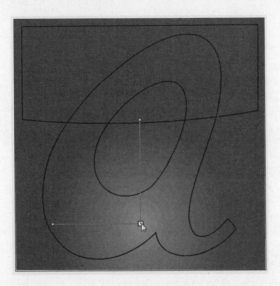

Figure 4-22. Position the gradient at the bottom of the shape with the Gradient Transform tool.

8. Click the path that makes the outer portion of the "a" shape. This is the second path you created. Click the **Solid Fill** button ☐ in the Fill and Stroke panel. Set this shape's color to white. Next, switch to the **Stroke** tab in the Fill and Stroke panel and set the type to **None**. This removes the black stroke around the shape. Select the shape that makes the hole in the "a", the third shape you created. You should still be on the **Stroke** tab in the Fill and Stroke panel, set the type to **None**, removing the black stroke around this shape. Switch back to the **Fill** tab and set the type to **Radial Gradient Fill**, which fills the shape with the default gradient. You want this gradient to be the same as the first shape, but instead of trying to match it by eye, click the saved swatch from Step 7. This sets shape's fill, matching the one from earlier. Finally, select the remaining shape and set its fill type to a **Linear Gradient Fill** ▨. Set this gradient to white fading to transparent white. Use the Gradient Transform tool ▣ to rotate the gradient so that it is white at the top of the

shape fading to transparent at the bottom (see Figure 4-23). Finally, switch to the `Stroke` tab and set the type to `None`, removing the stroke around the shape.

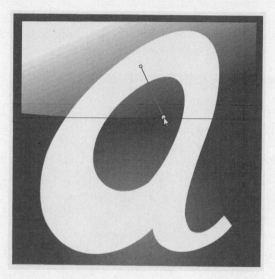

Figure 4-23. Adjust the gradient in the image.

Project review

The Create Bézier and Line tool is key to learn, and in this project you constructed various shapes with it. You saw how a click-and-release sets a straight vertex, whereas dragging out control handles from a vertex creates curve. You also learned how to hide and display (or, unhide) objects from the Layer panel. You learned how to set the starting properties of objects by having nothing selected and how to set the fill and stroke properties. Finally, this project showed you how to change the properties of shapes by setting different fills and removing strokes. In the next project, you explore the predefined shapes in Raven. You layer them to construct a stylized cartoon character.

Project 4.2—Create a Simple Character Using Simple Shapes

You do not have to make every object in Raven by setting individual vertices. You can use predefined shapes to make construction much quicker. Raven has five predefined shapes that can be used to construct images. Layering and combining these shapes enables you to quickly build complex images from simple pieces. The shapes can be drawn directly into the workspace or generated from properties defined by you. In this project, you explore ways that shapes can be used to create an image. You layer shapes to simulate weighted strokes, and you reuse sets of shapes to speed up the creation process. However, first you should understand the difference between objects and paths. See Figure 4-24 for the final character that you will make in this project.

Objects and paths are different elements in Raven. **Objects** are geometric shapes made with the Shape tool. The vertices that make up the object are not accessible while it is an object. They maintain their geometric shape even when moving control handles. Objects can be scaled, rotated, and skewed, but none of the individual vertices can be altered outside of the whole object. Paths, on the other hand, have all of their vertices accessible for editing. This means that each individual vertex can be edited apart from the whole path. A path does not maintain any set structural pattern.

Figure 4-24. Thi is the final image you will create in this project.

Key concepts in this project
- Shapes
- Transform tool
- Convert objects to paths
- Fill and Stroke properties

Find this file online at
http://aviary.com/artists/gettingstartED/creations/chapter_4_project_2.

1. Open Raven and select the default 625X625 dimension, and then click the **Create** button. When the application opens, a workspace and a canvas are presented in the center of the screen. Even though it appears as though you are working with a clean, white surface, it is actually transparent. The first step to build this file and something to consider when creating in Raven is a background. Select the Shape tool to open the Shapes fly-out. Here, you can choose the basic shape and set the parameters. Choose the default rectangular shape and draw a square around the canvas. Don't worry about the fill and stroke of this shape; you set those later. Click and drag to draw the rectangle that covers the entire canvas. A blue preview shape displays until you release the mouse button (see Figure 4-25). Be sure that the object covers the entire canvas because if there is any portion of the canvas not covered it will show as transparent in the final image. Everything that falls outside of the canvas will get cropped from the final image. Finally, name the layer that contains this rectangle Background. Then, click on the **Create Layer** button and drag the new layer above the Background layer.

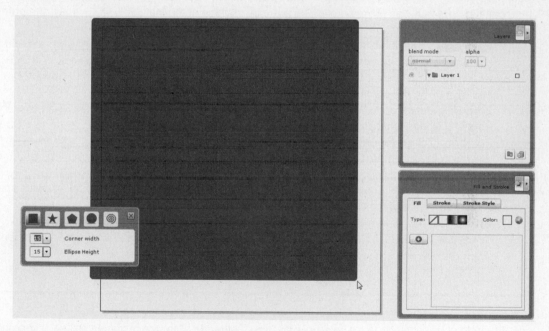

Figure 4-25. Draw a rectangle using the Rectangle Shape tool.

173

Figure 4-26. Raven has five predefined shapes.

Like in Phoenix, the shape tools are used to add predefined geometric shapes. Raven has five different tools that have their own parameters (see Figure 4-26). All the shapes are added in the same way. First, click the canvas at the start point location. While continuing to hold down the mouse button, drag out the shape and release the button to end it. Holding down the Shift button while drawing a shape constrains the shape's proportions. Double-clicking in the workspace with any of the shape tools selected brings up a parameter dialog where height-, width-, and shape-specific parameters can be set. Click OK generates the shape at the spot that was clicked. Following are explanations of the individual shapes and the parameters for each.

- **Rectangle**: This draws a rectangle or square. The corner width sets the point at the top and bottom edges where the corners start curving. Ellipse heights set the point at the left and right edges where the corners start curving. These settings can be adjusted using the Edit Paths by Nodes tool and by moving the corner control handles.
- **Star**: This draws a star shape. Vertex count sets the amount of arms the star will have. The Edit Paths by Nodes tool can be used to adjust the inner radius of the shape.
- **Polygon**: This draws a straight-sided geometric shape. Vertex count sets how many sides are drawn on the polygon. The Edit Paths by Nodes tool can be used to set the curvature of the sides on the shape.
- **Circle**: This draws an ellipse or circle. The Edit Paths by Nodes tool can be used to adjust the width and height of the circle.
- **Spiral**: This draws a regular spiral shape. The Edit Paths by Nodes tool can be used to adjust the number of rotations of the shape. The spiral's height and width will be equal when drawing the shape.

2. Add some shading to the rectangle that you just made. With the rectangle still selected, on the Fill and Stroke panel, click the `Radial Fill` button 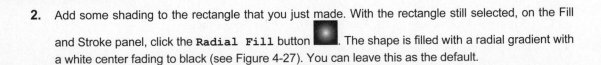. The shape is filled with a radial gradient with a white center fading to black (see Figure 4-27). You can leave this as the default.

Figure 4-27. Change the fill to a radial gradient.

3. Create the base shape for the body of your character. To start, to form the body of your character, use the Shape tool again, and draw a rectangle starting in the center and moving down. Try to size its width so that there is equal space on each side (see Figure 4-28). Don't worry if it extends beyond the backdrop because it will be cropped from the final image. Color this rectangle black by first setting the fill type back to solid by clicking on the `Solid Fill` button ⬜. Next, set the color by clicking the color box ᶜᵒˡᵒʳ: ⬜⬤ in the Fill and Stroke panel. This opens the Color Picker where you can choose the color.

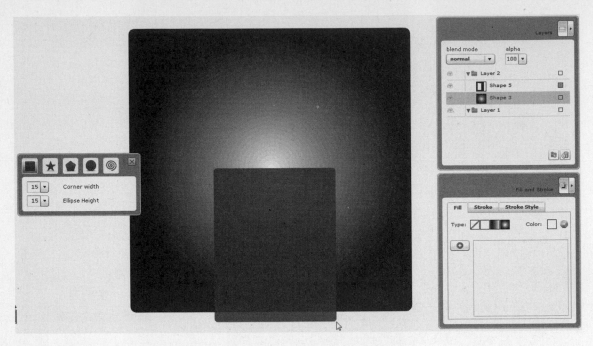

Figure 4-28. Add in the base shape.

4. Now, in the center of this rectangle, draw a triangle. To draw a triangle, you have to select the Polygon Shape tool ⬠ in the Shape fly-out panel. The default setting is to draw give **sides**; however, change this to three. Draw the triangle just like the rectangles (see Figure 4-29). Change this shapes color to white in the Fill and Stroke panel. If you find that you need to move the shape to get it in the right place, use the Select and move objects tool ⬚.

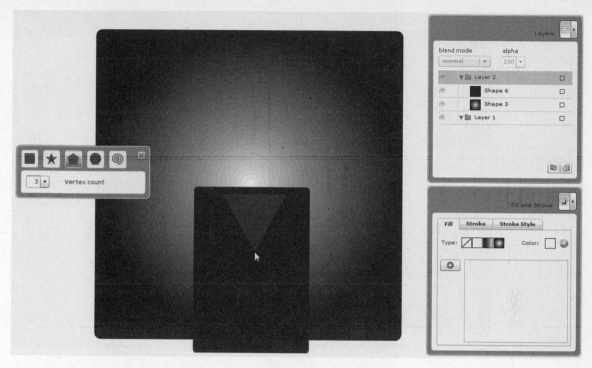

Figure 4-29. Layer simple shapes to build up the image.

5. Now, draw two more triangles. The first one should point down on top and smaller than the first triangle. The other should point up and overlap the first triangle (see Figure 4-30). Fill each of these with black. You can now see that the three triangles form a shirt and tie. Again, use the Transform tool to line up the triangles. It is amazing what a few shapes can imply.

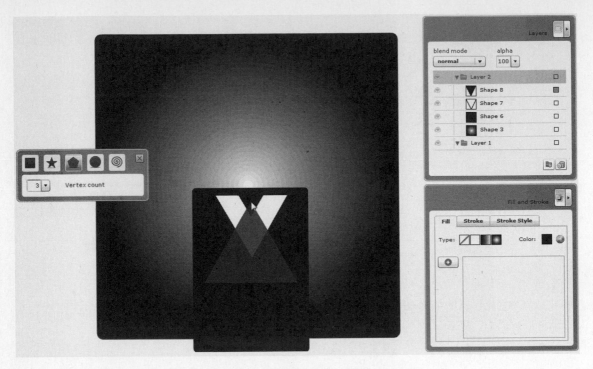

Figure 4-30. Use the shape's control handle to adjust the size of the triangle.

6. Name the layer that contains the body shapes Body. Then, create a new Layer by clicking the **New Layer** button ![folder icon] and dragging this layer above the others in the Layers panel. Select the Rectangle Shape tool and draw a short and long rectangle. It should be centered above the body shapes and be about two thirds the width of the background. This becomes the ears of the character. You can manually adjust several parameters of the shapes with the Edit Paths by Nodes tool ![node tool icon]. With the Edit Paths by Nodes tool activated, controls on the rectangle become noticeable. Move the two round controls in the upper, right corner to adjust the roundness of the corners in this shape (see Figure 4-31). Set them so that they are very round. These parameters can also be set before drawing the rectangle; you do this in the **Properties** panel by adjusting the **Corner Width** and **Ellipse Height** parameters. Next, change the Fill color to a blue hue. After you fill the shape with this color, save it as a swatch by clicking the **Add Swatch** button ![plus button]. You now have access to that swatch throughout this session of Raven, and it gives you uniform color throughout the image. Switch to the **Stroke** tab in the Fill and Stroke panel, and set the **Stroke color** to a darker blue. A stroke is the outline around the shape. You can set its color, width, and other parameters in the **Stroke** and **Stroke Style** tabs. Save the color as a swatch in that same manner as the fill color. Finally, in the **Stroke Style** tab of the Fill and Stroke panel, set the **Width** to 10. This makes the Stroke very wide and gives a bold graphic feel to the design (see Figure 4-32).

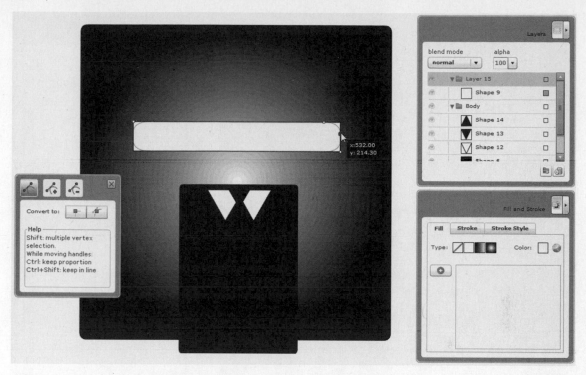

Figure 4-31. Add a bold stroke to the object.

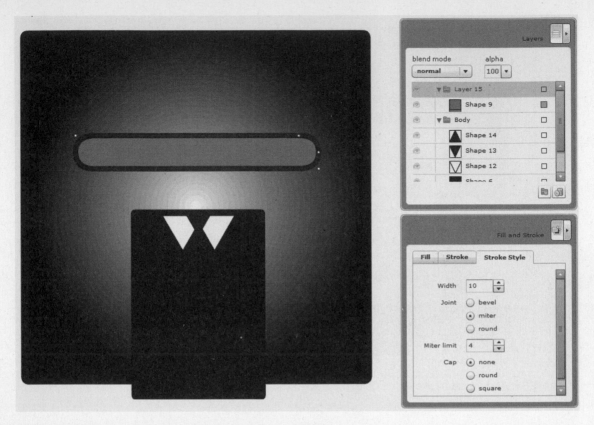

Figure 4-32. Set the fill and stroke properties for this shape.

7. The head of your character is built using three shapes. First, there is the base blue shape. Then, there is a shape that will be converted to a path and used for shading. Finally, the third shape is the stroke around the other shapes. Start with the Shape tool and draw a large rectangle in the center covering the previous shapes you made. A little of the blue rectangle you just made can be seen protruding from under this new shape, and it should also cover a little of the body shapes. Use the Edit Paths by Nodes tool again to round the corners like you did with the previous shape. Finally, set the `fill` to the lighter blue colored swatch by double-clicking the swatch in the Fill and Stroke panel. Then, switch to the `Stroke` tab and set the stroke type to `None` (see Figure 4-33).

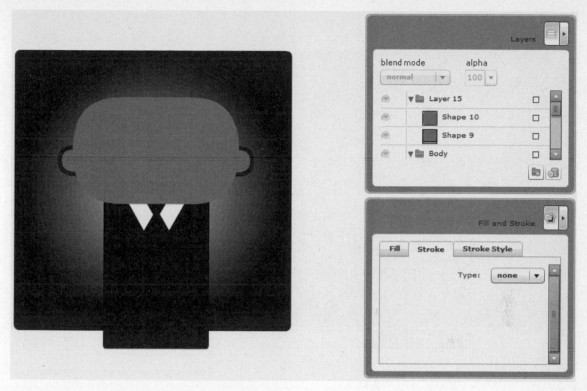

Figure 4-33. Start your head with a base shape.

8. With this head shape still selected, use the Copy **Edit ➤ Copy** and the Paste **Edit ➤ Paste** commands to make a duplicate of the head shape. Change the color of it to a darker blue, using the darker of the two color swatches Then, open the Color Picker by clicking on the color box ^{Color:} ⬜ ⚪ in the Fill and Stroke panel, and then set the **Alpha** of this shape to 50. Next, use the **Object ➤ Object to Path** command. As pointed out in the introduction of the project, this changes the shape to a path that gives you access to the vertices in the object. With the Edit Paths by Nodes tool, move the vertices at the top of the shape down until you have a curved shape, leaving the bottom vertices where they are (see Figure 4-34). You want to make the shape cover just the lower quarter of the base head shape.

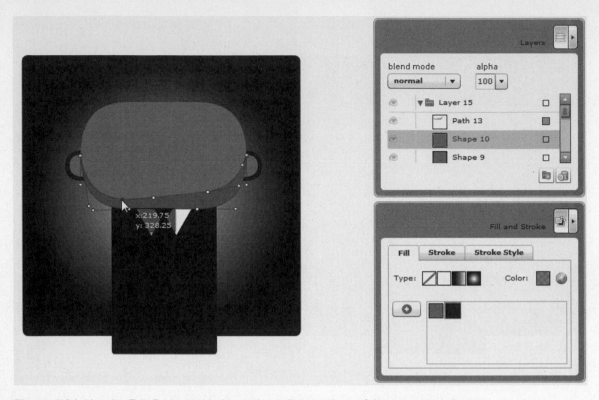

Figure 4-34. Use the Edit Paths by Nodes tool to adjust vertices of the converted shape.

9. The original head shape that was copied earlier should still be on the Clipboard, so use the Paste command again. However if it is not still copied, select it with the Select and Move Objects tool and use the **Edit ➤ Copy** command to place it on the Clipboard, so you can paste it with the **Edit ➤ Paste** command. This places a copy of the base head shape on top. Remove the **fill** by clicking on the **No Fill** button in the **Fill** tab. Add a blue stroke to the shape using the dark blue color that was used as the stroke around the ear shape and was saved as a swatch. Finally, set the **width** of this stroke to 10 in the **Stroke Style** tab. This wide stroke covers any inconstancies from moving vertices of the shade shape (see Figure 4-35).

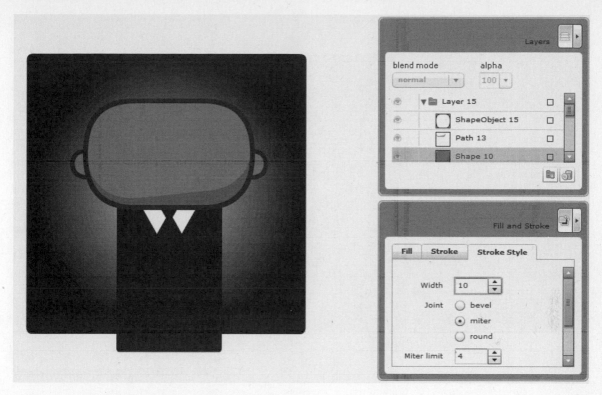

Figure 4-35. Paste the shape on top and remove the fill.

10. Add some hair to the character. Select the Star Shape tool that is located in the Shape tool fly-out panel. Set the **vertex count** to 9 or more and draw a star shape at the top of the head. The shape should have the dark blue, 10-pixel stroke set from the last shape. If not, set it and then set this shape's Fill color to the saved blue color used in the head shape. You want to place the hair shape behind the head. Now, you can either drag this shape in the Layer panel below the base head shape or you can use the menu command **Object ➤ Move down**. It takes about three iterations of this command to get the hair shape behind the head (see Figure 4-36). Finally, name the layer that contains all the head shapes Head. Then, create a new layer and drag it to the top of the layers.

Figure 4-36. Add a stroke to the star shape.

11. Make a mouth for your character. Start by selecting the Ellipse Shape tool ⬤ from the Shape fly-out panel. Then, draw a small ellipse in the mouth area of the head. Next, remove any stroke by setting the type to `None` in the `Stroke` tab. Then, switch to the `Fill` tab and set the color of it to the same dark blue as the outline used on the head (see Figure 4-37). This color should still be saved in the swatch. Next, copy and paste the oval and change the color of the copied oval to the same one that was used to fill the base head shape. Finally, using the Transform tool, scale the top oval so that a small portion of the darker oval peaks out from underneath. To do this, click the bottom, center control handle of the transform box and drag slightly upwards (see Figure 4-38). You can zoom into the workspace using the Zoom Level slider. This is located at the top right of the application and enables you to zoom in to get a better look at smaller details or you can zoom out to see the big picture.

Figure 4-37. Copy and reposition a shape to create the mouth.

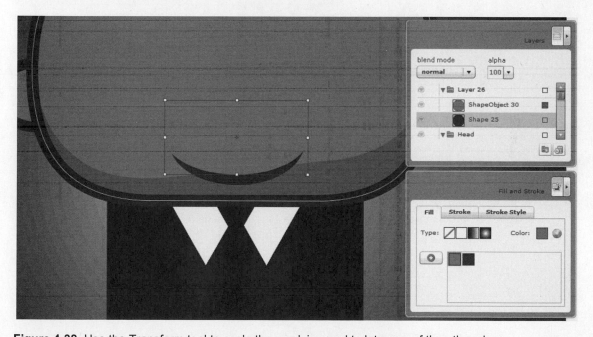

Figure 4-38. Use the Transform tool to scale the overlying oval to let some of the other show.

12. Add eyes to you character using a series of circles. With the Ellipse shape tool , draw only one of the eyes. You can duplicate it after it is done. Start by drawing a large circle while holding down the Shift key. By holding down the shift key while drawing a shape, you can constrain its proportions, which makes the height the same as the width. This makes the ellipse a perfectly round circle. Fill this circle with black. Next, add a smaller circle inside the upper, left section of the first circle and color it white. Draw a third white circle inside the lower, right area of the first circle (see Figure 4-39). These white circles will become highlights for the eyes.

Figure 4-39. Use several circles to make the eyes.

13. With the lower, white circle still selected, select **Object ➤ Object to path**. Use the Edit Paths by Nodes tool to push the vertices around until the circle is flatter on one side (see Figure 4-40). Remember, you can zoom into the workspace using the Zoom Level slider and the top. This makes it easier to make small adjustments such as manipulating the vertices of the eye highlight.

Figure 4-40. Convert the shape to a path to manipulate the object.

14. Select all three objects that make up the eye, the black center, and the two white highlights. Do this by clicking on each of the square icons in the Layer panel while holding the Ctrl button (Command ⌘ on Mac). Then, use the Copy and Paste commands to duplicate all three shapes that make up the eye. Next, select the Transform tool to position the duplicated eye to its proper location on the opposite side of the head (see Figure 4-41).

Figure 4-41. Copy the first eye and move it to the other side of the face.

15. Add a little personality to your character with a set of eyebrows. Use the Rectangle Shape tool to draw a brow and fill it with the dark blue color that was use as the stroke color on the head. Duplicate the brow with the Copy and Paste commands. Position the shapes with the Transform tool. Scaling and rotating the eyebrows changes the expression of your character. Flat, even brows show boredom, v-shaped brows impart anger, raised, angled out brows show surprise, and offset brows imply mischief (see Figure 4-42).

Figure 4-42. Eyebrows give a personality to your character.

Project review

In this project, you saw how convenient the shape tools are for creating objects. You can easily create images using them, and add styling with Fill color and stroke weights. You also learned that you can save color swatches to match the colors throughout the image. The `Object to Path` command lets you break out of the shape's predefined parameters so you can mold it to something new. Finally, you learned that copying and pasting sets of objects can save you time when there are repeating objects in your file. In the next project, you learn how to make an icon that is suitable to use in an application-launching dock. You set document sizes to control your output dimension, and you continue to explore gradients and the Gradient Transform tool.

Project 4.3—Create a PNG Dock Icon

Because vectors can be resized without losing any quality, it lends itself to the icon creation process. Raven can export as a PNG file, which makes this an ideal application to make an icon for application-launching docks, such as the Apple OS X Dock, Rocket Dock for Windows, or the Linux Cairo-Dock. In this project, you make a USB thumb drive icon and export it for use as a 128x128 PNG dock icon. See Figure 4-43 for the icon that you will be making with this project.

Figure 4-43. The finished dock icon created in this project.

Key concepts in this project

- Gradients
- Linear strokes
- Resizing documents
- Exporting PNG files

> *Find this file online at*
> *http://aviary.com/artists/gettingstartED/creations/chapter_4_project_3.*

1. Start by making the base shape for the icon. Launch Raven and start the file with the default 625x625 dimensions. After you have constructed the icon, you will be resizing it to 128x128 pixels. Keeping the file at the larger size will make it easier to work on. With the Rectangular Shape tool ▣, draw a rectangle in the center of the canvas. Use the Edit Paths by Nodes tool ⚞ to adjust

the corner radius by dragging the two round control handles (see Figure 4-44). Give the rectangle a large curve to the corners but not so large that ends are completely rounded.

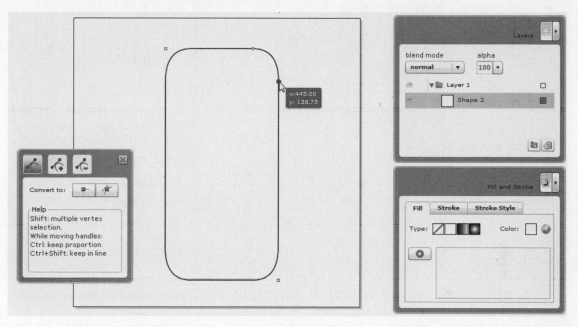

Figure 4-44. Use the Edit Paths by Nodes tool to set the roundness of rectangle corners.

2. Set the Fill color of this rectangle's Linear Fill gradient by clicking the `Linear Fill` button ▓. This fills the shape with the default gradient of white fading to black. You need to change the gradient color to bright green that fades to dark green. In the `Fill` panel, you can see the gradient colorbar. It is a long preview area with two triangles underneath it. The triangle icons are color stops and represent each individual color in the gradient. Double-click the first color stop icon. This opens the Color Picker panel so that you can set the color to dark green. Change the other color stop to bright green using the same method as the first. The rectangle now has the proper colors, but the gradient needs to transition from top to bottom and not left to right. You can change the parameters of a gradient directly on the shape with the Gradient Transform tool ▓. With the Gradient Transform tool selected, you can give a new control handle to the rectangle. By dragging the round control handle, you are able to change the rotation angle and length of the gradient. While dragging the square handle, you can set the gradient's center. Now, adjust the gradient so that the color starts dark green at the top and fades down into the bright green (see Figure 4-45). Finally, switch to the `Stroke` tab in the Fill and Stroke panel and set the Stroke to a dark green color. Then, switch to the `Stroke Style` tab and set the stroke `width` to 6.

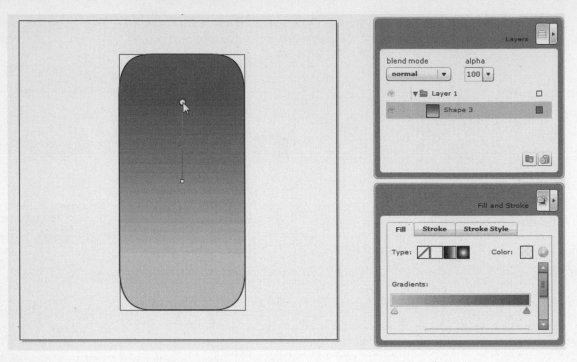

Figure 4-45. Color the shape with a linear gradient fill.

Figure 4-46. The colorbar is where you can set colors in a gradient.

The Gradient setting colorbar is the area where colors are set in the gradient (see Figure 4-46). The triangle icons are called color stops and can be dragged along the colorbar to set a gradient. You can add a color stop by clicking on an area under the colorbar, set color and Alpha by double-clicking a color stop and deleting a color stop by dragging it away from the colorbar. Spread sets how the gradient is drawn past the original area (see Figure 4-47). `Pad` continues the color in the extended region. `Reflect` mirrors the gradient in the extended region. `Repeat` repeats the gradient in the extended region.

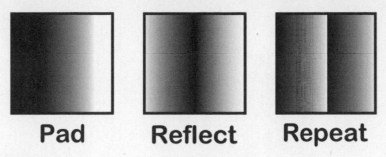

Pad　　**Reflect**　　**Repeat**

Figure 4-47. Spread mode

Figure 4-48. The Gradient Transform tool lets you change the parameters of a gradient directly on the object.

The Gradient Transform tool lets you set the direction of the gradient and the quickness of the color blending (see Figure 4-48). Click a shape that has a gradient fill and it lets you adjust it.

For linear gradients, one control bar displays with two control points: one on the end and one in the center. The one on the end changes the size and direction of the gradient. The center one controls the position of the gradient. There can also be up to eight additional control points between the end points that correspond to each color stop in the gradient. For radial gradients, two control bars appear. The center point controls the position of the gradient. The end points control the width and height of the ellipse that creates the gradient. The radial gradient can also have color stop control points. If you move one, both move at the same time.

3. Flatten the top of the rectangle by first using the `Object ➤ Object to Path` function. This gives you access to the vertices in the object. Next, select the Delete Path's Vertex tool 🖉, which is accessible from the Edit Paths by Nodes fly-out panel. Now, click the two top most vertices to remove them (see Figure 4-49). The path automatically adjusts to the missing vertices and flattens across the top. If it doesn't, you can use the Convert Anchor Point tool ⬉ and click on the two top vertices to convert them to straight.

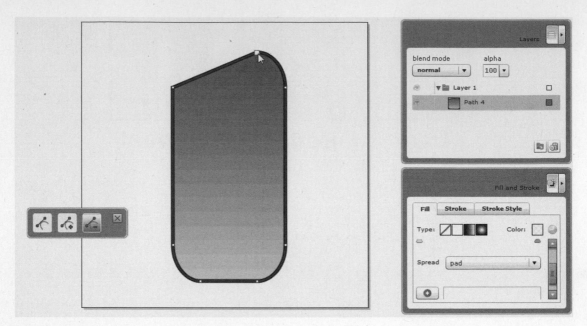

Figure 4-49. Convert the shape to a path and remove some vertices.

4. To identify this icon as a USB thumb drive, you need to make a USB logo for the front. This logo consists of a circle with a square, triangle, and another circle all connected by lines. Start by setting the fill and stroke for the shape you want to draw. In the **Fill** tab of the Fill and Stroke panel, change the fill to solid black. Then, switch to the **Stroke** tab and set the **type** to **None**. This makes the subsequent shapes black with no stroke. Using the Shape tools, draw each of the four shapes off to one side of the canvas so that you can work on them without interfering with the work you have done so far. Use the Transform tool to arrange the shapes, one circle centered under the other the shapes. The other shapes should be arranged left to right: circle, triangle, and square. See Figure 4-50 for the layout of the USB logo. Finally, adjust the scale of each shape so they are all approximately the same size.

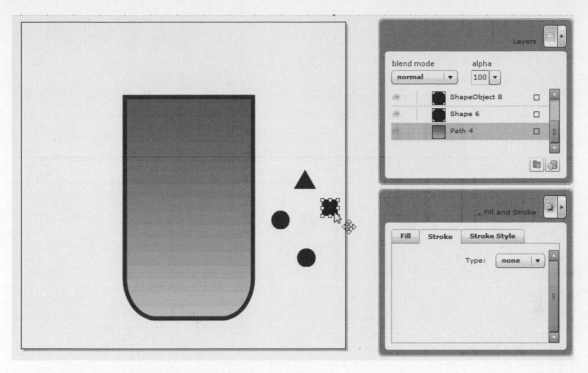

Figure 4-50. Construct the USB logo with the shape tools.

5. Connect the four shapes with lines using the Create Bézier and Lines tool . Start by setting the fill and stroke of these lines. In the Fill and Stroke panel's `Fill` tab, set the fill to `None`. In the `Stroke` tab, set the color to black, and in the `Stroke Style` tab, set the `width` to 2. The Create Bézier and Lines tool is a tool used to make lines, paths, and shapes. You make simple lines by first clicking on the lower circle to set the first vertex, which is an anchor point of this path. Next, click on the first shape and while holding down the mouse button, drag upward. You can see a red line or control handle extending from that vertex to the cursor. This control handle affects the curve of the line that is being made. You can see what the line would look like by the blue preview line. After you are satisfied with the line, release the mouse. From here, you can continue setting points in this path if you want to, but we are done. To end the path, you have to double-click on the last vertex. Finally, draw lines to the rest of the shapes to finish the USB logo (see Figure 4-51).

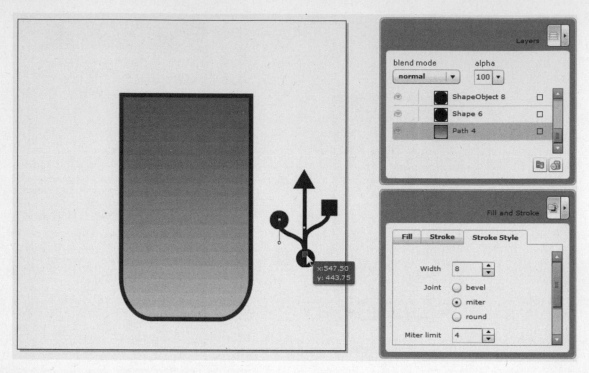

Figure 4-51. Connect the shapes with a path.

6. Center the logo that you just created on your green base shape. Using the Transform tool, select the entire logo by dragging around it, being careful not to select anything else. When dragging a selection around elements, if any sections of them fall inside the selection area, the element will be selected. After the logo is selected, move it to the center of the green base shape (see Figure 4-52).

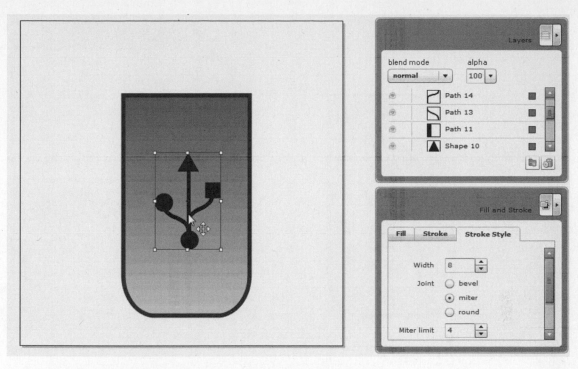

Figure 4-52. Position the logo to the center of the green base shape.

7. Use **Blend Modes** to create a highlight on the icon. Draw a rectangle using the Rectangle Shape tool about the same size of the green base shape and anywhere in the center of the image. Do not worry about placement or scale of this shape at the moment. Remove any fill the rectangle might

 have by clicking the **No Fill** button in the **Fill** tab from the Fill and Stroke panel. Switch to the **Stroke** tab and set the **type** to **Linear**. Switch to the **Stroke Style** tab and set the width to 8. Currently, the only way to adjust the gradient on a stroke is to adjust the shape. You need to rotate the rectangle using the Transform tool so that the white side of the gradient is facing up. Then, scale it so that it fits just inside the base shape of the icon. Finally, set the object's Blend Mode in the Layer panel to **Add** (see Figure 4-53). This **Blend Mode** makes the black areas transparent while the white is intensified.

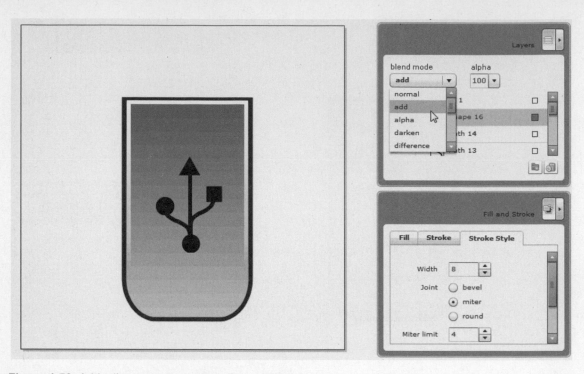

Figure 4-53. Add a linear gradient stroke for a highlight.

8. Create a glossy highlight to the icon. First set the properties for this element. In the Fill and Stroke panel's **Fill** tab, set the type to Linear Gradient. Then, remove the stroke by setting the **type** to None in the **Stroke** tab. Draw another rectangle slightly smaller and inside the base shape. Next, use the **Object ➤ Object to Path** function to gain access to the vertices in the object. Select the Edit Paths by Nodes tool and move the lower right vertex of the rectangle up about one third. Next, while still using the Edit Paths by Nodes tool, drag around the bottom two vertices to select both vertices. With the vertices selected, use the **Line to Curve** button ⬚ in the Edit Paths by Nodes tool fly-out panel to convert them to curves. Adjust the now available control handles to give an S curve to the bottom of the highlight element and make the sides and top straight. Finally, set the **Blend Mode** of this element to **Screen** in the **Layers** panel, which turns the black transparent, leaving only the white (see Figure 4-54). Then use the Gradient Transform tool to adjust the fill so that there is a subtle highlight across the shape.

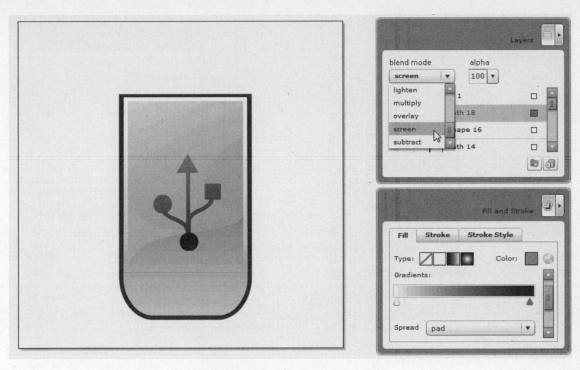

Figure 4-54. Add another gradient with a Blend Mode for a glossy shine.

9. Start constructing the plug end for the USB thumb drive icon. First, make a new layer. Layers are a great way to organize objects in a file. Click the **New Layer** button ![icon] to create a new layer nested within the current one. Drag this new layer to the top of the stack in the Layer panel. You can easily select all the objects that are contained in the layer. With the Rectangle Shape tool, draw a square shape slightly smaller in width than the base icon shape. Set the fill to a Linear gradient of light gray fading to medium gray, and use the Gradient Transform tool to make the gradient vertical (see Figure 4-55). Finally, set the Stroke **color** to dark gray and set the **width** to 8.

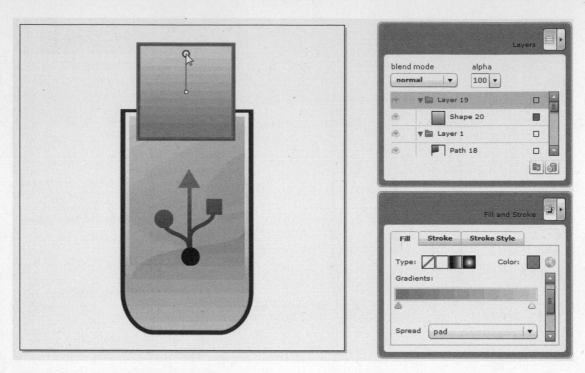

Figure 4-55. Use a square for the plug.

10. Next, you add more depth to the plug. Draw another rectangle inside the previous rectangle. This shape should have the same fill and stroke of the previous shape. Set the gradient direction in the opposite direction of the previous shape with the Gradient Transform tool (see Figure 4-56). Finally, remove the stroke by setting the `type` to none in the **Stroke** tab.

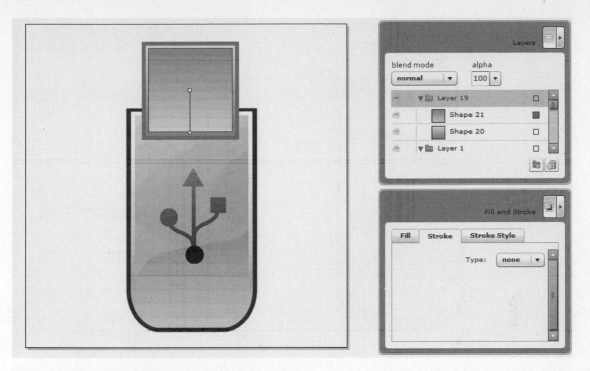

Figure 4-56. Add a smaller rectangle for more shading.

11. Add the two holes to the plug on this USB thumb drive icon. Draw a small rectangle and set its fill to a Linear Fill gradient of dark gray to transparent. Use the Gradient Transform tool to rotate the gradient so that the dark gray is on top. Next, copy and paste this shape using the **Edit ➤ Copy** and **Edit ➤ Paste** commands. Position the copied shape with the Transform tool on the other side of the plug (see Figure 4-57). Add a skinny, tall rectangle in between these two and make its fill color a solid dark gray (see Figure 4-58). Finally, select the layer containing the plug elements in the **Layers** panel and select **Object ➤ Move to bottom** to move the entire plug element behind the rest of the shapes.

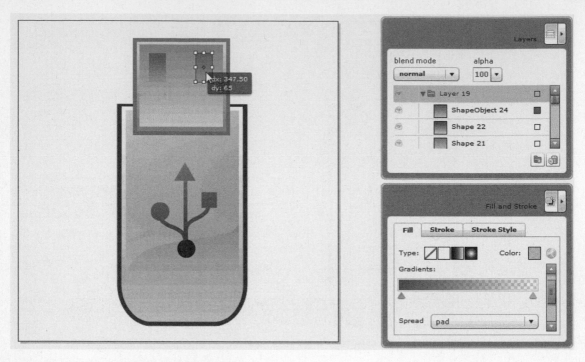

Figure 4-57. Add the holes in the plug end.

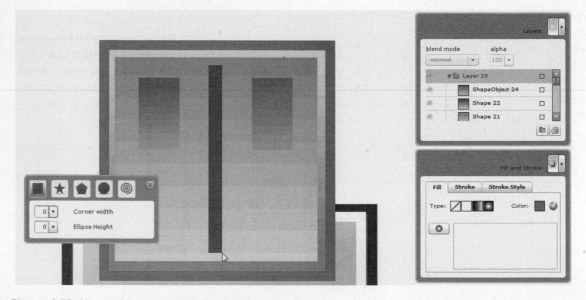

Figure 4-58. Use a skinny rectangle to separate the plug.

12. Add a shadow to the icon. With the Ellipse Shape tool, draw a wide oval at the bottom of the icon. Set the fill to radial gradient using the `Radial Fill` button 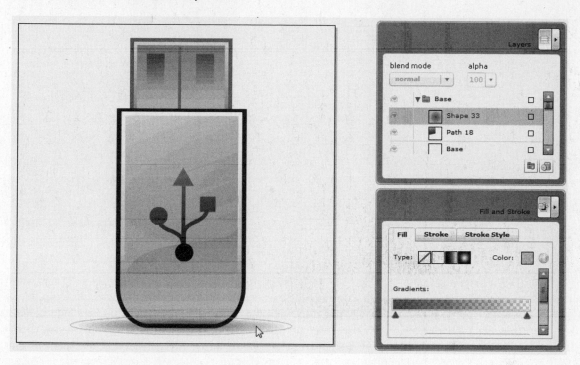. Set this gradient color to 50% opaque black fading to transparent black, which fills the ellipse with light black in the center fading to transparent on the edges (see Figure 4-59). Finally, select `Object` ➤ `Move to bottom` to move this to the bottom of the Layer stack.

Figure 4-59. Use a radial gradient for a drop shadow.

13. Size the file for the final icon size of 128x128 pixels. To format the image to this size, you have to set the document size to these dimensions using the `File` ➤ `Document Size` command. This opens the `Document setup` dialog where you can resize the file's output by setting the `Document Height` to128 and `Document Width` to 128. After the canvas has been resized to the smaller dimension, select the entire image with the Transform tool by dragging around it. Resize the icon image to fit inside the small canvas (see Figure 4-60). Be sure to hold down the Shift key while resizing the image to constrain the proportions, so it does not get distorted during the process.

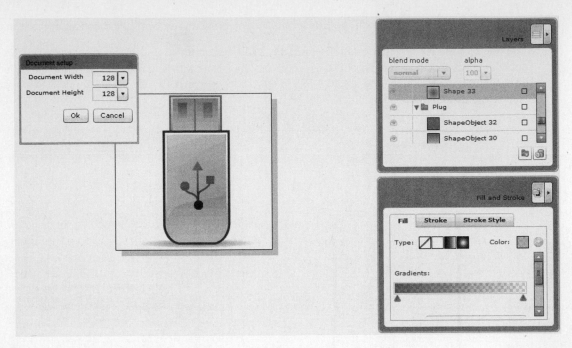

Figure 4-60. Resize the canvas to the standard dock icon size.

14. Export the image as a .PNG file. The PNG format retains all of the image's details and transparent area, making it ideal to use as a dock icon. Select **File ➤ Export ➤ Export Bitmap**. Make sure the format is set to **PNG (*.png)** and click the **Generate Image** button (see Figure 4-61). This starts the conversion process. After the download button is enabled in the next panel, click it and choose a location on your computer to save the file. Finally, the icon is ready to be used in your dock application (see Figure 4-62).

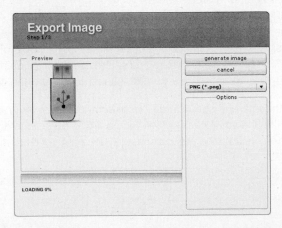

Figure 4-61. Use the **Export Bitmap** function to save the image as a PNG file.

Figure 4-62. The finished icon in action

Project review

In this project, you learned how create an icon that is suitable to use in an application launcher dock. You saw that gradients are easy to manipulate and can give your simple shapes added shading and depth. The `Object to Path` function gives you access to the vertices in your shapes, letting you mold the predefined shapes. You also saw how grouping objects into layers makes files easy to organize. Finally, you saw how to export your creation as a PNG file to your computer. In the next project, you learn how to use guides to make you shapes line up. You will see how to predefine a shape's dimensions and how to position shapes with the Align and Distribute commands.

Project 4.4—Create an Isometric Object

Many technical artists and game designers use an isometric perspective. This type of image shows the most area of an object, two sides, and a top. If you add cutouts and holes, even the interior of the object can be seen. In this project, you learn how to use the guides and the **Align and Distribute** function to line up objects. You will see the importance of rulers and predefined shapes to construct an isometric object. See Figure 4-63 for the final image made in this project.

Figure 4-63. The finished image you will make in this project.

Key concepts in this project

- Using guides and rulers
- Presetting shape objects
- Gradients
- Transform centers

> *Find this file online at*
> *http://aviary.com/artists/gettingstartED/creations/chapter_4_project_4.*

1. Start your image with a base shape. Create a new Raven file and select the default canvas size of 625x625. Select the Polygon Shape tool ⬠. The parameter Vertex count is presented; this is the number of sides that will be in the polygon. Set this parameter to 6, which is a hexagon. Hold the Shift key down and click the center of the canvas, and then drag upward to draw the hexagon shape. Because this shape is predefined as a hexagram, holding down the Shift key while drawing constrains the rotation angle instead of the `Height` and `Width`. Make this shape about three-quarters as big as the canvas, and then release the mouse button to commit the shape to the file (see Figure 4-64).

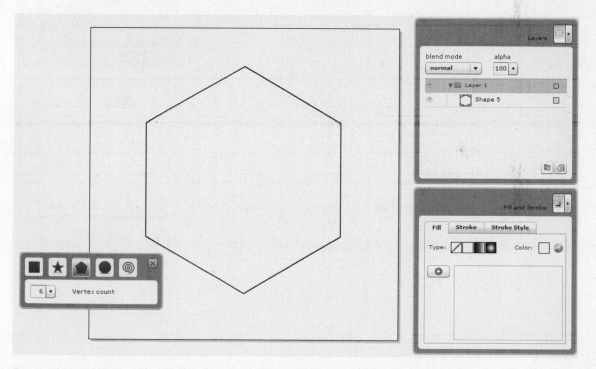

Figure 4-64. Hold down the Shift key while drawing a shape to constrain its orientation.

2. Next, you create a series of guides to help align all of the objects based on this hexagon shape. The **Object to guides** function automatically creates guides based on the shape. For shape objects, this function sets horizontal and vertical guides based at the center of the shape. For paths, this function sets the guides at each vertex. Select **Object ➤ Objects to guides**. This creates guides at the center of the shape. Then, select **Object ➤ Object to path** to convert the shape to a path. Finally, use the **Object ➤ Object to guides** again. Because the object has been converted to a path, it places guides at the bounds and vertices (see Figure 4-65).

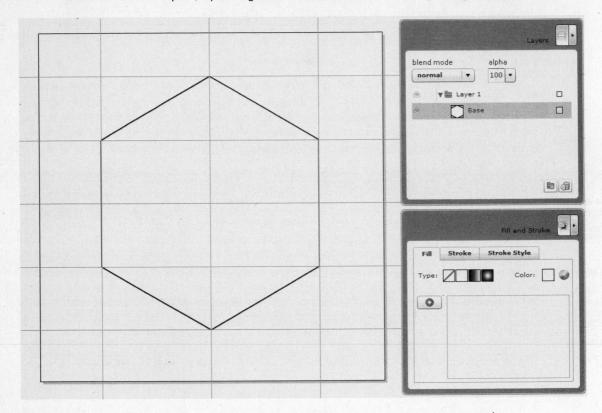

Figure 4-65. Have Raven create automatic guides with the **Object to Guides** command.

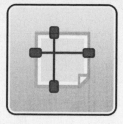

Figure 4-66. The Guide tool lets you adjust guides.

Guides are reference objects that help you align and position shapes, paths, and vertices in a file (see Figure 4-66). Objects snap to the guides. **Snapping** happens when an object comes close to a guide. It gets drawn into and aligns with it. Guides are seen only in the Raven application and do not show in the final output image. The Guide tool is used to position guides in the workspace. This is the only tool that can interact with a guide after they are set. There are two ways to create guides. The first method is to use the `Object` ➤ `Object to guides` function. This produces guides based on the selected object. The second method to add guides is by clicking the rulers at the top or left and dragging out a guide to the workspace. To turn off or on the visibility of the guides, use the `Rulers` ➤ `Show/Hide Guides`. Finally, to remove all the guides that are in a file, use the `Rulers` ➤ `Remove All Guides` function.

3. Draw the sides of the cube. In the `Stroke Style` tab of the Fill and Stroke panel, set the width of the hexagon's outline to 15. This gives the final cube a bold outline. Next, use the Create Bézier and Lines tool to create a rectangle starting in the upper left side, to the center, down to the bottom, back to the lower left, and closing the path back at the start point. It is easy to create straight lines because the path's vertices snap or are attracted to the guides. In the Fill and Stroke panel's `Stroke` tab, set the type to none. Then, in the `Fill` tab, set the type to a `Linear Gradient` with the colors set to bright red fading to dark red (see Figure 4-67). Draw a second rectangle on the right side mirroring the first, and then draw the rectangle at the top in the remaining area (see Figure 4-68). These shapes inherit the color of the first shape's red gradient.

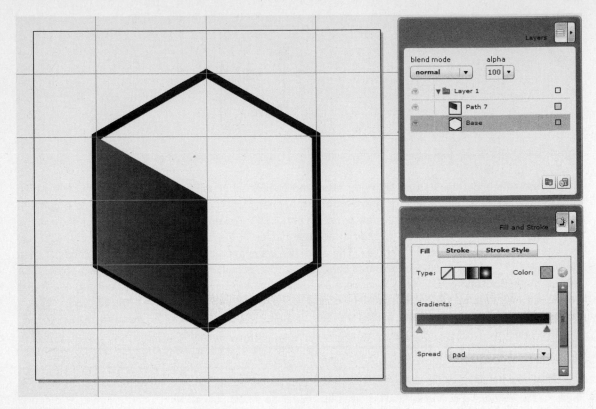

Figure 4-67. Paths snap to the guides.

Figure 4-68. Diagram of the order in which to draw the sides of the cube

4. Set the gradient directions to give the object a cube-like feel. Use the Gradient Transform tool to set the directions of the gradients. Side 1 should start with the bright red in the lower, left corner fading diagonally to the dark red in the top, right corner. Side 2 should have bright red in the top, left corner fading to dark red in the bottom, right corner. Finally, set the direction of side 3 with the dark red at the top fading down to bright red at the bottom (see Figure 4-69). You can use the **Rulers ➤ Show/Hide Guides** command if the guides get in your way. This temporarily hides them from view but doesn't delete them. Clicking the command again restores the guides to the file.

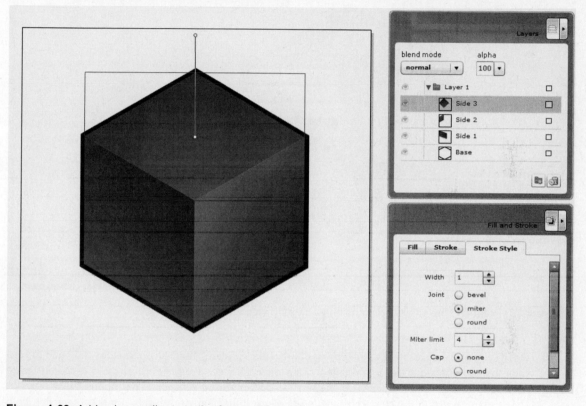

Figure 4-69. Add color gradients to the faces of the cube.

5. Add some decorations to the sides of the cube. You have to skew the decorations—in this case stars—so that they are lined up with the sides. A precise way of doing this is to set up a temporary reference square. Start by setting the fill and stroke for the shape that will be added. In the Fill and Stroke panel's **Fill** tab, set the type to No Fill. In the **Stroke** tab, set the type to solid and set the color to black. Finally, in the **Stroke Style** tab, set the width to 2. Next, select the Rectangle Shape tool, but instead of drawing the shape, click where you would like this square to be placed. Because you didn't drag the rectangle's dimensions, this will bring up the **Create Shape**

dialog. Here, you can predefine the shape's parameters. Set the **Corner Radius** parameter to zero and leave the Rectangle **width** and **height** at 200 (see Figure 4-70). Clicking **OK** draws the shape on the canvas with the parameters that you defined in the **Create shape** dialog, a 200 by 200 pixel square with sharp corners.

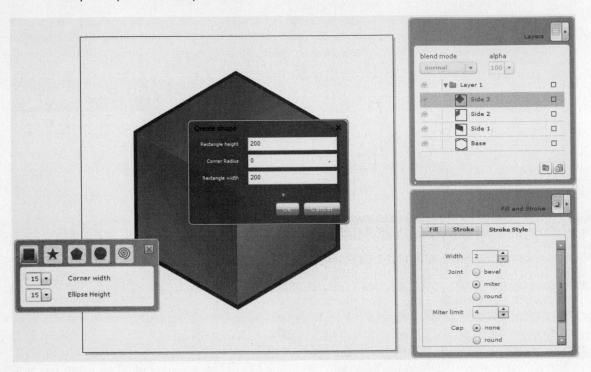

Figure 4-70. Predefine the shape's dimension by clicking with the Shape tool.

6. Next, you add a star shape to the center of the square. Select the Star Shape tool ★ and draw a star inside the square that you created in the previous step. To ensure the star is centered inside the square, open the **Object ➤ Align & Distribute** function. This opens the **Align & Distribute** dialog, which contains different aligning functions for objects. Start by selecting both the square and the star shape by using either the Move tool or the Transform tool and dragging a selection box around both. Then, click the **Align Center Horizontally** 🔲 and **Align Center Vertically** 🔲 buttons to center the star in the middle of the square (see Figure 4-71). With both shapes selected, use the **Edit ➤ Copy** command to copy them. Then, use the **Edit ➤ Paste** to copy them, and move them above the other shapes. Then, use the **Edit ➤ Paste** again to make a third set of the shapes and move them over to the base cube shape.

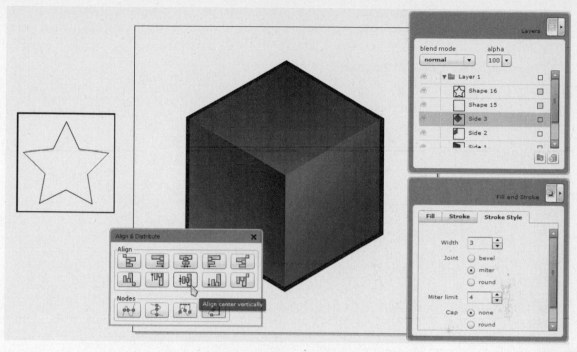

Figure 4-71. Create the stars for the side of the cube.

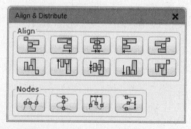

Figure 4-72. The `Align & Distribute` dialog

The align functions automatically position objects and align them with each other (see Figure 4-72). Following is a list of the different align and distribute commands.

Align right sides to left sides of objects.

Align the right sides of objects.

213

Align horizontal centers of objects.

 Align the left sides of the objects.

 Align left sides to the right sides of objects.

 Align top sides to the bottom sides of objects.

 Align the top sides of objects.

 Align vertical centers of objects.

 Align the bottom sides of objects.

 Align the bottom sides to the top sides of objects.

 Align selected vertices horizontally.

 Align selected vertices vertically.

 Distribute or equally space the selected vertices horizontally.

 Distribute or equally space the selected vertices vertically.

7. Select both the square and the star shape with the Transform tool . Then, align the top, left corner of these decoration shapes with the top, left corner on the side on the hexagon that is the base shape for the cube. Stretch the objects so that it is the same width and height as the side of the cube (see Figure 4-73). You should use the guides to help you line up the decoration shapes. If you have hidden the guides from earlier, remember to show them with the **Rulers ➤ Show/Hide Guides** command. Next, take the transform center icon; this is the small circle ✧ in the center of transformed objects. This is the Transform Center, and rotation and skewed transformations are base on this point. Drag the transform center to the top, left corner of the decoration shapes.

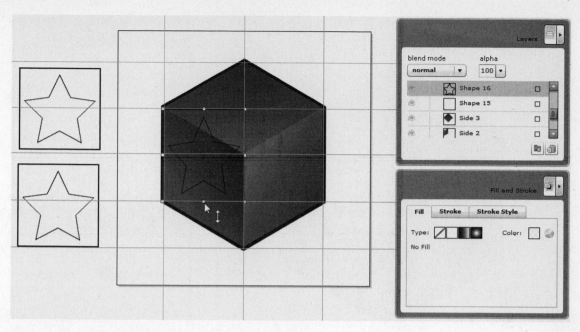

Figure 4-73. Line up the objects.

8. Now, drag downward on the right side of the objects when you see the cursor change to the double arrow. This skews the objects based on the transform's center and makes it easier to line up with the edges (see Figure 4-74). When you have lined up the edge of the objects with the edge of the cube, stretch the height to match the side and delete the square object, leaving just the star. To select only the square object, click in an empty area. This deselects any objects that might be selected. Then, hover over the object you want to select. You see a green highlight around the shape when you are on that object. Clicking selects it. Sometimes it can be hard to select an object that consists of just a stroke, so you can also use the Layers panel to select an object. Find the object you want to select in the Layers panel and click on the little box to the right of the object's name to select it. Finally, position the copies of the decorations on the two other sides of the cube. The top decoration needs to be rotated and skewed to make it line up (see Figure 4-75).

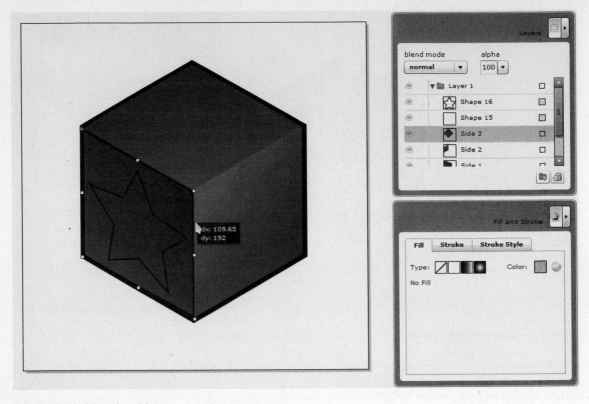

Figure 4-74. Align the sides.

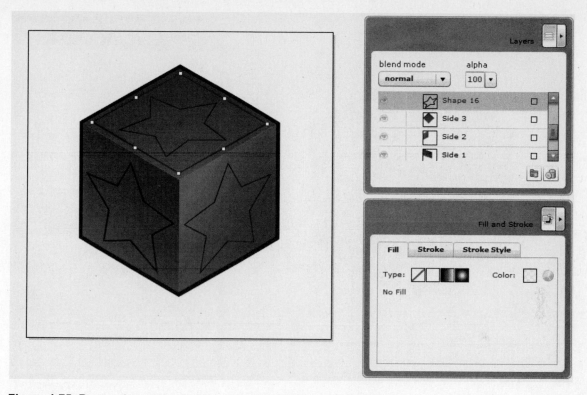

Figure 4-75. Repeat the previous steps to add stars to the other sides.

9. Color the star decorations by adding a gradient fill and a heavy stroke to them. With the Transform tool or Move tool selected, hold the Ctrl (Command ⌘ on the Mac) key down and click the box to the right of each object's name in the Layers panel. This selects the three-star decorations, and any fill and stroke changes are applied to all of the three-star decorations. In the Fill and Stroke panel, set the `Fill` for the stars to a Linear Fill with a gradient of light blue fading to dark blue. Then, switch to the `Stroke` tab and set the `type` to `solid` and the `color` to white. Then, switch to the `Stroke Style` tab and set the `width` to 8. Finally, use the Gradient Transform tool to rotate the gradients. Try to match the rotations that the sides of the cube have to the stars (see Figure 4-76).

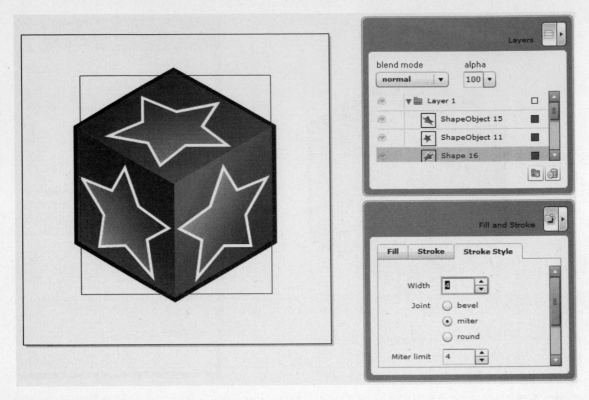

Figure 4-76. Add color to the stars.

10. Now, add the finishing touches. All raven files have a transparent background. Consequently, you have to add a background object to complete this image. Start by drawing a rectangle that is bigger than the canvas using the Rectangle Shape tool ▣. This object covers the cube so you need to move it to the bottom of the layer stack **Object ➤ Move to bottom** in the **Layers** panel. Set the gradient fill for this background to a Radial Fill ▣ of black fading to white. Next, use the Gradient transform tool ▣ and shrink the black center of the gradient so that it barely peeks out from under the cube, creating the appearance of a shadow underneath the cube (see Figure 4-77).

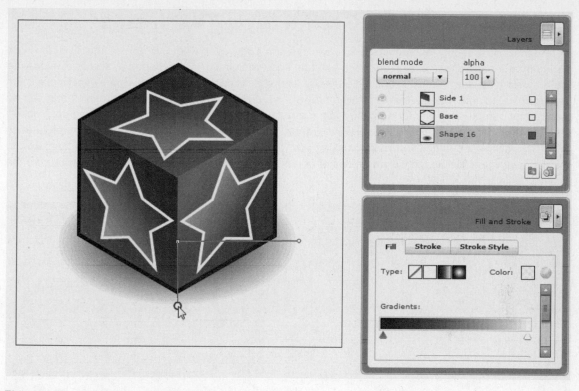

Figure 4-77. Add a background and shadow.

Project review

In this project, you learned how to make and use guides to align objects. You also added guides directly from shapes so you could easily align other objects to it. You saw that you didn't have to draw a shape direotly, but you could generate them with set parameters. You explored more techniques of the Transform tool, such as skewing and rotating from a different reference point. Finally, you set the fill and stroke properties of multiple shapes to unify parameters and speed up your creation process. In the next project, you construct a stylized text poster. You learn how to use imported resources as guides for manually tracing. You use smaller paths to build up the image. Finally, you will see how to use layers to organize your creation.

Project 4.5—Create a Graffiti Style Text Image

From comic illustrations to product design, vectors are used everywhere. Many of these images are started from a hand-drawn sketch on which you can trace your vector. Raven enables you to convert your line drawing to a clean vector image. The precise and sharp lines that vectors can give you make them ideal for professional looking images. In this project, you create stylized graffiti text graphics that can be used in any number of ways: for a t-shirt design, a package logo, a skateboard logo, and so on. You will see how to import a hand-drawn graffiti style graphic from which to trace. Tracing this resource is done using several smaller paths overlapping, making your paths easier to manipulate. Finally, you learn how to use the layer **Lock** function to isolate groups of objects and paths in your images. See Figure 4-78 for the final results from this project.

Figure 4-78. The final image made in this project.

Key concepts in this project

- Grouping objects with layers
- Create Bézier and Lines tool
- Setting parameters of multiple objects
- Layer locking and hiding.

> *Find this file online at*
> http://aviary.com/artists/gettingstartED/creations/chapter_4_project_5.
>
> *The starting resource is at*
> http://aviary.com/artists/gettingstartED/creations/graffiti.

1. First, you import the image you will use as a tracing guide. Launch Raven and at the splash screen, set the dimensions to 1000 x 750 (see Figure 4-79). Click the **Create** button to create the file with the canvas set to those dimensions. To get a bitmap resource into Raven, use the **File ➤ Import file** command. This opens the Resource Browser at the top of the application. The **Resource Browser** gives you access to resources for many different locations. You can find a link to the image used in the example in the sidebar. After you have found the resource, click **Import** to load the bitmap into your file. If the resource is bigger than your current document size, such as the one used in this example, you are asked how to handle the image. The dialog says, "Image is bigger than the current canvas. Do you want to resize it?" For this example, click **Yes,** and resize the resource to fit the document. Clicking No imports the resource at the original dimensions. To create your own image to trace from, you can draw it by hand and use a scanner to get it into your computer. Then use the **Resource Browser** to import it into Raven.

Figure 4-79. Set the starting dimensions from the splash screen.

2. Isolate the resource image from the rest of the image. You use this resource to help guide your paths, but you do not want it to interfere with your creation process. To keep the resources visible but out of the way, you will want to lock them. You can lock a layer in the Layers panel; this keeps it visible but you cannot interact with it. As you have seen in previous projects, a layer is a container that holds objects. All the parameters of objects inside a layer can be set as groups. You can change the stacking order, hide, unhide, lock, and set fills and strokes of multiple objects with layers. It is a great way to organize discreet elements in a file. Create a new layer in the **Layers**

panel by clicking the **Create New Layer** button . This makes a new layer nested in the current one. You need to drag this new layer to the top of the layer stack and name it Outline by double-clicking the layer's title. Finally, lock the layer with the resource image by clicking in the area

between the **Show/Hide Layer** button and the layer name (see Figure 4-80). You will see a

lock icon that shows the layer is locked. The Lock icon will be hidden when it is turned off only showing when the layer is locked.

Figure 4-80. Lock the resource layer.

3. Now, trace the resource with the multi-functioning Create Bézier and Lines tool . First, set the fill and stroke properties for the paths you will draw. In the Fill and Stroke panel, set the type to no fill in the **Fill** tab, and in the **Stroke** tab, set the color to bright red. This makes any paths you draw easy to see with the resource underneath it. Also any new paths you draw will have these properties, until you change them. When tracing an object like this, you want to make many individual shapes, instead of one or two large ones. Start off by picking a section that you want to trace. Then, use the Zoom Level slider to zoom into that section. You need the entire section you plan to trace in the view because scrolling while drawing a path can mess up your path. Next, use the Create Bézier and Lines to create a path around the section (see Figure 4-81). Then, pick a section adjacent to the first and trace it with a path, slightly overlapping with the first path. You need these paths to overlap a little, so there are no gaps. Continue around the resource you are tracing in the same way.

Figure 4-81. Use the Bézier and Line tool to trace the sketch.

4. As you can see in Figure 4-82, the paths are small, manageable pieces that overlap. You can fine-tune each path with the Edit Paths by Nodes tool after you create each. Ideally, you want the path to follow the contours of the resource image (see Figure 4-83). Remember that the Edit Paths by Nodes tool has keyboard-controlled modifiers. If you hold down the Ctrl key (Command on the Mac) while adjusting a control handle, the opposite handle moves in unison. Holding down the Shift and Ctrl keys while adjusting a vertex's control handles makes them symmetrical, which makes it easier to form smooth curves.

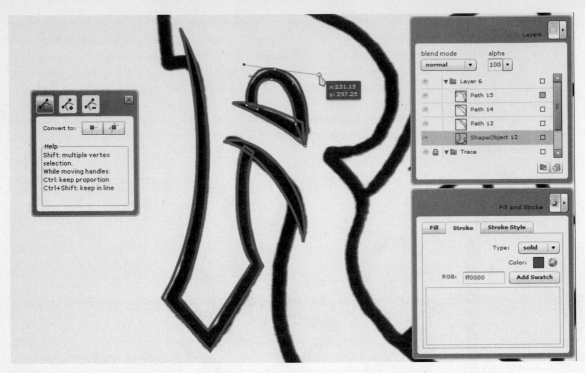

Figure 4-82. Manually trace the resource, and use the Edit Paths by Nodes tool to adjust the paths.

Figure 4-83. The overlapping paths that make up the outline

5. After the entire trace is done, use the Transform tool and drag a selection around all the objects. This selects all the pieces you just created, but not the resource image layer because it is locked. With the paths selected, you can set the fill and stroke for all. In the `Fill` tab, set the fill to solid, black and in the `Stroke` tab, select `none` for the `type`. Finally, you can delete the layer that contains the sketch as it is no longer needed (see Figure 4-84).

Figure 4-84. The result of manual tracing and uniform fill

6. Make shapes that will be the fill color of the text. Create a new layer using the `Create New Layer` button , drag this layer to the top in the Layers panel and name it Fill. Then, lock the layer that contains the traced outline. Set the properties for the paths you will draw. Set the `Fill type` to `none` in the Fill and Stroke panel, set the `Stroke type` to solid, and set the `color` as red. This makes the paths easy to see angst the outline. Using the Create Bézier and Lines tool, draw paths that will become the fill for the letters. You will move this Fill layer behind the outline so you want it to extend slightly over the outline so the outline will completely cover the fill paths. The way to do this is to follow the center line of the outline (see Figure 4-85). Continue to create paths for each letter.

Figure 4-85. Create object paths to use as a fill for the letters.

7. Set these fill paths to a colored gradient. Start by selecting all the fill paths by using the Transform tool. Drag a selection around all the paths, and when the other layer is locked, you select only the ones on the Fill layer. With the paths selected, set the `Stroke type` to none in the `Stroke` tab and in the `Fill` tab, set the type to Linear. Set the Gradients color to yellow fading to light orange (see Figure 4-86).

Figure 4-86. Fill the objects with a linear gradient.

8. Prepare the file to create some highlights. Drag the Fill layer below the Outline layer (see Figure 4-87). This makes the outline cover the fill and makes the image look better. Do not worry about any of the holes in the letters; you will change their fills to match the background later. Make a new layer using the `Create New Layer` button; drag this above the rest of the layers, and name it Highlights. Finally, lock the Fill layer so you can't accidentally alter it while working on the rest of the file.

227

Figure 4-87. Set the gradient's color.

9. Create highlights on the letters. Start by setting the fill and stroke properties. In the `Fill` tab of the Fill and Stroke panel, set the type to Linear Gradient and set the `color` to white at 100 `Alpha` fading to white with a 0 `Alpha`. Switch to the `Stroke` tab and set the type to `none`. Then, with the Create Bézier and Lines tool, draw shapes that are slightly smaller than the outline shapes. These will become highlights on the letters (see Figure 4-88). Remember to zoom into a section that you are drawing your highlight paths on to make it easier to follow the shape accurately. You also have to fine tune these paths with the Edit Paths by Nodes tool because it is hard to get a path perfect on the first try.

Figure 4-88. Use the Create Bézier and Lines tool to create highlight objects.

10. Set the gradient rotations and prepare the layer for some extra details. Use the Gradient Transform tool to adjust the gradient so that they blend with the white in top right to transparent to the bottom left (see Figure 4-89). Next, make a new layer using the **Create New Layer** button . Drag this new layer to the top of the layer stack and name it Details. Finally, lock the Highlight layer to keep from altering it.

Figure 4-89. Set the gradient in the highlights.

11. To give the letter a bit more character, you can add dark orange dots at the bottom of each. Start by setting the fill and stroke of these dots. In the Fill and Stroke panel's **Fill** tab, set the type to solid and the color to a dark orange, which is slightly darker than the orange that was used in the Fill layer's gradient. Then, switch to the **Stroke** tab and set the type to none. Next, select the Ellipse Shape tool ⬤ and while holding down the Shift key, draw several small circles in the bottom quarter of the letters. You can overlap them or leave them separate, whichever you prefer. Continue until all the bottoms of the letters are decorated with the dots (see Figure 4-90).

Figure 4-90. Add dots to the bottom of each letter.

12. Make a background for the letters. Create a New layer, drag it to the very bottom of the layers, and name it Background. Lock the layer that contains the dots, so it won't get in your way. Then, use the Rectangle shape tool ▣ to draw a rectangle that extends outside the canvas (see Figure 4-91). Do not worry about the Stroke or the corner radius of this shape because everything that falls outside the canvas will not be included in the final image.

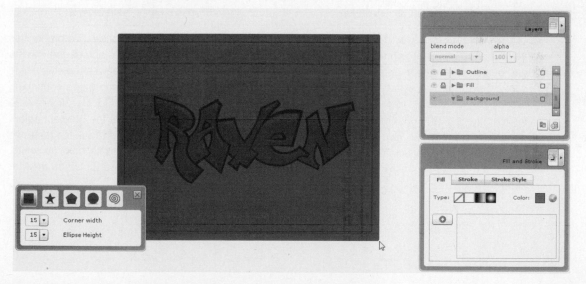

Figure 4-91. Use the Rectangle shape tool to create a background.

231

13. Set the fill of the background shape to a Radial Fill gradient. Set the gradient color to light blue fading to dark blue. Then, use the Gradient Transform tool to adjust the gradient so that the light blue center color radiates equally from the center of the image (see Figure 4-92).

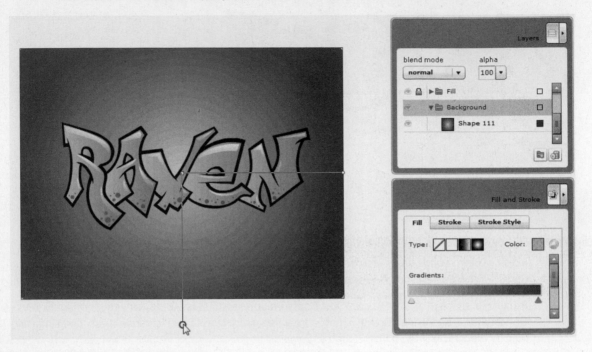

Figure 4-92. Set the radial gradient.

14. Use the Create Bézier and Lines tool to draw a star burst shape behind the letters. To create this pattern, start your path outside the canvas. Draw the next segment that crosses across the canvas and passes through the approximate center. Next, draw a short segment parallel with the side of the canvas, and then a segment across the canvas (see Figure 4-93). Repeat these steps continuing around the canvas closing the shape when you reach where the path was started. See figure 4-94 for a diagram of this pattern. Finally, set this path's Fill to Radial Gradient. Make the gradient colors dark blue to light blue. This is the opposite of the background rectangle's fill and makes these two shapes stand out from each other. Switch to the `Stroke` tab and set the stroke color to white. Finally, switch to the `Stroke Style` tab and set the width to 4, creating a border between the star burst path and the background rectangle.

Figure 4-93. Create a radiating shape.

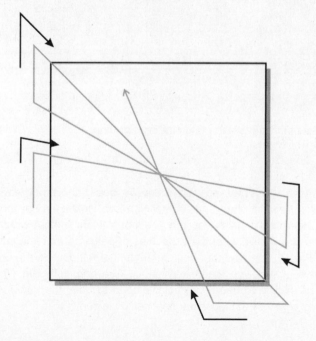

Figure 4-94. A diagram of the shape

15. To complete the image, you need to color the holes in the letters to match the background. Unlock the Fill layer so you can select the paths that are in the holes. With the Move tool, select one of the hole paths. When you hover over the shape, its boarder turns green, letting you know that you can select that path. After you select it, in the `Fill` tab of the Fill and Stroke panel, set the fill type to `solid` ion. It is easy to match the color of the background by using the Color Picker's Eye Dropper tool. With the Color Picker open, instead of picking a color manually from the color area, move the cursor your image. The cursor changes to an eye dropper, letting you sample color directly from your image. Click an area of you image that you think would be the color that would show through the hole of the letter and click `OK` in the Color Picker to set it (see Figure 4-95). Continue this process to color the other holes to finish the image.

Figure 4-95. Color the holes in the letters to match the background.

Project review

In this project, you saw how you can manually trace a drawing to achieve a clean and professional looking image. You learned that you can isolate groups of objects or paths with layers. Locking those layers gives you the freedom to work without worrying about accidentally altering other objects. You preemptively set the properties of paths so that you could create groups with the same fill and stroke. Finally, you saw that any elements that fall outside the canvas are clipped from the final image. In the next project, you create a mock-up of a graphic t-shirt. You explore the style of simulated hand-cut objects. You also use a set color palette to unify the colors throughout the image. Finally, you import a bitmap resource to place your final design in context.

Project 4.6—Designing a Graphic for Screen Printing

Most t-shirt designs are made with a vector-editing application, and Raven is well suited for this task. T-shirts are printed using a method called screen printing. It is a process that involves pushing ink through a mesh fabric stretched over a frame. There is a stencil either laying on this screen or embedded into it. Where the stencil is open, the ink flows through onto the t-shirt, and where it is closed, it is blocked from it. In this project, you simulate hand-cut screen printing stencils with the Create Bézier and Lines tool. You create a color palette that unifies colors throughout the image. Finally, you place your image onto a t-shirt bitmap resource to check the final output of the image (see Figure 4-96).

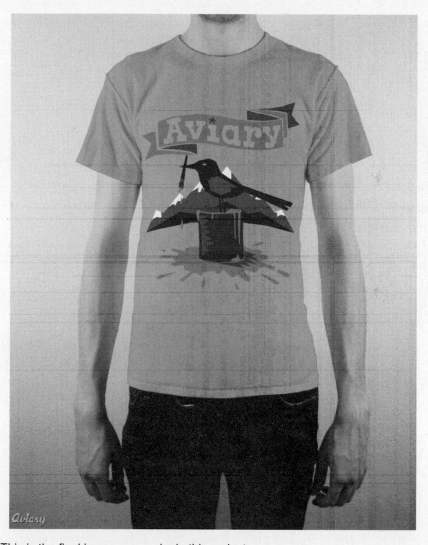

Figure 4-96. This is the final image you make in this project.

Key concepts in this project

- Create Bézier and Lines tool
- Save colors as swatches
- Import bitmaps

> *Find this file online at*
> *http://aviary.com/artists/gettingstartED/creations/chapter_4_project_6.*
>
> *The starting file is at*
> *http://aviary.com/artists/gettingstartED/creations/t-shirt_resource_ch4_p6.*

1. Launch Raven and set your file size. You want to have your canvas similar in dimension as your final product and because this image will go on a t-shirt, you want the canvas to be taller than it is wide. Start this project by launching Raven and set the dimensions of your image to 800 `wide` and 1000 `high` in the splash screen (see Figure 4-97).

Figure 4-97. Set the canvas size from the `Start` dialog.

2. Before you start creating your design, create your color palette for this file. Screen printing can print only one color at a time and is limited in its color amount. To maintain a set amount of colors in the file, we set up a palette to use in this creation. Start by opening the Color Picker. Pick a base color that will be the color of the shirt in the final image (see Figure 4-98). Next, click the OK button to set this as the current color. Click the **Add Swatch** button ⊕. This adds the current color to one of the color swatch wells below. After a color is saved as a swatch, it is available in the color swatch area in the `Fill` and `Stroke` tabs of the Fill and Stroke panel. Continue picking colors and adding them as swatches. This example used four shades of blue and two red colors.

- Base blue (shirt): b2bec6

- Light blue: 567990

- Mid blue: 434a5b

- Dark blue: 163c53

- Coral: ef7049

- Maroon: a0472c

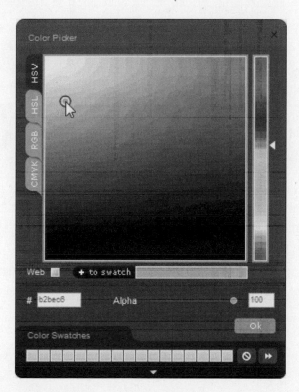

Figure 4-98. Predefine your color palette.

3. Set some guides to help you see the canvas and keep your design symmetrical. To manually set guides, click on one of the rulers and you can drag out a guide. Dragging from the top ruler, set the horizontal guides and the ruler to the left to set the vertical guides. Drag a guide at each side of the canvas. With these guide in place, you will always know where the canvas is even when it is covered by objects. Finally, set a vertical guide in the approximate center (see Figure 4-99). Remember, you can toggle the visibility of the guides by using the **Rulers ➤ Show/Hide Guides**.

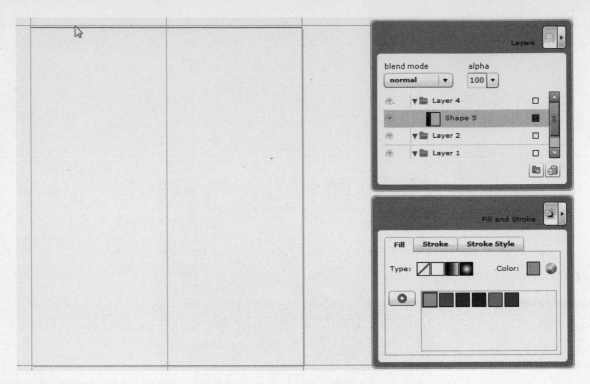

Figure 4-99. Set some guides to help with the layout of the design.

4. Create a background with the Rectangle Shape tool , covering up the entire canvas. Color this shape the base blue, which is going to be the color of the shirt (see Figure 4-100). Finally, lock this layer by clicking on the area next to the Eye icon in the layer panel.

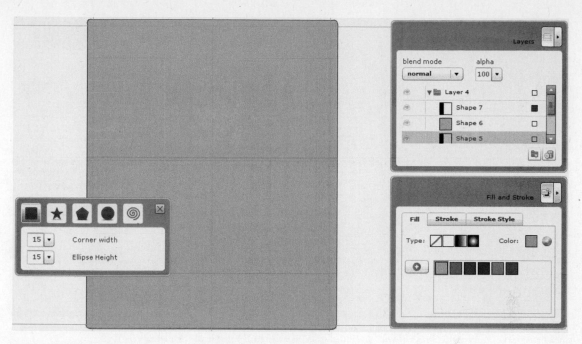

Figure 4-100. Create a background rectangle on which to work.

5. Begin creating your design using straight edges. You start by making a banner across the top of the design. Make a new layer by using the **Create New Layer** button , drag this layer to the top of the layer stack and name it Banner. Select the Create Bézier and Lines tool and start drawing your design. Screen printing stencils used to be hand-cut with a sharp knife. Due to the nature of this technique, it was hard to produce smooth curves, so the edges of the designs would tend to have straight edges. You will exaggerate this to create a stylized design. To simulate this effect, click and release the mouse button when creating vertices that produce straight line segments (see Figure 4-101). The great feature of this technique is that you do not have to worry about objects lining up, and the variation in angles adds personality to the design.

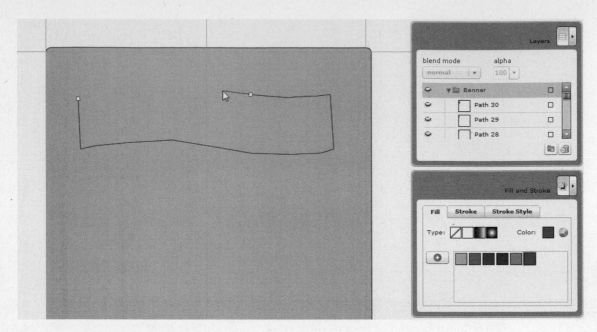

Figure 4-101. Draw your shapes with minimal curves to give the look of hand-cut stencils.

6. Continue drawing the banner, building up the image by stacking objects on top of each other, working from the background objects and working forward to foreground objects. Color each object using the color swatches that you set up earlier. Using the blue base shirt color, simulate cutting holes into your design, for example, the insides of the letters of the banner (see Figure 4-102). After you have constructed the banner, create a new layer naming it Back. Move it to the top of the layer stack, and lock the Banner layer by clicking the area between the eye and the layer title.

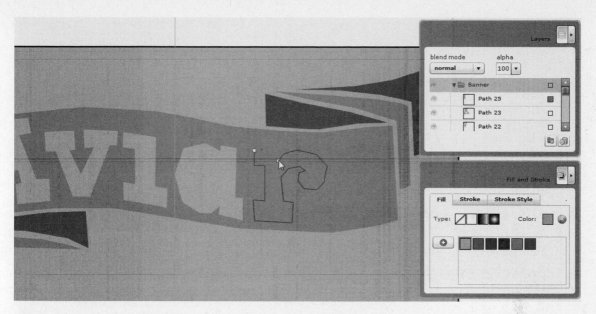

Figure 4-102. Use the base blue color to create cutouts in your design.

7. Create background elements. On the Back layer, continue using the Create Bézier and Line tool to create mountains. Start with the light blue color to draw the silhouette of the mountains. Then, use the dark blue color to create hills in front of the mountains. Finish them off by adding snow to the peaks (see Figure 4-103). After the mountains are done, make a new layer by clicking the **Create New Layers** button. Name this layer Bird and drag it to the top of the layer stack. Finally, lock the layer that has the mountains.

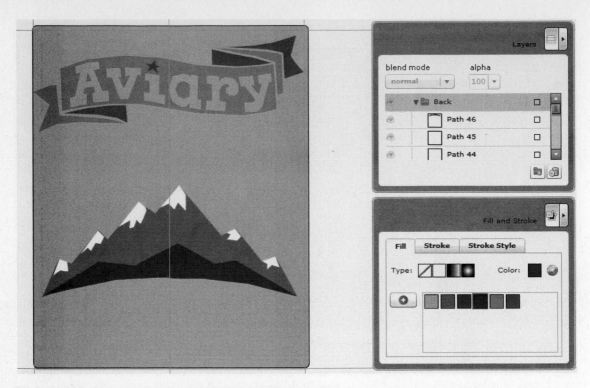

Figure 4-103. Create a set of mountains for the background.

8. On this new Bird layer, you create a bird standing in a paint bucket, with a paint brush in its mouth. Start by using the Create Bézier and Line tool with the coral color to make a splatter. Then, use the mid blue to make the paint bucket shape, with a highlight of light blue on the left. Finally, switch back to the coral color to add paint dripping from the top of the bucket (See Figure 4-104).

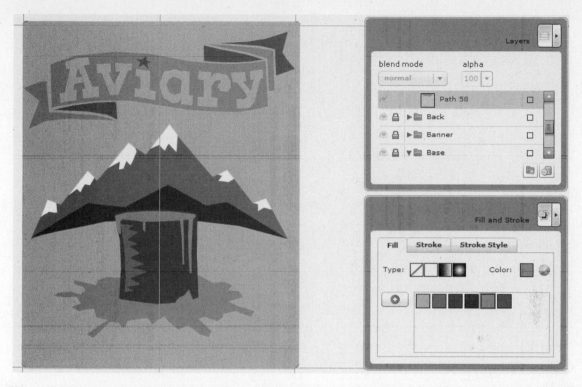

Figure 4-104. Use the color swatches when creating paths to maintain a unified color scheme throughout the image.

9. Create some shading on the splatter and in the paint bucket with the maroon color. Also add some extra drips around the paint splatter. Next, create a silhouette of a bird in the dark blue color centered over the top of the paint bucket. The bird might be easier to make out of several smaller paths, one each for the body, head, tail, and beak. Create a wing shape on the body of the bird and color it light blue. Finally create an eye on the bird coloring it the base blue color (see Figure 4-105).

Figure 4-105. Make the bird silhouette and add details to the bucket.

10. Use the dark blue color to create a set of legs for the bird. Using the same color, create a handle of a paint brush in the bird's beak. Then, use the light blue to make a ferrule and mid blue for the bristle of the brush. Finally, use the coral color to put a bit of paint at the end of the brush and a few drips (see Figure 4-106).

Figure 4-106. Import the image of your shirt.

11. Import a t-shirt image to place your design on. After you have the design finished, unlock the base blue rectangle that you used as the background and delete it. Next, use the `File ➤ Import file` command to open the `Resource Browsers`. Then, navigate to the image of the blank t-shirt. You can find the t-shirt resource used in this file by searching for t-shirt resource ch4 p6 in the `Resource Browser's Aviary Library` tab (see Figure 4-107). If you made a design that used a different color for the shirt, you can open the t-shirt resource ch4 p6 file in the Phoenix, select the Color layer by holding the Shift key while clicking on the preview image in the Layers panel, and then use the Paint Bucket tool to fill the selection with the color you used in your file.

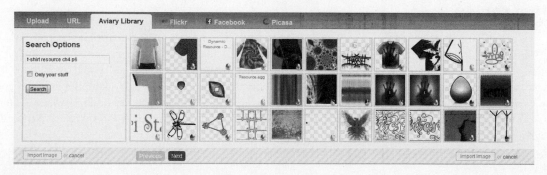

Figure 4-107. Import the t-shirt resource into the file.

12. Now, import shirt into the file at the top most layer on the `Layers` panel. Move this resource to the bottom of the stack by using the `Object ➤ Move Bottom`. Then, lock the layer so that it won't interfere with the rest of the file. Position the graphic on the t-shirt resource. Because the shirt resource is locked, use the Transform tool and drag around the design. This selects the entire design, letting you transform it in one piece (see Figure 4-108). Scale and position the graphic on the shirt.

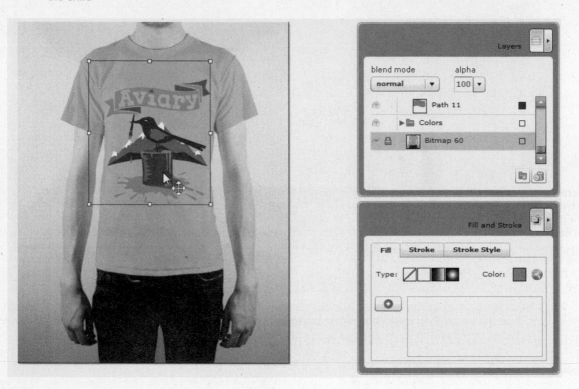

Figure 4-108. Fine-tune the position of the graphic on the t-shirt.

Project review

In this project, you learned how to change the way you use the Create Bézier and Line tool to create a stylized cutout design. You also saw how creating a limited color palette for your image is a way to maintain a constant color scheme throughout an image. Again, you saw the advantages of grouping objects and paths into layers. You saw how to lock layers to keep them out of your way. You learned how to find a specific resource in Aviary's `Library` tab in the resource Browser. Finally, you created a mock of a t-shirt design suitable to present to a client, or to prepare for a printer. In the next project, you learn how to control Raven's `Bitmap to Vector Trace` functions. You make an inspirational poster graphic by layering several traces of the same image and adding text.

Project 4.7—Create a Graphic Inspirational Poster with Raven Trace

Raven trace is an incredible online bitmap-to-vector converter. Raven Trace analyzes a bitmap and, depending on the settings you choose, can output a one-color, grayscale, or full-color vector. After a bitmap has been converted, you can edit it like any other vector shape. Bitmap-to-vector conversion has been available in desktop graphics applications for some years, but Raven has made it available for free online. In this project, you make several differently colored traces and stack them to create a poster style image. See Figure 4-109 for the results from this project.

Figure 4-109. The final image you make in this project.

Key concepts in this project

- Understanding Raven Trace
- Changing attributes of multiple objects
- Striped fills with gradients.

> *Find this file online at*
> *http://aviary.com/artists/gettingstartED/creations/chapter_4_project_7.*

1. Prepare your file for tracing. Find an image that you would like to use for this project, and find out what its dimensions are. Right-click the image and choose **Properties** form the context menu. A pop-up dialog with the image's **height** and **width displays**. Write this down so you can set the document size in Raven. Launch Raven and set the height and width the same as the image that you will use in this trace file. For this example, the **height** is 1060 pixels and the **width** is 1600.

   Next, pick four colors and save them as swatches. Click the color box ^{Color:} in the Fill and Stroke panel to open the Color Picker so that you can pick the colors that you will use in the file (see Figure 4-110). After you pick a color, use the **Add Swatch** button to save a swatch of that color. Continue this process until you have chosen four colors. For this example, pick four colors with the same hue (color) but with different values ranging from dark to light. You don't have to pick the same hue for the image, but doing so does give you a unified look.

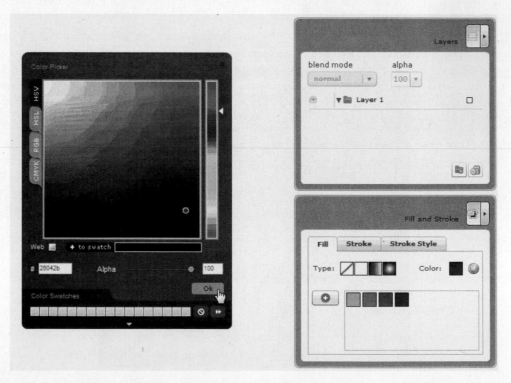

Figure 4-110. Pick the four colors you will use in the file and save a color swatch of each.

2. Next, you import the image you want to trace. Now that you have your swatches ready, you need to import your image into the file. Start by using the **File ➤ Import File**, which opens the Resource Browser. Locate the image you want to trace. If you want use the image from this example, switch to the **Aviary Library** tab and type Start Chapter 4 Project 7 in the search box. This search filters the files so you can find the image easily (see Figure 4-111). When you have found the image you are going to use, click the **Import File** button to bring the image into your file.

Figure 4-111. Import your Image to be traced.

3. Prepare your bitmap images. Raven's **Trace Bitmap** function is an advanced process that analyzes a bitmap image and literally traces the value and color areas with paths. After an image is converted, you can manipulate the paths and vertices like any other vector file. The Trace Bitmap function has many parameters to adjust how the functions convert the bitmap. For this file, you layer several successively smaller traces to create an inspirational poster. To start, you must have four copies of the bitmap image so you can make a trace of each. Select the bitmap image with the Transform tool ▣ and use the **Edit ➤ Copy** command to place a copy of the bitmap onto your computer's Clipboard. Next, use the **Edit ➤ Paste** command to add a copy of the bitmap to the file. It will be directly on top of the original so you should be able to see that the image was added; however, you can see if there is a copy in the Layer panel. Hide this copy by clicking the **Show/Hide Layer** button 👁. Repeat this process two more times, until you have four bitmaps with three of them hidden (see Figure 4-112).

Figure 4-112. Make three copies of the bitmap resource.

4. Now to get familiar with the Trace Bitmap function's parameters. Select the bitmap that is visible with the Select and Move tool ⬈✛ . Then, use the `Object ➤ Trace Bitmap` command to open the `Convert to Path` dialog. You will see a thumbnail image in the top, left, and a preview image underneath. On the right are two tabs. One is for `Black and White Trace` parameters and one is for `Color Trace` parameters. Switch to the `Black and White` tab (see Figure 4-113). The first set of parameters runs a noise reduction function on the image before the trace. You typically do not need this unless you have a complex or noisy image that produces too many vertices. If you need to activate these controls, check the `Use Noise Reduction` check-box to enable the parameters.

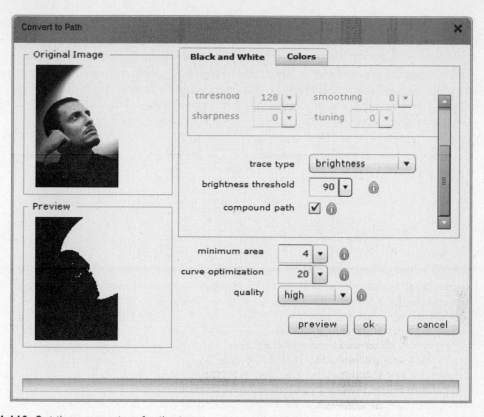

Figure 4-113. Set the parameters for the trace.

5. The next set of parameters sets how the trace is performed. The **Trace Type** setting lets you choose from a standard **Brightness trace**, which produces solid objects, or **Edge Detection**, which traces only the edges in an image. The **Brightness Threshold** setting adjusts the amount of the image that is included in the trace. A high setting produces more of the image as a filled object, whereas a lower setting produces less. The compound path setting, if enabled, produces a trace that is one complete object. Any of the areas that are not traced are hollow so that anything underneath shows. When **Compound Path** is disabled, the resulting trace produces separate objects and any space not in the trace is filled with white (see Figure 4-114).

Figure 4-114. Trace type and noise reduction parameters.

6. The next set of parameters is applied during the trace. The **Minimum Area** setting discards any object in the trace that is smaller in pixels than the number set. The **Curve Optimization** setting sets the amount that Raven tries to convert straight vertices to curved ones. **Quality** sets how many vertices are in the final trace. The High and Medium quality parameters produce tighter traces and more vertices. Too many vertices in a file can become a problem because the more vertices a fill has, the more computer process is used to render the file. A file with a lot of vertices can significantly slow Raven down, especially on slower computers (see Figure 4-115).

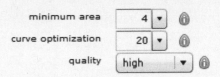

Figure 4-115. The post trace optimization parameters.

7. Click the **Preview** button at the bottom of the **Trace** dialog to see a rough thumbnail image of the resulting trace (see Figure 4-116). Here, you can see if you need to adjust any of the parameters. When you are ready to trace the bitmap, click **OK** and then wait for the trace to complete.

Figure 4-116. A rough preview of the Trace output.

8. Perform the **Trace** function on the first bitmap. In the parameters for this example, set the **Brightness Threshold** to 85 and be sure the **Compound Path** is checked. Then, set the **Quality** to medium, and click the **OK** button to perform the trace. The resulting path or paths are added to the file and organized under a single layer in the **Layers** panel. The bitmap image that

was used in the trace is deleted from the file, which is why you made the copies earlier (see Figure 4-117). You need to set the color of the trace. You can do this in one command instead of selecting each shape individually. Start by having either the Transform tool or the Select and Move tool selected because this technique won't work with any of the other tools. Then, select the entire layer containing the trace by clicking on the square selector icon next to it in the **Layers** panel.

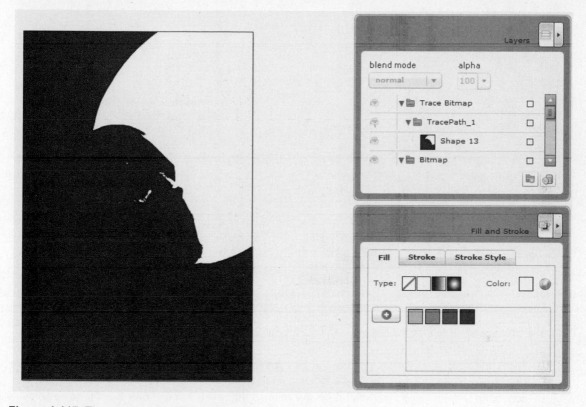

Figure 4-117. The result of the first trace

9. Create a Striped fill pattern. With the paths in this layer selected in this first trace, set the type to **Linear Gradient** in the **Fill** tab of the Fill and Stroke panel. Set the colors in the gradient to the lightest color from the trace blending to the next second lightest color. Next drag the color stop controls so that they are close together in the center of the colorbar. This produces a quick transition between the two colors. Then, set the **Spread** to **Repeat**. Finally, select the Gradient Transform tool and shrink the length of the gradient by moving the control handle closer to the center of the gradient. You can see that the shorter the gradient, the thinner the stripes appear in the fill. Adjust the gradient to a 45-degree angle and make it very short to create many small stripes (see Figure 4-118).

Figure 4-118. Create a Striped Fill pattern with the Repeat Spread method.

10. Trace the next layer. Unhide one of the bitmaps in the bottom layer, and then select it with the Select and Move tool. Run the Trace function on this bitmap with the **Object** ➤ **Trace Bitmap** command. For this layer, you want a smaller path so that when it is laid over the first trace some of that layer will show underneath. You use the exact same setting as the first trace except for the **Brightness Threshold**. The parameter settings for this trace are **Brightness Threshold** of 65, **Compound Path** is checked, and **Quality** set for Medium. Click **OK** to convert the bitmap into a vector. Again, use the Select and Move tool to select all the paths in the TracePath_1 layer by clicking on the small box next to the title. Finally, color the trace results by setting the type to Solid and the color that is the second lightest color in the **Fill** tab of the Fill and Stroke panel (see Figure 4-119).

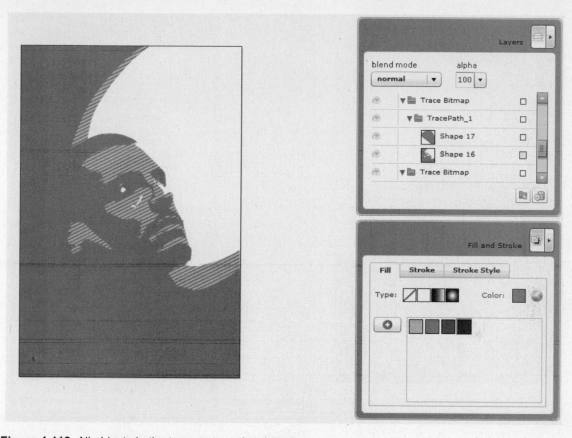

Figure 4-119. All objects in the trace get a color change.

11. Continue creating traces. Unhide another copied bitmap from the bottom layer. Using the same process as in Step 10, trace this bitmap. The parameter settings for this trace are **Brightness Threshold** of 45, **Compound Path** is checked, and **Quality** to Medium. Finally, color this trace result the third color (see Figure 4-120).

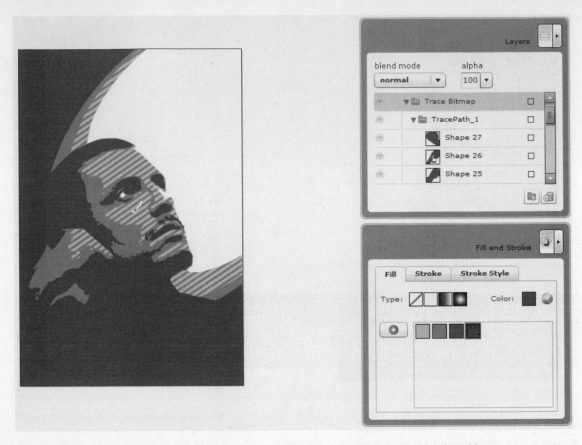

Figure 4-120. Create traces with a smaller threshold setting to produce a multi-colored image.

12. Unhide the last bitmap, and run a trace on it using the same process as before. The parameter settings for this trace are **Brightness Threshold** of 25, **Compound Path** is checked, and **Quality** to Medium. Finally color this trace the darkest color. The resulting image has four traces of different colors and thresholds, stacked on top of each other as you can see in Figure 4-121.

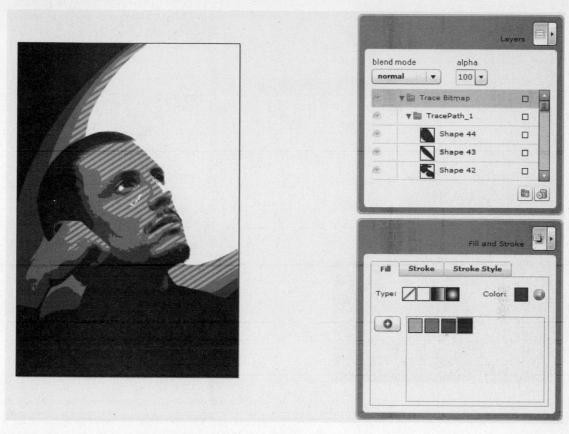

Figure 4-121. The traces are layered on top of each other.

13. Add an inspirational word to the bottom of the image. You have to resize the document to give room for the inspirational word. Select **File ➤ Document size** to open the **Document setup** dialog. The **Document Height** and **Width** settings are populated with the current document size. Add 150 to the **Document Height** setting and click **OK** (see Figure 4-122). This adds 150 pixels to the bottom of the canvas. Raven's canvas resizing is applied to the bottom and right sides.

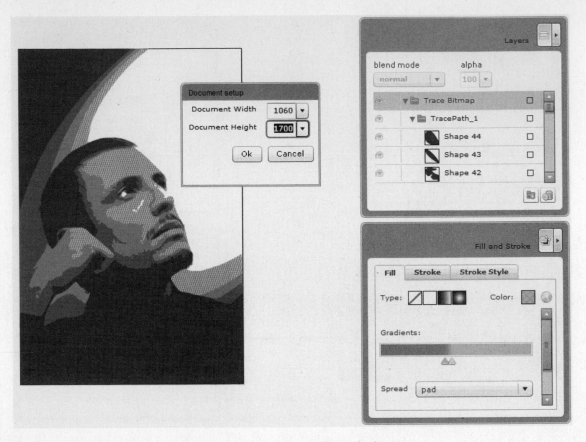

Figure 4-122. Resizing the canvas to add an inspirational title to the image.

14. Use the Rectangle Shape tool to add a shape filling in the new empty canvas area at the bottom of the image (see Figure 4-123). Color this shape the darkest color from the traces. Do not worry if the shape goes outside of the canvas because the overflow does not end up in the final image.

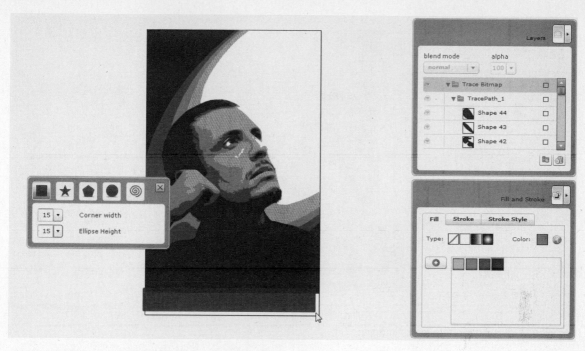

Figure 4-123. Add color to the empty canvas area.

15. Use the Text tool ⊤ to add an inspirational title to the image. Click the Text tool and open the Text fly-out menu where the tool parameters are located. Chose a bold font from the font dropdown menu. You have access to all of the fonts currently installed on your computer. Next, set the color of the text to one of the lighter shades used in your traces. Double-click the area that you want to add the text, and a text box with an active input cursor displays. Type the word that you want to add to the poster. In this example, use the name application RAVEN (see Figure 4-124). Finally, use the Transform tool ▨ to scale and position the text object in the area at the bottom of the image.

Figure 4-124. Add the title to the image.

16. Add a paper texture to complete the poster effect. Import a paper texture (the one used in this file is located at www.CGTextures.com). Use the `File ➤ Import File` command to open the `Resource Browser`. Locate the paper texture bitmap and import it into Raven. Set the `Blend Mode` of this bitmap to `Multiply`, which lets the grain of the paper show in the trace image you just made. Finally, if you need to, use the Transform tool to position the texture so it covers the entire image (see Figure 4-125).

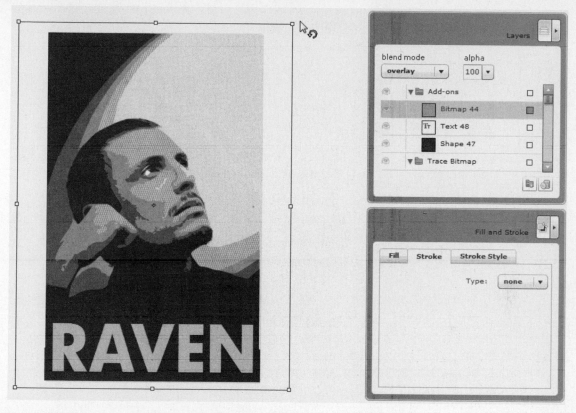

Figure 4-125. Use a resource to impart a paper texture to the traced images.

Other trace methods

In this project, you saw how to create a layered trace image. However Raven's Trace function can do so much more. You saw the trace feature in its simplest form, one color Brightness trace. There are other trace functions and advanced setting that that enables you to create traces of edges. You can also use the Trace to create a grayscale conversion of a bitmap. Finally, there is a full color bitmap-to-vector conversation. You will soon get acquainted with these other results of Raven's Trace function.

Edge detection trace

This method has all the same settings as the basic Brightness trace, but the results follow the edges of the bitmap, producing a vector outline of the image. Edge detection works best on bitmaps that have a high contrast (see Figure 4-126). Use this method to simulate a line drawing or stack the results on top of the original to enhance the edge of the image (see Figure 4-127).

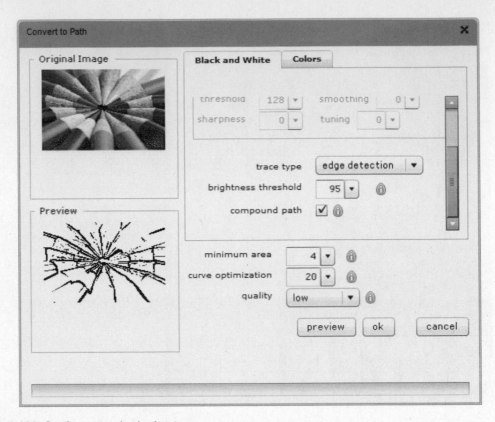

Figure 4-126. Set for a standard edge trace.

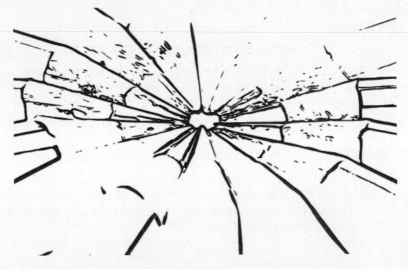

Figure 4-127. The results of an edge detection trace.

Color and grayscale trace

The `Colors` tab in the `Convert to Path` panel is where you can find the parameters to perform a color or grayscale trace (see Figure 4-128). This produces multiple paths one or more for each color. These paths are stacked on top of each other. Be careful with how many colors you use in a trace because each path adds vertices, and the more vertices a file has, the longer it takes to render.

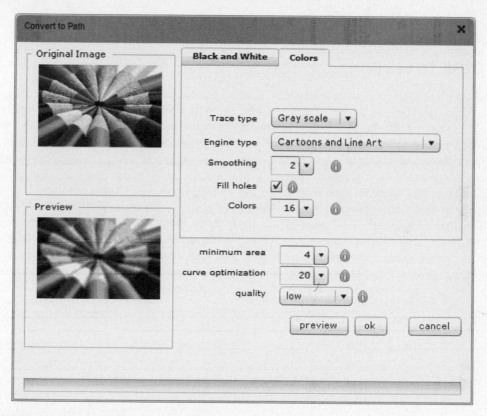

Figure 4-128. The `Colors` tab and parameters.

The `Trace type` sets either a grayscale or a color trace. The `Gray scale` setting produces a trace that has no color, but only shades of black and white. The `Engine type` sets a different method for simplifying colors. `Smoothing` sets the amount of blur applied to the image before the trace. The `Fill holes` setting will spread the different objects in the trace so that their edges overlap and fill the gaps between them. `Colors` set the amount of different colors that are used in the trace. The more colors in a trace, the more time it takes to complete it.

Project review

In this project, you learned how to use Raven's `Trace Bitmap` function to create a stylized poster image. The `Brightness` method gives you a single color path based on the value in a bitmap, which is useful for manually layering traces. You saw that the `Repeat` spread method of a Linear Gradient can produce a striped fill pattern. Finally, you used a bitmap resource and `Blend Modes` to give your image a paper texture.

Chapter review

Raven has real-world applications: icon creation, poster design, screen printing, and more. In this chapter, you learned the importance of paths and how to handle the Create Bézier and Line tool. This multi-functioning tool is key to creating complex and dynamic vector images. You then explored the versatility of Raven's shape objects to create perfect shapes and even build images. Guides are important utility objects that help you line up paths in several projects. Even though Raven is a vector application, it can also handle bitmaps. These bitmaps augment your vector creations; you use them as guides to draw paths. You converted them to vectors to build up images. You even used a bitmap with Blend Modes to give your image rich texture. Raven is a powerhouse vector editor accessible from any Internet-connected computer. You never again have to be away from or pay too much for these capabilities. In the next chapter, you explore Aviary's effect editor Peacock. This intricate application is arguably the most powerful and complex application that Aviary has made. You learn a new method of constructing image files. Peacock uses a hub-and-connector method to chain multiple effects together with amazing results, and Peacock has over 65 hubs that when chained together in various ways can replicate almost any kind of digital imaging effect.

Chapter 5

Creating Images with Peacock

Peacock is a powerful effect construction application. Effects, as they are referred to in Aviary, are a process that alters the pixels in an image. Effects can range from simple color manipulation to distortions to complex pattern generators like the AutoPainter. These effects can be layered or connected into chains. Each effect in a chain adds its effect from the previous and passes the results to the next. Units called hubs produce effects in Peacock. **Hubs** are compositional units that perform one specific effect and have their own specific parameters (see Figure 5-1). For example, there is a hub that performs a blur effect and there is a hub that performs bilateral smoothing. Even though these two perform similar effects, their inner workings are much different, so each effect is contained in a hub with different parameters. Peacock's hubs are grouped into six different categories based on similar functions. These categories include `Generators`, `Effects`, `Controllers`, `Resources`, `Blackboxes`, and `(User Interface) UI Elements`. **Generator hubs** are hubs that generate an output image. You must always start a file with a `Generator` hub because it gives you resources. **Effect hubs** alter or manipulate the input. **Controller hubs** are utility hubs splitting inputs, outputs, orientation, and sizing. **Resource hubs** are imported images that can be used in a file. **Blackbox hubs** are precompiled Peacock files that are groups of hubs designed to be reused. These files are also used as `Custom Filters` in Phoenix. **UI Elements** are controls used with Blackbox hubs to add functionality. To create any effect imaginable, you can add any number of these hubs and connect them in an almost unlimited fashion.

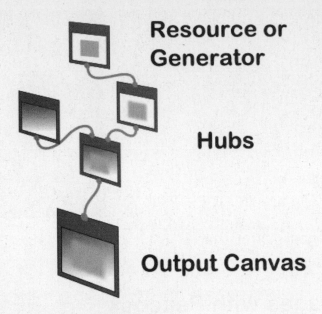

Figure 5-1. Layout of a Peacock file and effect chains

Peacock Application Overview

When you first launch Peacock, you see a gray area in the center of the application; this is the workspace. The **workspace** is an area to compose and test your file (see Figure 5-2). Every file starts with a Canvas hub; this hub displays the output of the file. You cannot delete the Canvas hub. You can drag hubs to the workspace area to add them into the file. The View Navigator is in the lower, right section of the workspace. The **View Navigator** displays all the hubs used in a file. A small square represents each hub and its relative location. The white rectangle is used to navigate around the workbench by dragging it inside the navigator window. The slider sets the zoom level in the workspace. You can zoom in and out of the workspace within a 10%–500% zoom range. Additionally, you can pan around the workspace by holding down the Space bar and dragging the workspace around.

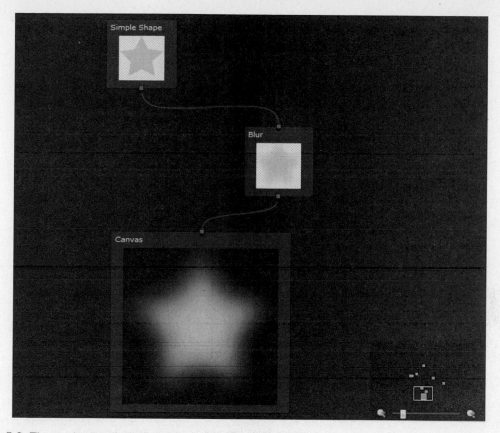

Figure 5-2. The workspace and View Navigator with a few hubs

On the left side of the application are five tabs (see Figure 5-3). Clicking any of them opens a Sidebar drawer containing hubs. These sidebars separate the hubs into six different categories based on their functions (see Figure 5-3). Hubs can be dragged from the sidebars and dropped onto the workspace to be added to the file. When the sidebar is open, you can find additional information about any particular hub by clicking on it in the sidebar. This information is displayed at the top of the sidebar. You can also filter the hubs in a specific sidebar by typing in the search box at the top of the sidebar. Clicking the `Clear` button resets the hub search filter.

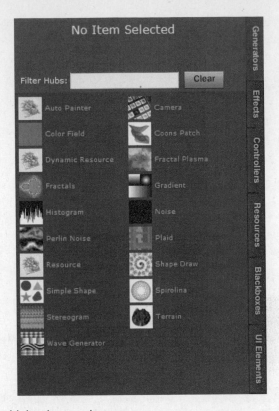

Figure 5-3. The Generator sidebar is open here.

After a hub is dropped onto the workspace, it expands and exposes its connector pins and preview window (see Figure 5-4). Hubs have either one or more Input and Output pins. The pins on the hubs show how they can be connected. You can connect an Output pin to an Input pin. Clicking one of the pins and dragging to another makes a connector line display between the hubs, indicating that they are now connected. Information from one hub is pushed out from the output and can be fed into any other hub's inputs via the connector lines. The information that passes through a hub receives that hubs effect, and the result is passed on to the next hub in the chain. You cannot connect an output to a hub that has been used previously in the same chain. You can tell which pins cannot be connected because they become transparent when dragging a connector.

At the top of each hub, you see its title that displays the type of hub. **Input pins** are plugs where connector lines can be attached to the hub and are found on the top of a hub. **Output pins**, which are at the bottom, are plugs that connector lines can be pulled from the hub and connected to other hubs in the effect chain. An Input pin is where information is brought into a hub; after the hub's effect is preformed on the input, that information is pushed out from the hub through an Output pin. **Connector lines** are conduits for information into or out of a hub and can be connected only from an Input pin to an Output pin. Hubs are connected linearly, so hubs can be connected only to one further down in the chain. A connection line can never be looped and connected to a hub earlier in the chain. Input and Output pins are grayed out if they are not allowed to be connected to. The **Delete** and **Hide/Show** buttons display only when the mouse cursor is over the hub. Double-clicking the **Trashcan** button deletes the hub. The **Hide/Show** button enables or disables the hub in the chain.

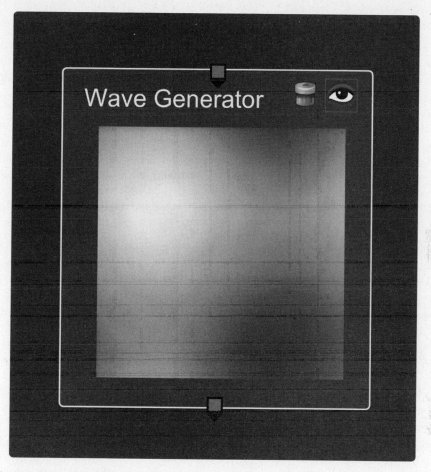

Figure 5-4. The anatomy of a hub

One important factor to be aware of is that many hubs can output their own image dimensions. The default dimension that most hubs use is the Canvas' size. Changing the Canvas hub's dimension can affect the dimension of many of the other hubs in a file. Alternately, a hub's dimension can be changed to a **Fixed Size**, which can be different than the Canvas and is isolated to the specific hub. This is helpful when using memory-intensive hubs; you can reduce the size of the input to reduce the render times of some complex hubs such as the AutoPainter. Some hubs with more than one input can be set so the hub's dimension matches the **Input Size**. You can also set a hub's dimensions to a **Custom Size**, which is sometimes referred to as **Dynamic Size**. **Custom Size** is a dimension that is set by a hub other than an input or the Canvas. A Custom Size hub is a utility hub found in the **Controller** sidebar; its sole purpose is to control other hubs' dimensions. After a Custom Size hub is added to a file, you can set other hubs to match its dimension. The Custom Size hub lets you dynamically control the output dimensions of sets of hubs. At anytime, you can change the Custom Size hub and any hubs set to that Custom Size hub will automatically update to the new size. Finally, not all hubs have dimension parameters. Hubs such as Blur and Auto Level add an effect but do not alter the size.

On the right side of the application is the **Properties** panel. This panel has three tabs: **Properties**, **Parameters**, and **Comments**. The **Properties** tab displays all the available properties and settings for the hubs. Clicking any hub that is on the workspace brings up its properties in this panel. Any parameter settings are set here, and the results are updated in the hub. This area changes in accordance with whatever hub is selected. All hubs, except the Canvas, have a **Randomize** button and a **Reset to Default** in the Properties panel. Some hubs do not have any properties. The **Parameter** tab lists all the parameters for the hub. Next to each parameter are one or more checkboxes; checking them exposes Input or Output parameter pins for use with UI Elements. See Chapter 9 for more information on parameters and UI Elements. There is also a set of checkboxes, which let you set which parameters are included in the **Randomize** feature. The **Comments** tab is an area where you can add comments to a hub. You can use this area to leave notes about a specific hub. Hubs with comments display an asterisk (*) by their title.

Finally, at the top of the application is the Menu bar and the HTML Save bar (see Figure 5-5). The Menu bar has menus for file control commands. The **File** Menu includes **Save**, **Import Resource**, and **Preferences**. The **Edit** menu has commands for **Copy**, **Paste**, **Undo**, and **Duplicate**. The **View** menu has commands for viewing the Canvas window and centering the workspace on the Canvas hub. The **Feedback** menu lets you send a bug report or suggestions to the developers. The **Help** menu displays the current version of Peacock you use. Enabling the **Selection Only** button renders the hubs in the chain up to the hub that is selected and not beyond it. This is a convenient feature when testing parameters in a large file; you don't have to render the complete file. Next to the **Selection Only** button is a **Pause** button. The **Pause** button disables the files rendering. Use this if you need to set several parameters and don't want to wait for a render between each adjustment. Next are the dedicated undo and redo buttons. Finally, the **Memory Meter** displays the total memory that your computer has committed to Peacock. This is mainly used for the developer to diagnose bugs that might crop up in the application. If you report a bug, be sure to include the **Memory Meter's** output in your bug report. The **Flush** button tries to release unused memory back into your computer. The **Memory Meter** function might not be in future updates of Peacock; it is a tool to help develop the application. The HTML Save bar is where you save files, add tags and descriptions, and set permissions. After a file is saved, you are shown a preview and links so you can share your creation on your blog or social networking site.

Figure 5-5. You control your file on he Menu and Save bars.

Project 5.1—Creating a Picture Frame to Display an Image

With just a few hubs, you can make an image that stylishly displays any of your pictures. In this project, you create a dark wood frame with a matte to show off your imported image. You learn how files are constructed in Peacock and create several chains of effects and combine them to produce an image. You explore how Generator hubs produce outputs that you can manipulate with effect and controller hubs. Changing just a few parameters of these few hubs can make a rich image. See Figure 5-6 for the final image and Figure 5-7 for the hub layout made in this project.

Figure 5-6. Learn the basics of Peacock in this project.

Key hubs used in this project

- Gradient hub
- Kaleidoscope hub
- Drop Shadow hub
- Repeat hub

> *The file for this project can be found at*
> `http://aviary.com/artists/gettingstartED/creations/chapter_5_project_1.`

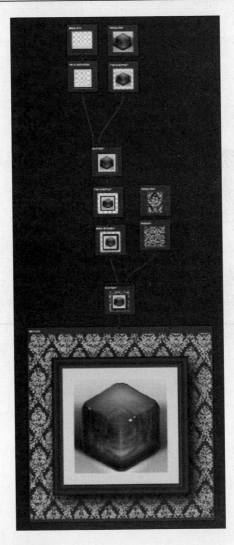

Figure 5-7. The layout of hubs in this file

1. Start by launching Peacock; open the **Generators** hub sidebar and drag out a Gradient hub to the workspace. A connector line automatically connects the Gradient hub to the Canvas (see Figure 5-8). The first hub that is added to a file is always connected to the Canvas by default. The hub pushes its output to the Canvas through this connector line. The gradient hub produces a linear or radial gradient similar to the ones you can make with Phoenix and Raven. On the right side of the application, you see a **Properties** panel with a series of parameters. This is where you adjust the gradient's parameters.

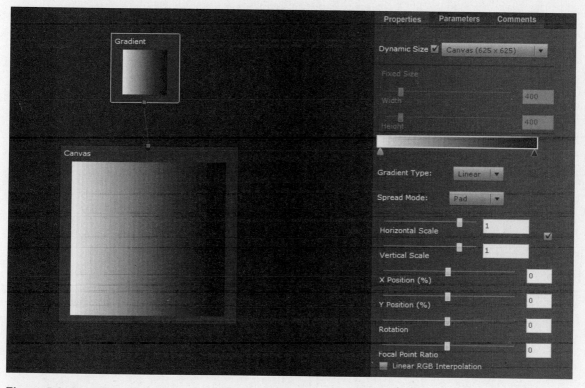

Figure 5-8. The first hub in a file automatically connects to the Canvas.

2. Set the gradient's output to create a base for the frame in the image. You make one side of the frame with the gradient and use other effects to wrap into the frame shape. You need a horizontal gradient to simulate the wood and matte to make the bottom edge of the frame. Start by setting the left color stop's **Alpha** to 0, and drag it to just past the middle of the colorbar. To do this, you need to double-click the triangle icon under the colorbar. This is a color stop and represents a color in the gradient. It opens the Color Picker used to set **color** and **Alpha**. Notice that the gradient is vertical. To change it to a horizontal gradient, change the **Rotation** parameter to 90. You can use the slider to set this, but because you are sure that you want a quarter turn, typing 90 in the text box is much faster. You want to simulate contours in the side of the frame so add some light and dark brown color stops in the wooden section of the gradient. See Figure 5-9 for

reference, use alternating light and darks browns to simulate high and low areas in one side of the frame.

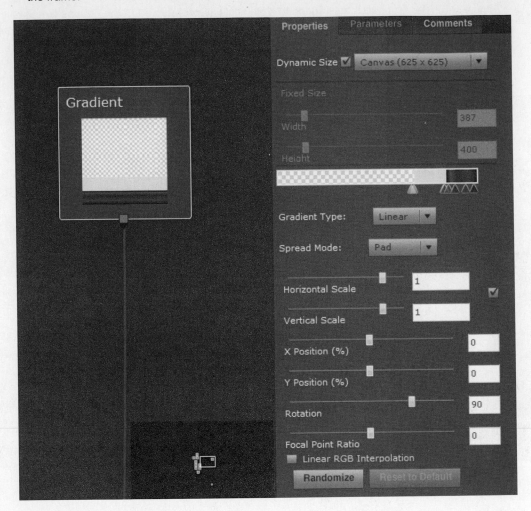

Figure 5-9. Set the Gradient hub.

Figure 5-10. The Gradient hub

The Gradient hub makes a linear or radial gradient fill pattern (see Figure 5-10). This hub creates a multi-colored fill that blends from one color to the next. The gradient fill can have up to ten separate colors but can have many more color transitions by altering the **Spread Mode**. Following is a list of the hub's parameters.

- **Gradient setting colorbar**: This is an area where colors are set in the gradient (see Figure 5-11). The triangle icons are called color stops and can be dragged along the colorbar to set the gradient. There can be up to 10 different color stops. To add a color stop, click on an area under the colorbar. To set **color** and **Alpha**, double-click a color stop to open the Color Picker. Finally, to delete a color stop, drag it away from the colorbar.

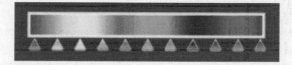

Figure 5-11. The colorbar for setting a gradient's color

- **Gradient Type**: Gradient type can be set to linear, which blends in one direction or a radial where the color blends outward from a center point (see Figure 5-12).

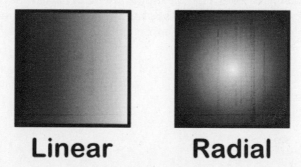

Figure 5-12. The difference between linear and radial gradients

275

- **Spread Mode**: Sets how the gradient is drawn past the original area. If a gradient is shrunk and is smaller than the size of the output, this parameter sets how the gradient is drawn to fill in the area (see Figure 5-13).

Figure 5-13. Spread modes for a gradient continuing in the extended regions

- **Horizontal/Vertical Scale**: Scales the gradient in the respective directions.
- **X Position (%)**: Sets the horizontal center of the gradient.
- **Y Position (%)**: Sets the vertical center of the gradient.
- **Rotation**: Sets the rotational angle of the gradient.
- **Focal Point Ratio**: Sets the center point of radial gradients. This pushes the center point of a radial gradient toward one of the edges in the gradient.
- **Linear RGB Interpolation**: Changes how quickly each color in a gradient blends into its neighboring color.

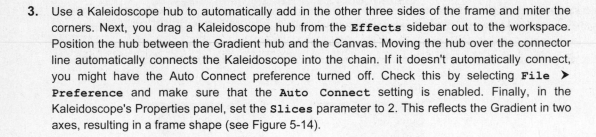

3. Use a Kaleidoscope hub to automatically add in the other three sides of the frame and miter the corners. Next, you drag a Kaleidoscope hub from the **Effects** sidebar out to the workspace. Position the hub between the Gradient hub and the Canvas. Moving the hub over the connector line automatically connects the Kaleidoscope into the chain. If it doesn't automatically connect, you might have the Auto Connect preference turned off. Check this by selecting **File ➤ Preference** and make sure that the **Auto Connect** setting is enabled. Finally, in the Kaleidoscope's Properties panel, set the **Slices** parameter to 2. This reflects the Gradient in two axes, resulting in a frame shape (see Figure 5-14).

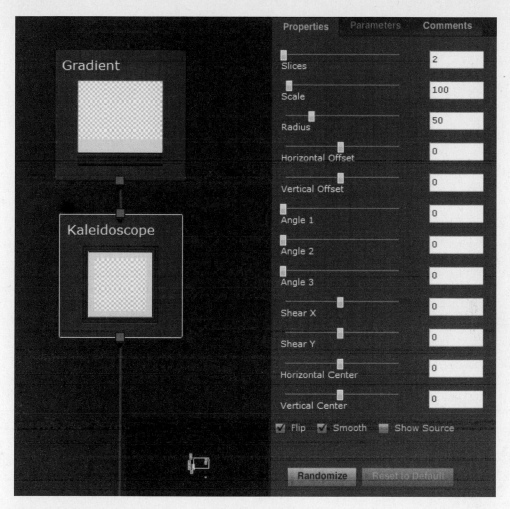

Figure 5-14. Use the Kaleidoscope to create the frame shape.

Figure 5-15. The Kaleidoscope hub reflects the input image across multiple axes.

The Kaleidoscope is used to create intricate radiating patterns by mirroring slices of the input image across multiple axes (see Figure 5-15). The Kaleidoscope cuts a virtual slice from the input image and rotates it around a center point. This slice can be rotated, scaled, and stretched, which gives a variety of patterns from a single input image. The number of slices can be set to produce a tighter pattern. Following is a list of the hub's parameters.

- `Slices`: Sets the number of slices the hub takes from the image. A slice is a section on one side of the mirroring axis. The final image has a number of visible slices that equals two times this value and four times this value when Flip is enabled (see Figure 5-16).

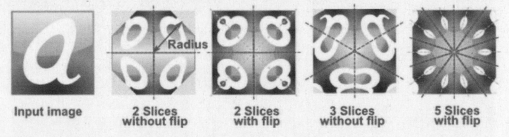

Figure 5-16. Examples of slices with and without the flip modifier option

- `Scale`: Scales the input image before the kaleidoscope mirroring is applied.
- `Radius`: Sets the radius of the Kaleidoscope effect.
- `Horizontal / Vertical Offset`: Offsets the input image before it is sliced and flipped.
- `Angle 1`: Rotates the input image before it is sliced and flipped.
- `Angle 2`: Rotates the input image before it is sliced and flipped. This appears to do the same as Angle 1.
- `Angle 3`: Rotates the Kaleidoscope after it is sliced and flipped.
- `Shear X / Y`: Shears the input image on the X or Y axis, much like skew.
- `Horizontal / Vertical Center`: Moves the kaleidoscope.
- `Flip`: Splits each new slice and then flips it to mirror original slice.
- `Smooth`: Smoothes the slice's junction.
- `Show Source`: Draws the source under the kaleidoscope.

4. Set up a hub so that you can blend two effect chains together. Drag a Blender hub out from the **Controllers** sidebar. Again, move this hub over the connector between the Kaleidoscope hub and the Canvas, and the Blender is automatically connected (see Figure 5-17). The Blender hub acts like the Layers panels in Phoenix and Raven. The inputs are stacked like layers and can have **Blend Modes** and **Alphas** applied to each. Inputs that are connected to the left Input pin are at the top of the layer stack, whereas moving to the right places the input lower in the stack. You have to manually arrange hubs in your file as you add more. You can move a hub that is on the workspace by clicking and dragging it to a new location. You can also select multiple hubs by dragging around the ones you want to select. To deselect any hubs, just click an empty area of the workspace. You see that this hub is different in that it has ten Input pins and one Output pin. The Blender does just that. It takes several inputs and blends them together using different **Blend Modes**. This is similar to layers in Phoenix and Raven.

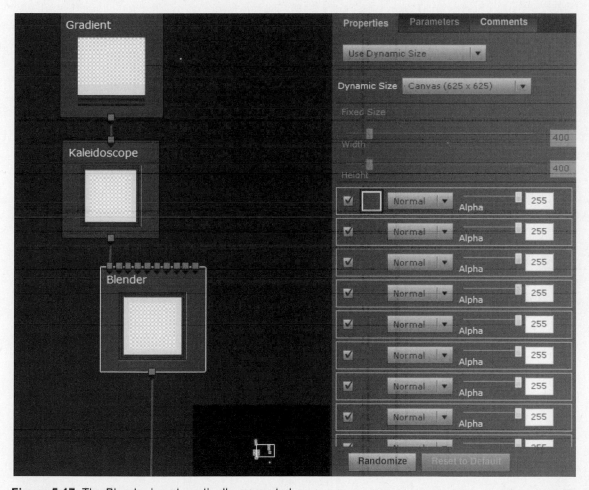

Figure 5-17. The Blender is automatically connected.

Figure 5-18. The Blender hub combines several effects together.

The Blender hub combines multiple inputs using different Blend Modes; this hub acts similarly to the Layers panel in Phoenix and Raven (see Figure 5-18). The hub layers up to ten different inputs, each with its own `Blend Mode` and `Alpha` settings. By default, the layers are stacked from top to bottom. The image attached to the left most Input pin is the top layer, while the image connected to the right most Input pin is the bottom layer. The following is a list of the hub's parameters.

- `Show/Hide Layer`: When unchecked, this checkbox hides the layer from the blender. This essentially turns on or off the layer.

- `Blend modes`: Here you can see a small preview of the input bitmap and select the `Blend Mode` and `Alpha`. By default, the order of the hubs you connect to the Blender from left to right corresponds to the order in which they appear on the list from top to bottom. However, you can drag and drop the input bitmaps in the Properties panel to reorder them.

- `Alpha`: This sets the `Alpha` or transparency of the layer. A specific `Alpha` amount can be typed directly into the textbox. The `Alpha` range starts at 0, completely transparent to 255, which is completely opaque.

5. Import the image you want to appear in the frame you just made. Like the other applications, you can import images into the file with the `Resource Browser`. Select `File ➤ Import Resource` to open the Resource Browser, navigate to the image that you want to frame, and then select it. To use the example in this project, go to the `Aviary Library` tab in the `Resource Browser`. Then, type Tigers Eye Cube in the search box, and make sure the `Only My Stuff` option is unchecked. This filters all the available files on Aviary using the word in the title or description. You are able to find the file in the results of this search (see Figure 5-19). Click the `Import` button to bring the file into Peacock. Open the `Resources` sidebar, and find the imported image as a Resource hub. Drag it out to the workspace above the Blender hub. Finally, click the Output pin on the resource, and drag a connector to one of the open Input pins on the blender hub (see Figure 5-20). Because the Resource is connected to a pin that is to the right of the one the frame is connected to, it appears below the frame.

Figure 5-19. Import an image with the Resource Browser.

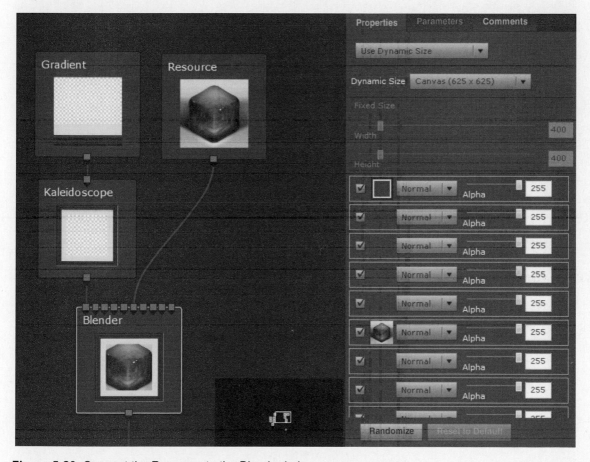

Figure 5-20. Connect the Resource to the Blender hub.

6. If the image that was imported doesn't fit in the frame, you need to resize it. Use the Transformer hub to resize it. The Transformer scales, rotates, and skews the input. Drag a Transformer hub from the **Controllers** sidebar, so that it is in between the Resource and the Blender hubs. It automatically connects into the chain. Next, change the **Horizontal** and **Vertical Scales** until the image fits into the frame. Both the **Vertical** and **Horizontal Scale** settings move in unison. However, if you need to scale the image in different amounts in either the horizontal or vertical directions, uncheck the box to the right of the scale sliders. This checkbox to the right of the scale is the **Proportional Lock** sliders locks the two parameters together. When it is enabled, both sliders are set to the same value. In this example, a **Horizontal** and **Vertical Scale** of 80 makes the image fit into the frame, but this depends on the size of the opening in the frame (see Figure 5-21).

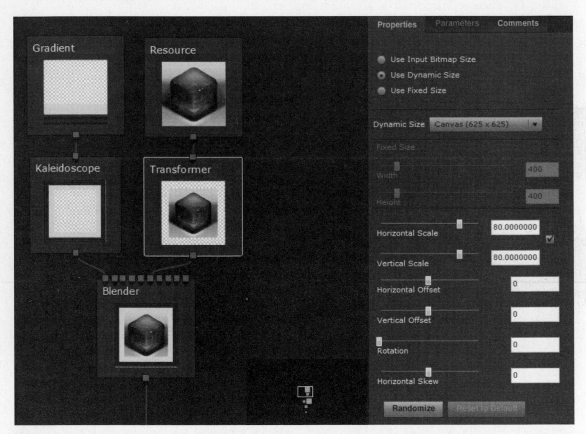

Figure 5-21. Use a Transformer hub to size the resource.

Figure 5-22. The Transform hub performs scaling, skew, and rotation.

The Transform hub changes the input image's dimensions, position, rotation, skew, or alignment (see Figure 5-22). The following is a list of the hub's parameters.

- `Horizontal/Vertical Scale`: Increases or decreases the Horizontal and Vertical Scale of the image. The tick box next to these parameters sets the `Proportional Lock`. When enabled, `Horizontal Scale` and `Vertical Scale` always move together. When disabled, you can set `Horizontal Scale` and `Vertical Scale` independently of each other.
- `Horizontal/Vertical Offset`: Moves the image horizontally or vertically.
- `Rotation`: Sets the rotation angle of the image.
- `Horizontal/Vertical Skew`: Skews the image horizontally or vertically.
- `Align`: Align the image to the selected spot.
- `Fit to Output`: This automatically scales the input image to the size of the output setting. For example, if an input is 1024 x 768 pixels and the output size is 600 x 600, checking the `Fit to Output` option sizes the input to 600 x 600 pixels. There is no guessing on the `Horizontal Scale` and `Vertical Scale`.
- `Proportional`: When used with the `Fit to Output` setting, this keeps the resizing proportional.
- `Smooth`: This option slightly smoothes the hard edges of transformed images. This is noticeable only in extreme transformed images.
- `Seamless`: This option wraps any pixels that fall over an outer edge of the transformers to the opposite edge.

7. Size the picture and the frame. You need to scale down the frame and picture so that you can put a wall texture behind them. Now that you have the frame and the picture combined in the blender hub, any transformations you add after the Blender hub transform them as one unit. Drag another Transformer hub from the `Controllers` sidebar and connect it between the Blender and the Canvas hubs. Next, set the `Scale` so that the combined frame and picture fits into the composition. In this instance, 75% gives you enough room around the frame to add a wall texture and a shadow behind the frame and picture (see Figure 5-23).

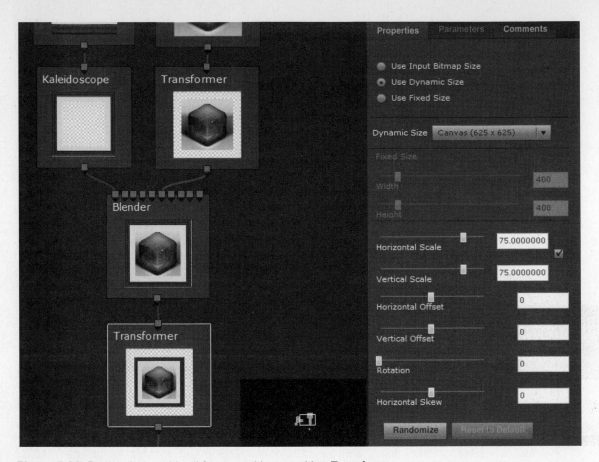

Figure 5-23. Resize the combined frame and image with a Transformer.

8. Add a shadow behind the Frame to give it some dimension. Drag a Drop Shadow hub from the **Effects** sidebar, and connect it between the second Transformer and the Canvas. The Drop Shadow hub creates a blurred shadow behind the input object. If there is no open area in the input, then you do not see any drop shadow, which is why you want to scale down the frame before adding this hub. Because the picture frame has an open area around it, the drop shadow fits around and gives the frame some depth by simulating a cast shadow. The default shadow is a little anemic for the image, so start by setting the **Horizontal** and **Vertical Blur Radius** to around 50. This makes the shadow's edges blend further out from the center. Next, set the **Distance** to 24 to offset the shadow from the picture frame. Finally, set the **Strength** to 1.2, which makes the shadow a little darker (see Figure 5-24).

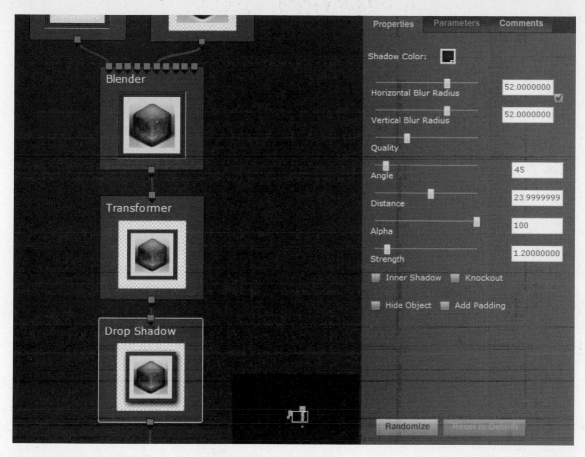

Figure 5-24. Add depth to the picture frame with a drop shadow.

Figure 5-25. The Drop Shadow hub produces a soft offset shadow behind an image.

The Drop Shadow hub adds an outer or inner shadow to the image based on its borders (see Figure 5-25). This shadow appears as if it underneath the object. You can set how blurry the edge of the shadow is and how far it is offset from the object, `Alpha`, and `color`. This effect works only if there are transparent areas in the image or the `Inner Shadow` option is enabled. Following is a list of the hub's parameters.

- `Shadow Color`: Sets the color of the shadow.
- `Horizontal/Vertical Blur radius`: Sets the amount of blur the shadow gets.
- `Quality`: The quality of the shadow's blur; you can lower quality if you want a quicker rendering file.
- `Angle`: Sets the angle at which the shadow drops.
- `Distance`: Sets the distance at which the shadow drops.
- `Alpha`: Sets the shadow transparency; 100 `Alpha` means an opaque shadow.
- `Strength`: Sets how quickly a shadow fades out at the edges; a low setting makes for a soft shadow, whereas a high setting produces a hard, stroke-like shadow.
- `Inner Shadow`: Puts the shadow inside the image itself.
- `Knockout`: Hides the object and cuts a silhouette of the object out of the shadow.
- `Hide Object`: Hides the object.
- `Add Padding`: Adds an extra Canvas area around the object so that the entire shadow is shown. Use this feature if you need a quick resizing of the output. Most of the time you should use the Transformer or Crop hubs instead of the padding feature because they offer more control.

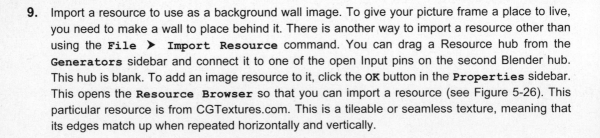

9. Import a resource to use as a background wall image. To give your picture frame a place to live, you need to make a wall to place behind it. There is another way to import a resource other than using the `File ➤ Import Resource` command. You can drag a Resource hub from the `Generators` sidebar and connect it to one of the open Input pins on the second Blender hub. This hub is blank. To add an image resource to it, click the `OK` button in the `Properties` sidebar. This opens the `Resource Browser` so that you can import a resource (see Figure 5-26). This particular resource is from CGTextures.com. This is a tileable or seamless texture, meaning that its edges match up when repeated horizontally and vertically.

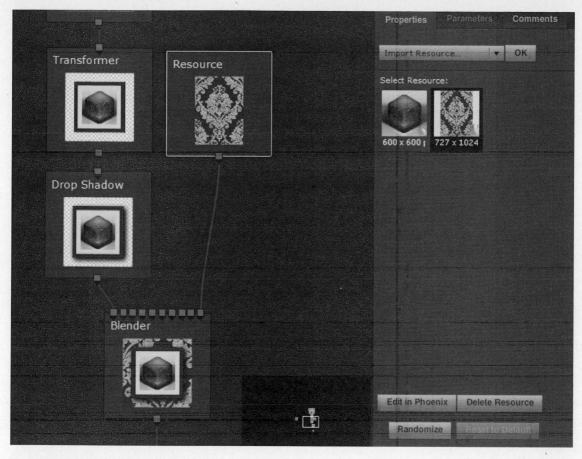

Figure 5-26. Import a background image.

10. Scale and tile the resource so that it fits with the composition. Drag out a Repeat hub from the **Effects** sidebar. Connect it between the background resource and the second blender. The Repeat hub copies the input image horizontally and vertically, and scaling the results down exposes more of the tiling texture. Note that adding the hub made no change to the background image; you have to set the `Scale` parameter to get the tiling effect. Slide the `Scale` control down until the background looks the way you want. For this example, a `scale` of 13 gives a good result (see Figure 5-27).

287

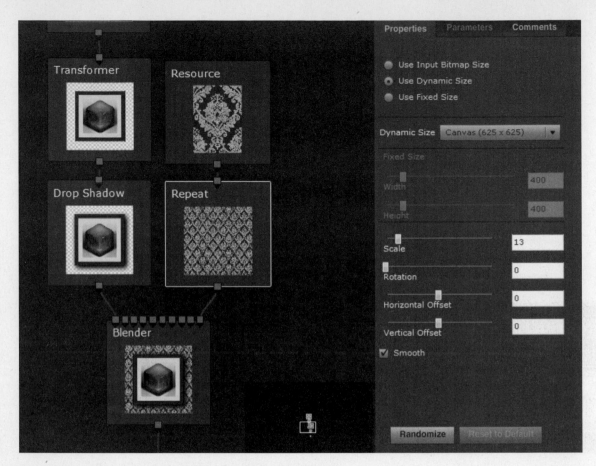

Figure 5-27. Tile the background image with the Repeat hub.

Figure 5-28. The Repeat hub is a simple tiling effect.

The Repeat hub tiles an input image (see Figure 5-28). The Repeater hub treats the input image as a tile and repeats that tile horizontally and vertically to fill the hub. When the scale of the image is reduced, the tiles are repeated to the edges of the hub. This repeated tile and the pattern can be rotated and still repeat to fill the entire hub. Following is a list of the hub's parameters.

- `Scale`: Sets the scale of the input image. The smaller the setting, the more tiles are exposed.
- `Rotation`: Set the rotation angle of the repeating effect.
- `Horizontal/Vertical Offset`: Offsets the repeated tiles in the respective direction.
- `Smooth`: Smoothes the image before applying the repeat effect.

Project review

In this project, you constructed an image from the myriad of hubs that Peacock has to offer. You learned how to add hubs to a file and connect them to form chains of effects. The Blender hub lets you combine hubs and acts like the layers in the other applications. You can scale, skew, or rotate your input images with the Transformer hub. In this project, you scaled your picture frame to allow room for a background. Finally, you saw how to quickly tile a seamless resource using the Repeat hub. In the next project, you make a text effect by combining several effects. Fractal Plasma hubs give the effect texture, bevels impart dimension, and threshold produces highlights.

Project 5.2—Create a Jelly Effect for Text

Typology is the use of text and the arrangement and altering of letter glyphs to create an image where the words become more than elements to pass information. For as longs as there have been letters, people have used them to create art. From illuminated text to modern logos, type plays an important role in design. In this project, you create a simple effect to change a text element to look like jelly. With Peacock's 60+ hubs, you examine how just a few of them can embellish a simple silhouette of a text element. See Figure 5-29 for the final image and Figure 5-30 for the hub layout from this project.

Figure 5-29. The final image that you make with in project.

Key hubs used in this project

- Bevel hub
- Fractal Plasma hub
- Masker hub
- Threshold hub

> *The file for this project can be found at*
> *http://aviary.com/artists/gettingstartED/creations/chapter_5_project_2.*
>
> *The starting resource can be found at*
> *http://aviary.com/artists/gettingstartED/creations/start_chapter_5_project_2.*

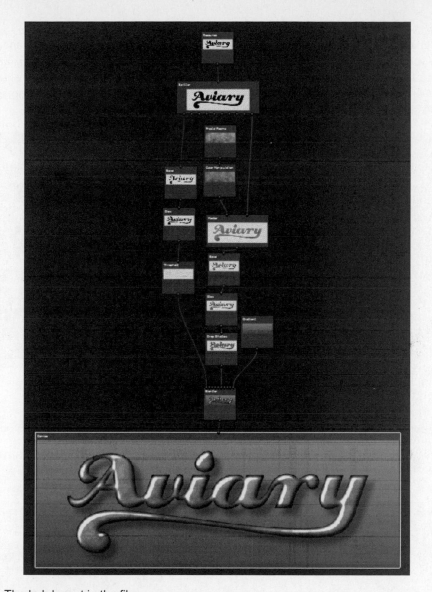

Figure 5-30. The hub layout in the file

1. Launch Peacock, import your text silhouette, and size the Canvas. You can make this text in Phoenix (see Chapter 2), use Aviary's Screens capture add-on Talon to grab one from the Web, or use the image from this project. Import the image with the `File ➤ Import Resource` command. This opens the `Resource Browser` where you can locate the file and import the image. If you want to use the image from this project, open the file listed in the sidebar as the starting resource, and then click the `Open in Effects Editor` button to open the file. Because this resource is the size you want the final image to be, set the Canvas to that size. The

easiest way to do this is to copy the size of the resource by right-clicking the hub and choosing `Copy Fixed Size` from the context menu. Next, right-click the Canvas hub, and set it to the size you just copied (see Figure 5-31). The reason you want to set the Canvas size when you start a file is that most hubs have output sizes, and these output sizes are set by default to match the Canvas size. Consequently, if you change the size of the Canvas after setting some hubs, it could change these hubs' output dimensions, and the resulting image is altered.

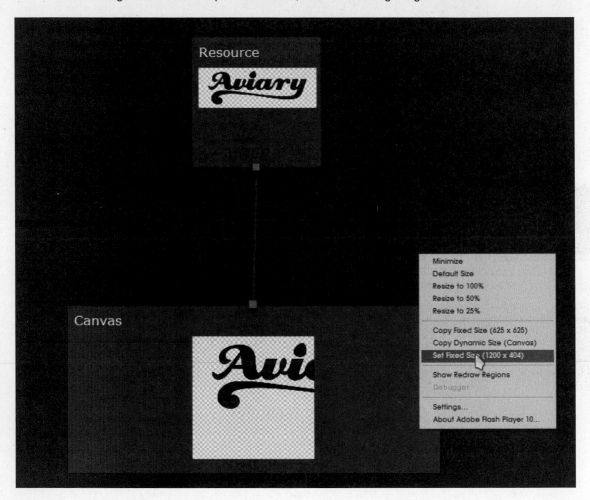

Figure 5-31. Size the Canvas to fit the resource.

2. To use this text resource in different effect chains later, you need to create multiple outputs. Drag a Splitter hub from the `Controllers` sidebar over the connector between the Resource and the Canvas. This hub automatically adds to the chain (see Figure 5-32). The Splitter hub takes the input and splits it into ten Output pins. You can resize hubs to make the pins easier to select or to give a larger preview by dragging the edges of the hub. Next, drag a Blender hub from the

Controllers sidebar between the Splitter and the Canvas. Move the connection to one of the middle Output pins on the Splitter and a middle Input pin on the Blender (see Figure 5-33). This particular hub setup is useful; a Splitter followed by a Blender lets you create several independent effect chains and mix them back together in the Blender with **Blend Modes**. You use this hub setup quite often because of its usefulness.

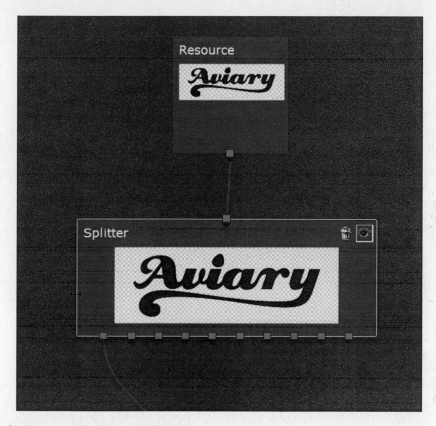

Figure 5-32. Split the output of the text element.

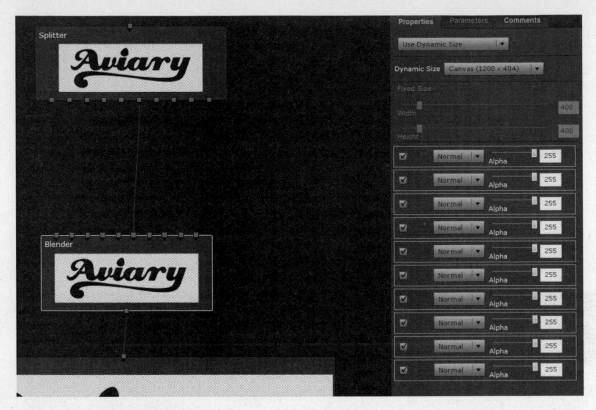

Figure 5-33. Add in a Blender hub.

3. Create a mask of the text element so that you can add a texture overlay. A **mask** is a function where information from one image is used to set the `Alpha` in another. You take the values in the text element and use those to set the `Alpha` in a texture, which creates a cutout of the texture in the shape of the text. Drag a Masker hub from the `Controllers` sidebar and connect it between the Splitter and the Blender. Make sure that the output from the Splitter is attached to the right `Mask Bitmap` Input pin (see Figure 5-34). You can check the name of an Input or Output pin by hovering over it to bring up a tool tip. This Masker hub takes the output from text hub and converts that into a stencil for the output of a texture hub to come.

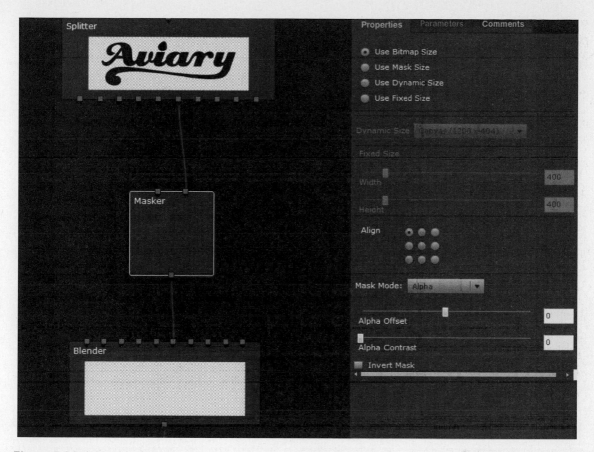

Figure 5-34. Add a Masker hub.

Figure 5-35. The Masker hub creates a stencil based on an input image.

A Masker hub uses the brightness from an image and uses that information to set the Alpha levels in another image (see Figure 5-35). The two images are overlain and the luminosity or one of the RGBA channels of the masker image is translated into **Alpha** levels in the masked image. This effect is preformed at a one-to-one ratio so images that are not the same size create gaps or clipping in the mask. Following is a list of the hub's parameters.

- **Align**: When images don't match the output size, this aligns them to the selected spot.
- **Mask Mode**: This sets the channel that the Masker hub uses for the mask.
  - **Alpha**: Uses the Alpha channel of the mask input.
  - **Luminance**: Uses the luminance of the input bitmap for masking information. Luminance is a combination of RGB channels together.
  - **Red/Green/Blue**: Uses the selected color channels to determine transparency.
- **Alpha Offset**: Masks intensity. Negative values show more area. Positive values show less.
- **Alpha Contrast**: Sets the contrast value of a grayscale mask. This adjusts the amount of the mask that falls between opaque and transparent.
- **Invert Mask**: Inverts the mask.

4. Generate a rough texture to feed into the Masker hub. Add a Fractal Plasma hub from the **Generators** sidebar to the left **Input Bitmap** Input pin on the Masker hub. The Fractal Plasma hub generates a multi-colored texture. Set the **Roughness Factor** parameter to 0.85. This increases the intensity of the noise in the plasma and imparts a rougher texture to the text. You can also change the **Random Seed** parameter if you want to generate a new noise texture. The **Random Seed** parameter is used in several hubs and is a number used to produce a re-creatable random number output (see Figure 5-36). Peacock uses seeded random numbers generators instead of true random because with seeded ones you get a constant output so you can re-create the same settings in a hub. Note that when the Fractal Plasma's output passes through the Masker hub, it shows only where the Resource image is solid and is transparent where the resource is transparent.

Figure 5-36. Add a Fractal Plasma to give your image some texture.

Figure 5-37. The Fractal Plasma hub creates a multi-colored pattern.

Fractal Plasma is a type of fractal that creates a random color field (see Figure 5-37). This type of texture is used in three-dimensional applications to simulate landscape elevations and natural textures. The Fractal Plasma hub can use several different formulas to generate the pattern. However, most of the time you use the default Simple formula because it gives a great result in the quickest time. Following is a list of the hub's parameters.

- `Random`: This is the formula that generates the Fractal Plasma.
    - `Simple`: This is a fast seedable random number generator.
    - `Linear Congruential Generator (LCG)`: 32-bit random number generator.
    - `Mersenne Twister`: This is a more complex random number generator that is slower.
    - `Native (not seedable)`: This uses the native random number generator and is not seedable. This means that the plasma looks different after each refresh.
    - `Experimental I`: This generator does not return random numbers but just counts upwards.
- `Random Seed`: Number used to initialize the random number generator.
- `Roughness`: This setting enhances the contrast in the turbulence of the plasma.
- `Roughness Factor`: This setting creates more turbulence in the plasma.
- `Horizontal/Vertical Scale`: Stretches the plasma in the corresponding direction.
- `Grayscale`: The color information is ignored, resulting in black and white plasma.
- `R G B`: Turns on/off the corresponding color channel.
- `Alpha Channel`: Turns on/off the `Alpha` channel of the plasma. This creates varied `Alpha` settings for each pixel.
- `Smooth`: When the plasma is stretched, this setting smoothes the output.

5. In this step, you make the color from the Fractal Plasma more consistent. Drag a Color Manipulation hub from the `Effects` sidebar and add it between the Fractal Plasma and the Masker hubs. The Color Manipulation hub enables you to change the `Hue`, `Saturation`, `Contrast`, and `Brightness` of the input image. It can also `Tint` the entire image with a single color. Change the color to a light green by first clicking the color box in the lower, right. This brings up the simple `Color Picker` dialog so you can choose the color. Next, set the `Tint` slider all the way to the right, which sets it to maximum. This changes the Fractal Plasma's output

to an overall green color, which shows in the masker hub. Finally, set the `Contrast` to -0.01 to reduce some of the harsher values in the texture (see Figure 5-38).

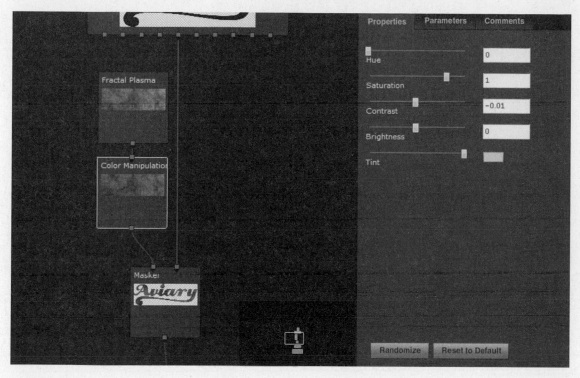

Figure 5-38. Change the color of the Fractal Plasma with a Color Manipulation hub.

Figure 5-39. The Color Manipulation hub alters color and brightness values.

The Color Manipulation hub changes the various values that affect colors within the image (see Figure 5-39). This hub enables you to do color correction on your images, such as with the `Hue & Saturation` and the `Brightness & Contrast` functions found in Phoenix. You can even invert all the colors in an image by setting the `Contrast` setting to -2. Following is a list of the hub's parameters.

- `Hue`: Shifts the hue of the image.
- `Saturation`: Affects the saturation, or the amount of pure color in the image. A setting of 0 removes all color from an image leaving a grayscale version.
- `Contrast`: Changes the contrast or how much difference there is between the values of in and image.
- `Brightness`: Changes the lightness or darkness in the image.
- `Tint`: Adds an overall color to the image, and overrides any color changes set by the Hue parameter.

6. Create shading on the text object with a bevel. Add a Bevel hub from the `Effects` sidebar in between the Masker and the Blender hubs. The Bevel hub creates a colored highlight and shadow on opposite sides of an object. This is to give the impression of light hitting one side of an object and casting a shadow on the other side. The Bevel is effective for creating a three-dimensional effect. Set the `Highlight Color` to a light green (#ccffcc), and leave the rest of the parameters at their default settings (see Figure 5-40).

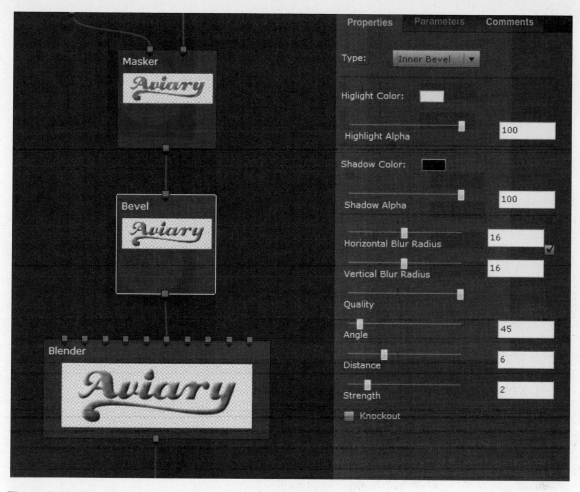

Figure 5-40. The Bevel hub gives the image three-dimensional depth.

Figure 5-41. The Bevel hub creates a highlight and a shadow on the opposing edges of an object.

A Bevel hub creates depth to a shape by giving the illusion of light and shadow on a shape (see Figure 5-41). The Bevel hub can be used to give an object some depth and simulate a raised effect. Depending on the strength setting it can produce a smooth or a hard chiseled bevel. The following is a list of the hub's parameters.

- `Inner Bevel`: Applies the bevel to the inside of the shape boundaries.
- `Outer Bevel`: Applies the shadow and highlight outside of the shape.
- `Full Bevel`: A combination of Inner and Outer Bevel, it applies the shadow and highlight inside and outside of the shape.
- `Highlight Color`: Enables you to choose the color of the highlight on the bevel.
- `Alpha`: Adjusts the `Alpha` of the highlight.
- `Shadow Color`: The color of the shadow on the bevel.
- `Alpha`: The total opacity that is applied on the shadow color.
- `Horizontal/Vertical Blur`: Sets the radius of the blur on the bevel.
- `Quality`: Sets the quality of the blur on the bevel.
- `Angle`: Sets the angle that the bevel is drawn on the shape.
- `Distance`: Sets the distance from the edge that the bevel effect ends.
- `Strength`: Sets how strong the edge of the bevel is.
- `Knockout`: Hides the shape and renders the bevel.

7. Darken the edge of the text shape to give it more depth. Drag out a Glow hub from the **Effects** sidebar and add it to the chain between the Bevel and Blender hub. The Glow hub creates a colored halo around the edge of an object. For this image, however, you want the Glow to radiate into the interior of the object. To do this, check the box next to the `Inner Glow` option. Finally, set the `Glow Color` to black to create a darker edge around the shape (see Figure 5-42).

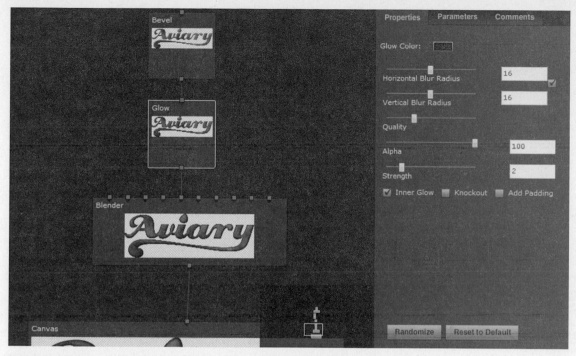

Figure 5-42. Use a Glow hub to add a subtle inner shadow around the shape.

Figure 5-43. The Glow hub produces a colored halo around an image.

The Glow hub is used to apply an inner or outer glow (see Figure 5-43). The glow effect radiates from the edges of a shape. This effect does not work well on thin lines or objects with low opacity edges. Following is a list of the hub's parameters.

- `Glow Color`: Enables you to change the color of the glow. There is a set of default colors, but you can also use a hex value for the color.

- `Horizontal Blur Radius`: The `Horizontal Blur Radius` adjusts how far the glow extends in the horizontal direction, or the length of the glow's blur.

- **Vertical Blur Radius**: **Vertical Blur Radius** is just like the **Horizontal Blur Radius**, but it is applied in the vertical direction.
- **Check Box**: Links the values of **Vertical** and **Horizontal Blur** so that they remain the same.
- **Quality**: Adjusts the quality of the blur. The higher the value, the greater the amount and quality of glow generated.
- **Alpha**: Adjusts the opacity of the glow.
- **Strength**: Sets how strong the glow is drawn. Higher settings extend the glow farther from object before fading off.
- **Inner Glow**: Checking the **Inner Glow** checkbox applies the glow to the *inside* of the input image.
- **Knockout**: Does not show the input shape, but does show the glow that is applied to the input image.
- **Add Padding**: Expands the size of the hubs so none of the glow is clipped at the edges.

8. Add a shadow behind the text to set it off from the background. Drag out a Drop Shadow hub from the **Effects** sidebar onto the workspace and add it in between the Glow hub and the Blender. To give the illusion of more space between the text object and the background, set the **Distance** setting to 31. This offsets the shadow farther from the text. Next, lighten the drop shadow by setting its **Alpha** to 70. Finally, reduce the **Strength** to 0.6. This gives you a distant, soft drop shadow (see Figure 5-44).

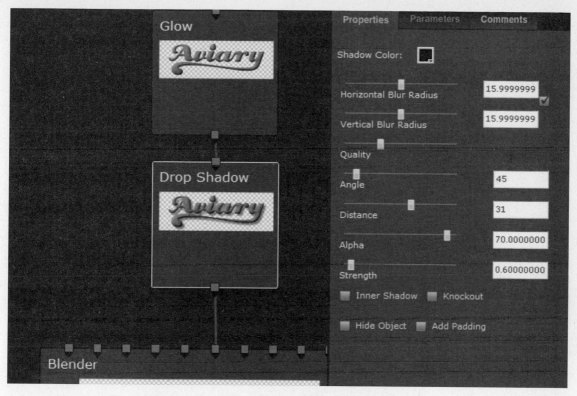

Figure 5-44. Add a drop shadow to lift the text object off of the background.

9. Create a glossy highlight to overlay the text. Drag out a new Bevel hub from the `Effects` sidebar, but drop it in an empty area of the workspace to the left of the existing hubs. Because this is a glossy highlight to the image, it is on top of the rest of the image, so you construct this chain of hubs on the left side. This keeps the file organized by not having connectors overlap. You manually connect this hub into the chain by dragging out connector lines from the first Output pin on the Splitter, and the first Input pin on the Blender (see Figure 5-45).

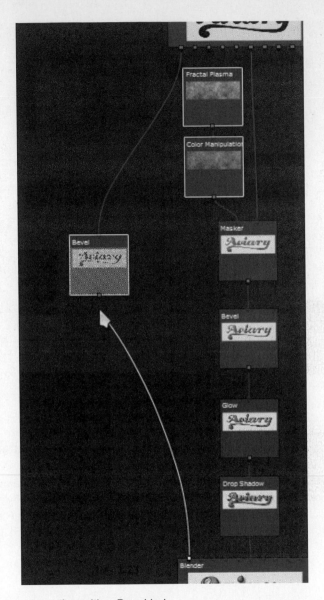

Figure 5-45. Make a new connection with a Bevel hub.

10. Create a bold bevel on the text silhouette. Set the **Strength** parameter in the Bevel hub to its maximum of 255. This makes a harsh highlight on the text shape. You use this highlight to create the gloss. Next, set the **Horizontal** or **Vertical Blur Radius** to 8. The checkbox to the right of the parameters is the **Proportional Lock** for both settings. With it enabled, both the sliders move in unison and save a step when you want the horizontal and vertical setting the same (see Figure 5-46).

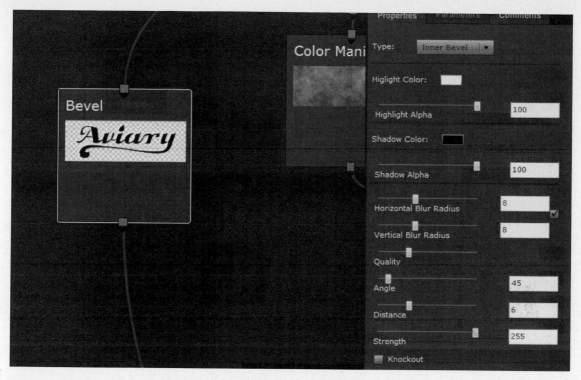

Figure 5-46. Set the parameters in the Bevel hub.

11. Cover the edges of the Bevel's highlight with a Glow hub. Add a new Glow hub from the `Effects` sidebar and connect it in between the second Bevel and the Splitter hubs. Create an offset from the edge of the shape and the highlight. To do this, enable the `Inner Glow` option. Then, set the `Glow Color` to black. Set both `Blur Radius` options to 7, shrinking the glow. Finally, set the `Strength` to the maximum of 255, to create a hard edge around the text (see Figure 5-47).

307

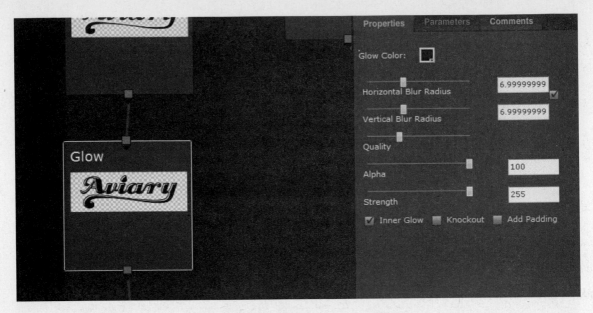

Figure 5-47. Simulate an offset of the Bevel's highlight with an inner glow.

12. Extract the highlight in this effect chain to produce the gloss. Drag out a Threshold hub from the **Effects** sidebar, and connect it between the second Glow hub and the Splitter hub. The Threshold hub converts the input image to either a background or a foreground color. This is determined by the Threshold parameter; any value that is darker than the threshold is set to the foreground color while any value that is lighter is set to the background color. You set the **highlight** to white and smooth it while everything else is transparent. Start by setting the **Background Alpha** setting to 0. This makes everything but the highlight transparent. To smooth the output, set the **Smoothing** setting to 12. Finally, to give the edge of the highlight a little more fidelity, set the **Edge Sharpness** setting to 72 (see Figures 5-48 and 5-49).

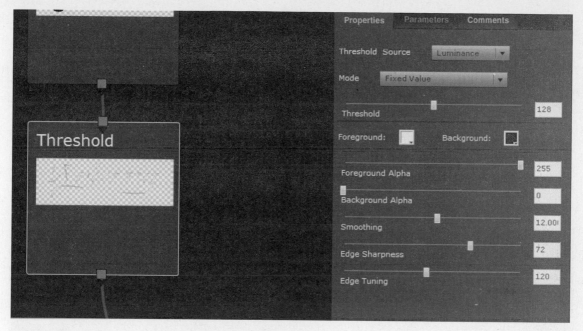

Figure 5-48. Extract the highlight with a Threshold hub.

Figure 5-49. The Threshold hub converts an image into a two-color image.

The Threshold hub converts an image to two values: foreground or background. Any pixels higher than the set `threshold` become the foreground color, and pixels below threshold become the background color. The foreground and background can be transparent, which is useful for simple masking. Following are the parameters for this hub.

- **Threshold Source**: Sets the `Channel` that the threshold uses.
- **Mode**: Sets algorithms that are used to produce `threshold`.
- **Threshold**: Set the `threshold` level in `Fixed Value` mode.
- **Foreground/Background**: Sets the `foreground/background color`.

309

- **Foreground/Background Alpha**: Sets the **foreground/background Alpha**.
- **Smoothing**: Blurs the edge between the two threshold regions.
- **Edge Sharpness**: Sharpens the edge between the two threshold regions.
- **Edge Tuning**: Fine-tunes the edge by enlarging or shrinking the threshold area slightly.

13. Next, enhance the highlight by setting its **Blend Mode** to Add. Select the **Blender** hub to open its parameters in the **Properties** panel. Find the layer that contains the highlight. You see a small preview to help you locate the layer you want. In the **Blend Mode** dropdown menu, find the **Add Blend Mode** and select it (see Figure 5-50). The **Add Blend Mode** intensifies the light parts of an input and ignores all the dark. This produces a bright highlight.

Figure 5-50. Set the **highlights Blend Mode** to Add.

14. Make a gradient fill for the background to the image. Drag out a **Gradient** hub from the **Generators** sidebar. Connect this hub to the last Input pin on the **Blender** hub so that it displays behind the other elements. Set the gradient's **color** to light red blending to dark red. Finally, set the **Rotation** to 90, making it a horizontal gradient (see Figure 5-51).

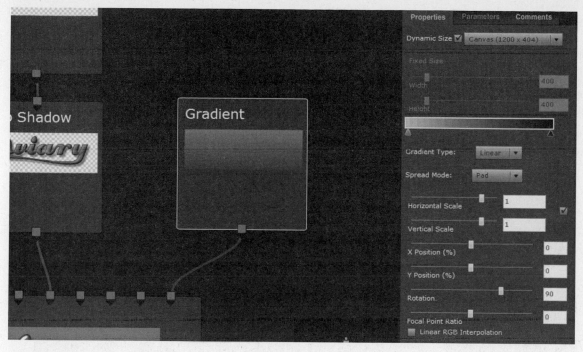

Figure 5-51. Add a Gradient hub to create a background for the text object.

Project review

In this project, you learned how to add outputs from an image using the Splitter hub. A Masker hub uses the values of one image to set the **Alpha** of corresponding pixels in another image. You saw how you can alter the colors and even colorize images with the Color Manipulation hub. Thresholds can be used to extract certain areas from an image if you set one of the color's **Alpha** settings to 0. Finally, you learned how to use a Glow hub to produce an effect that extends into the object. In the next project, you learn how to create an image out of smaller pieces. You use the AutoPainter hub, arguably the most powerful hub in Peacock, to make an image out of these pieces.

Project 5.3—Create an Image out of Repeated Block Objects

Peacock is good at creating patterns; many of the hubs are designed to create repeated, mirrored, and generated patterns. You can also use that power to build interesting images out of repeated objects. In this project, you make small blocks that resemble familiar toys, and then use the power of the AutoPainter to construct a larger image out of the blocks. See Figure 5-52 for the final image and Figure 5-53 for the hub layout from this project.

Figure 5-52. This is the final image that you will create in this project.

Key hubs used in this project

- Terrain hub
- Edges hub
- AutoPainter hub
- Splitter hub

The file for this project can be found at
http://aviary.com/artists/gettingstartED/creations/chapter_5_project_3.

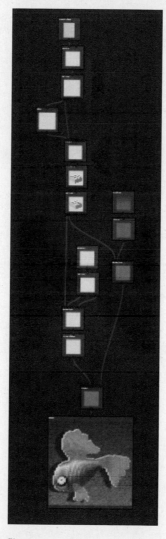

Figure 5-53. The layout of hubs in this file

1. Launch Peacock and start by setting the Canvas dimension to the large size of 1800 x 1800, and uncheck the **Adapt Display Size to Input Bitmap** option (see Figure 5-54). The reason you want to make this file this large is to give the image enough pixels to show the details. If you were to leave it at the smaller size, the blocks that the image is built with would blend too much. Furthermore, it is a good rule of thumb to set the Canvas size at the start of a file because many hubs' dimensions are directly linked to the Canvas size. Changing the size of the Canvas in the middle of file construction changes many of the hubs outputs and breaks the final results.

Figure 5-54. Enlarge the Canvas size so that there are enough pixels to show the detail in the final image.

2. Create a top view of the toy block with a Simple Shape hub. Drag a Simple Shape hub from the **Generators** sidebar. Being that it is the first hub introduced, it automatically connects to the Canvas. In its default state, the hub produces a black square. You want to change this to a tall, light rectangle with six white circles. Start by changing the hub's dimensions to 900 **Width** and 1200 **Height**. Next, change the **Shape Type** to Circle, which changes the square shape to a circle. Change the circle's color by setting the **Fill Color** to white. Next, set the **Background Color** to a light gray (#cccccc). Scroll to the bottom of the **Properties** panel and set the **Columns** to 2 and **Rows** to 3. Check the **Clip Cells** option to enable it; you should now see six white ellipses. The settings repeat the simple shape horizontally by the **Column** amount and vertically by the **Row** amount, producing the six ellipses. Finally, to push these back into circles,

uncheck the **Proportional Lock** checkbox to the left of **Horizontal** and **Vertical Scale** sliders. With the **Proportional Lock** disabled, you can change these settings separately. Set the **Horizontal scale** to 70and leave the **Vertical** at 100 (see Figure 5-55).

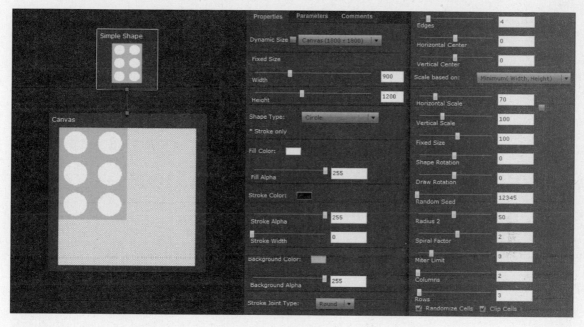

Figure 5-55. Set up the Simple Shape hub to create the top-down view of the toy block.

Figure 5-56. The Simple Shape hub creates several useful shapes.

Use the Simple Shape hub to create regular and irregular shapes (see Figure 5-56). The Simple Shape hub is anything but simple. It gives you complete control over various shape attributes. You can choose from nine different base shapes. Use the many parameters to mold and alter them even more. Following is a list of the parameters for this hub.

- **Shape Type**: Select the basic shape.

- **Circle**: This produces a circle or ellipse shape.
- **Regular Polygon**: This produces a multi-sided shape with evenly length sides. The numbers of sides are set with the **Edges** parameter.
- **Irregular Polygon**: This produces a multi-sided shape with random side lengths. The numbers of sides are set with the **Edges** parameter.
- **Regular Star**: This produces a star shape with evenly spaced arms. The numbers of sides are set with the **Edges** parameter.
- **Irregular Star**: This produces a star shape with randomly spaced arms. The numbers of sides are set with the **Edges** parameter.
- **Ring**: This produces a circle or ellipse shape with a hole in the center.
- **Egg**: This produces an oblong shape with a large radius on one end.
- **Line**: This produces a straight line. This shape has no fill and its color and weight are controlled by stroke parameters only.
- **Archimedes Spiral**: This produces a spiral line. This shape has no fill and its color and weight are controlled by stroke parameters only.

- **Fill Color**: Sets the fill color of the shape.
- **Fill Alpha**: Sets the fill Alpha of the shape.
- **Stroke Color**: Sets the **outline color**.
- **Stroke Alpha**: Sets the **outline Alpha**.
- **Stroke Width**: Sets the **outline width**.
- **Background Color**: Sets the color around the shape.
- **Background Alpha**: Sets the **Alpha** around shape.
- **Stroke joint type**: Sets the corner types on shapes with corners (see Figure 5-57).

Figure 5-57. Examples of the miter types

- **Edges**: Sets the amount of sides of polygons and stars.
- **Horizontal and Vertical Centers**: Sets the center of the shape.
- **Scale Based on**: This sets the scaling function of the shape based off of one of the following parameters:
    - **Maximum (Width, Height)**: Sets the size of the shape to the size of whichever is bigger, height or width of the hub.
    - **Minimum (Width, Height)**: Sets the size of the shape to the size of whichever is smaller, height or width of the hub.
    - **Width**: Sets the size of the shape to the width of the hub.
    - **Height**: Sets the size of the shape to the height of the hub.
    - **Diagonal**: Sets the size of the shape to the diagonal dimension of the hub.
    - **Fixed Size**: Sets the size of the shape using the **Fixed Size** parameter.

- **Horizontal and Vertical Scale**: Lets you set the scale of the object. Uncheck the box next to it to scale each direction individually.
- **Fixed Size**: Sets the size of the shape when using **Fixed Size** as the **Scale Based** on parameter.
- **Shape Rotation**: Rotates the shape and then scales it to horizontal/vertical scale dimensions. No matter the rotation, the shape fits within the area of the horizontal and vertical scale. This parameter distorts the shape to fit within the dimensions (see Figure 5-58).
- **Draw rotation**: Rotates the shape around center. The shape is sized to the horizontal and vertical scales and then rotated. This setting does not distort the shape (see Figure 5-58).

Shape Rotation: Draw Rotation:

Scales then rotates shape   Rotates then scales the shape.

Figure 5-58. The difference between Shape and Draw Rotation parameters

- **Random seed**: Number used to initialize the random number generator used for the irregular shapes.
- **Radius 2**: Sets the inner radius of irregular polygons, rings, spirals, eggs, irregular stars, and regular stars (see Figure 5-59).
- **Spiral Factor**: Sets how tightly the **Archimedes Spiral** is wound.

Figure 5-59. How the **Radius** parameter is used in the shapes.

- **Miter limit**: Sets the angle at which a mitered corner changes to a beveled corner on the stroke.

- **Columns**: Sets the amount of shapes tiled in the horizontal direction.
- **Rows**: Sets the amount of shapes tiled in the vertical direction.
- **Randomize Cells**: When there are multiple rows and or columns of irregular shapes, it gives a random setting for each shape.
- **Clip Cells**: When enabled, the repeated shapes are clipped instead of overlapping.

3. Turn your simple shape into a three-dimensional looking object. Drag a Terrain hub form the Generators sidebar, and connect it between the Simple Shape and the Canvas hubs. Make sure that the Simple Shape is connected into the Elevation Map, which is the first Input pin on the Terrain hub. The Terrain hub converts the brightness (luminosity) of an input bitmap into a three-dimensional elevation map: the lighter the pixel in the input bitmap, the higher the corresponding elevation. In this file, the gray background is an elevation and the six white circles are a higher elevation, which gives the appearance of a toy block. Start by setting the **elevation** to 500, which sets the height of the object. Then set the **shadow intensity** parameter to 5, which produces a soft shadow on the object. Finally, set the **Light Angle** parameter to 250, which produces a darker gray color on front of the toy block (see Figure 5-60 and Figure 5-61).

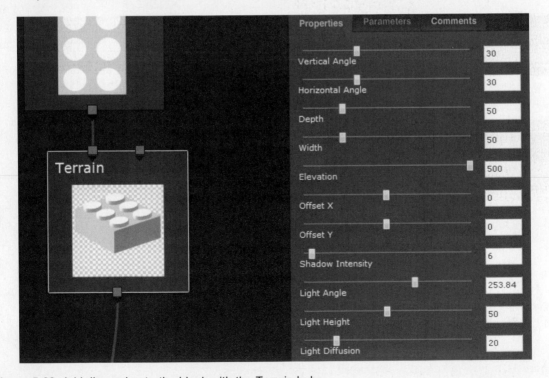

Figure 5-60. Add dimension to the block with the Terrain hub.

Figure 5-61. The Terrain hub produces a three-dimensional elevation map base on the luminocity of an image.

The Terrain hub creates a terrain map based on luminosity information from an input image. The resulting image is an object where the lighter areas from the input image build up and produce a taller section than the darker areas. This object is by default angled into an isometric perspective. This means it looks as though it is turned, so a corner is pointing at the screen and is tilted downward so that the top is shown. The parameters are:

- **Vertical Angle**: Sets the amount the terrain is skewed vertically.
- **Horizontal Angle**: Sets the amount the terrain is skewed horizontally.
- **Depth**: Sets how deep the terrain is drawn (see Figure 5-62).
- **Width**: Sets how wide the terrain is drawn (see Figure 5-62).
- **Elevation**: Sets the height of the terrain. This is relative to the luminance of the height map (see Figure 5-62).

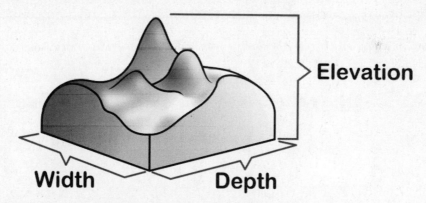

Figure 5-62. Diagram of the dimensions produced by the Terrain hub.

- **Offset X**: Sets the horizontal center of the terrain.
- **Offset Y**: Sets the vertical center of the terrain.
- **Shadow Intensity**: Sets how dark the shadow is rendered on the terrain.
- **Light Angle**: Sets the angle of the light that is rendered on the terrain.

319

- **Light Height**: Sets how high above the terrain the light source is. At 100, the light is directly over the terrain and shadows do not show up.
- **Light Diffusion**: Sets how soft the light is rendered on the terrain.
- **Shadow Diffusion**: Sets how soft the shadow is rendered on the terrain.
- **Resolution**: Sets how detailed the terrain is rendered. The higher the resolution, the longer it will take to render.
- **Side Color**: Sets the color of the side of the terrain.
- **Front Color**: Sets the color of the front of the terrain.

4. Set up a Splitter and Blender so you can add a darker edge to the object; this makes the individual block show up better in the final image. Start by dragging out a Splitter hub from the **Controllers** sidebar, and insert it between the Terrain hub and the Canvas. Next, drag out a Blender hub, and connect it between the Splitter and the Canvas hubs. You now have a Splitter connected into a Blender, which lets you layer multiple effects (see Figure 5-63).

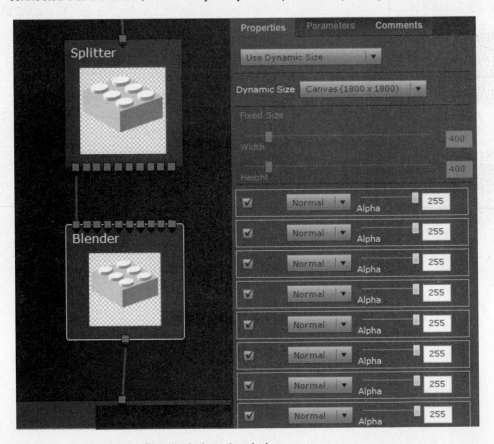

Figure 5-63. Add a Splitter and a Blender hub to the chain.

5. Next, drag out an Edges hub from the **Effects** sidebar and connect it in between the Splitter and the Blender hubs. Make sure that the Edges hub is connected to the first Output pin on the Splitter and the first Input pin on the Blender. This ensures that the effect produced from the Edges hub lies on top of any other objects that are attached to the Blender hub. In the Edges hub **Properties** panel, set the **Foreground** color to a medium gray (#666666). Then set the **Background Alpha** to 0, which produces only a trace of the edge of the object. Now, adjust the **Edge Tuning** until you like the results, 35 works well for this example. Finally, make a separate connection from the Splitter hub directly to the Blender (see Figure 5-64). Doing this shows the original toy block object with the darker edges over the top (see Figure 5-65).

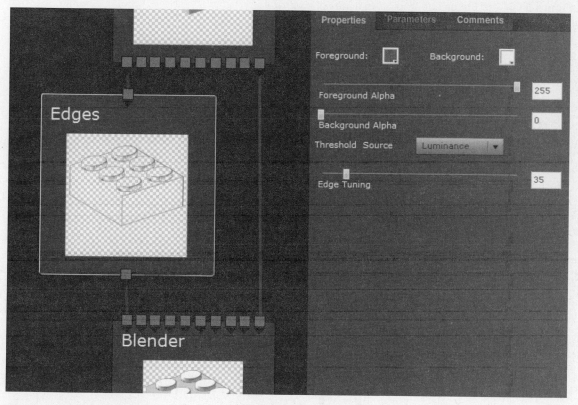

Figure 5-64. Trace the edges of an object with the Edges hub.

Figure 5-65. The Edges hub traces the edges of an image.

The Edges hub traces the outer edge of shapes, based on the contrasting values in an image. This effect draws the foreground color anywhere the contrast between pixels exceeds the threshold setting; every where else is colored with the background color. The result produces a two-colored image that highlights the edges in an image. Following are the parameters for this hub.

- **Foreground/Background Color**: Sets the Foreground or Background color.
- **Foreground/Background Alpha**: Sets the Foreground or Background opacity.
- **Threshold Source**: Sets which channel is used to produce the edge effect.
- **Edge Tuning**: Fine-tunes the threshold range by expanding or shrinking the effect.

6. Before you add the AutoPainter hub into this chain, which is used to assemble the toy blocks, you must resize the block object. The reason this is done is because the AutoPainter draws the entire input image many times. The larger the input image, the more pixels that the hub has to render, and thus a longer render time. It is recommended to reduce the size to the smallest possible while maintaining important details. Start by connecting a Transformer hub from the **Controllers** sidebar in between the Blender and the Canvas. Then, select the **Use Fixed Size** option, and set the **Width** and **Height** to 75. This sets the output dimensions to 75 x 75 pixels, which is an ideal size for the AutoPainter hub. Next, reduce the **Horizontal** and **Vertical Scales** until the block object fits just inside the hub's new dimensions. For this file, use 4 (see Figure 5-66).

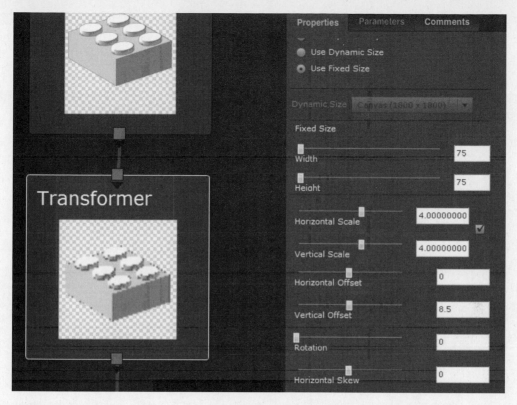

Figure 5-66. Resizing the block object makes it more manageable for the AutoPainter hub.

7. Add the AutoPainter hub to the chain and set It up to create your image. The AutoPainter hub is an advanced tiling hub. It tiles an input image, called a brush, across the Canvas. The brushes' `scale`, `Alpha`, `spacing`, `rotation`, and more can be adjusted and can be controlled by different bitmap images. Start by dragging an AutoPainter hub from the `Generators` sidebar, and connect it to the chain between the Transformer and the Canvas hubs. The output from the Transformer hub needs to be connected to the first `Brushes Input pin` on the AutoPainter because this is used as the brush. In the `Properties` panel, you see that the AutoPainter has so many parameters that they are separated into four different tabs: `Output`, `Brush`, `Painting`, and `Maps`. Next, select the `Painting` tab, which is where the spacing parameters are located. Then, set the `Horizontal Order` to `Right to Left` and the `Vertical Order` to `Bottom to Top`. The brushes are now drawn from the bottom, right and finishing at the top, left, which gives the impression of stacked blocks. Then, set the `Horizontal Spacing` so that the column of blocks touches the edges of the next column; this will be around 37. This setting is determined by the size of the toy blocks; you might have to adjust this setting if they are not quite lined up. Do the same for the `Vertical Spacing`, lining up the tops to the bottoms of the next row of blocks, which is around 18. Next, set the `Vertical Delta` setting to 68, so that each successive row of blocks line up to the block in the row that was below it originally. The `Vertical` and `Horizontal Deltas` are used to offset the each brush when it is draw. For

323

example, a brush image is drawn, and if the vertical delta is set to 10, the next brush is drawn 10 pixels higher vertically than the last and continues like that. This gives the impression that the toy blocks are stacked up in rows and columns. Finally, set the `Vertical Padding` to 200, which extends the blocks to the edges of the Canvas (see Figure 5-67).

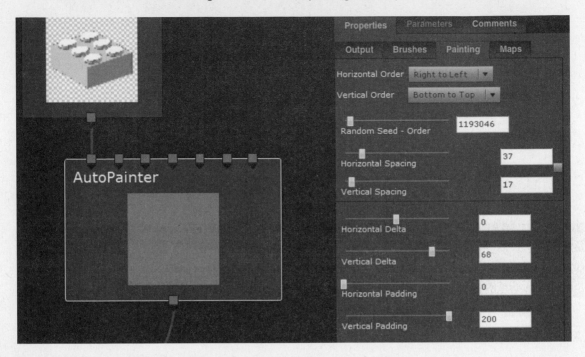

Figure 5-67. The AutoPainter hub does all the hard work.

8. Set the AutoPainter to accept color from the image you add later. Switch to the **Brushes** tab in the AutoPainter. Set the **Brush Colorization** Mode to **Overlay**, which sets how color from the input map is applied to the brushes (see Figure 5-68). The overlay mode imparts color to each brush but still maintains the details in the individual brushes.

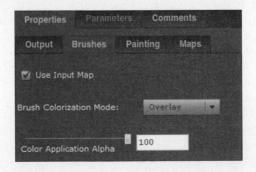

Figure 5-68. The Brushes tab

9. Switch to the `Output` tab where you remove the background fill. The AutoPainter hub draws a background fill by default; this fills the spaces where brush might not cover. However, you want to add your own Background to the image, so you need to remove this fill. In the `Output` tab, set the `Background Alpha` to 0 (see Figure 5-69).

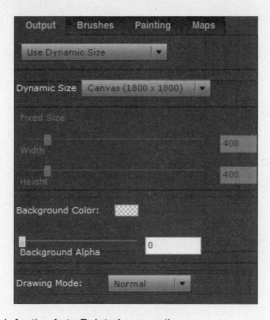

Figure 5-69. The `Output` tab for the Auto Painter's properties

10. Finally, switch to the `Maps` tab, scroll down to the `Minimum Opacity` setting, and set it to 0. This sets the brushes' Alphas according to the brightness of any image that is connected to the Opacity Input pin. Then, set the `Opacity` to 2, which sets each brush's `Alpha` to either 100 or 0 Opacity. Finally, set the `Opacity Source` setting to `Alpha`, which uses the `Alpha` levels from the image that is connect to the `Opacity Map Input pin` instead of the brightness values (see Figure 5-70).

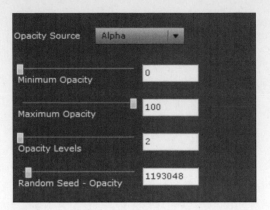

Figure 5-70. Set the `Opacity` of the brushes.

Figure 5-71. The AutoPainter hub is a highly customizable pattern generator.

AutoPainter is a powerful pattern-making hub. Its versatility comes from the various parameters that can be controlled by external bitmaps (see Figure 5-71). The AutoPainter takes information from the input, scale, rotation, offset, and opacity map's corresponding pixel, applies the information to the brush, and then renders it on the Canvas. This is repeated across the entire Canvas in the order set by the hub. Following are the parameters for this hub.

- **Input pins on the Autopainter hub**: There are seven Input pins on the hub; each is for a different function in the hub. The only Input pin that requires a bitmap to be connected is the brush. Following is a list of the Input pins:
    - **1-Brush**: The image used as the brush or the base image that is repeated by the hub.
    - **2-Input Map**: Used as the color that will be applied to the painting that comes from the brushes.
    - **3-Scale Map**: The bitmap that the AutoPainter hub uses to control the scale of the brushes that are rendered in the hub.
    - **4-Rotation Map**: The bitmap that the AutoPainter hub uses to control the rotation of the brushes that are rendered in the hub.

- **5-Offset Map**: The bitmap that the AutoPainter hub uses to control the horizontal and vertical offset of the brushes that are rendered in the hub.
- **6-Opacity Map**: The bitmap that the AutoPainter hub uses to control the opacity of the brushes that are rendered in the hub.
- **7-Brush Index Map**: The bitmap that the AutoPainter hub uses to control the index of the brushes that are rendered in the hub.

The **Output** tab has the parameters that control the hubs dimensions, background fill colors, and Blend Modes of the brushes:

- **Size Menu**: Selects any of the inputs, dynamic, or fixed size for the hub to copy its size.
- **Dynamic Size Menu**: Choose from Canvas or Custom Size.
- **Fixed Size**: Manually sets the size of the hub.
- **Background Color/Background Alpha**: Sets the background that is behind the rendered brushes.
- **Drawing Mode**: This sets the Blend Mode of the brushes when they are drawn across the hub using any of the native Blend Modes.

The **Brushes** tab is where the controls for the brush's color **Blend Modes** from the Input map and indexing are located.

- **Input Map:** Turns on/off the color information being fed from the input map source. However, disconnecting the input map achieves the same effect.
- **Brush Colorization Mode**: Sets how the color information is blended onto the brush. Imagine the brush on a layer and the color information on another layer above it. The **Colorization Mode** determines how the color from the input map is blended onto the brush.
- **Color Application Alpha**: Sets how much of the input map's color will affect the brush.
- **Brush Index Source**: Sets what channel from the bitmap connected to the index map Input pin is used for the indexing order.
- **Column/Row**: Sets how the brush is divided.
- **Minimum/Maximum Brush Indexes**: Sets which indexed pieces of the brush can be used.
- **Random Seed**: Number used to initialize the random number generator, used for random effects of the indexed brush.

The **Painting** tab has parameters to control how the repeated brushes positioned by the hub.

- **Horizontal/Vertical Order**: Sets the order that the brushes are drawn.
- **Random Seed**: Number used to initialize the random number generator, used for random effects of the brush order.
- **Horizontal/Vertical spacing**: Sets the amount of distance between each brush. These settings can be locked together with the checkbox on the right.
- **Horizontal and vertical delta**: Offsets the placement of the brushes in the respective direction. This is an incremental offset so that each successive column/row is offset more than the last.

- **Horizontal and Vertical Padding**: Sets how much the brush pattern extends out from the hub. When the offset or delta settings move the brushes leaving empty spaces, the padding can extend the brushes out from the columns or rows to fill the voids.
- **Horizontal / Vertical Offset**: Sets the center of the brush pattern.

The **Maps** tab contains the parameters to control the different bitmaps that are connected to the Offset Map, Scale Map, Rotation Map, and Opacity Map Input pins.

- **Offset source**: Sets what channel information is used from the bitmap connected to the offset map Input pin to produce the offset.
- **Maximum/Minimum Horizontal and Vertical offset**: Sets the range of the displacement.
- **Random Seed**: Number used to initialize the random number generator.
- **Scaling source**: Sets what channel from the bitmap connected to the scale map Input pin the scaling information uses in the scaling process.
- **Maximum/Minimum Scaling**: Sets the range of scaling of the brush.
- **Random Seed**: Number used to initialize the random number generator.
- **Rotation Source**: Sets what channel from the bitmap connected to the rotation map Input pin the Rotational information uses in this effect.
- **Maximum/Minimum Rotation**: Sets the allowable range of rotation of the brush.
- **Rotation Delta**: Sets the rotation delta, which incrementally rotates the brush as it is rendered.
- **Random Seed**: Number used to initialize the random number generator.
- **Opacity Source**: Sets what channel from the bitmap connected to the opacity map Input pin the opacity information uses in this effect.
- **Maximum/Minimum Opacity**: Sets the range of opacity of the brush.
- **Opacity levels**: Sets how many distinct levels of opacity there are in this function.
- **Random Seed**: Number used to initialize the random number generator.

11. Import the image you want to use the toy blocks effect on. Use the **File ➤ Import Resource** function to import the image you want to use. For this example, we used an image of a fish with a transparent background. To find this image, search for Fishy in the **Aviary Library** tab of the Resource Browser. Make sure you uncheck the option **Only your Stuff** so it searches all Aviary's public images. When you find the image, click the **Import** button to insert it into the file. Then, drag this image from the **Resource** sidebar and connect it to the second Input pin titled **Input Map** on the AutoPainter hub. The **Input Map** imparts its color to the brushes. If you decide to use a different image for this project, you want it to have some transparent areas so that you can see some of the blocks details (see Figure 5-72).

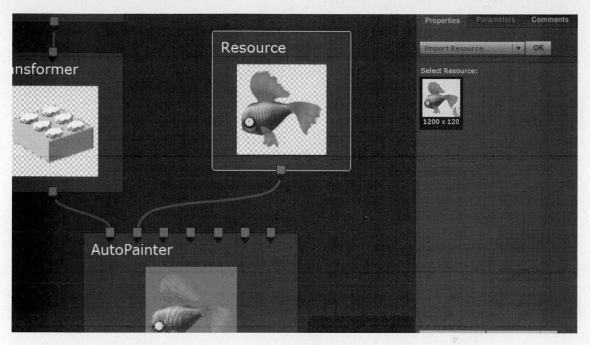

Figure 5-72. Import a resource image to be drawn with the toy blocks.

12. Split the resource so that it can be used for the Opacity map in the Autopainter. Drag a Splitter hub from the **Controllers** sidebar and connect it between the Resource and the AutoPainter. Then, make another connection from the Splitter to the sixth Input pin, the `Opacity Map` (see Figure 5-73). The AutoPainter takes the image that is connected to the `Opacity Map` pin and uses that information to perform opacity actions set in the **Properties** panel. You now see your image made up of the toy blocks.

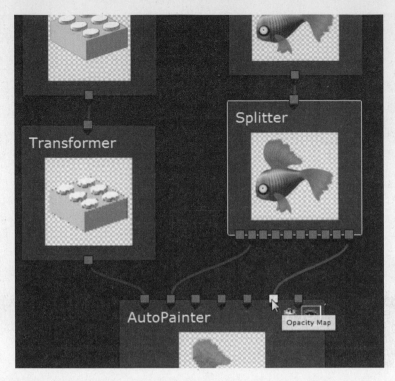

Figure 5-73. Split the Resource and make a connection to the `Opacity Map` pin.

13. Add some depth to the new block object by making a shadow of the toy block image. Drag a Drop Shadow hub from the **Effects** sidebar in between the AutoPainter and Canvas hubs. Set the **Horizontal** and **Vertical Blur Radius** to 28, the **Angle** to 170, **Distance** to 135, and the **Strength** to 0.5. This produces a shadow that appears to be cast on a wall behind the block object (see Figure 5-74). You make the wall for this shadow in the next steps.

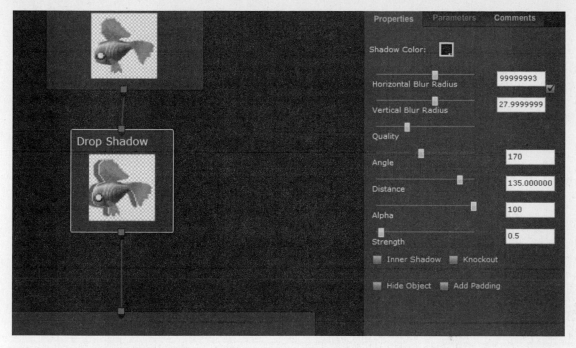

Figure 5-74. Add a drop shadow.

14. Add a Blender hub from the **Controllers** sidebar, after the Drop Shadow hub. This is used to layer in a background for your image (see Figure 5-75).

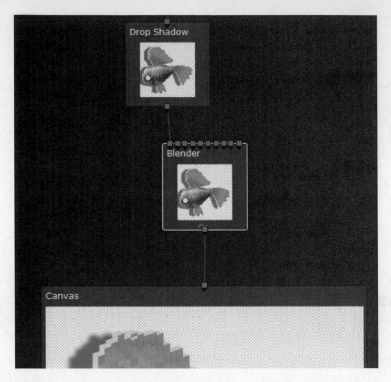

Figure 5-75. Add a Blender hub.

15. Drag a Gradient hub from the **Generators** sidebar, and connect it to an open Input pin on the new Blender hub. Set the **color** in this gradient to light blue blending to dark blue, and the **rotation** to -90, which creates a vertical gradient behind the block object (see Figure 5-76).

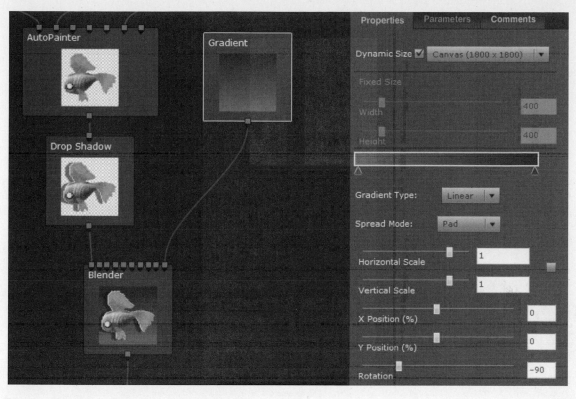

Figure 5-76. Use a Gradient as a background.

16. Create some variation in the gradients color with a Noise hub. Drag a Noise hub from the **Generators** sidebar, and connect it between the Gradient and the Blender. The Noise hub creates a random black and white static fill. To let the gradient's color show through this noise, set the **Merging Blend Mode** parameter to **Overlay** and set the **Merging Alpha** to 70 (see Figure 5-77). This Noise hub imparts a variety to the gradient and is apparent in the background after it is connected to a new AutoPainter hub (see Figure 5-78).

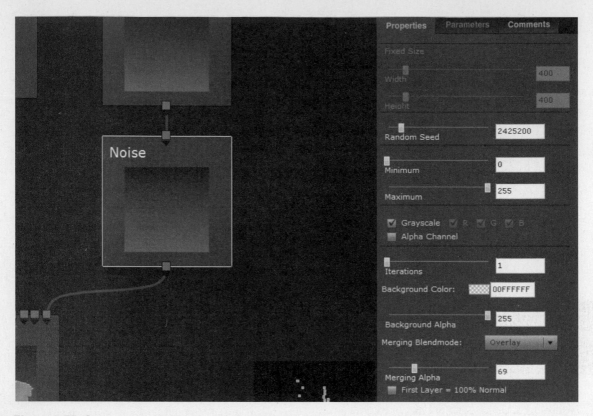

Figure 5-77. Create some variation in the background.

Figure 5-78. The Noise hub generates a static pattern.

Creates a black and white or color static noise fill. The texture that this hub generates is useful to impart randomness to your images. The Noise hub has an input that lets you overlay the noise on the image without having to use a Blender hub. Following are the parameters for this hub.

- **Random Seed**: Number used to initialize the random number generator.
- **Minimum/Maximum**: Sets the range of black (minimum) and white (maximum) that is rendered in the noise.
- **Grayscale**: The color information is ignored, resulting in a black and white noise.
- **R/G/B**: Turns on/off corresponding color channel.
- **Alpha Channel**: Turns on/off the **Alpha Channel** to plasma.
- **Iterations**: Intensifies the generated noise.
- **Background Color**: Sets the background color (maximum); set with hex color.
- **Background Alpha**: Sets the **background Alpha**.
- **Merging Blend Modes**: Chooses how generated noise and the input bitmap are blended.
- **Merging Alpha**: Sets the **Alpha** of the generated noise over the input bitmap.
- **First Layer = 100% Normal**: Sets the generated noise as the only output. The input bitmap is not blended with the noise.

17. Duplicate the toy block effect to the background image. Drag a Splitter hub from the **Controllers** sidebar and connect it between the Transformer and the AutoPainter hubs just below the toy block image hub. This splits the output of the toy block image so that you can use it as a brush in a second AutoPainter hub. Then select the AutoPainter hub, and use the **Edit ➤ Duplicate** function to duplicate the hub including all its settings. Next, move this new AutoPainter to the right, and connect an output from the new Splitter to the first **Input pin (Brush)** on this duplicated hub. Then, connect the output from the Noise hub to the second **Input pin (Input Map)** on the AutoPainter (see Figure 5-79). Next, connect the output of the new AutoPainter to the second Blender that is before the Canvas. Finally, in the AutoPainter's Properties panel, go to the **Maps** tab and set the **Minimum Opacity** parameter back to 100. The background is drawn with the same toy block as the fish object. Duplicating the AutoPainter hub produces the same spacing as the other block object. See Figure 5-80 for a close-up showing the blocks in the final image.

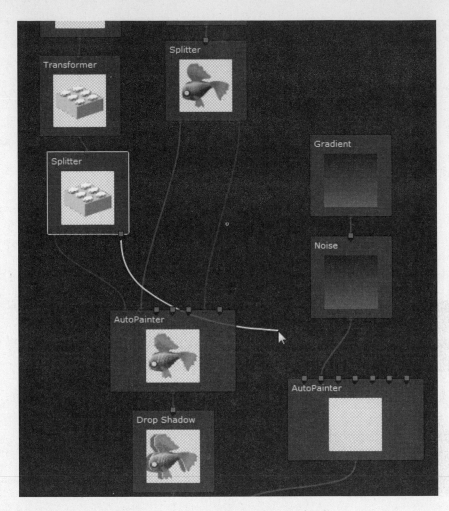

Figure 5-79. Duplicate the AutoPainter and connect the background to it.

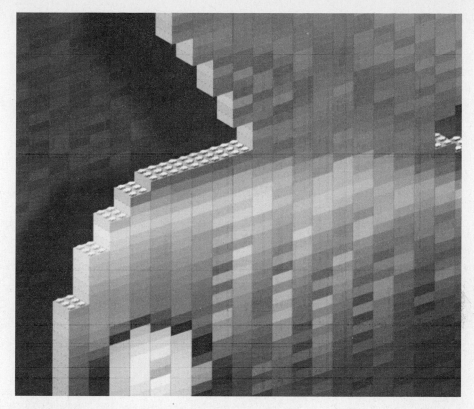

Figure 5-80. Closeup of the toy blocks that make up the image

Project review

In this project, you saw how you can create detailed images by using the AutoPainter hub. The Terrain hub turned a simple shape into a three-dimensional image, which then was resized for use by the AutoPainter. You learned the basic of the powerful AutoPainter hub. This hub can take the information from multiple bitmap images to alter the way the AutoPainter draw brushes across the hub. Finally, you learned that you can duplicate a hub to be reused elsewhere in a file. This also duplicates the parameter settings, which saves you time matching parameters. In the next project, you see how to warp a texture into a sphere using the Coons Patch hub. You also learn how to pin the connector line to help organize your files.

Project 5.4—Create a Textured Sphere

Peacock can do more than just simple pattern and texture construction. It is capable of performing many complex deformations and distortions. You can use the various generator hubs and the deformation effect hubs to build complex images. You learn the basics of the Coons Patch hub. This hub lets you warp an input image into complex shapes, such as a sphere. You then layer several effects to enhance the spherical shape, highlights, shading, reflection, and a background. See Figure 5-81 for the final image and Figure 5-82 for the hub layout for this file.

Figure 5-81. The final image made in this project.

Key hubs used in this project

- Wave Generator hub
- Coons Patch hub
- Masker hub
- Bevel hub

The file for this project can be found at http://aviary.com/artists/gettingstartED/creations/chapter_5_project_4.

Figure 5-82. Hub layout for this file

1. Launch Peacock, and import a texture you want to make into a sphere. Use **the File ➤ Import Resource** command to open the Resource Browser. Locate the file that you want to use, and import it into Peacock. The image used in this file was found at www.CGTextures.com. Drag the Resource hub from the **Resources** sidebar onto the workspace. The hub automatically connects itself to the Canvas because it is the first hub added to the chain (see Figure 5-83).

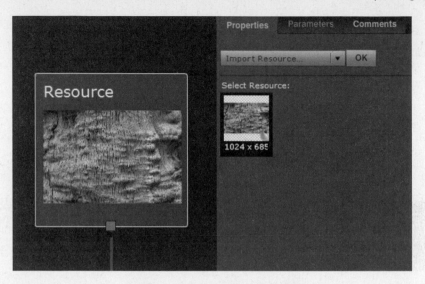

Figure 5-83. Import the texture that you want to be wrapped onto a sphere.

2. Add some shading to this texture before performing the sphere distortion. Start by dragging a Blender hub from the **Controllers** sidebar, and connect it between the Resource and Canvas hubs. Move the connection between the Resource hub and the Blender to the last Input pin on the Blender hub (see Figure 5-84).

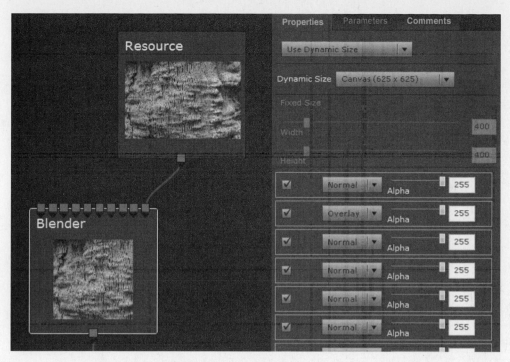

Figure 5-84. Add a Blender hub to the file.

3. Next, drag a Wave Generator hub from the `Generators` sidebar, and connect it to the first Input pin on the Blender. The Wave Generator hub creates black and white gradient fills based on mathematical formulas. These fills vary in shape like linear gradients, wave gradients, and even checkerboards. Leave the Wave Generator hub's parameters in their default settings. Finally, select the Blender hub, and set the layer with the Wave Generator's `Blend Mode` to `Overlay` (see Figure 5-85). This lightens the texture in the upper left, darkens it in the lower right, and gives shading to the texture when it is wrapped into a sphere (see Figure 5-86).

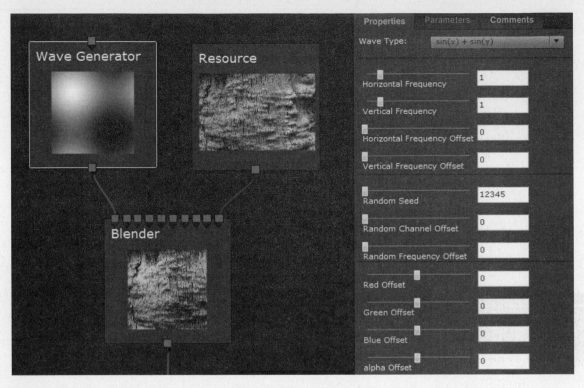

Figure 5-85. Use a Wave Generator to add highlights to the texture.

Figure 5-86. The Wave Generator produces a mathmatically-based fill pattern.

Creates a mathematical wave based pattern. The Wave Generator hub produces a black and white pattern that smoothly transitions from light to dark. The patterns are versatile building blocks for many different effects. You can create more complex patterns by offsetting horizontal and vertical frequencies. The following are the parameters for this hub.

- **Wave Type**: This sets the basic pattern that the hub draws (see Figure 5-87).

- $\text{sin}(x) + \text{sin}(y)$: Alternating black and white gradient dots (A).
- $\text{sin}(x+y)$: Repeating diagonal gradient (B).
- $\text{sin}(x + 2* PI * \text{sin}(y))$: Repeating vertical sin wave gradient (C).
- $\text{sin}(y + 2* PI * \text{sin}(x))$: Repeating horizontal sin wave gradient (D).
- `Square Wave (Checkers)`: Hard edge black and white checkered pattern (E).
- `Sawtooth Wave x+y`: Diagonal gradient pattern (F).
- `Triangle Wave x+y`: Diamond gradient pattern (G).
- `Sawtooth Wave x`: Horizontal gradient pattern (H).
- `Triangle Wave x`: Smooth horizontal gradient pattern (I).
- `Sawtooth Wave y`: Vertical gradient pattern (J).
- `Triangle Wave y`: Smooth vertical gradient pattern (K).

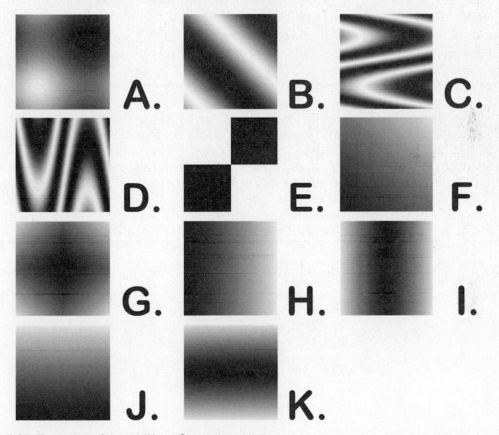

Figure 5-87. Examples of the 11 Wave Generator patterns.

- `Horizontal Frequency`: Sets how much the pattern is repeated in the horizontal direction.
- `Vertical Frequency`: Sets how much the pattern is repeated in the vertical direction.
- `Horizontal Frequency Offset`: Offsets the frequency in the horizontal direction.
- `Vertical Frequency Offset`: Offsets the frequency in the vertical direction.

- **Random Seed**: Number used to initialize the random number generator for random effects.
- **Random Channel Offset**: Randomly offsets each of the RGB channels.
- **Random Frequency Offset**: Randomly offsets the frequencies of each of the RGB channels.
- **Red Offset**: Offsets the red channel.
- **Green Offset**: Offsets the green channel.
- **Blue Offset**: Offsets the blue channel.
- **Alpha Offset**: Offsets the Alpha channel.
- **Color Input Row**: Sets the horizontal line in the input bitmap that the color information is pulled from.
- **Grayscale**: The color information is ignored, resulting in black and white plasma.
- **RGB**: Turns on/off corresponding color channel.
- **Alpha Channel**: Turns on/off the **Alpha** channel to plasma.
- **Smooth Input Colors**: Smooth the input bitmap before the color information is passed to the Wave Generator.

4. Distort the texture into a sphere. Drag a Coons Patch hub from the **Generator** sidebar, and connect it between the Blender and the Canvas. The Coons Patch maps the input bitmap onto a distortable grid. Its default setting produces a 10 x 10 grid with white lines and a black background. Each grid square is filled with the corresponding color from the input bit map. To get more detail from the bitmap into the Coons Patch, you have to increase the grid's rows and columns. However, the more there are, the longer it takes to render the hub. To make this file easy to work with, set the row and columns to 100 while constructing the file. After you are done, go back in and set them to 400. Start by setting the **Stroke** and **Background** colors to 0 **Alpha** by clicking the color selector, and setting the **Alpha** slider to 0 in the Color Picker. Next, set the **rows** and **column** settings to 100 (see Figure 5-88). The hub now takes longer to render but it shouldn't be so long that it interrupts your workflow.

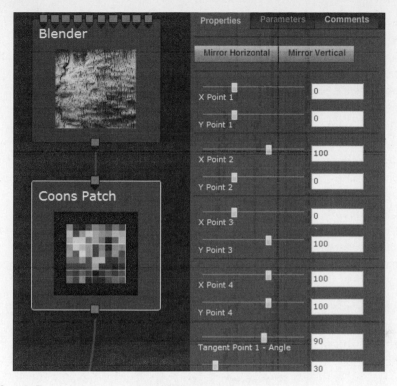

Figure 5-88. A Coons Patch hub is a versatile distortion tool.

Figure 5-89. The Coons Patch hub warps the input image controlled by four control points.

A Coons Patch is a surface that is stretched across four boundary curves (see Figure 5-89). The patch's layout is controlled by curves fitted to four X/Y points. Each curve is adjusted by a pair of control or tangent points. The Coons Patch can map an input image directly onto the grid that is generated between the boundary curves. Increasing the Row and Columns in the patch increases the resolution of the mapped image. Following are the parameters for this hub.

- **Stroke**: Pulls up color to set color and opacity of grid lines.

- **Background**: Pulls up color to set color and opacity of background.
- **Stroke width**: Sets thickness of grid lines.
- **Horizontal/Vertical center**: Changes center position of Coons Patch.
- **Scale**: Scales the Coons Patch.
- **Columns**: Sets the amount of columns in the Coons Patch.
- **Rows**: Sets the amount of rows in the Coons Patch.
- **Grid Distortion X**: Distorts the grid in the horizontal orientation. This distortion gradually changes the spacing of columns.
- **Grid Distortion Y**: Distorts the grid in the vertical orientation. This distortion gradually changes the spacing of rows.
- **Draw Rows**: Toggles on/off the grid lines in rows.
- **Draw Columns**: Toggles on/off the grid lines in columns.
- **Line Only**: With this option enabled, the Coons Patch draws only straight lines from the four X/Y points. Any tangent point and length settings are overridden.
- **Show Guides**: Draws points, labels, and handles for visual reference in setting the Coons Patch (see Figure 5-90).

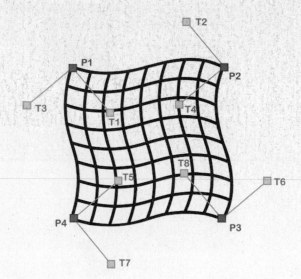

Figure 5-90. Diagram that shows the X points, Y points, and the tangent points

- **X Points / Y points:** Position of each corresponding point in reference to the grid. These can be set from -200 to 200 (see Figure 5-90).
- **Tangent Points Angles:** Sets the angle of the tangent points, relative to the originating point (see Figure 5-91).

**Tangent Point
Angle**

Figure 5-91. The tangent angle is based on 360 degrees of rotation.

- **Tangent Points Lengths**: Sets the length of the tangent points relative to the originating point (see Figure 5-92).

**Tangent Point
Length**

Figure 5-92. The tangent length is the distance from the X/Y point to the the tangent point.

5. Next, you distort the Coons Patch into a sphere shape. Scroll down to the **X point 1** parameter, and set it to 49.9. This sets the horizontal position of the top, left anchor point. The reason that you don't set this to 50 is that the Coons Patch gives you an error message if two anchor points have the same coordinates, so you avoid that by using the 49.9 setting. Next, scroll down to the **Tangent point 1 - Length** and set it to 0. Then, scroll down to the **Tangent Point 3 - Angle**, and set it to 270, and set **the Tangent Point 3 - Length** to 70. You see that the upper, left section of the Coons Patch grid is rounded (see Figure 5-93). You could go through and set each of the eight anchor points and 16 tangent parameters. However, there is an easier way. Go up to the **Mirror Horizontal** button and click it; this mirrors the setting from the left side on the Coons Patch to the right. The mirroring function copies the X/Y points, tangent angles, and tangent lengths, and then reverses the parameters and pastes them to

opposite side of the Coons Patch. This takes a lot of guess work and calculating out of matching setting. Next, click the **Mirror Vertical** button to mirror the setting from the top to the bottom. You have a textured sphere. On rare occasions, the mirroring might not produce the correct results the first time, so you might need to click the mirror buttons again to fix it. Finally, set the **Row** and **Column** parameters to 400 to increase the detail in the text, and wait for it to render.

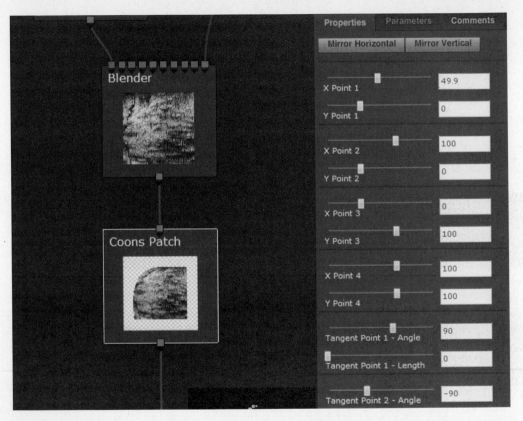

Figure 5-93. Use the **Mirror Horizontal** and **Vertical** buttons to create a symmetrical distortion.

6. Create a dark edge around the sphere shape with a Drop Shadow hub. Connect a Drop Shadow hub from the **Effects** sidebar in between the Coons Patch and the Canvas. Check the **Inner Shadow** option to draw the shadow inside the sphere. Set the **Horizontal** and **Vertical Blur Radius** to 20, which fades the edges more. Increase the **Distance** parameter setting to 40, **Alpha** to 50, **Strength** to 11, and the **Angle** to 225, which produces strong shading around the bottom of the sphere. Finally, you can set the **Quality** to 100 to smooth out any rough transitions in the shadow (see Figure 5-94).

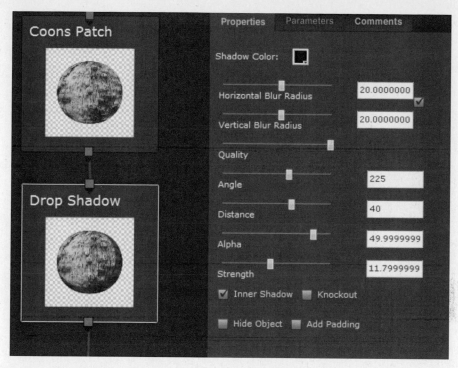

Figure 5-94. Add some shading with a `Drop Shadow` set to `Inner Shadow`.

7. Drag a Bevel hub from the `effects` sidebar, and add it into the chain between the Drop Shadow and the Canvas. The idea with adding the bevel is to add a little highlight and enhance the shadow area a bit more. Start by reducing the `Highlight Alpha` to 45 and increasing the `Horizontal` and `Vertical Blur Radius` to 40 and the `Strength` to 8 (see Figure 5-95).

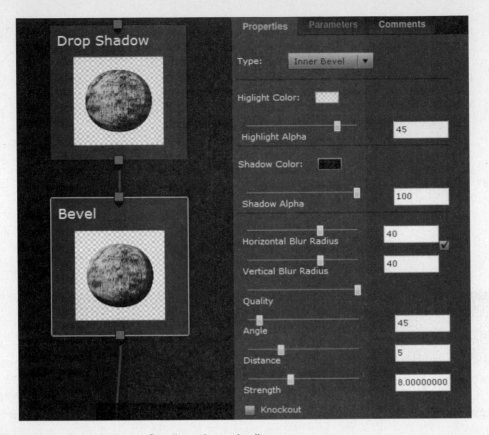

Figure 5-95. Add a Bevel hub to refine the sphere shading even more.

8. Add a Splitter and Blender from the `Controllers` sidebar in between the Bevel and the Canvas (see Figure 5-96). Doing this opens up new Output and Input pins so that you can add in a reflection, shadow, and background.

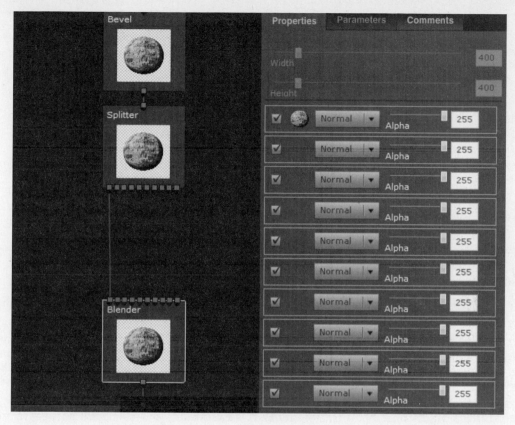

Figure 5-96. Add a Splitter and a Blender to add space for a reflection and background.

If you need more space between pins or a larger preview, any hub can be resized. Hover over any edge on a hub and the cursor changes to a double arrow, where you can click and drag to resize the hub (see Figure 5-97).

Figure 5-97. Resize a hub by dragging the edges.

You can size a hub to several predefined sizes by right-clicking the hub and selecting one from the context menu. To access the context menu, use the right mouse button to click the hub to bring it up.

- `Minimize`: Resizes hub to minimum size; approximately 60 x 60 pixels.
- `Default Size`: Resizes hub to default size; approximately 132 x 108 pixels (this is not the same as the initial size of hub).
- `Resize to 100%`: Sizes hub to set dimensions.
- `Resize to 50%`: Sizes hub to 50% set dimensions.
- `Resize to 25%`: Sizes hub to 25% set dimensions.

9. Drag a Transformer hub from the `Controllers` sidebar, and connect it between a middle Output pin on the Splitter and a middle Input pin on the Blender hubs. This connection becomes a reflection of the sphere, but first it needs to be flipped vertically. A `Rotate/Flip` hub can easily flip an image but it cannot position it. The Transformer easily positions and scales images, but there is no flip option. You can flip an image with a little scaling trick. Setting the Vertical or Horizontal scale to -100 flips the object in the respective direction. Uncheck the `Proportional Lock` checkbox, and set the `Vertical Scale` to -100. Then, adjust the `Vertical Offset` to about 425 so that the reflected sphere lies under the original (see Figure 5-98).

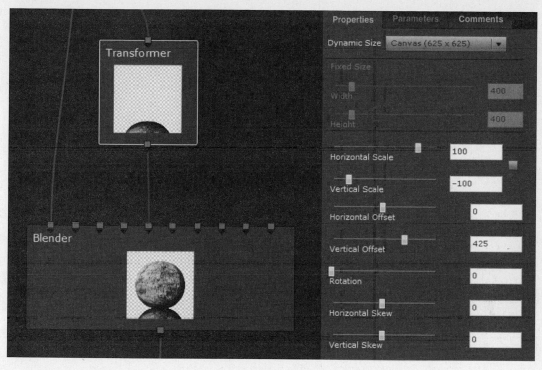

Figure 5-98. Use a Transformer hub to flip and position a copy of the sphere as a reflection.

10. Use a Masker and Gradient to fade out the flipped reflection. Add a Masker hub from the **Controllers** sidebar in between the Transformer and the Blender. Set the **Mask Mode** to **Luminosity** in the Masker hub. Then, add a Gradient hub from the **Generators** sidebar to the second Input pin on the Masker hub. Set the **Rotation** parameter to 90. Finally, drag the white color stop to the right, which adjusts the fade of the reflection. See Figure 5-99 for reference.

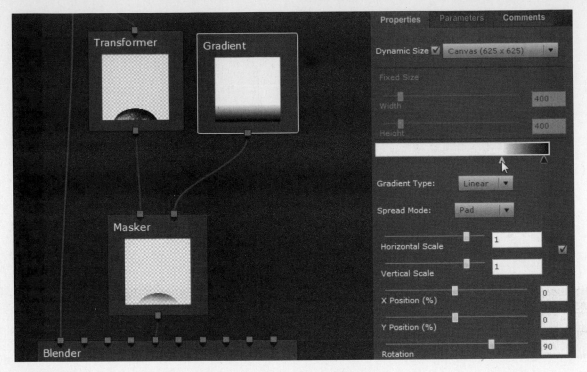

Figure 5-99. Use a Masker and a Gradient to fade out the reflection.

11. Create a Shadow under the sphere. Drag out a Gradient hub from the `Generators` sidebar, and connect it to an Input pin on the Blender between the original sphere and the reflection. Start by setting the color to opaque black fading to transparent black, and then set the `Gradient Type` to `Radial`. Next, adjust the `Horizontal Scale` to 0.75 and `Vertical Scale` to 0.16, which makes a short elliptical shadow. Finally, adjust the `Y Position` so that the shadow is positioned under the original sphere; a setting of 35 works well in this example (see Figure 5-100).

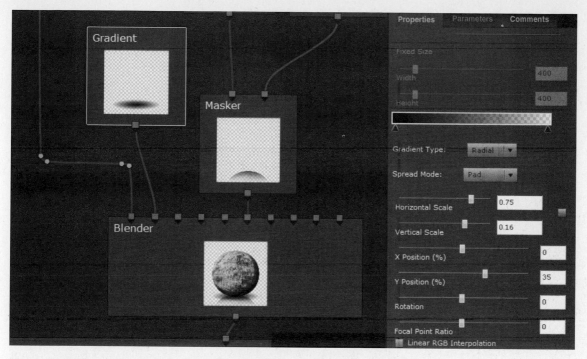

Figure 5-100. Use a Gradient to add a cast shadow.

 In a file that contains many hubs or one that has many crossing connections, you can position the connection lines themselves. Hold the mouse over a connector line to highlight it in white (see Figure 5-101).

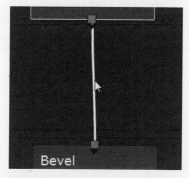

Figure 5-101. Highlight a connector line by hovering the mouse over the line.

Clicking the connector line sets a connector pin. Connector pins are points that you can use to position the lines (see Figure 5-102). Use them to keep the connections organized.

Figure 5-102. Dragging a connector line sets a connector pin to hold the line in place.

You can set as many connector pins as you need to position your connector lines (see Figure 5-103).

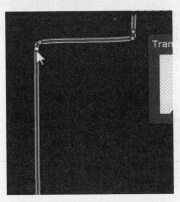

Figure 5-103. Use multiple connector pins to place the connector line anywhere.

12. Make a background for the sphere. You need to have a surface under the sphere that the shadow and the reflection is being reflected on. To make this surface look like it is under the sphere, you want to have a two gradient representing a flat surface under the sphere and a vertical surface behind the sphere representing a wall. This can easily be done with a single Gradient hub with the **Spread Mode** set to Repeat. Connect a Gradient hub from the **Generators** sidebar to the last Input pin on the Blender hub. Set the colors in the gradient to light blue fading to dark blue, and set the **Rotation** parameter to 90. Next, set the **Spread Mode** to Repeat and the **Y Position** to -30 (see Figure 5-104).

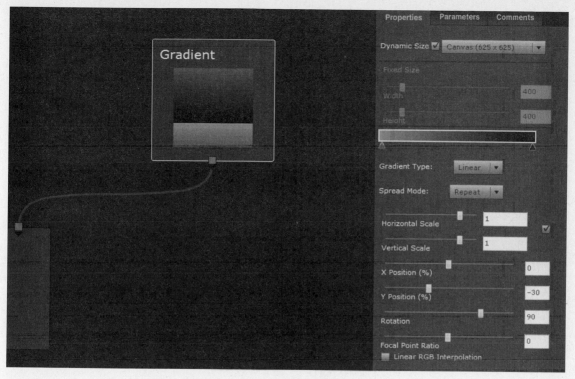

Figure 5-104. Add a Gradient as a background to the sphere.

Project review

In this project, you learned how to use the Coons Patch to warp a texture into a sphere shape. You can also use this hub to mold images into any number of shapes. You saw how layering of several similar effect producing hubs can give you more control. In the project, you used a Wave Generator, Drop Shadow, and a Bevel hub to give the sphere shading. You could have done this with a single Bevel hub, but that gives you a few parameters to adjust. With three hubs making the effect, you have access to many more, which lets you fine-tune effects. You can organize files by resizing hubs and arranging connector lines by using connector pins. Finally, you used a single Gradient hub to create a repeated gradient fill, simulating a more complex background to your image.

Chapter review

In this chapter, you took the first step to understanding Aviary's effect editor Peacock. This application can be intimidating at first with all the slider, numbers, and technical terminology. However, when you crack the shell, you find incredible power and freedom to create. You learned about the general layout of the application and how files are created by chaining hubs together. These chains let you layer, separate, and blend effects in complex ways. The first project showed you how easy it is to construct an image from just a few hubs. Out of Gradient and Kaleidoscope hubs, you created a frame to display an image. You saw how an imported resource can be made into a customizable texture with the Repeat hub. In the second project, you used a Masker hub to cut out textures and used it as an overlay. You saw how a Bevel hub can be used differently to create a glossy highlight. In the third project, you created a toy block element and use the powerful AutoPainter hub to paint and image the blocks. You saw what role the output dimension of a hub can play to enhance the speed a file is drawn. In the last project, you learned how you can warp images with the Coons Patch hub. Layering similar effects gave you much finer control over the effects. In the next chapter, you continue exploring the intricate Peacock. You learn how to create textures from scratch. Using the vast array of hubs, you combine them to make several simple textures. These textures give you resources to create more complex images.

Chapter 6

Creating Textures and Tiles in Peacock

Peacock was initially designed to create patterns and effects for Phoenix, and it has powerful tools for creating these patterns and textures. The program has many uses. For example, If you develop websites, you can create a seamless tile in Peacock for repeating across a page's background. Peacock is also a perfect application for creating textures for three-dimensional (3D) modeling applications. Of course, you can also render patterns for use in your Phoenix images. With a good knowledge of the parameters and the Seamless hub, you can create tiled images; Tile, Repeat, and even the AutoPainter hubs offer tools to arrange these textures. Peacock is powerful, but it can be difficult to use for those starting out with computer graphics. In this chapter, we go over some simple examples so that you can quickly master this graphic powerhouse.

Project 6.1—Brushed Aluminum

Brushed aluminum or brushed metal is a design texture made Apple OS X made popular in the mid 90s. It has since fallen out of favor for use in Apple interfaces, but is useful for 3D textures and more. It is a simple texture to create, but imparts rich details. In this first project, you learn how to use Noise, Gradient, and Polar Tiling hubs to create this rich texture. See Figure 6-1 for the results image and Figure 6-2 for the hub layout for this brushed aluminum texture project.

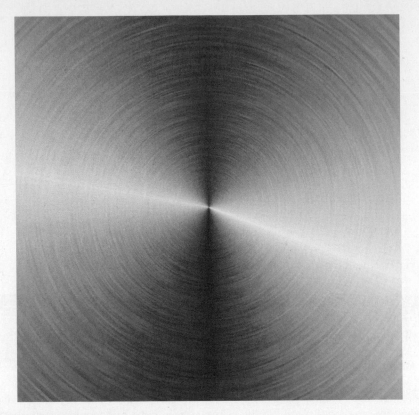

Figure 6-1. Brushed aluminum texture

Key hubs used in this project

- Noise hub
- Motion Blur hub
- Gradient hub
- Polar Tiling hub

> *Find this file online at*
> *http://aviary.com/artists/gettingstartED/creations/chapter_6_project_1.*

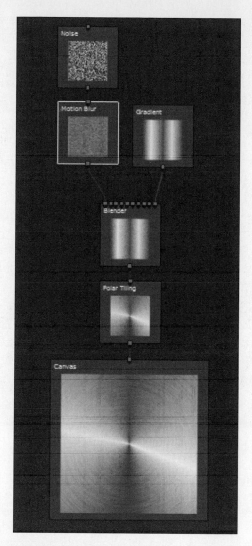

Figure 6-2. Overview of the hub layout in this file

1. First, you will give the brushed aluminum some color with a subtle gradient. Launch Peacock, and then drag a Gradient hub from the **Generators** sidebar onto the workspace. The Gradient hub automatically connects to the canvas because it is the first hub introduced to the file. Set the color in the Gradient to gray (#888888), fading to light gold (#fff4c4), fading back to gray (#888888), fading to light blue (#cfeeff), and ending back at the first gray color (#888888). See Figure 6-3. To change a color, double-click the color stops under the colorbar to display the **Color Picker** dialog where you can choose the color. The color stops are the triangle icons under the colorbar. They can be moved around by dragging them along the colorbar, deleted by dragging them away from the colorbar, and added by double-clicking the colorbar.

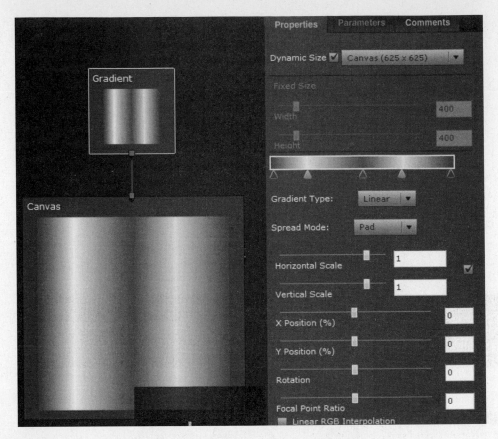

Figure 6-3. Use a Gradient hub to give slight color and shading to your texture.

2. Curve the gradient into a radial pattern. Next, drag a Polar Tiling hub from the **Effects** sidebar and connect it in between the Gradient and Canvas hubs. The Polar Tiling hub distorts the input image into a radial pattern. This distortion stretches the input image so that it is curved around the hub and radiates out from a center point. Set the **Longitude Tiles** and **Latitude Tiles** parameters to 1, which does not allow the gradient to repeat itself as it is distorted. You can experiment with the **Longitude Tiles** parameter to get a more dramatic effect as it repeats the gradient. Finally, check the **Bilinear interpolation** setting, which improves the overall look of the Polar distortion by increasing the resolution at the edges of the hub (see Figure 6-4).

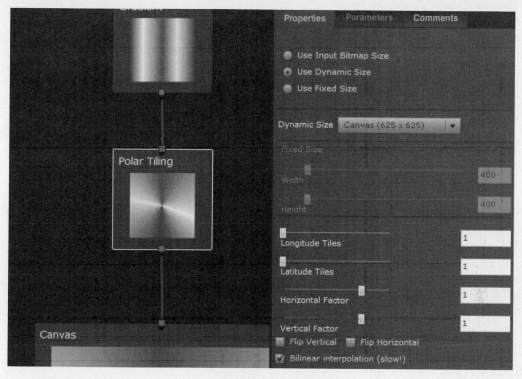

Figure 6-4. Add a Polar Tiling hub to alter the gradient.

Figure 6-5. The Polar Tiling hub curves your input image into a circular shape.

The Polar Tiling hub circularly distorts an image around a center point (see Figure 6-5). You can use this hub to create a variety of effects ranging from micro planets to radial patterning. Following is a list of parameters associated with the Polar Tiling hub.

- **Longitude Tiles**: Sets the amount of spoke tiles.
- **Latitude Tiles**: Sets the amount of ring tiles.

- **Horizontal / Vertical Factor**: Stretches the distortion in the respective direction.
- **Flip Vertical / Horizontal**: Flips the distortion horizontally and vertically
- **Bilinear interpolation (slow!)**: Increases the quality of the resolution of the effect. This increases the render time.

3. Add a Blender hub to the file so you can layer a texture over the gradient. Drag a Blender hub from the **Controllers** sidebar and connect it in between the Gradient and Polar Tiling hubs. The Blender enables you to layer different images and combine them with different blend modes. This hub acts similar to the layers in Phoenix and Raven. Move the connecting line of the Gradient to the last Input pin on the Blender hub (see Figure 6-6).

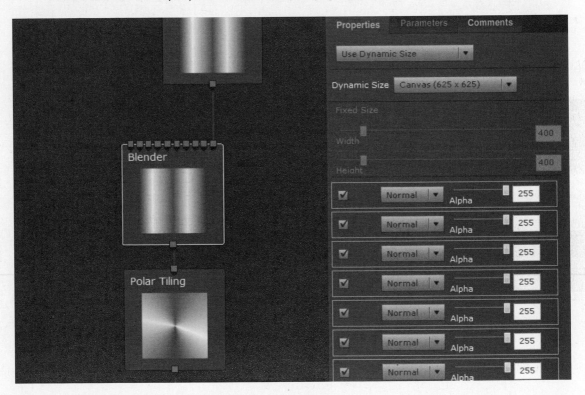

Figure 6-6. Add a Blender hub to the file.

4. Use a Noise hub as a base for the brushed texture. Drag a Noise hub from the **Generators** sidebar and connect it to the first input pin on the Blender hub. Leave the parameters of the Noise hub at their default settings. Select the Blender hub to bring up its parameters in the **Properties** panel. Set the **Blend Mode** of the layer that the Noise hub is connected to **Overlay** by selecting it from the dropdown menu, which lets some the gradient color show through. Finally, set the **Alpha** to 128 to reduce the effect of the Noise hub (see Figure 6-7).

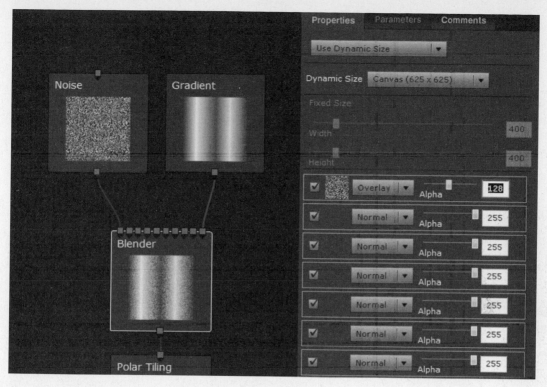

Figure 6-7. Add a Noise hub for texture.

5. A Motion Blur stretches the noise texture into the brushed effect that completes the texture. Drag a Motion Blur hub from the **Effects** sidebar and connect it in between the Noise and Blender hubs. The Motion Blur hub blurs the input image in a single direction, which imparts a sense of motion. Set the **Angle** to 0 or 180 because both produce a horizontal blur. Then, set the **Blur Amount** to 30 to increase the blurring (see Figure 6-8).

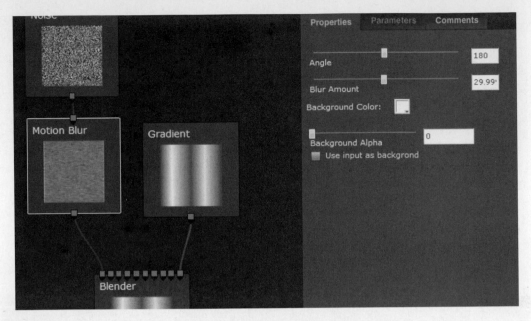

Figure 6-8. Add a Motion Blur hub to the Noise hub to achieve the brushed effect.

Figure 6-9. The Motion Blur hub produces a blurring effect in a single direction.

This effect produces a blur in a single direction (see Figure 6-9). It can be used to simulate blurring due to motion. Following is a list of the parameters associated with this hub.

- **Angle**: Sets the angle of the motion blur effect
- **Blur Amount**: Sets the amount of blur applied
- **Background Color**: Sets the color of the background. This background shows only if the Blur amount is large enough to displace the pixels at the edges, exposing the underlying layer.
- **Background Alpha**: Sets the Alpha of the background color.
- **Use input as background**: This option enables you to set the original image from the input pin to be set as the background, so when you apply blur, the original image is always shown behind the blur.

Project 6.2—Techno Tile

In this next project, you create a texture of evenly spaced holes. This texture easily fits as a background for a technology website, or by altering the size of the holes; it can be made into a metal grate texture. You will see how easy it is to create a repeating pattern with the Repeat hub, and will also layer simple shapes to construct a bevel around each hole. See Figure 6-10 for the final texture created and Figure 6-11 for the hub layout in this project.

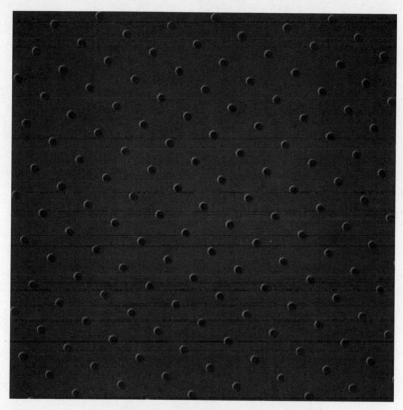

Figure 6-10. This texture works well as a background for a technology website.

Key hubs used in this project

- Repeat hub
- Masker hub
- Gradient hub
- Simple Shape hub

> *Find this file online at*
> *http://aviary.com/artists/gettingstartED/creations/chapter_6_project_2.*

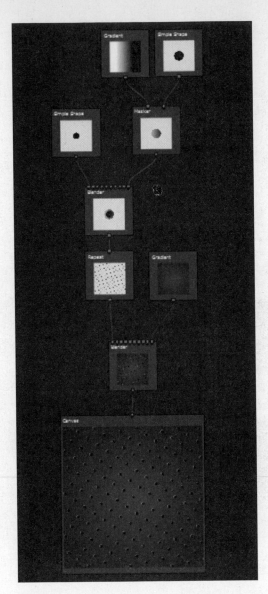

Figure 6-11. This is the hub layout for this file.

1. Create a single hole so it can be tiled across the hub later. Launch the Peacock file and then drag a Simple Shape hub from the **Generators** sidebar. It automatically connects to the canvas because it is the first hub introduced into the file. Set the **Shape Type** parameter to Circle, and the **Horizontal Scale** and **Vertical Scale** to 20, which makes a small black circle. The **Proportion Lock** check box to the right of the **Horizontal Scale** and **Vertical Scale** sliders locks the two scale values together. This makes it easy to match the height and width of

objects (see Figure 6-12). However, if you need an elliptical shape, you need to uncheck the **Proportion Lock** and set the **Height** and **Width** settings independently. For this project, leave it as a circle.

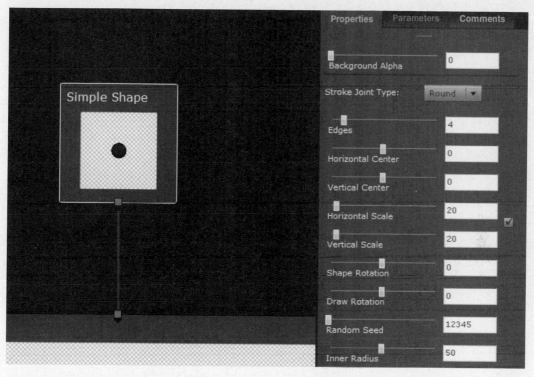

Figure 6-12. Start with a Simple Shape hub for the holes.

2. Add a Blender hub to the file so you can layer the base for the bevel around the hole. Drag a Blender hub from the **Controllers** sidebar and connect it in between the Simple Shape and Canvas hubs. Next, add a second Simple Shape hub to the workspace and connect it to the last input pin on the Blender hub. Set the **Shape Type** to Circle and the **Horizontal Scale** and **Vertical Scale** to 30 in this second Simple Shape hub (see Figure 6-13). Now, you should have two black circles; one is larger than the other.

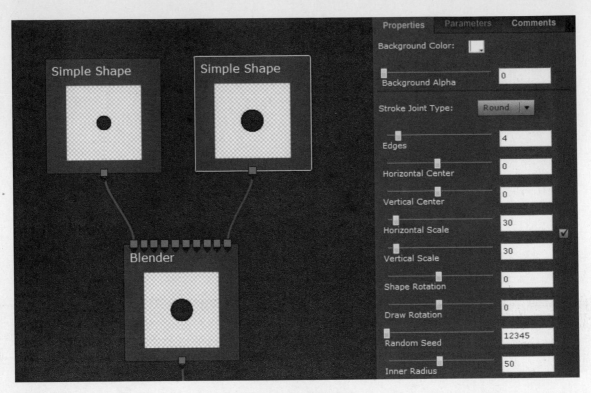

Figure 6-13. Add a Blender hub and another Simple Shape hub.

3. Add a Masker hub, so that you can isolate a gradient fill for the bevel around the hole. Drag a Masker hub from the **Controllers** sidebar and connect it in between the second, larger Simple Shape and the Blender hubs. The Masker hub takes the **Alpha** or **Luminosity** values from one input image and uses it as the **Alpha** information in the second image. In essence, one image cuts out sections in the other. Be sure to connect the Simple Shape to the second Mask Bitmap Input pin on the Masker hub (see Figure 6-14).

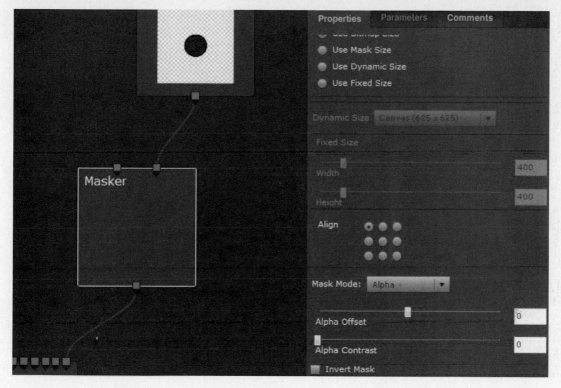

Figure 6-14. Add a Masker hub to the second circle.

4. Add a small gradient to the Masker hub to color the bevel. Next, add a Gradient hub from the **Generators** sidebar to the first Input pin on the Masker hub. Set the **Horizontal Scale** and **Vertical Scale** of the gradient to 0.55. This shrinks the range of the Gradient so that the result from the Masker hub is a circle that has a gradient of medium gray fading to dark gray (see Figure 6-15). Again, the **Proportion Lock** checkbox to the right of these sliders locks them together so that they move in unison.

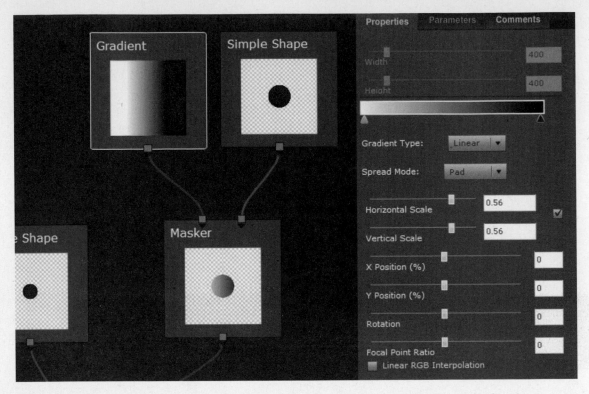

Figure 6-15. Add a Gradient hub to the Masker to simulate a bevel around the first circle shape.

5. Drag a Repeat hub from the **Effects** sidebar and connect it between the Blender and Canvas hubs. Set the **Scale** to 8, which repeats the shape of the hole across the canvas. It is repeated and fills the canvas. The Repeat hub treats the input image as a tile that repeats horizontally and vertically. The scale parameter sets the size of the tile and a smaller setting makes more of the tile appear in the hub. Finally, set a **rotation**. In this example, it is set to 35 (see Figure 6-16).

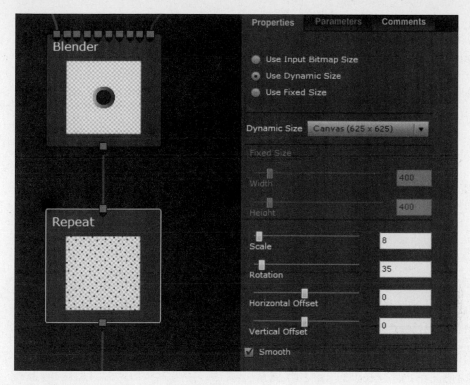

Figure 6-16. Multiply the "Holes" with a Repeat hub.

Figure 6-17. The Repeat hub produces a tiled and rotated pattern from the input bitmap.

The Repeat hub repeats the input image across the canvas.

The Repeat hub treats the input image as a tile and it repeats it horizontally and vertically (see Figure 6-17). The amount of tiles shown is controlled by the scale of the tile. Following is a list of the parameters for this hub.

- **Scale**: Sets the scale of the input image. The smaller the setting, the more tiles are drawn.**Rotation**: Sets the rotation angle of the repeating effect.
- **Horizontal / Vertical Offset**: Offsets the repeated tiles in the respective direction.
- **Smooth**: Performs a Smoothing on the image before applying the repeat effect.

6. Finally, create a background and place it behind the holes. Next, drag a Blender hub from the **Controllers** sidebar and connect it between the Repeat and Canvas hubs. Then, add a Gradient hub from the **Generator** sidebar to the last input pin on the Blender hub you just added. Set the Gradient color to medium gray (#888888) fading to slightly darker gray (#454545), the **Gradient Type** to **Radial**, and the **Horizontal Scale** and **Vertical Scale** to 1.4. This draws a dark gray background behind the holes (see Figure 6-18). You can experiment with any background; for example, try the brushed aluminum texture from the last project as the background.

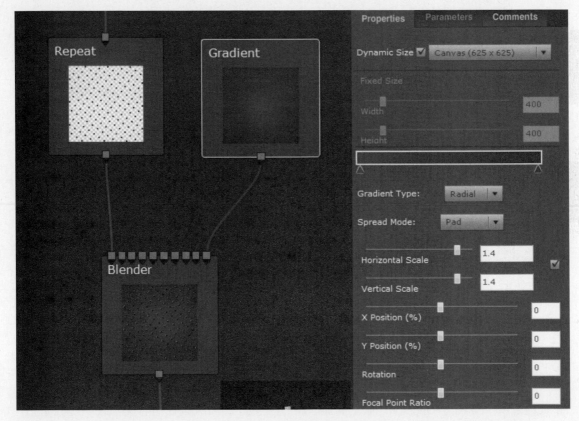

Figure 6-18. Use Blender and Gradient hubs to fill in the space around the holes.

Project 6.3—Create a Fine Wood Texture

Wood, unlike the first two textures, has a natural pattern and grain. Several hubs in Peacock can simulate these natural and realistic patterns. In this project, you use the built-in distortion parameter in the Plaid hub to create grain in a wood texture. The Fractal Plasma hub imparts some natural patterning to the texture, and the Color Manipulation hub is used to color the wood. See Figure 6-19 for the final texture and Figure 6-20 for the hub layout from the project.

Figure 6-19. This wood texture can be used as a texture for a 3D model.

Key hubs used in this project
- Plaid hub
- Edges hub
- Color Manipulation hub
- Fractal Plasma hub

> *Find this file online at*
> `http://aviary.com/artists/gettingstartED/creations/chapter_6_project_3.`

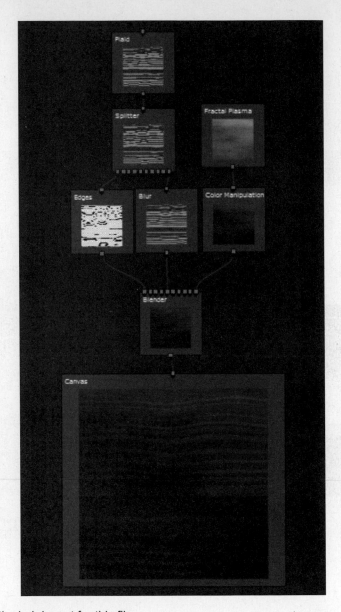

Figure 6-20. This is the hub layout for this file.

1. First, you use a Fractal Plasma hub to add variety to your wood texture. Launch Peacock and add a Fractal Plasma hub from the **Generators** sidebar to the workspace. The Fractal Plasma hub generates a random multi-colored field. Set the **Roughness Factor** parameter to 0.6 to bring out more noise detail in the hub. Next, set the **Horizontal Scale** parameter to 3, which lengthens the pattern horizontally. Finally, drag the **Random Seed** slider around until you are

happy with the resulting output (see Figure 6-21). The `Random Seed` in this file is set to 6234776 and gives you the same pattern as in this example.

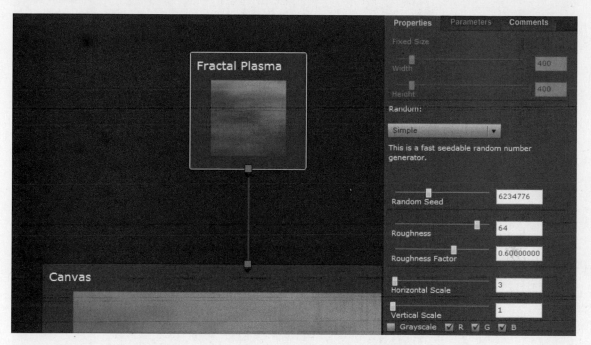

Figure 6-21. Use a Fractal Plasma hub to give the image a natural looking texture.

2. Change the Fractal Plasma to a woody color. Drag a Color Manipulation hub from the `Effects` sidebar and connect it in between the Fractal Plasma and Canvas hubs. This is where you set the overall color of the wood texture. Select a brown color (#633800) with the Color Selector in the bottom right. Next, set the `Tint` slider to 100, will changes the color of the Fractal Plasma to the brown color that you chose. Fine-tune the color with the `Contrast` and `Brightness` sliders to achieve a good wood color. In this example, the `Contrast` is set to 1 and the `Brightness` is set to 35 (see Figure 6-22).

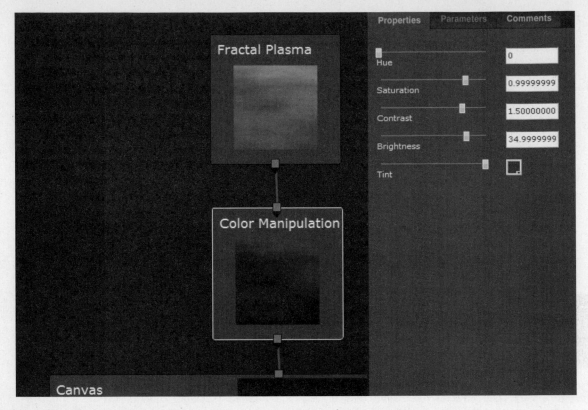

Figure 6-22. Use a Color Manipulation hub to set the overall color of the wood.

3. Use a Blender hub so you can layer the wood grain effect. Add a Blender hub from the **Controllers** sidebar and connect it in between the Color Manipulation and the Canvas hubs. Reconnect the Color Manipulation hub to the last input pin on the Blender if it isn't already there (see Figure 6-23).

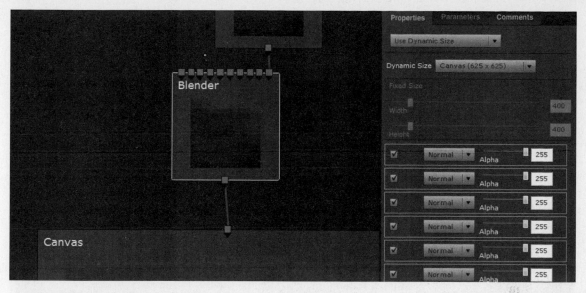

Figure 6-23. Add a Blender hub to the file.

4. Use the Plaid hub's distortion parameter to give a distinctive wood grain effect to the wood pattern. Drag a Plaid hub from the **Generators** sidebar and connect it to a middle Input pin on the Blender hub. The Plaid hub generates a series of colored stripes orientated horizontally, vertically, or both. Set the **Mode** to **Horizontal Stripes**, set the **Horizontal Stripes** to 60, and set the **Size Variation** to 100. This produces several horizontal stripes of varying widths. To give these stripes a bit of a wave effect, set the **Distortion Strength** to 50 and the **Distortion Size** to 30. Finally, check the **Grayscale** option to remove the color from the stripes (see Figure 6-24). You can experiment with these settings to give the wood a different look.

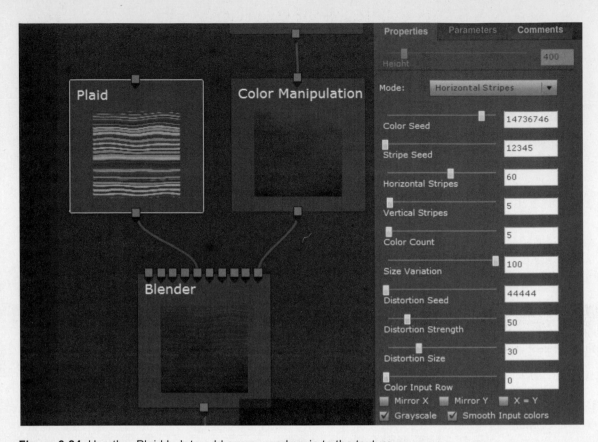

Figure 6-24. Use the Plaid hub to add some wood grain to the texture.

Figure 6-25. The Plaid hub creates striped patterns.

The Plaid hub creates several different types of striped patterns (see Figure 6-25). These stripe patterns can consist of either vertical, horizontal, or a combination of both combined with different Blend Modes. The plaid pattern's color can be controlled by an input bitmap. Following is a list of parameters that control the plaid pattern.

- `Mode`: Sets the base pattern for the plaid.
    - `Vertical Stripes`: Produces a set of vertical stripes only.
    - `Horizontal Stripes`: Produces a set of vertical stripes only.
    - `50% Crossover`: Blends Vertical and Horizontal stripes with 50% opacity on each.
    - `Darken Crossover`: Blends Vertical and Horizontal stripes with a darken Blend Mode.
    - `Lighten Crossover`: Blends Vertical and Horizontal stripes with a lighten Blend Mode.
    - `Difference Crossover`: Blends Vertical and Horizontal stripes with a difference Blend Mode.
    - `Add Crossover`: Blends Vertical and Horizontal stripes with an add Blend Mode.
    - `Subtract Crossover`: Blends Vertical and Horizontal stripes with a subtract Blend Mode.
    - `Multiply Crossover`: Blends Vertical and Horizontal stripes with a multiply Blend Mode.
    - `Screen Crossover`: Blends Vertical and Horizontal stripes with a screen Blend Mode.
    - `Overlay Crossover`: Blends Vertical and Horizontal stripes with an overlay Blend Mode.
    - `Weave Crossover`: Blends Vertical and Horizontal stripes by randomly alternating each
- `Color Seed`: Number used to initialize the random number generator that produces colors.
- `Stripe Seed`: Number used to initialize the random number generator that produces stripes.
- `Horizontal Stripes`: Sets the number of horizontal stripes.
- `Vertical Stripes`: Sets the number of vertical stripes.
- `Color Count`: Sets the number of separate colors in the pattern.
- `Size Variation`: Sets the amount of variation in the size of stripes.
- `Distortion Seed`: Number used to initialize the random number generator that produces the distortion.
- `Distortion Strength`: Sets the amount of distortion in the pattern.
- `Distortion Size`: Sets the size of the distortion.

- **Color Input Row**: Sets the horizontal line in the input bitmap that the color information is pulled from.
- **Mirror X**: Flips and tiles the pattern horizontally.
- **Mirror Y**: Flips and tiles the pattern vertically.
- **X = Y**: Switches the horizontal and vertical information.
- **Grayscale**: Discards the color information leaving a black and white pattern.
- **Smooth Input Colors**: Performs a smoothing operation on the input bitmap before passing on the color information to the plaid pattern.

5. Enhance the edges of the grain effect by splitting the output of the plaid and layering an edges effect. Add a Splitter hub from the **Controllers** sidebar in between the Plaid and Blender hubs. This gives you 10 outputs from the Plaid hub. Make sure the connection is from the last Output pin on the Splitter to a middle Input pin on the Blender. This gives you room to add in the edges effect. Add an Edges hub from the **Effects** sidebar and connect it from the first Output pin on the Splitter to the first Input pin on the Blender hub (See Figure 6-26). The Edges hub layers a black and white striped pattern that follows the edges of the strips from the Plaid. Leave the parameters; they are the default settings that will give you the result you want.

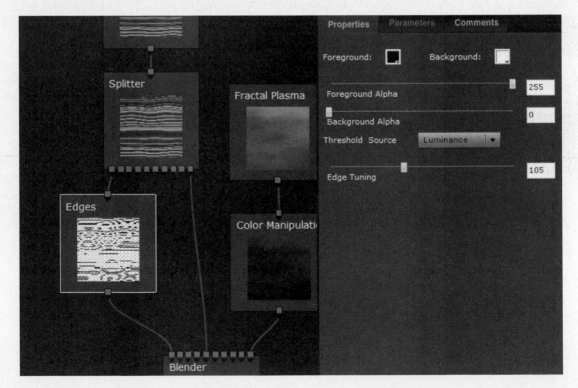

Figure 6-26. Use a Splitter and an Edges hub.

6. Finally, set the Blend Mode to layer the edges, grain, and color effects together. Set the Blend Mode of the Plaid layer to **Overlay** and the **Alpha** to 85, letting the stripes show through the edge effect. Then, on the Edges layer, set the Blend Mode to **Overlay** and the **Alpha** to 38 (see Figure 6-27). This lets the color from the Fractal Plasma layer show through the Plaid and Edges layers, giving the impression of a wood grain. This is just one way to create a wood texture. Experiment with parameters and other hubs to create different variations of the wood texture. You can also open other users' wood texture files to see other methods to create this type of pattern.

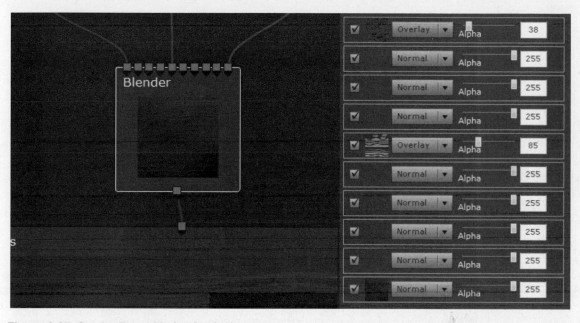

Figure 6-27. Set the Blend Modes for the layers.

Project 6.4—Create a Lava Crackle Texture

The crackle texture can be used to simulate many natural textures, such as lava, ice, and animal fur. This texture can also be used as an overlay to add age to images simulating distress or wear. At first glance, there isn't an apparent way to create this texture with Peacock because there isn't a Crackle hub. However, you will see how to use a little known parameter with the Stippling hub that enables you to produce this crackle texture. See Figure 6-28 for the final image created in this project and Figure 6-29 for the hub layout.

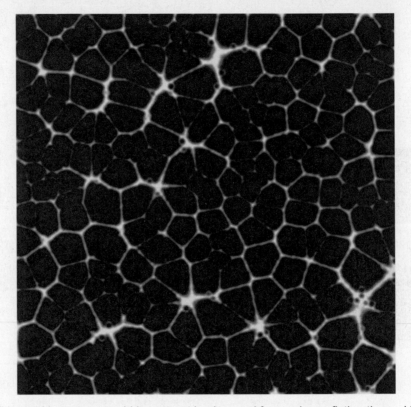

Figure 6-28. This crackle texture would be a great background for a science fiction themed image.

Key hubs used in this project

- Noise hub
- Stippling hub
- Extrapolator hub
- Color Remapper hub

> *Find this file online at*
> `http://aviary.com/artists/gettingstartED/creations/chapter_6_project_4`.

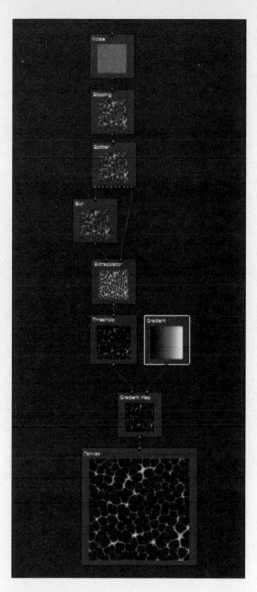

Figure 6-29. The hub layout for this file

1. Mix a Noise hub and Stippling hub to create the base texture for the crackling effect. Launch Peacock and drag a Stippling hub from the `Effects` sidebar onto the workspace; it automatically connects to the canvas. You should not see any changes in you file because there is not a generator of resources in the file for the Stippling effect to work on. Next, drag a Noise hub from the generator sidebar and connect it to the first input pin on the Stippling hub. When the Stippling hub has some input, it produces a series of dots based on that input. The reason you use the

Noise hub to feed into the Stippling hub is that it produces relatively uniformly spaced dots. Select the Stippling hub to bring up its parameters in the **Properties** panel. First set the **Minimum Distance** to 74 and the **Max Distance** to 88, which spaces the dots out. Next, check the **Show Distance Map** function, which draws a gradient around each of the dots. Finally, set the **Override Probability** to 0.2 to tighten the pattern (see Figure 6-30).

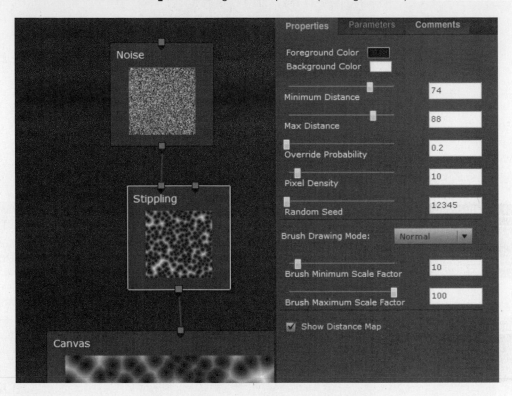

Figure 6-30. To give the Stipple hub something to work with, use a Noise hub.

Figure 6-31. The Stippling hub

The Stippling hub creates an image of dots where the density is controlled by the input image (see Figure 6-31). This hub also lets you set an input image as a brush that is used in place of the default dot shape. The hub also has an alternate display feature that draws a gradient around each dot and overrides any input image brush. Following is the list of parameters for this effect hub.

- **Foreground / Background color**: Sets the foreground color, background color, and Alpha.
- **Minimum Distance**: Sets the minimum distance allowed between dots or brushes.
- **Maximum Distance**: Sets the maximum distance allowed between dots or brushes.
- **Override Probability**: Controls the probability of how close a dot can be placed.
- **Pixel Density**: Sets how tightly the dots are placed.
- **Random Seed**: The number used to initialize the random placement of the dots.
- **Brush Drawing Mode**: Sets the Blend Mode of the brushes when used. The hub uses only internal Blend Modes.
- **Brush Minimum / Maximum Scale Factor**: Sets the scaling of the brush when used. Maximum controls the scale of the brushes in the light areas. Minimum controls the scale of the brushes in the dark areas.
- **Show Distance Map**: Displays a gradient around each dot that corresponds to the proximity to other dots. This feature overrides any brushes.

2. Next, to sharpen and enhance the contrast of the Stippling hub's output, you have to add a series of hubs. Start by adding a Splitter hub from the **Controllers** sidebar and connect it in between the Stippling and Canvas hubs, giving you 10 outputs from the Stippling hub. Next, add a Blur hub from the **Effects** sidebar connecting it between the Splitter and the Canvas hubs. Set the **Horizontal** and **Vertical Blur Radius** to 10. You can see how you will convert this blur into a sharpening effect (see Figure 6-32).

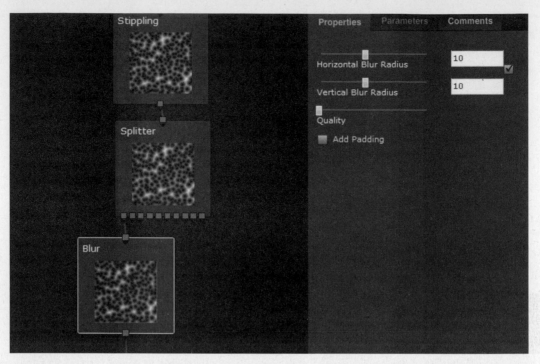

Figure 6-32. Add in a Splitter and Blur hub as the first step to sharpening the Stippling effect.

3. To complete the sharpening of the Stipple pattern, use an Extrapolator hub. Drag an Extrapolator hub from the `Effects` sidebar and connect it in between the Blur and Canvas hubs, making sure that it is connected to the first Input pin on the Extrapolator. Then, make a connection from the Splitter to the other Input pin on the Extrapolator hub. The Extrapolator hub essentially tries to extrapolate the difference between two inputs, or make them the same. In this file, there is one input with a heavy blur being extrapolated from the original, so the hub attempts to move the original to the blurred version. However, if you reverse the extrapolation, it sharpens the output. Set the `Factor` parameter to -2 and the `Multiplier` to 13, which produces a heavy sharpening and contrast on the image (see Figure 6-33).

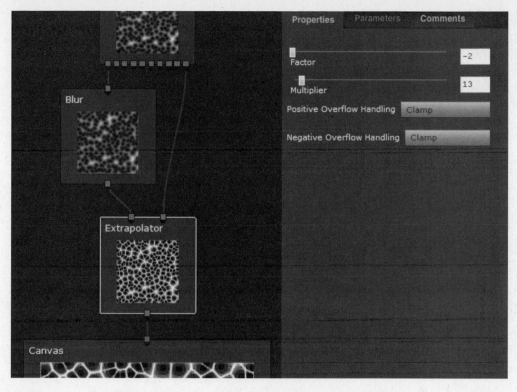

Figure 6-33. Use an Extrapolator hub to enhance contrast and to sharpen the image.

Figure 6-34. The Extrapolator hub can perform many various color, tonal, and sharpening effects.

The Extrapolator hub attempts to make two inputs the same; reversing the effect pushes the images in the opposite direction (see Figure 6-34). For example, image A is extrapolated from image B, which is a blurred version of image A. The Extrapolator hub attempts to make image A look like image B. The resulting image becomes blurrier the higher the factor is set because image A tries to become like image

B. So, if you set the factor in the opposite direction, away from point B, the image becomes sharper because image A tries to become everything that image B is not. Following is a list of the Extrapolator's parameters.

- **Factor**: Sets how much the mask bitmap is extrapolated against the input bitmap.
- **Multiplier**: Sets how much the extrapolation is multiplied.
- **Positive / Negative Overflow Handling**: Sets how the hub handles pixels that exceed the maximum and minimum values. Options are:
  - **Clamp**: The pixels that overflow the limited values of 0–255 will not exceed but be locked at the maximum (255) or Minimum (0) values
  - **Wrap**: The pixels that overflow the limited values of 0–255 are wrapped. So a value of 260 is set to 5 (260 – 250 = 5)
  - **Mirror Wrap**: The pixels that overflow the limited values of 0–255 are inversely wrapped. So a value of 260 is set to 250 (255 – (260 – 255 = 5) =250)

4. Clean up the results from the extrapolation. Drag a Threshold hub from the **Effects** sidebar and connect it in between the Extrapolator and Canvas hubs. Here, the Threshold hub is used to reduce the amount of the gray values in the image and defines the crackle pattern. Set the **Threshold** to 178, **Smoothing** to 5, **Edge Sharpness** to 165, and the **Edge Tuning** to 190, leaving a black and white crackle texture (see Figure 6-35).

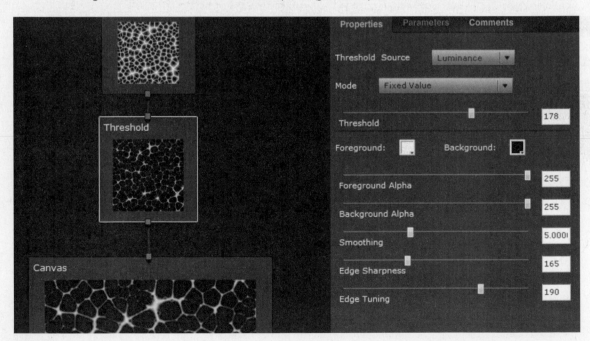

Figure 6-35. Use a Threshold hub to refine the image.

5. Now, you need to add color to the black and white crackle pattern. Drag a Color Remapper hub from the **Effect** sidebar and connect it in between the Threshold and Canvas hubs. Be aware that the hub's name in the sidebar is Color Remapper, but the title on the hub has not been changed yet and reflects the old name, which is Gradient Map. This hub is referred to as the Color Remapper in this project. Ensure the **Threshold** is connected to the first Input pin on the Color Remapper hub. Next, add a Gradient hub from the **Generators** sidebar to the second Input pin of the Color Remapper. The Color Remapper maps the colors from one input to the luminosity of another. In this case, it maps a gradient you set to the black and white crackle pattern. Select the Gradient hub and set the colors to black (#000000), to maroon (#330000), to red (#ff0000), to orange (#ff9900), to yellow (#fff82a), and white (#ffffff). At this point, you can adjust the colors by eye because there are many random variables in the effect (see Figure 6-36). In this example, the orange, gold, and white color stops are further to the right of the colorbar to get the desired results. Furthermore, by using totally different colors in the gradient, you change the material that the crackle simulates. Changing to blues would make it look like ice.

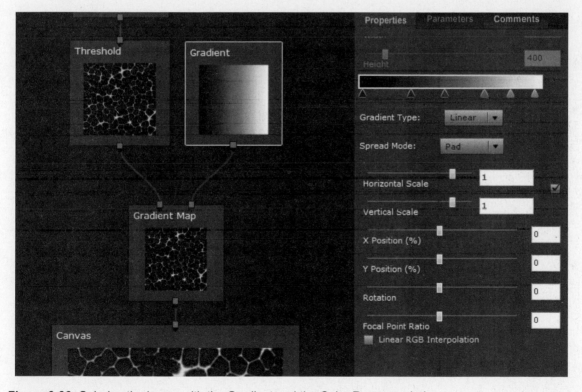

Figure 6-36. Colorize the image with the Gradient and the Color Remapper hubs.

Figure 6-37. The Color Remapper maps the colors from one image to the luminosity of another.

The Color Remapper hub maps color from one image to another (see Figure 6-37). This hub takes a horizontal row of pixels from an input image connected to the second input pin (colors) and remaps them to the luminosity for the bitmap attached to the first Input pin (Input bitmap). Following is a list of the Color Remapper's parameters.

- **Red / Green / Blue adjust**: Adjusts the intensity of each channel in the input bitmap before the color information is applied
- **Color Input Row**: Sets the horizontal line in the input bitmap that the color information is pulled from
- **Palette Offset**: Sets the start point of the color palette that is applied to the input bitmap.
- **Smooth Colors**: Performs a smoothing effect to the color bitmap before applying the colors to the input bitmap.
- **Revert Color Order**: Reverses the color order of the applied color.
- **Sort by Luminance**: Sorts the input colors by luminance before applying color.

Project 6.5—Create a Sandstone Texture

Stone is a natural material that is easy to create with Peacock. The new Convolution hub has an effect emboss that with a few other hubs creates a realistic stone texture. In this project, you will see what the Convolution hub can do and how to enhance the results to simulate stone texture. You set how to use the Color Remapper in conjunction with Fractal Plasma hubs to create a detailed color pattern to the texture. See Figure 6-38 for the final image and Figure 6-39 for the hub layout from this project.

Figure 6-38. This stone texture would be useful when creating architectural images or 3D models.

Key hubs used in this project

- Fractal Plasma hub
- Convolution hub
- Auto Levels hub
- Color Remapper hub

Find this file online at
http://aviary.com/artists/gettingstartED/creations/chapter_6_project_5_2.

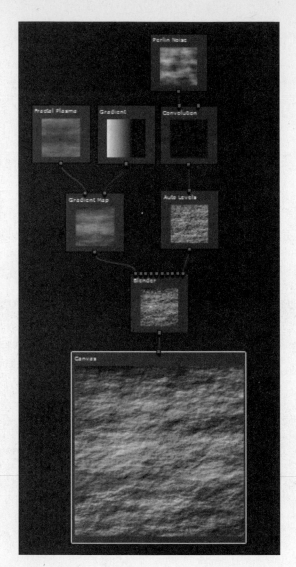

Figure 6-39. The hub layout for this file

1. Use the Perlin Noise hub to produce the base texture for the stone texture. Launch Peacock and add a Perlin Noise hub from the **Generators** sidebar. Perlin Noise produces a naturalistic grayscale fill; this type of noise is developed to produce realistic textures in computer graphics. First, uncheck the **Proportional Lock** to the right of the **Horizontal Scale** and **Vertical Scale** sliders. Then, set the **Horizontal Scale** to 0.4 and the **Vertical Scale** to 0.22; this stretches the Perlin Noise horizontally. Finally, to give the noise finer detail, set the **Octaves** parameter to 8 (see Figure 6-40). Each **Octave** doubles the amount of detail in the Perlin Noise

hub; however, each added octave increases the render time slightly. It is good practice to use only the amount of `Octave` detail that is needed for the effect.

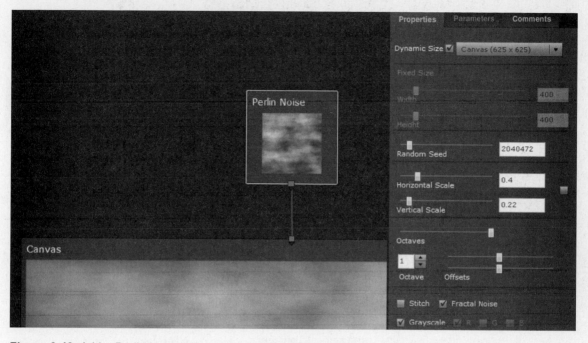

Figure 6-40. Add a Perlin Noise hub to give the stone a natural look.

Figure 6-41. The Perlin Noise hub produces realistic noise textures.

The Perlin Noise hub creates a random cloud-like noise (see Figure 6-41). This effect was developed for generating height maps for 3D landscapes. You can use this hub to create a variety of cloud-like noise patters. The output can range from a static noise to a gentle random gradient. The Perlin noise produces two distinct patterns: a soft pattern or a hard edged Fractal Noise pattern. Following is a list of parameters associated with this hub.

- **Random Seed:** Number used to initialize the random number generator used by this effect.
- **Horizontal/Vertical Scale**: Stretches the Perlin Noise in the corresponding direction.
- **Octaves**: Sets how many octaves are used to generate Perlin Noise. The higher the octave level, the more detail is generated.
- **Select Octaves**: Selects the octave that is affected by the octave offset setting.
- **(Octave) Offsets**: Offsets the selected octave.
- **Stitch**: Makes the Perlin Noise a seamless tile.
- **Fractal Noise**: Changes the style of the Perlin Noise.
- **Grayscale**: The color information is ignored, resulting in black and white plasma.
- **R G B**: Turns on/off corresponding color channel.
- **Alpha Channel**: Turns on/off the Alpha channel to Perlin Noise.

2. Next, you emboss the Perlin Noise results to give some depth to the texture. Drag a Convolution hub from the **Effects** sidebar and connect it between the Perlin Noise and Canvas hubs. Make sure that the Perlin Noise is connected to the first Input pin on the Convolution hub. The Convolution hub alters each pixel in an image based on a 3x3 or 5x5 matrix, commonly referred to as a kernel. This hub looks at each pixel, and then uses the kernel to multiply the surrounding pixels to calculate the pixel's new value. Altering the numbers in the matrix performs different operations such as sharpen, blur, and mean. This is a complex effect, so the best way to understand it is to play with the numbers in the matrix. However, for this project, leave the presets parameter on **Emboss** and change only the **Bias** to 30 (see Figure 6-42).

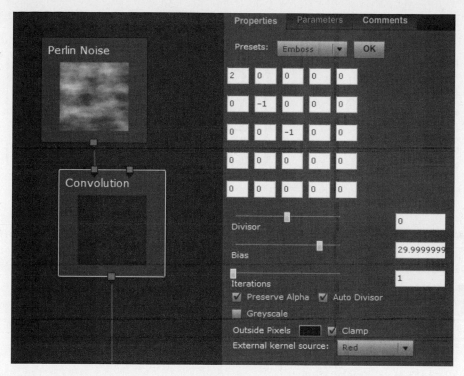

Figure 6-42. The Convolution hub has multiple functions and is a programmable hub.

Figure 6-43. The Convolution hub applies the convolution matrix (kernel) to each pixel's value.

The Convolution hub uses a 3x3 or 5x5 matrix or kernel to alter the pixels in an image (see Figure 6-43). The hub looks at each pixel separately, multiplies the surrounding pixels with the kernel, and adds the results. The original pixel is replaced with this new number. For example, in Figure 6-43, there is a convolution being performed on the center pixel with a value of 2. The convolution matrix or kernel is multiplied to the surrounding pixels to calculate the value of the center pixel. So, the new value of the center pixel is ((2*0 = 0) + (2*0 = 0) + (3*1 = 3) + (2*0 = 0) + (3*0 = 0) + (2*1 = 1) + (3*0 = 0) + (2*0 = 0) +

(2*0 = 0)) = 5. The convolution moves to the next pixel, performs the same action on it, and continues on all pixels in an image (see Figure 6-44).

Figure 6-44. Example of a convolution on a single pixel

- **Presets**: Preset effects. After selecting the effect, you must click the OK button for it to take effect.
    - **Emboss**: Enhances the edges, creating a light and dark side.
    - **Sharpen**: Enhances details by adding contrast to edges.
    - **Blur**: Creates a blur.
    - **Blur More**: Creates a stronger blur.
    - **Mean**: Creates a light blur.
    - **Laplacian**: Traces edges.
- **Divisor**: The result of the pixel calculation is divided by this setting.
- **Bias**: This value is added directly to the pixel calculations.
- **Iterations**: This is how many times the calculations are performed.
- **Preserve Alpha**: This setting uses the pixels' opacity when calculating each pixel with the kernel. Normally just the luminosity is used in calculations.
- **Auto Divisor**: When enabled, it will try to automatically set the best divisor setting for this effect. It is recommended that you leave this option enabled.
- **Grayscale**: No color information is passed to the output.
- **Outside Pixels**: Sets the color of edge pixels if they are displaced.
- **Clamp**: Locks the edge pixels and won't be displaced.
- **External Kernel Source**: When a bitmap is connected to the kernel map, it sets the channel uses the information. The External Kernel works best with a 3x3 or 5x5 pixel image. It is basically the same as the internal matrix (kernel).
- **External Bias**: This value is added directly to the kernel bitmap pixel calculations.

3. Enhance the levels from the Emboss effect with an Auto Levels hub. Drag an Auto Levels hub from the **Effects** tab and connect it in between the Convolution and Canvas hubs. This brightens the image and exposes the texture (see Figure 6-45). The Auto Levels hub stretches the luminosity values from the input image so that the lightest values are pushed to white and the

darkest to Black. This works like the Levels command in Phoenix. There are no parameters in the **Properties** panel to set.

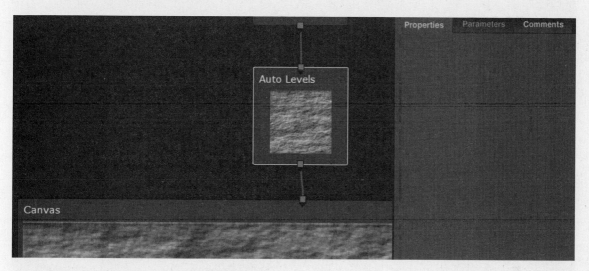

Figure 6-45. Auto Levels brighten the Convolution.

4. Layer color on the texture with Fractal Plasma and Blender hubs. Add a Blender hub from the **Controllers** sidebar in between the Auto Levels and Canvas hubs. Reconnect the Auto Levels output to the last Input pin on the Blender hub. Next, drag a Fractal Plasma from the **Generators** sidebar and connect it to the first Input pin on the Blender hub. Set the **Roughness Factor** to 0.7 and the **Horizontal Scale** to 3.8 to create a rough horizontal color texture (see Figure 6-46). Finally, you can adjust the **Random Seed** slider until you find a setting that produces a texture that you like. In this file, it is set to 3060708.

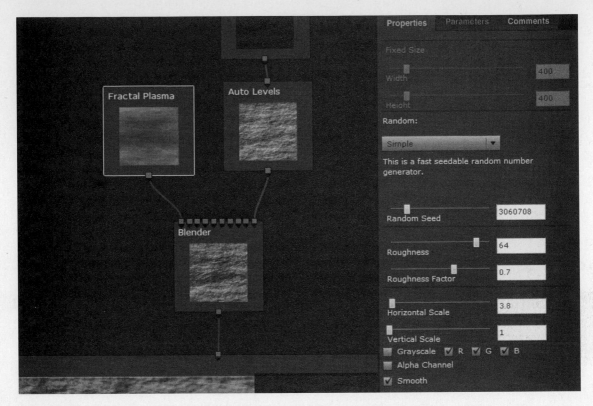

Figure 6-46. Use a Blender and Fractal Plasma hub to add color to the texture.

5. Set the color to blend with the emboss effect. Select the Blender hub to bring up its parameters in the **Properties** panel. Then, set the Blend Mode of the Fractal Plasma layer to **Overlay**. This combines the layers together letting details from both hubs show (see Figure 6-47).

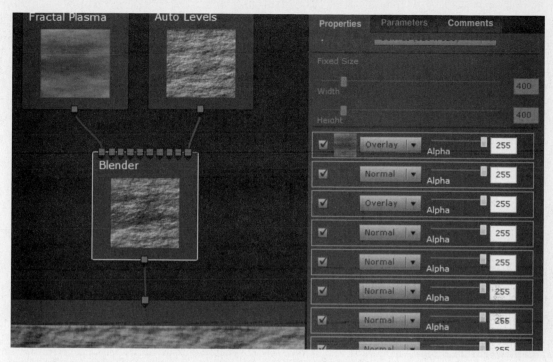

Figure 6-47. Set the Blend Mode of the **Fractal Plasma** to **Overlay**.

6. Adjust the color of the Fractal Plasma to look more like rock colors. Drag a Color Remapper hub from the **Effects** sidebar and connect it in between the Fractal Plasma and the Blender. The title of the hub might say Gradient Map because it has yet to be updated. Next, add a Gradient from the **Generators** sidebar and add it to the second Input pin on the Color Remapper. The Color Remapper takes the colors from the Gradient and uses them to colorize the Fractal Plasma. You want to set the Gradient colors to ones that resemble colors of rocks. Set the **Gradient color** to white (#ffffff) fading to light brown (cccc99#), fading to brown (#663300), and ending with dark brown (#330000). Finally, drag the color stops around until you get a nice balance of darks and lights in your image (see Figure 6-48). Experiment with the colors in the Gradient to colorize your rock texture differently. There are many different ways to create a stone texture with Peacock. It is recommended that you explore others files on Aviary to see other ways to create them.

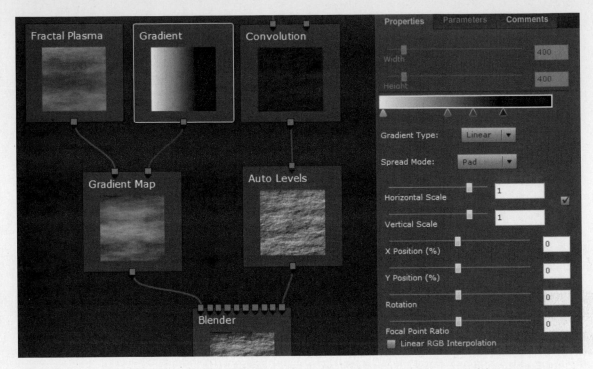

Figure 6-48. Use the Color Remapper hub along with a Gradient to change the color of the `Fractal Plasma`.

Project 6.6—Create a Grass-Like Texture

Grass can be difficult to create in a graphics programs. To make a convincing grass texture, you have to have a natural randomness, but have full control of how it is drawn in your image. Peacock has several hubs that make this task easy. You will see how to harness the powers of the Shape Draw hub to construct a single blade of grass. Then, you use the AutoPainter to draw thousands of these blades to make a grass texture. See Figure 6-49 for the final texture and Figure 6-50 for the hub layout from this project.

Figure 6-49. Changing the color of this texture can make it work for hair or fur.

Key hubs used in this project

- Simple Shape hub
- Shape Draw hub
- Color Bounds hub
- AutoPainter hub

Find this file online at
http://aviary.com/artists/gettingstartED/creations/chapter_6_project_6.

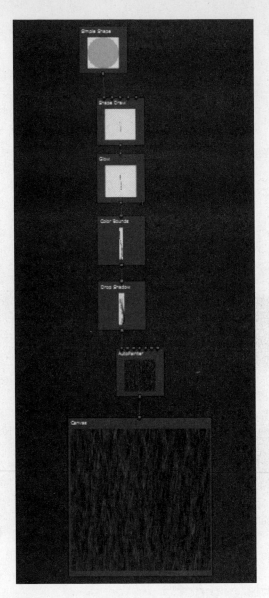

Figure 6-50. Hub layout for this file

1. Use a Simple Shape hub as a base for the blade of grass. Launch Peacock and drag a Simple Shape hub from the **Generators** sidebar and drop it onto the workspace. The hub automatically connects to the Canvas. Then, uncheck the **Dynamic Size** option, which enables you to set the fixed dimension of the hub. Set both the **Height** and **Width** to 50 pixels to make a small hub (see Figure 6-51). The reason that you set the hub's dimension this small is because you will use a Shape Draw hub and AutoPainter, both of which are process-intensive hubs. The larger the

input image size in these hubs, the longer it takes to render the output. Finally, set the **Shape Type** to circle and set its **Fill Color** to a bright green (#66ff00).

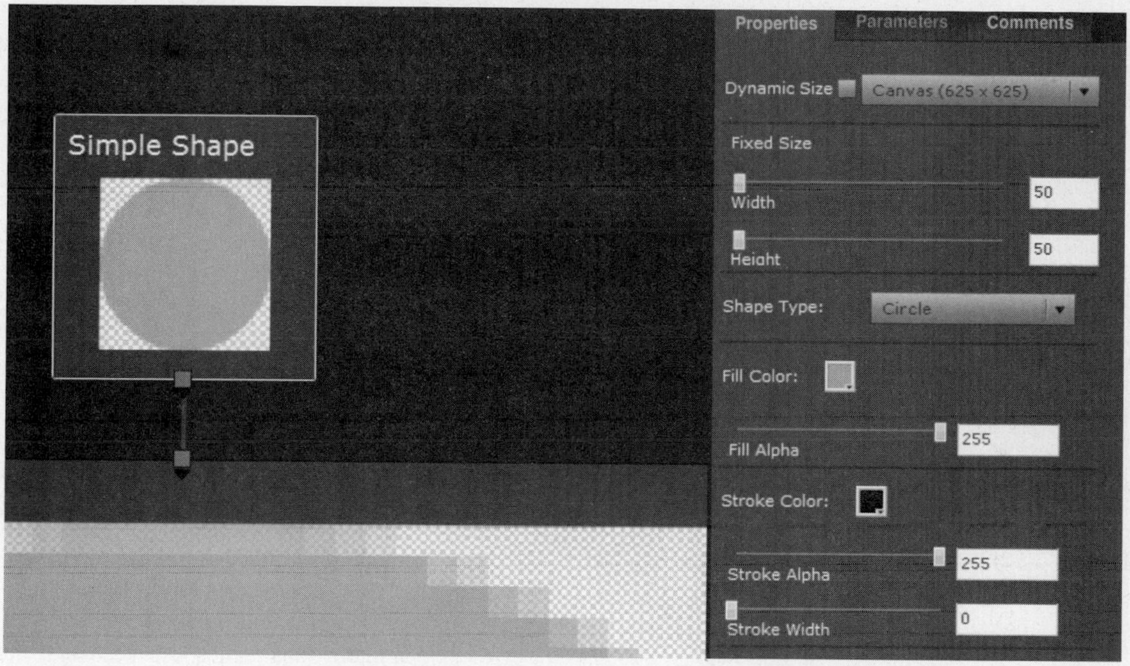

Figure 6-51. Set the Simple Shape's dimension very small to make it easier to handle with the Shape Draw hub.

2. Use the power of the Shape Draw hub to create a single blade of grass. Add a Shape Draw hub from the **Generators** sidebar and connect It In between the Simple Shape and the Canvas hubs. The Shape Draw hub copies the input image commonly referred to as a brush, and then places these copies along a path. There are seven different shapes of paths and several parameters to alter the copies to create complex objects. The **Shape Draw** parameters are grouped by functions in five tabs. You use only the first four for this project; the fifth tab contains parameters for input bitmap controls of the brushes. The initial output of the Shape Draw hub is a circular path of brush copies with a white background. Select the **Output** tab where the hub dimensions and background are set. Change the **Background Alpha** to 0; this removes the white background color. Switch to the **Brush** tab. The Brush tab contains the parameters that control size, Alpha, rotation, and offset of the brushes. Start by unchecking the **Proportion Lock** to the right of the **Start Scale** and **End Scale** sliders. Next, set the **Start Scale** to 4 and the **End Scale** to 30. This starts the brush copies at 4% of the original scale and incrementally gets larger where it ends the brushes at 30%. Then, uncheck the **Proportion Lock** check box to the right of the **Opacity** sliders so they slide independently. Finally, set the **Start Opacity** to 10 and leave the **End Opacity** at 100. This starts adding the brushes at 10% **opacity** or **Alpha** on the path, and it incrementally become more opaque until it ends at

405

100% **Alpha** (see Figure 6-52). The next step shows the setting of the parameters in the two remaining tabs.

Figure 6-52. Use a Shape Draw hub to make a blade of grass.

3. The next two tabs control the path and the interaction between the copied brushes and the path. Switch to the Shape tab. This is where you set the parameters that control the path that the brushes will follow. In the **Shape** tab, set the **Shape Type** to Curve to create a two-point path that has curves at each end. This is similar to a Bézier curve in Raven. You should not see the path directly, but you will see how the brushes are drawn on to it. Set the **Horizontal Scale** and **Vertical Scale** to 50, and set the **Rotation** to 90. This shortens the path and rotates it so it is vertical. Set the **Left Tangent Offset** to 15 and the **Right Tangent Offset** to – 15, this will give the curve an S shape. You can think of the Left and Right Tangent Offset as the control handle on a Bézier curve. Each directly affects the amount of curve at each end of the path. Switch to the Draw tab. The Draw tab contains all the parameters that control how the brushes are drawn onto the path. Set the **Spacing** to 0.7, which controls the distance between the brushes (see Figure 6-53). This tightens the brushes to look like a single shape.

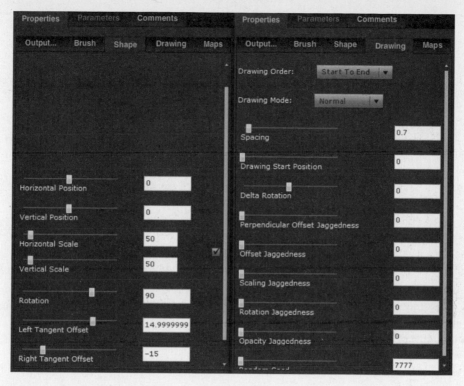

Figure 6-53. The parameters setting in the **Shape** and **Drawing tabs** in the Shape Draw hub.

Figure 6-54. The Shape Draw hub copies and inputs images or brushes along a path set by the hub.

The Shape Draw hub uses the input bitmap brush and copies it along a path (see Figure 6-54). There are seven different path shapes and several parameters that control the brush, path, and interaction between them. These are as follows:

This hub has five Input pins; each uses its input bitmap in a specific way. The following list explains what each of these input pins do:

- **Brush**: This is the brush used to draw the shape. This image is going to be repeated along the path.
- **Scale Map**: This is the bitmap that the Shape Draw hub uses to control the scale of the brushes drawn.
- **Rotation Map**: This is the bitmap that the Shape Draw hub uses to control the rotation of the brushes drawn.
- **Offset Map**: This is the bitmap that the Shape Draw hub uses to control the offset of the brushes drawn. This moves the brushes vertically and horizontally.
- **Opacity Map**: This is the bitmap that the Shape Draw hub uses to control the opacity of the brushes drawn.

The Shape Draw hub's parameters are separated into five different tabs that correspond to similar functions. The first tab is the **Output** tab and it controls the dimensions and background color of the output.

- **Dynamic size**: Sets the size to be the same as the canvas.
- **Background color**: Sets the color of the background.
- **Background Alpha**: Sets the transparency of the background.

The second tab is the **Brush** tab. The parameters here control attributes of the brush as it is draw along the path that is set in the **Shape** tab.

- **Start/End Scale**: Controls the scale of the brush on the beginning and on the end of the path. The check box locks the two sliders together.
- **Start/End Rotation**: Controls the starting and ending rotation of the brush.
- **Start/End Opacity**: Controls the starting and ending opacity of the brush.
- **Opacity Levels**: Selects how many levels of opacity you want the brush to have.
- **Orient To Path**: When this option is enabled, the rotation of the brush is matched with the direction of the path. When it is disabled, the brush keeps its original rotation.
- **Center Horizontal/Vertical Offset**: Sets the center point that is used for the draw position of the brush. The **Shape** tab controls what shape of the path and adjusts its properties.

- **Shape**: Sets the shape of the path the brush is drawn along. Possible options are Circle, Line, Square, Spiral, Curve, Fractal Path, and Drawn path.
- **Horizontal/Vertical Position**: Sets the position of the drawn shape on the canvas.
- **Horizontal/Vertical Scale**: Sets the scale of the drawn shape in both directions. Check box locks the sliders together.
- **Rotation**: Sets the rotation of the drawn shape.

Each shape has specific parameters that can alter their properties.

- **Circle**: Creates a circular or elliptical path.
  - **Revolutions**: Sets the number of times the shape is drawn along the circle.
- **Line**: Creates a straight path.
- **Square**: Creates a square or rectangular path
- **Spiral**: Creates a spiral path that moves out from a center point.
  - **Spiral Grow Factor**: Sets the distance between each of the spirals' rotations, progressively.
  - **Spiral Length Factor**: Sets the value that increases the distance between each brush in the spiral.
  - **Spiral Point Count**: Sets the length of the spiral.
- **Curve**: Create a curved line similar to a Bézire curve (see Chapter 4 for more information on Bézier curves).
  - **Left Tangent Offset**: Sets the distance of the tangent that defines the beginning of the curve from the curve itself.
  - **Right Tangent Offset**: Sets the distance of the tangent that defines the beginning of the curve from the curve itself.
- **Fractal Path**: Creates a random distorted path.
  - **Resolution**: Sets the level of detail of the fractal path.
  - **Distortion Factor**: Sets the level of distortion applied to the fractal path.
  - **Random Seed**: Random number used to initialize the render.
- **Drawn Path**: Creates a path based on a user drawn path. With this shape a drawing area will appear under the shape menu, this is where you can draw your path for the brushes to follow.

The **Drawing** tab controls various parameters that control the interaction between the brushes and the path.

- **Drawing Order**: Sets the order in which the hub lays the brush. Start-to-end and end-to-etart are opposites. Random sets the brush randomly with no specific order.
- **Drawing Mode**: Sets the Blend Mode used for the brush when it's drawn on the hub.
- **Spacing**: Sets the spacing between each individual brush. Setting the spacing to be very close increases the render time dramatically.
- **Drawing Start Position**: Sets where along the path the brushes start drawing.
- **Delta Rotation**: Rotates the brush incrementally. Basically, each successively drawn brush is rotated by this percentage.
- **Perpendicular Offset Jaggedness**: Randomly increases the distance of the brush from the path.
- **Offset Jaggedness**: Randomly moves and offsets some brushes.
- **Scaling Jaggedness**: Randomly scales some brushes up and down.

- **Rotation Jaggedness**: Randomly rotates some brushes.
- **Opacity Jaggedness**: Randomly changes the opacity of some brushes.
- **Random Seed**: Number used to calculate the random factor of the previous parameters.

The **Maps** tab this is where the control parameters for the various input bitmaps are set. Each of the different map controls has an **Input Line** parameter. The information passed to the Shape Draw hub from the input maps is only taken from one-pixel horizontal row. The **Input Line** parameter controls where vertically from the input bitmap the horizontal row is sampled.

- **Offset Source**: Sets which channel provides the map information.
- **Minimum/Maximum Perpendicular Offset**: Sets the range of the offset.
- **Position Source**: Sets which channel provides the map information.
- **Minimum/Maximum Position Offset**: Sets the range of the position offset.
- **Scaling Source**: Sets which channel provides the map information.
- **Minimum/Maximum Scaling Offset**: Sets the range of the brush's scaling.
- **Rotation Source**: Sets which channel provides the map information.
- **Minimum/Maximum Rotation Offset**: Sets the range of the rotation applied to the brush.
- **Opacity Source**: Sets which channel provides the map information.
- **Minimum/Maximum Opacity Offset**: Sets the range of the opacity.

4. Create some shading on the blade of grass. Drag a Glow hub from the **Effects** sidebar and connect it in between the Shape Draw and Canvas hubs. First, check the **Inner Glow** check box to make the glow radiate in to the center of the shape. Then, set the **Glow Color** to a dark green (#3300) and set the **Horizontal** and **Vertical Blur Radius** to 3.5 (see Figure 6-55). It gives a darker edge on the grass blade that fades to the lighter green in the center.

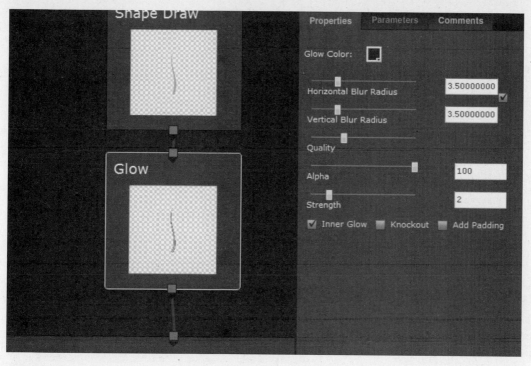

Figure 6-55. Use a Glow hub to add shading to the grass object.

5. Use a Color Bounds hub to automatically remove the extraneous space around the grass blade. Drag a Color Bounds hub from the **Effects** sidebar and connect it in between the Glow and Canvas hubs. The Color Bounds hub finds specified pixels in an image and performs various functions based on those pixels. Check the **Crop Input** function this crops the output of the hub determined by the color specified. You want to select the background color in this case transparent and tell the hub to remove it. Then, double-click **the Detect Color box** to open the **Color Picker**, and set the **Alpha** to 0. Finally, uncheck the **Find Color** option to crop the output and all the extraneous transparent pixels (see Figure 6-56). The **Find Color** option does not remove the **Detect Color,** but is used in the Blackbox files.

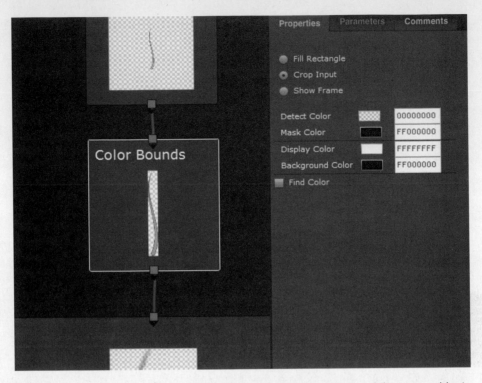

Figure 6-56. Use a Color Bounds hub to remove the extraneous space around the grass object.

Figure 6-57. The Color Bounds hub can be used to auto crop an image.

The Color Bounds hub performs various functions on the input image based on the boundaries set by a specific color. All colors can be set with the Color Picker or the RGBA Hexadecimal color code. Following is a list of the parameters for the Color Bounds hub.

- **Fill Rectangle:** Draws a rectangle that covers all of the colors specified by the **Detect Color** setting.
- **Crop Input:** Crops the image to the color set by the **Detect Color** setting (see Figure 6-57).

- **Show Frame:** Draws a rectangle that encloses all the color specified by the **Detect Color** setting.
- **Detect Color:** Sets the color that the hub uses to determine the bounds of the effect.
- **Mask Color:** Sets the color that the hub uses to set the mask colors.
- **Display Color:** This sets the color of the rectangle when the **Fill Rectangle** option is enabled or frame color when the **Show Frame** option is enabled.
- **Background Color:** Sets the background color when the **Fill Rectangle** option is enabled.
- **Find Color:** Sets whether the bounds will include the **Detect Color** or exclude the **Detect Color**.

6. Add a shadow to the grass blade to help separate the individual blades after the AutoPainter copies them. Drag a Drop Shadow hub from the **Effects** sidebar and connect it between the Color Bounds and Canvas hubs. Set the **Horizontal** and **Vertical Blur Radius** to 14, the **Distance** to 25, and the **Strength** to 1.5. Notice that because you have a fairly large distance setting for the drop shadow that it is getting cut off by the boundary of the hub. To fix this, check the **Add Padding** option (see Figure 6-58). This expands the dimension of the hub so it includes the entire drop shadow. This is a handy option and can save you from adding several Transformer and Crop hubs.

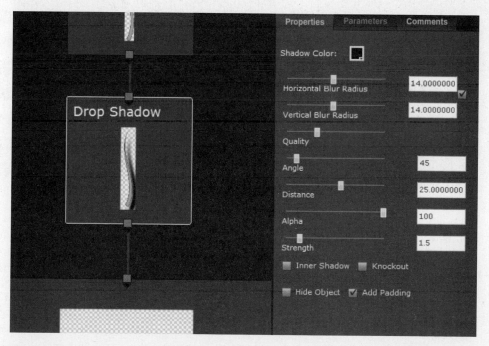

Figure 6-58. Add a Drop Shadow to the grass object to help separate them when copied.

413

7. To do the heavy work of copying and positioning the blades of grass, add an AutoPainter hub from the `Generators` sidebar in between the Drop Shadow and the Canvas hubs. In the `Output` tab, set the `Background Alpha` to 0 to remove the default black background. Next, switch to the `Painting` tab, set the `Horizontal Order` to `Inside Out` and the `Vertical Order` to `Top to Bottom`. The `Order` settings define in what order the objects are drawn on the canvas. In this file, the horizontal objects are drawn in the center and move outwards, whereas the vertical objects start at the top and move toward the bottom. The reason that it is done this way is to give the impression of the grass growing up from the canvas; having no order would produce a look of grass piled haphazardly on top of the canvas. While still in the Painting tab, set the `Horizontal Spacing` to 8, the `Vertical Spacing` to 12, and the `Horizontal Padding` and `Vertical Padding` to 40. The `Spacing` settings set the distance between the blades of grass, and the `Padding` settings take the grass to the edges of the hub (see Figure 6-59).

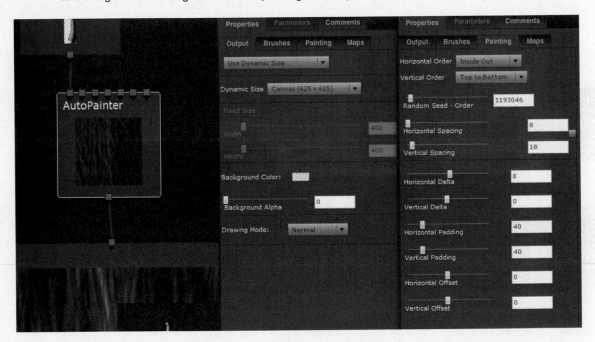

Figure 6-59. An AutoPainter hub fills the canvas with the grass object.

8. Set the rest of the parameters to complete the effect. Switch to the Maps tab to give the grass some variety, set the `Minimum` and `Maximum Horizontal Offset` values to 200 and −200, respectively. This randomly moves the grass 200 pixels horizontally. Next, set the `Minimum`value and `Maximum Vertical Offset` values to 20 and −20, respectively. This randomly moves the grass 20 pixels vertically. Then, set the `Minimum Scale` to 70, `Maximum Scale` to 140, sizing the grass randomly from 70% to 140%. Finally, set `Minimum Rotation` to −15 and set the `Maximum Rotation` to −15. This randomly rotates the grass 30 degrees and gives the grass some varied sizes; positions, rotations, and a more natural look (see Figure 6-60).

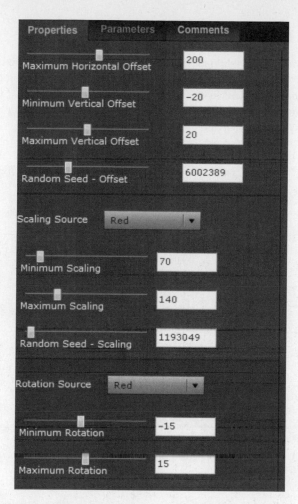

Figure 6-60. The Maps tab on the AutoPainter hub

Project 6.7—Camouflage Texture

Peacock can be used to create graphic patterns. These patterns can range from simple (such as a retro striped pattern) to complex (such as a camouflage texture like the one in this project). Though this pattern might look complex, it is easy and fast to construct in Peacock. In this project, you use the Perlin Noise hub to create organic shapes, and then you use the Threshold hub to carve out and color portions of the shape. Finally, you will layer and color them to produce a camouflage pattern. See Figure 6-61 for the resulting texture and Figure 6-62 for the hub layout made in this project.

Figure 6-61. The final result is a camouflage pattern that can be tiled.

Key hubs used in this project

- Perlin Noise hub
- Threshold hub
- Color Field hub

> *Find this file online at*
> *http://aviary.com/artists/gettingstartED/creations/chapter_6_project_7.*

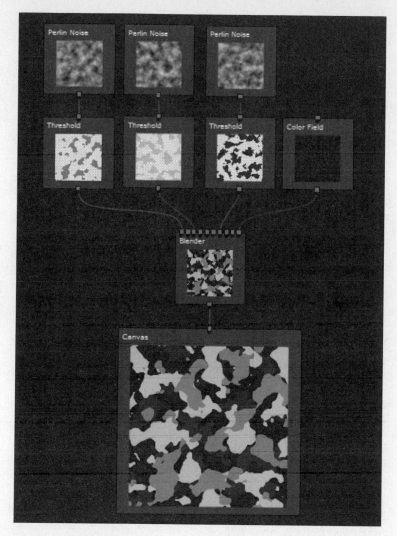

Figure 6-62. The hub layout for this file

1. Use a series of Perlin Noise hubs to create the base for the camouflage pattern. Launch the Peacock file and drag a Perlin Noise hub from the **Generators** sidebar onto the workspace. The hub automatically connects with the Canvas because it is the first hub added in the file. Set the **Horizontal Scale** and **Vertical Scale** to 0.15. Check the **Stitch** parameter, which makes the Perlin Noise tillable (see Figure 6-63).

417

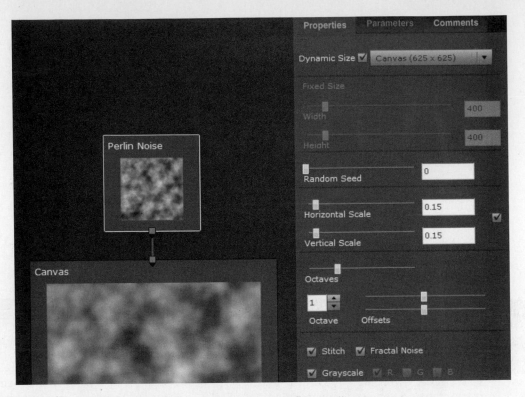

Figure 6-63. Perlin Noise is used as the base of the camouflage pattern.

2. Carve the camouflage shapes out of the Perlin Noise hub with the Threshold hub. Drag out a Threshold hub from the **Effects** sidebar and add it in between the Perlin Noise and the Canvas hubs. Adjust the **Threshold** parameter until you get a shape that resembles the basic shapes in camouflage; in this example, it is set to 110. Next, set both the **Foreground** and **Background** to a bright blue color and the **Foreground Alpha** to 0. If you left the **Foreground** at its default white color, you get a slight halo around the shape, which is the reason to set both the **Foreground** and **Background** colors the same. Finally, set the **Smoothing** parameter to 1.5 to smooth the edges of the shapes (see Figure 6-64).

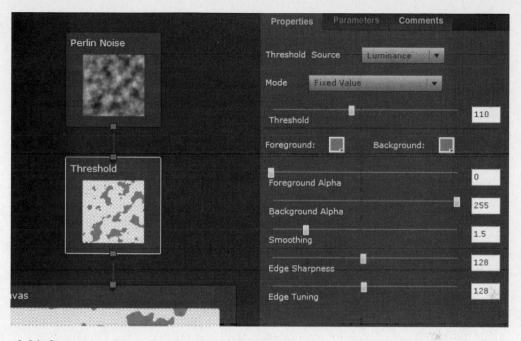

Figure 6-64. Carve out colored shapes with the Threshold hub.

3. Add a Blender so you can layer several duplicated effect chains. Drag a Blender hub from the **Controllers** sidebar and connect it in between the Threshold and the Canvas hubs (see Figure 6-65).

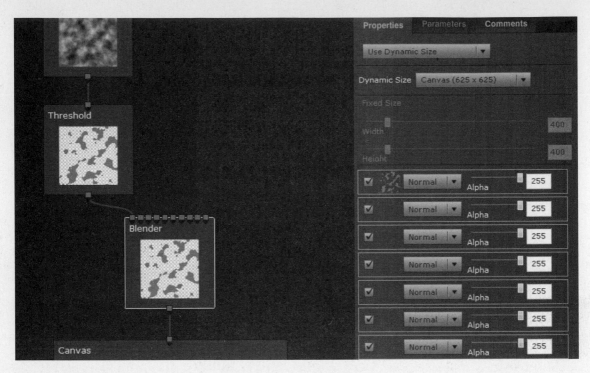

Figure 6-65. Add a Blender hub so that you can build more shapes.

4. Duplicate the Perlin Noise and the Threshold hubs to quickly create more camouflage shapes. Select both the Perlin Noise and Threshold hubs by holding down the Shift key while clicking on them. You know that they are both selected if there is a white highlight around each hub. Next, select `Edit ➤ Duplicate or use the` keyboard shortcut Ctrl+D (command+D on the Mac). The two hubs and their parameter settings are be copied. Drag these two new hubs over to the right of the first two and make sure the duplicated Perlin Noise hub is connected into the duplicated Threshold hub. Then, connect them both into the Blenders second or third Input pin. Select the duplicated Perlin Noise hub and drag the `Random Seed` slider to change the pattern in the noise (see Figure 6-66). This produces a new pattern in the hub; you can continue to adjust this until you get shapes that you like. Next, select the Threshold hub and set the `Foreground` and `Background` color to a lighter blue than the previous pattern. Be sure the `Foreground Alpha` is still set at 0.

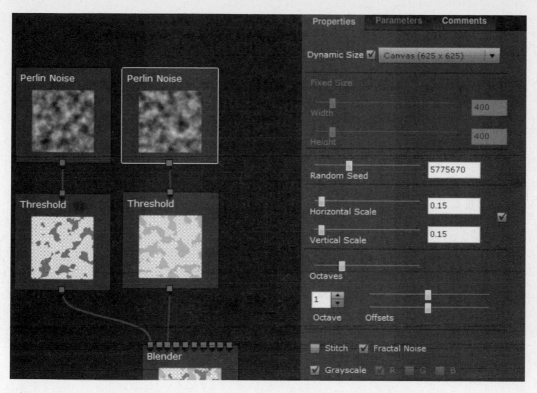

Figure 6-66. Copy and adjust the Perlin Noise and Threshold hubs to save time.

5. Repeat the process from step 4. Duplicating the Perlin Noise and Threshold hubs and connecting them to the Blender uses the sixth or seventh Input pin. Adjust the **Random Seed** parameter in the Perlin Noise to change the pattern a third time. Finally, select the Threshold and set the **Foreground** and **Background** color to a dark blue, making sure that the **Foreground Alpha** is set to 0 (see Figure 6-67).

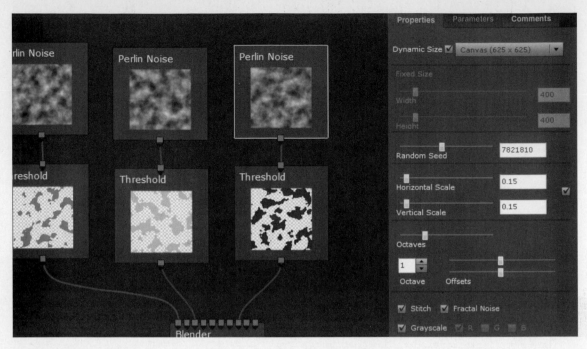

Figure 6-67. Repeat the steps to make a third set of camouflage shapes.

6. You have a two-color camouflage pattern, but there are still holes that show. At this stage, you can do one of two things. First, you can select the canvas and set the Background Color to a medium blue. This fills in the empty space around the camouflage shapes. Or, you can use a Color Field hub attached to the last Input pin on the Blender to fill the background. There isn't an advantage or disadvantage to either method for this file because you are just filling the background with color. Use the Color Field so that you can see how to use the hub. Drag a Color Field hub from the **Generators** sidebar and connect it to the last Input pin on the Blender hub. Set the color of the hub to a medium blue (see Figure 6-68).

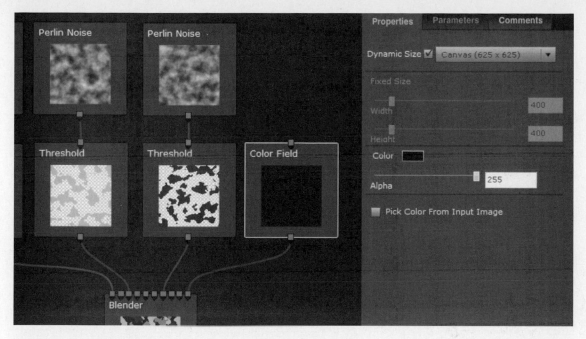

Figure 6-68. Use a Color Field to fill in the background.

Figure 6-69. The Color Field hub fills an area of similar pixels with a single color.

The Color Field hub fills the entire canvas with a single color (see Figure 6-69). This hub is good to use for backgrounds or color toning overlays. The hub can be used to sample a color from an input image as its fill color. Following are the parameters for the Color Field hub.

- **Dynamic Size:** Uses a custom size or canvas for sizing a hub.
- **Fixed Size:** If the **Dynamic Size** option is turned off, then the hub size can be set by Width and Height sliders.
- **Color:** Sets the fill color.

423

- **Alpha:** Sets the **Alpha** of a fill color.
- **Pick Color from Input Image:** Uses a sampled pixel from an input image for the fill color.
- The section that follows is shown only when the **Pick Color from Input** option is enabled.
- **Show Source + Crossbars:** This option displays the input image in the hub and draws a set of cross bars showing the color that gets sampled by the Color Field hub.
- **X Position (%):** Sets the X position of the sampled pixel.
- **Y Position (%):** Sets the Y position of the sampled pixel.
- **Capture Mouse Coordinates:** Uses mouse input to set the sample pixel.
- **Smoothing:** Performs a smoothing operation on the input image before it is sampled.

Project 6.8—Create a Seamless Tile from Any Texture

Peacock is well suited for creating seamless textures and tiles. A **seamless tile** is an image that if copied and placed end to end and or side by side, the texture continues without any disruption to the pattern. In this project, you learn how to create seamless tiles from an image. Any of the previous texture projects can be made seamless with this method. This technique works great with photographic images, but not so well with vector or sharp graphic images. This is due to the way that the Seamless hub creates these tiles. The Seamless hub takes a portion of the image from one side and overlays and blends it on the opposite side. This makes the edges line up when tiled. See Figure 6-70 for the resulting image and Figure 6-71 for the hub layout for this project.

Figure 6-70. This is the final image you will make in this project.

Key hubs used in this project

- Resource hub
- Seamless hub
- Tile hub
- Repeat hub

Find this file online at
http://aviary.com/artists/gettingstartED/creations/chapter_6_project_8.

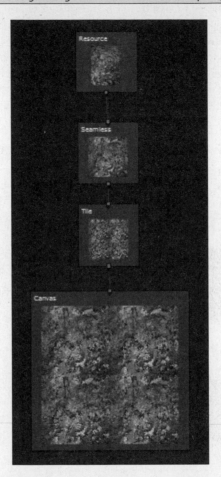

Figure 6-71. The final layout for a seamless tile

1. Pick an image that you would like to make into a seamless tile. Launch Peacock and import an image you want to make seamless. Use the `File` ➤ `Import Resource` command to open the `Resource Browser`. Navigate to the image you want to import, and then click `OK`. Next, open the `Resources` sidebar and drag the imported resource onto the workspace (see Figure 6-72). It automatically connects to the Canvas hub because it is the first hub introduced to the file.

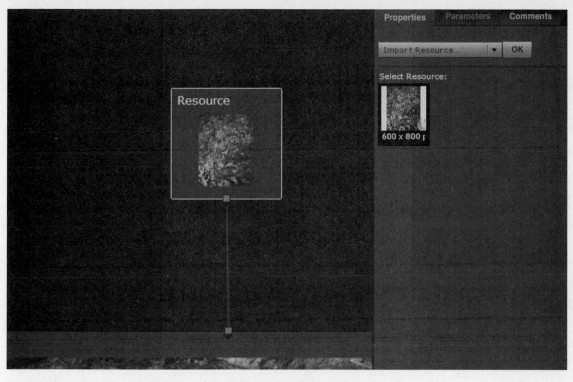

Figure 6-72. Import the image you want to make seamless.

2. Now, you create a tillable image with the Seamless hub. Drag a Seamless hub from the `Effects` sidebar and connect it between the Resource and Canvas hubs. The Seamless hub copies a portion of the edges, pastes them to the opposite sides, and blends them with the image. This ultimately shrinks the size of the output image. Experiment with the `Horizontal Blend` and `Vertical Blend` so that you get a good mix of the original image and the blended edges. In this particular file, the `Horizontal Blend` is set at 32 and the `Vertical Blend` at 73 (see Figure 6-73).

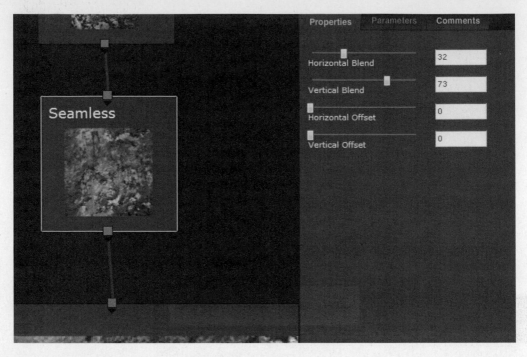

Figure 6-73. The Seamless hub makes the texture tillable.

Figure 6-74. The Seamless hub creates tillable images.

The Seamless hub creates seamless edges on an image to make it tillable (see Figure 6-74). The way that the hub produces a seamless edge is by copying a portion of one edge and moving to the opposite edge. The copied portion is overlapped and the inside edges are faded to help blend it. This shrinks the output dimensions of the hub because of this overlapping. Following are the parameters for this hub.

- **Horizontal / Vertical Blend:** Sets the amount of area used in the blend to create the seamless tile.
- **Horizontal / Vertical Offset:** Sets the amount of offset of the seamless hub.

3. The Tile hub repeats the input image in several different ways. Add a Tile hub from the **Effects** sidebar and connect it in between the Seamless and Canvas hubs. The default property of the Tile hub mirrors the input image horizontally and vertically. This means a copy of the image is flipped horizontally and placed to the right side of the image. Then, those two tiles are flipped vertically and placed below the first two (see Figure 6-75). At the bottom of the Properties panel for the Tile hub, uncheck the two mirror properties: Horizontal and Vertical. This makes the tiles output only one tile, so it looks exactly like the Seamless hub's output. You need to increase the number of times this image is tiled. Set the **Horizontal** and **Vertical Tile** parameter to 2 to increase the number of times the input image is repeated in the respected direction (see Figure 6-76). Alternatively, you can use the Repeat hub to achieve a similar effect. The Repeat hub is much quicker, but it has a few options to adjust the tile patterning.

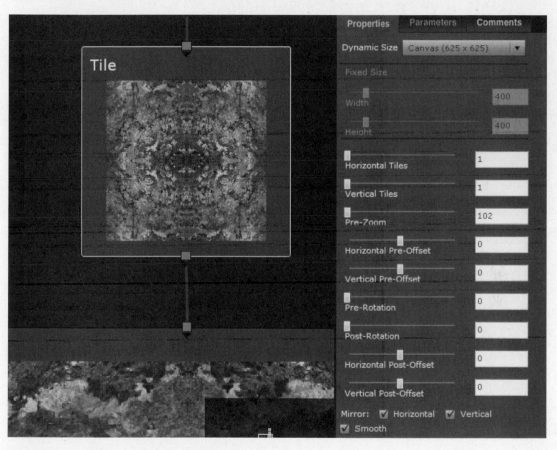

Figure 6-75. The default state of the Tile hub

429

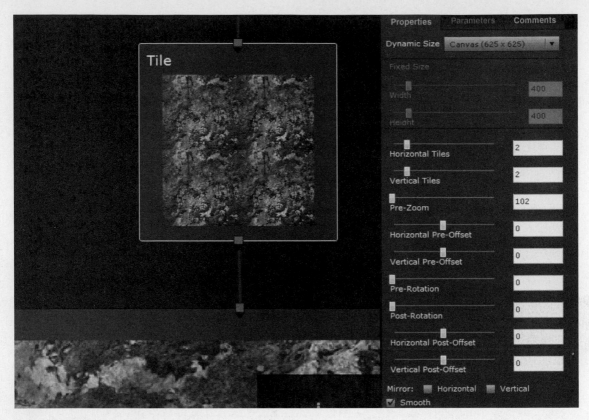

Figure 6-76. Multiple tiles without mirroring

Figure 6-77. The Tile hub creates a repeated image based on the input.

The Tile hub can create various tiled patterns. This hub will use the input image as a tile and repeat it in a variety of layouts. The tiles can be positioned scaled and rotated before and after the tiling process. Below are the parameters for the Tile hub.

- **Horizontal / Vertical Tiles**: Sets the number of times to repeat the input image horizontally and vertically (see Figure 6-77).
- **Pre-Zoom**: Zooms the image before applying the tile effect.
- **Horizontal / Vertical Pre-Offset**: Offsets the input image before applying the tiling effect.
- **Pre-Rotation**: Rotates the input image before applying the tiling effect.
- **Post-Rotation**: Rotates the tile after applying the effect.
- **Horizontal / Vertical Post-Offset**: Offsets the tile after applying the effect.
- **Mirror Horizontal**: Flips and tiles the image horizontally (see Figure 6-78).
- **Mirror Vertical**: Flips and tiles the image vertically (see Figure 6-78).
- **Smooth**: Performs a smoothing process to the image before applying the tiling effect.

Mirror Horizontally   **Mirror Vertically**   **Mirror Horizontally & Vertically**

Figure 6-78. The mirror parameter flips and tiles the image.

431

Project 6.9—Create a Smoke / Cloud Generator

The Shape Draw hub has an interesting feature that enables you to draw the path that you want he brushes to follow. This enables you to create several interesting and interactive effects. In this project, you will make a smoke / cloud effect brush. Of course, this is not a true brush like one you might have created in another graphic program, but it does simulate it. You can alter what brushes you use to create smoke and other various textures to produce different effects. Reduce the displacement and use a star shape to make fur or reduce the blur to make ice. Your imagination is the only limit of this effect, so experiment and explore. See Figure 6-79 for an example of the final results and Figure 6-80 for the hub layout created in this project.

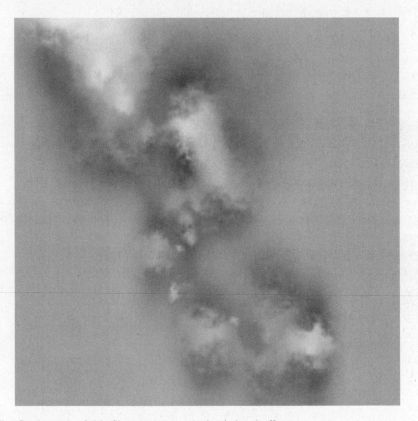

Figure 6-79. The final result of this file creates a smoke / cloud effect.

Key hubs used in this project

- Simple Shape hub
- Shape Draw hub
- Displacement Map hub
- Fractal Plasma hub

Find this file online at
http://aviary.com/artists/gettingstartED/creations/chapter_6_project_9.

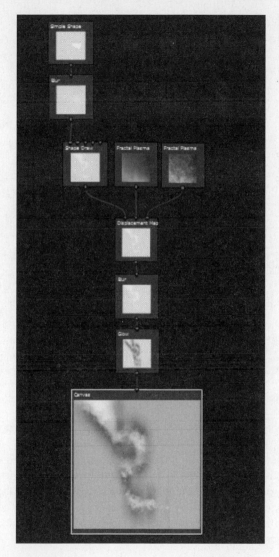

Figure 6-80. The hub layout for this file

1. Color the Canvas hub's background to resemble the sky. Launch Peacock, and select the Canvas hub to bring up its parameters in the **Properties** panel. Set the **Background Color** to a light sky blue color (# 67CFFF) by double-clicking the color box, and then choose the color with the **Color Picker** dialog. Finally, uncheck the **Adapt Display Size to the Input**

Bitmap parameter to see the blue color in the canvas (see Figure 6-81). This setting lets the canvas automatically resize itself to match the dimensions of the input.

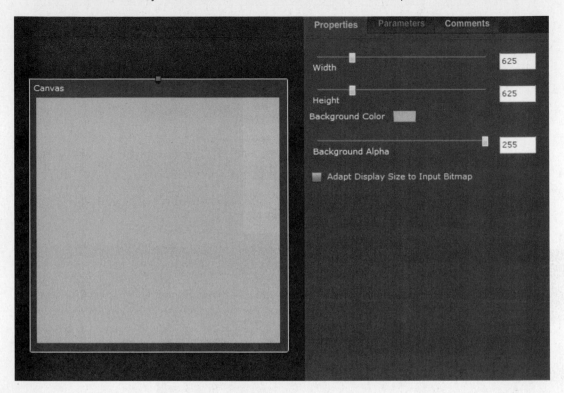

Figure 6-81. Set the Canvas hub's background color.

2. Create the base shape for the smoke with a Simple Shape hub. Drag a Simple Shape hub from the **Generators** sidebar to the workspace. It connects itself to the Canvas hub. For this file, you want to start with an offset irregular shape. The irregular shape gives some randomness to the smoke; the offset helps to randomize the placement of the smoke. Set the **Shape Type** to **Irregular Polygon**. Then, set the **Horizontal Center** to 20 and the **Horizontal Scale** and **Vertical Scale** to 35, making a small offset black polygon (see Figure 6-82). You can set the **Fill Color** of the shape to white at this time; however, for this example it is left black until later so you can see the steps better.

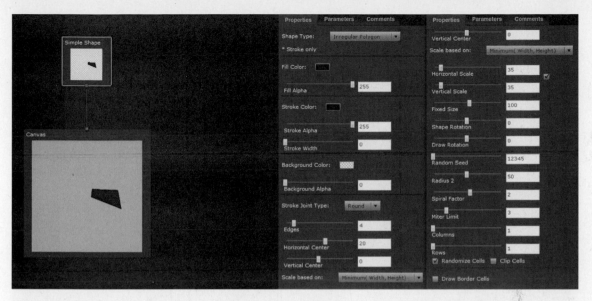

Figure 6-82. Set up an irregular shape as the base for the file.

3. Next, add a heavy blur to soften the shape. Drag a Blur hub from the **Effects** sidebar and connect it in between the Simple Shape and Canvas hubs. The idea is to create a fluffy base shape for the smoke / cloud effect, so set the **Horizontal Blur Radius** and **Vertical Blur Radius** to 190 (see Figure 6-83).

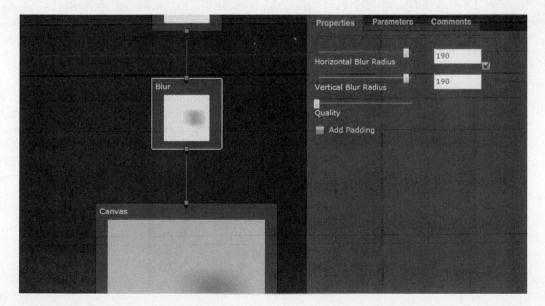

Figure 6-83. Add a heavy blur to the shape.

4. Add a Shape Draw hub to create the smoke shape, and then set the brush parameters. Drag a Shape Draw hub from the **Generators** sidebar and add it in between the Blur and Canvas hubs. First, set the **Background Alpha** to 0 in the **Output** tab to remove the default white background color. Uncheck the **Proportion Lock** option to the right of the **Start Scale** and **End Scale** sliders; this lets you set the Scale sliders differently. Set the **Start Scale** to 50, leaving the **End Scale** at 100. Finally, set the **Start Opacity** and **End Opacity** values to 50 (see Figure 6-84).

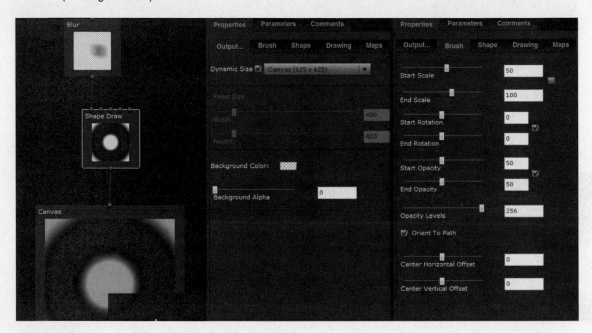

Figure 6-84. Shape Draw hub with drawn path option

5. Use the Drawn Path shape in the Shape Draw hub to create a custom path for the smoke. Set the **Shape** to **Drawn Path**, which opens an area under the parameter. Draw a line that you want the final smoke / cloud effect to take in this area. For this example, a squiggly, diagonal line was drawn, but you can draw any shape. Finally, in the **Drawing** tab, set the **Spacing** to 9, the **Delta Rotation** to 3, **Scaling Jaggedness** to 20, and **Rotation Jaggedness** to 20. The result is a fluffy, dark object that takes the shape of the Drawn Path (see Figure 6-85). Your image will look slightly different because your drawn path will be different than the one used in this example.

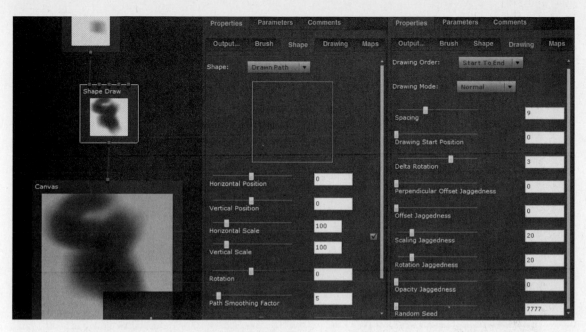

Figure 6-85. Draw a path for the brushes to follow.

6.   Next, you create a heavy distortion to the smoke with a Displacement Map hub. Drag a
     Displacement Map hub from the **Effects** sidebar and add it in between the Shape Draw and
     Canvas hubs. Make sure the Shape Draw hub is connected to the first Input pin on the
     Displacement Map hub. Leave this hub's parameters at the default settings. The Displacement
     Map moves pixels horizontally or vertically based on values form input bitmaps. This hub can be
     used to distort images like in this example. The Displacement Map hub needs to have at least
     one input image to make the effect work. Drag a Fractal Plasma hub from the **Generators**
     sidebar and connect it to the second Input pin on the Displacement Map hub; this is the
     Horizontal Displacement Bitmap. Set the **Roughness Factor** of the Fractal Plasma to
     0.45. The **Displacement Map** sifts the pixels horizontally based on the Fractal Plasma values
     (see Figure 6-86).

437

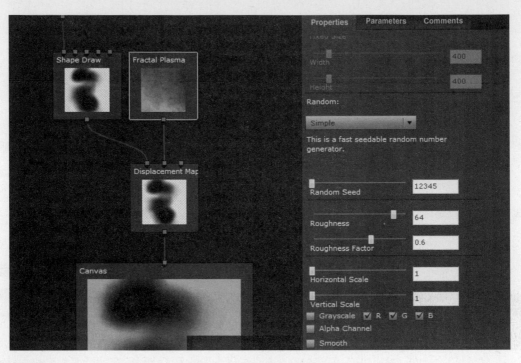

Figure 6-86. To create wispiness, use a Displacement Map hub.

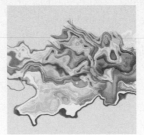

Figure 6-87. The Displacement Map hub shifts the pixels in an image based on values from horizontal and vertical input bitmaps.

The Displacement Map hub offsets the input image based off of input bitmaps. There are three Input pins on the hub. The first is the Input Bitmap; it is the image on which the displacement is performed. The second Input pin is the Horizontal Displacement Bitmap; the bitmap connected to this pin displaces the input bitmaps pixels horizontally based on its values. The third Input pin is the Vertical Displacement Bitmap; the bitmap connected to this pin displaces the input bitmaps pixels vertically based on its values.

- **Horizontal / Vertical Source** : Selects the source channel used for the displacement. When using colored images, you can try any of the colors for different results. With grayscale images, any of the color channels do the same. The best to use in this case is luminance. Alpha uses the alpha source (if any) and has the same effect as disconnecting the hub.
- **Horizontal/Vertical Fit**: Fits the input displacement bitmaps to fit the current hub size (if they are bigger or smaller). Scale to Fit fits the bitmap perfectly on the hub, and Scale Proportions scales it proportionally.
- **Horizontal/Vertical Displacement**: Sets the amount of displacement in each direction. The check box enables or disables proportional scaling (the two sliders at the same time or just one).
- **Edge mode:** Sets how the hub handles the edge pixels that are displaced by the effect.
  - **Clamp:** The pixels are clamped to the edge and stretched until they reach the displaced area.
  - **Wrap:** The displaced pixels are wrapped to the opposite edge of the hub.
  - **Replacement Color:** Fills the empty area where edge pixels are displaced.
  - **Ignore:-** No alterations to the displaced edge pixels.
- **Replacement Color:** Sets the replacement color when the **Edge Mode** is set to Replacement Color.
- **Replacement Alpha:** Sets the transparency of the replacement color when the Edge Mode is set to Replacement Color.
- **Iteration:** Sets how many times the displacement filter is applied. This multiplies the displacement.

7. Add a second Fractal Plasma to the Displacement Map to shift the pixels of the smoke even more. Drag another Fractal Plasma from the **Effects** sidebar and connect it to the last Input pin on the Displacement Map hub. Set this new Fractal Plasma hub's **Roughness Factor** to 0.8. This completes the displacement effect and creates puffy smoke shapes. You can also move the **Random Seed** slider to create new random plasma; this helps keep the smoke from getting a repeating pattern (see Figure 6-88).

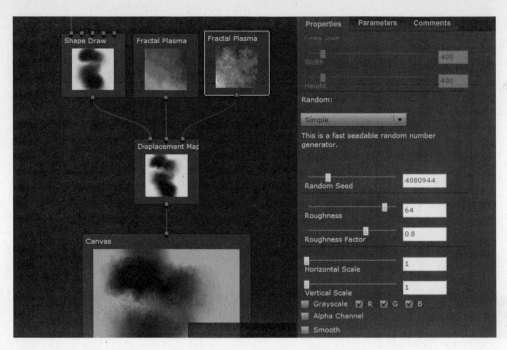

Figure 6-88. Add a second Fractal Plasma to the Displacement Map hub.

8. The displacement effect left some hard edges that might detract from the smoke, so you can add a slight blur to smooth them out. Drag a second Blur hub from the **Effects** sidebar and connect it in between the Displacement Map and the Canvas hubs. Set the **Horizontal** and **Vertical Blur Radius** to 2 and the quality to its maximum setting. The result is a slight softening of the edges created in the previous step. You can increase the blur radius if you would like a softer smoke (see Figure 6-89).

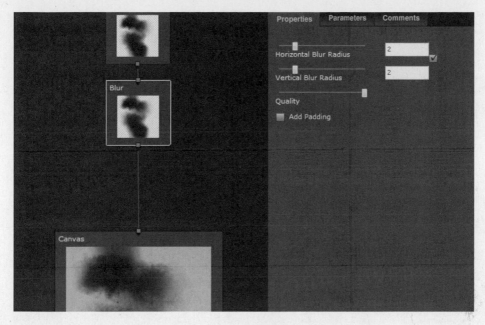

Figure 6-89. Soften the edges of the displacement effect with another Blur hub.

9. At this point, you can change the color of the smoke. Select the Simple Shape hub that the file was started with and set the **Fill Color** to white (see Figure 6-90). The smoke color changes to white. You can play with different colors to create interesting smoke, mist, or cloud shapes. The Canvas hub moves temporarily so you can see the results of the color change in it.

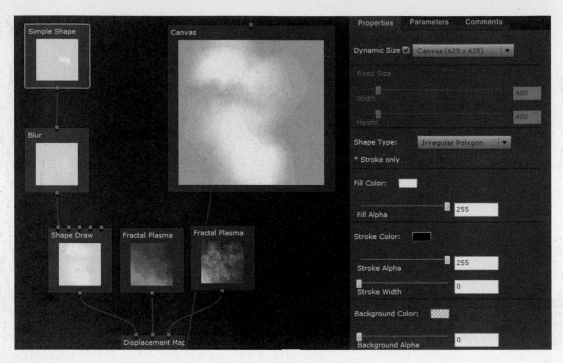

Figure 6-90. Set the Fill Color of the Simple Shape to white and change the color of the smoke.

10. Now, you add some depth to your smoke with a dark glow. Drag a Glow hub from the **Effects** sidebar and connect it in between the second Blur and the Canvas hub. Set the **Glow Color** to dark gray (#354854), the **Vertical Blur Radius** to 115, and the **Strength** to 1.5. This adds shading to the smoke and darkens the less opaque areas in the smoke (see Figure 6-91). Now that the smoke is finished, you can easily change its shape by drawing a new path in the Shape Draw hub. You can literally draw smoke into an image. Furthermore, you can change the color of the Simple Shape and the glow to give it a totally different look.

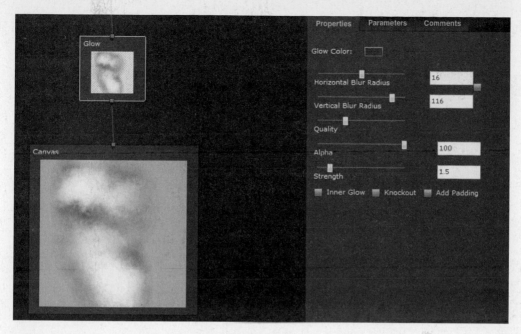

Figure 6-91. Use a dark colored Glow hub to give the smoke cloud some dimension.

Chapter Review

In this chapter, you saw how you can make a variety of textures using Peacock. Man-made, natural, and even graphic textures are in reach with this application. In the first texture, you saw how you can layer gradient and noise to create a brushed metal effect; however, add a Polar Tiling hub and it turns into a more dynamic texture. With the second texture, you explored how to layer shapes to create beveling effects that impart a machine-made feel. The Repeat hub enables you to tile and rotate the shapes to create a techno texture. You found how you can easily make a wood texture with the Plaid hub and its distortion parameter. Next, you learned how you could use a little known feature of the Stippling hub to create a crackling texture. The Color Remapper enabled you to create an intricate coloring of the pattern. You also learned how to use the Emboss feature of the complicated Convolution hub to create a stone texture. In the next project, you saw how the normally difficult task of creating a grass texture is easy with the Shape Draw and AutoPainter hubs. You saw that Peacock can also make graphic patterns with ease as you made a camouflage pattern. Then, you learned how to take any image into a seamless texture and how to use the tile hub to tile the results making a textured fill. Finally, you learned how to create a customizable smoke effect.

Peacock has over 60 hubs to create images. The projects in this chapter covered just a few of the most used hubs. Experiment, explore, and enjoy this incredible application. In the next chapter, you are introduced to Aviary's color palette creator application, Toucan. You will see how to find, organize, and export sets of colors for use in the other Aviary applications. You learn how to use color formulas to build harmonious color schemes and how to sample colors directly from imported images. Toucan shows you how colors interact and relate to each other.

Chapter 7

Selecting and Managing Colors with Toucan

From unifying colors in web pages to setting images up for print, color is an important aspect of design. Color is an often-overlooked aspect of image creation, but the proper use of colors can make an average image into a masterpiece. Color schemes can evoke different emotions and reactions. A splatter of red on an image can conjure thoughts of anger or rage, whereas the same splatter colored light blue can create a soothing peaceful feeling. Color is the first feature in an image that you notice, and then you notice the subject and details. You can easily pick out images that have captivating colors; you get an immediate reaction to them. This demonstrates the importance of well chosen and implemented colors. However, attention to color is usually neglected in images for various reasons. How can you tell how different colors interact with each other? How do you keep track of the colors used in an image? After you compile a set of colors, how do you use them in other applications? These are all easy with Aviary's color palette creator, Toucan. In this chapter, you learn how to use Toucan to construct color palettes that can be used in other Aviary tools. You see how to organize color schemes, explore harmonies, and create unify schemes to be used throughout images and applications.

Toucan Overview

Toucan is an application dedicated to creating color palettes. It is more advanced than the `Color Picker` that is used inside the application, but has most of the same features. Toucan is designed to give you advanced tools to organize and create color palettes for your images. It gives you many different ways to choose, sample, or set colors, and it makes it easy to manage them. A color palette is a set of colors that can be saved and used again. Figure 7-1 shows an example of a 20-color palette. These color palettes can be accessed and used in the other Aviary applications. You explore just how that works and how useful it can be as you make your way through the chapter.

Figure 7-1. The color palette with 20 color wells

After you launch Toucan, you are presented with the palette builder's interface. The palette color wells are at the top of the interface. When the application is first opened, you have randomly generated colors in three color wells. The active color well is highlighted with a gray bar under it (see the right-most color in Figure 7-1), and any color selected in the application changes the color of the selected color well. At the top left, there are three application function buttons. **The New Document button** is used to reset the application to its default state. **The import Image button** is used to import images into Toucan, where colors can be sampled and added to your palette. The **Send Feedback** button **enables you to contact the developers directly about bugs or suggestions**. At the top right, four buttons control the palette's color wells. The **Invert Palette** button reverses the order that the colors appear in the palette. You can also manually drag the colors around to different color wells to organize them. The **Plus** and **Minus** buttons add or subtract colors from the palette. You can have as few as two and as many as 20 colors in a palette. Finally, the **Full Screen Preview** button opens the palette viewer, where you can see the current palette colors on different backgrounds. This enables you to see what your colors look like on a white, medium gray, or black background. You can then see if you need to alter any colors so they show up in your various images.

Along the right side of the application are a color chooser and several sliders for setting colors using different color spaces (see Figure 7-2). The color chooser area lets you pick a color's saturation and value visually. The base hue that is displayed can be changed with the slider below. Underneath this, a textbox displays the selected color's hexadecimal code, which is used in HTML, CSS, and other Internet-related projects. You can type in a color code to have it selected in the chooser. Below the color chooser, there are four different sets of sliders each corresponding to a different color space. You can set the color using any combination of these sliders or by typing in set values in the corresponding textboxes to the right of the sliders.

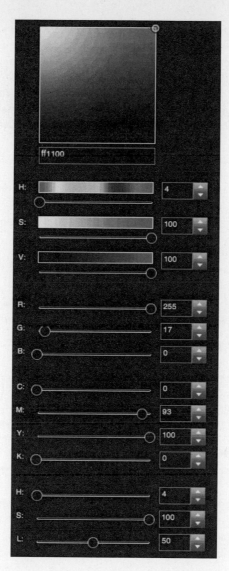

Figure 7-2. Color sliders sidebar

You can use four different color spaces when picking a color sample in Toucan. A **color space** is a way to map colors so they can be specified in a mathematical way. Most color spaces have three to four components that combine to identify a specific color, such as RGB or CMYK. Each color space produces a slightly different range of colors and each is suitable for different purposes. For example, CMYK is almost exclusively used in the print industry, whereas RGB is mainly used in digital graphics. The following is a list of the four color spaces in Toucan and the color components associated with each.

- **HSV** defines the color space by a combination of hue, saturation, and value.
  - `Hue`: The color of the selected sample.
  - `Saturation`: The intensity or amount of hue (color) of the sample.
  - `Value`: The lightness or darkness of the hue (color) of the sample.
- **RGB** defines the color space by a combination of red, green, and blue color values. This is an additive method used in computer screens and light projections.
  - `Red`: Controls the amount of red in the sample.
  - `Green`: Controls the amount of green in the sample.
  - `Blue`: Controls the amount of blue in the sample.
- **CMYK** defines the color space by a combination of cyan, magenta, yellow, and key color values. This is a subtractive method used in mixing paints and print processes.
  - `Cyan`: Controls the amount of cyan of the sample.
  - `Magenta`: Controls the amount of magenta of the sample.
  - `Yellow`: Controls the amount of yellow of the sample.
  - `Key (Black)`: Controls the amount of black of the sample.
- **HSL** defines the color space by a combination of hue, saturation, and lightness.
  - `Hue`: Controls the hue, which is the color of the selected sample.
  - `Saturation`: Controls the saturation of the current hue. **Saturation** is the intensity or amount of hue (color) of the sample.
  - `Lightness`: Controls the lightness of the current hue.

Next, look at the four main sections that take up the majority of the screen: `Color wheel`, `Clipboard`, `Image Picker`, and `Color deficiency preview`. Clicking the title bars of any of the sections expands and shows its parameters. The `Color Wheel` is by default opened and shows a large multi-colored circle on the screen (see Figure 7-3). This is where the main color sample is selected. The main selected color is shown on the color wheel by a large circle icon and subordinate colors are represented by smaller circle icons. There can be different amounts of subordinate colors depending on the `Params` setting. By default, there can be only two subordinate colors. Directly underneath the color wheel is the `Black Amount` slider where the overall value of the color wheel's color is set. A setting of 100 produces no black in your sample, whereas a setting of 0 produces only black in the sample. To the right of the color wheel is the sample preview bar, which displays all the sampled colors. At the top is the main color sample, whereas the ones underneath are the subordinate colors generated according to the different color formulas set with the `Type` menu. There are two buttons beneath the preview bar. The first of the two buttons, `To palette` , adds all the current selected colors to the color wells in the palette at the top of the application. The second button, `To clipboard` , sends the current selected colors to the temporary holding area `Clipboard` under the Color Wheel. Finally, to the right is where the color selection function and parameters are set. Use the `Type` dropdown menu to set the color selection function. Again, this controls what subordinate colors are generated. The parameters for each type of color selection formula changes accordingly. See the sidebar for information on the different color formulas.

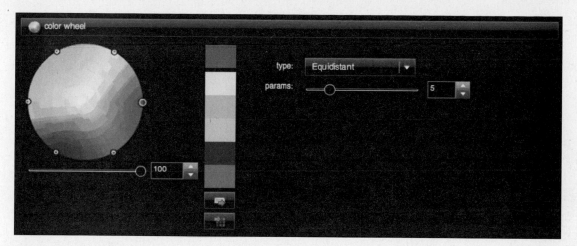

Figure 7-3. The color wheel picks several colors based on different color functions.

Toucan lets you automatically generate color schemes with various color formulas. These color formulas let you pick a base color and then find subordinate colors based on that base color. There are six different color formulas in Toucan, and each gives you different color schemes.

- In the Equidistant type (see Figure 7-4), the subordinate samples are spread equal distances around the circumference of the color wheel. It starts and ends at the main sample.
  - `Sample #`: Sets the amount of subordinate samples.

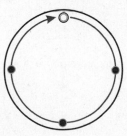

Figure 7-4. The Equidistant color formula

- In the Circular type (see Figure 7-5), the subordinate samples are spread in a circular direction from the main sample.
  - **Sample #**: Sets the number of subordinate samples.
  - **Sample °**: Sets the distance between samples in degrees based on the center of the color wheel.
  - **Sample S**: Sets the saturation of the subordinate samples. This does not affect the saturation of the main sample.
  - **Sample V**: Sets the value of the subordinate samples. This does not affect the saturation of the main sample.
  - **CW/CCW**: Sets the direction the subordinate samples spread from the main sample, CW = clockwise and CCW = Counter Clockwise.

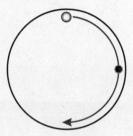

Figure 7-5. The Circular color formula

- In the Circular Proportional type (see Figure 7-6), the subordinate samples are spread to the center of the color wheel from the main sample.
  - **Sample #**: Sets the number of subordinate samples.
  - **Sample °**: Sets the distance between samples in degrees based on the center of the color wheel.
  - **Sample V**: Sets the value of the subordinate samples. This does not affect the saturation of the main sample.
  - **Pos/Neg**: Sets the orientation of the subordinate samples, pos = to the center of the color wheel and neg = away from the center based on the main sample.
  - **CW/CCW**: Sets the direction the subordinate samples spreads from the main sample, CW = clockwise and CCW = Counter Clockwise.

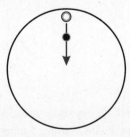

Figure 7-6. The Circular Proportional color formula

- In the Alternate type (see Figure 7-7), the subordinate samples are spread equal distances around the circumference of the color wheel. Every other subordinate sample is affected by the parameters.
  - `Sample #`: Sets the number of subordinate samples. It is constrained to only odd-numbered samples (1, 3, 5, and so on).
  - `Sample S`: Sets the saturation of the odd subordinate samples. This does not affect the saturation of the main sample and the even subordinate samples.
  - `Sample V`: Sets the value of the odd subordinate samples. This does not affect the value of the main sample and the even subordinate samples.

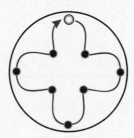

Figure 7-7. The Alternate color formula

- In the Opposite function (see Figure 7-8), the subordinate samples are set on the opposite side of the color wheel and radiate out in an alternating circular direction.
  - `Sample #`: Sets the number of subordinate samples.
  - `Sample A`: Sets the distance between samples in degrees base on the center of the color wheel.
  - `Sample S`: Sets the saturation of the subordinate samples. This does not affect the saturation of the main sample.
  - `Sample V`: Sets the value of the subordinate samples. This does not affect the saturation of the main sample.

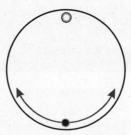

Figure 7-8. The Opposite color formula

- In the Deviance type (see Figure 7-9), the subordinate samples are set in a line from the edge to the center of the color wheel offset by the Sample ° amount.
  - `Sample #`: Sets the number of subordinate samples.
  - `Sample °`: Sets the angle of the subordinate samples based on main sample.

- **Sample V**: Sets the value of the subordinate samples. This does not affect the saturation of the main sample.

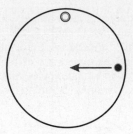

Figure 7-9. The Deviance color formula

The next section is **Clipboard**. The **Clipboard** area is a temporary place to store color samples (see Figure 7-10). You can drag colors to the **Clipboard** or send them with a click of the **To clipboard** button in the Color Wheel panel. The most recently added colors show in the last added area, whereas all colors saved to the clipboard show in the clipboard color area. The three sliders along the bottom let you filter the display range for hue, saturation, and value. Each slider has two circular control handles; one is used to set the start point and the other to set the end point of the filter. The checkboxes to the left of each slider reverse the selection range of the filter. The double-arrow button resets all the filter ranges.

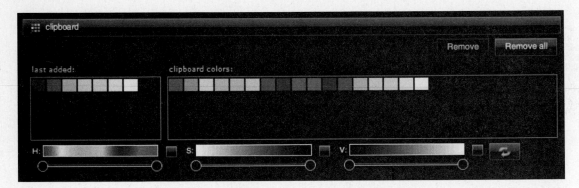

Figure 7-10. The Clipboard is used as a temporary holding area for color samples.

The next section is the **Image Picker**. This section lets you import an image and then take color samples directly (see Figure 7-11). Use the **Import Image** button at the top of the application or the button in the section itself to load an image for sampling. After an image is loaded into the Image Picker section, you are able to pick colors directly by clicking the image. Notice that the cursor change to an eyedropper, which shows you that you are sampling colors. Any color that is under the cursor is previewed in the **Color** box to the right of the image. Clicking the image pushes the sampled color to the selected color well in the palette. If you need a simplified version of the image to sample, use the `Pixel Width` slider to convert the image into larger color averaged tiles.

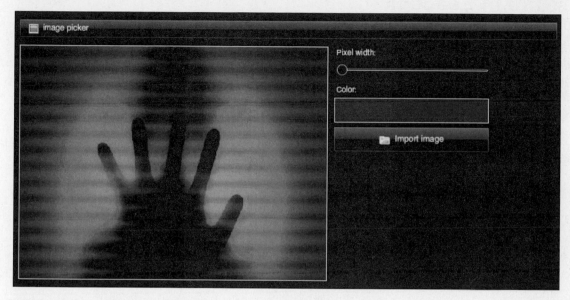

Figure 7-11. The Image Picker section

The `Color Deficiency Preview` displays the current color palette as seen by an observer with color deficiencies or color blindness (see Figure 7-12). You can choose different types of color deficiency filter from the box on the right. This does not change your palette in any way and is only a preview for color deficiencies. Therefore, you can make sure that if you're choosing colors for a website, you can be certain that visitors are still able to navigate the site if they have a color deficiency.

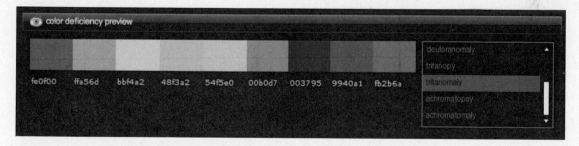

Figure 7-12. The color deficiency section

Project 7.1—Create a Color Palette for a Tie-Dye Texture in Peacock

Choosing colors can be a difficult aspect of creating an image. When buried in the midst of creating an image, you can lose sight of color interactions and end up with skewed and jarring colors. When creating images in the various Aviary applications, colors can be chosen with a Color Picker, but it only gives you a limited view of color interactions. You find that Toucan gives you more flexibility and power when picking colors. It lets you choose and fine tune colors with larger previews and fewer distractions. Additionally, Toucan has six different color formula functions that help you pick sets of colors. Using these functions, you can quickly generate and arrange harmonious color schemes. In this project, you use Toucan's color formula to create a rainbow color scheme, and then you use the palette in Peacock to create a tie-dyed color pattern. See Figure 7-13 for the final image made with this project.

Figure 7-13. This is the final image that you will make in this project.

Key features used in this project

- Adding color wells
- Using Color Wheel and formulas
- Import palette for use in Peacock

> *The color palette is available online at*
> *http://aviary.com/artists/gettingstartED/creations/chapter_7_project_1_colors.*
> *Find the file for this project online at*
> *http://aviary.com/artists/gettingstartED/creations/chapter_7_project_1.*

1. You create a color palette that starts with red then moves through the other colors. Launch Toucan and add five new color wells to the palette by clicking the **Add Color** button ⊕ at the top right five times (see Figure 7-14). You now have eight total color wells in your palette: the five you just added along with the three default color wells. The new color wells are set to the last selected color. If you find you have more than eight color wells, you can remove them with the **Remove Color** button ⊖ .

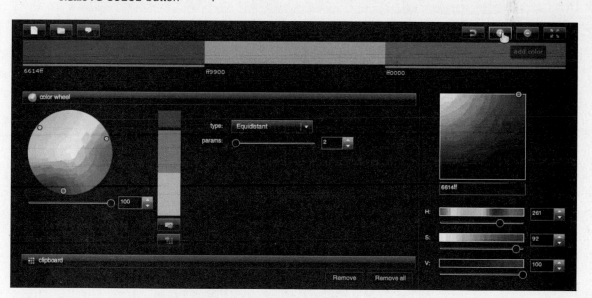

Figure 7-14. Add color wells to the palette.

2. Set up the color formula to pick the subordinate colors. Make sure that the **Equidistant** option is selected in the type dropdown menu. The **Equidistant** function picks subordinate colors equally spaced around the circumference of the color wheel. At the default setting, the function picks only two subordinate colors. To add more subordinate colors, set the **Params** slider to 7 (see Figure 7-15). Seven subordinate colors and one main color are enough to fill the eight color wells of the palette.

455

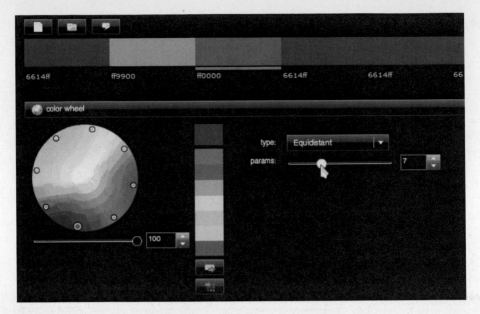

Figure 7-15. Set up the color function parameters.

3. Set the base color in the color wheel. Next, set the **Black Amount** slider just under the color well to 100 if it isn't already. Then, pick a bright red color at the right edge of the color wheel. The seven subordinate colors spread out equally around the wheel giving you a rainbow of colors (see Figure 7-16). The colors are shown to the right in the sample preview bar.

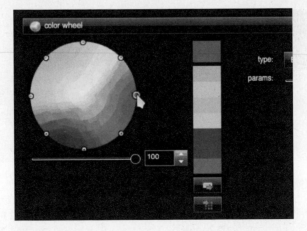

Figure 7-16. Set the main color.

4. Copy these colors to the palette. Press the **To palette** button directly under the sample preview bar (see Figure 7-17). This copies the sampled colors to the palette, filling the available

color wells. If there aren't enough color wells in the palette, it fills only the available ones in order from top to bottom and corresponding right to left in your color palette. At this point, you can fine-tune any of the colors from the palette by selecting the color and using the color wheel or sliders to make adjustments.

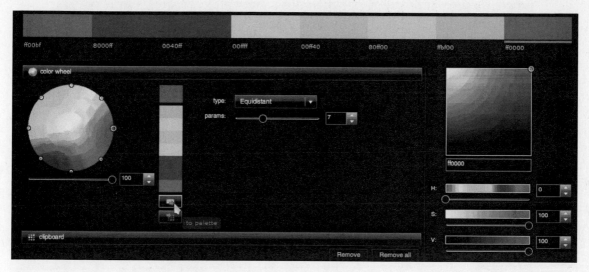

Figure 7-17. Copy the colors to the palette.

5. Save your color palette so that you can access it in the other Aviary applications. Click the `Save As` button in the blue Save bar at the top of the application. The `Save to Aviary` dialog slides open here, and you can name the file, add a description, add tags, and set permissions. The name is the only required field. Make sure you title your Toucan file something that you can remember and that is descriptive, so that others might be able to find the file after you have saved it (see Figure 7-18). It is good practice to add a description and tags to your file, so that you can find and use them later with the search function.

Figure 7-18. Save the color palette.

6. Use the color palette in the Peacock file. Launch Peacock and drag a Gradient hub from the **Generators sidebar** (see Figure 7-19). It automatically connects to the Canvas hub because it is the first hub introduced to a Peacock file.

Figure 7-19. Add a Gradient hub in a new Peacock file.

7. Import the palette you just created and use it to set the colors in the **Gradient** hub. Each color stop represents a color in the gradient, which is represented by the triangle-shaped icon. These color stops can be moved by dragging, added by double-clicking an empty area of the colorbar, or deleted by dragging them away from the colorbar. Double-click a color stop to open the **Color Picker**. Click the double arrow icon ⏩ at the bottom to open the **Toucan palette browser**. The palette browser has a search bar where you type the name of the color palette you just saved in Toucan. If you get too many results and your palette is hard to find, check the **only my palettes** option to filter the palettes that you have made. After you find the palette, click the blue arrow ◀ to the left of the palette, and it is loaded into the color swatch area of the Color Picker (see Figure 7-20). You can now close the palette browser by clicking the double arrow icon ⏪ again. Now that you have the palette loaded as swatches, they are there every time you

open the **Color Picker** during this session. Pick the red color and click **OK** to add it to the gradient. Keep going through and adding a color stop for each color consecutively until you have each of the eight colors in the gradient. Finally, add the red color at the end, making it nine color stops in total starting in red moving through the colors and ending in red.

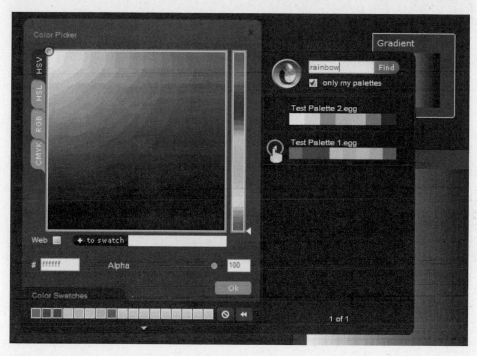

Figure 7-20. Load your Toucan palette into the Color Picker.

8. You want the gradient's color to transition as smooth as possible. Adjust the color stops so that they are evenly spaced by dragging the triangle color stop icons. Then, set the **Rotation** parameter to 90, so the gradient is tiled properly when you add the Spiral Tiling hub later (see Figure 7-21).

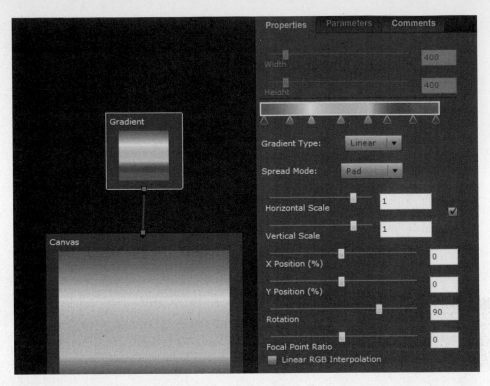

Figure 7-21. Rotate the gradient 90 degrees.

9. Add texture to the gradient by blending a Perlin Noise hub over it. Drag a Blender hub from the **Controllers** sidebar, and connect it in between the Gradient and the Canvas hubs. Move the connection of the Gradient hub to the last **Input pin** on the Blender hub. Then, drag a Perlin Noise hub from the Generators sidebar, and connect it to the first **Input pin** on the Blender. In the Properties panel of the Perlin Noise hub, ensure the **Proportion Lock** checkbox is off, set the **Horizontal Scale** to 0.05, leave the **Vertical Scale** 0.5, and uncheck the **Fractal Noise** checkbox. Finally, check the **Stitch** option, which produces a tilable texture. You have a vertical black and white pattern, reminiscent of zebra stripes (see Figure 7-22).

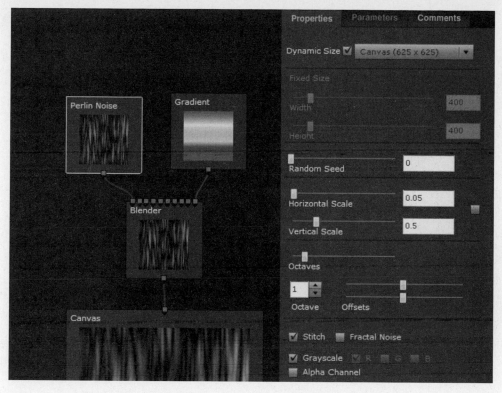

Figure 7-22. Add a Blender and a Perlin Noise hub to add texture to the gradient.

10. Select the Blender hub, and set the Perlin Noise layers Blend Mode to Add (see Figure 7-23). This Blend Mode combines the Perlin Noise and gradient outputs making the white areas intense.

461

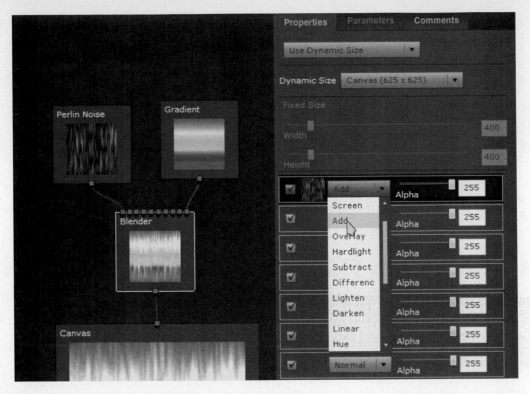

Figure 7-23. Set the blend mode to Add.

11. Complete the tie-dye look by twisting the pattern. Drag a Spiral Tiling hub from the **Effects** sidebar, and connect it between the Blender and Canvas hubs (see Figure 7-24). The hub distorts the gradient in a spiral radiating from the center of the Canvas, creating the tie-dyed look.

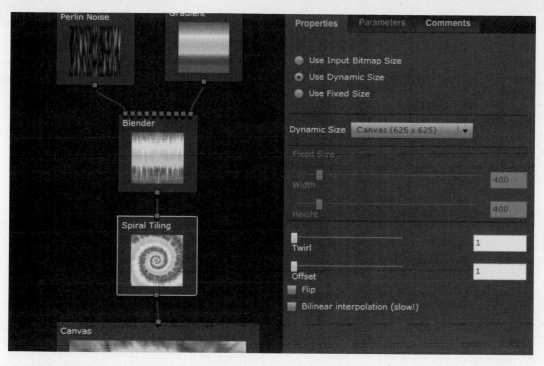

Figure 7-24. Insert a Spiral Tiling hub to give the image a tie-dye look.

Project Review

In this project, you saw how easy it is to use the power of Toucan's color formulas to produce coherent color palettes. These color formulas take out much of the legwork of choosing colors, which speeds up the process. You learned how to add color wells, copy colors to the color palette, and save them to be used in other applications. Then, you imported the color palette for use in making a tie-dye texture with Peacock Aviary's effects editor. In the next project, you use Toucan to sample colors from an image so that you can match color in a web page mock up.

Project 7.2—Matching Colors in a Mock Up of a Website Interface

Matching colors is important to maintaining a unified theme across different projects. Whether it is creating a drawing, logos, or websites, constant color can unify any related design projects. This is extremely evident in product or company branding. Colors evoke emotions; for example, blue is peacefulness, red denotes activity or action, pink has a soft sweet feel, and so on. Companies like to define a color to impart these emotions or ideas to them or their products. Colors also make quick identification of a brand; for example, the rich blue of Facebook or the red of Coca-Cola are more likely to be identified than a company that changes color schemes. If you ever find yourself designing for a company, it is likely that it has a set color scheme, which you are required to use. Toucan makes it easy to grab colors from images so that you can match preexisting colors schemes. In this project, you sample colors from an image, which enables you to make a web page mock up that matches the color scheme of the original. See Figure 7-25 for the final mockup made with this project.

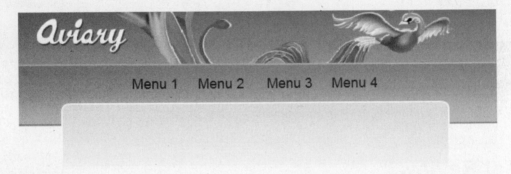

Figure 7-25. The final mockup with matched colors

Key features used in this project

- Importing images into Toucan
- Sampling colors
- Simplifying colors in an image

> The color palette for this project is online
> http://aviary.com/artists/gettingstartED/creations/chapter_7_project_2_colors.
>
> Find the file for this project online at
> http://aviary.com/artists/gettingstartED/creations/chapter_7_project_2.
>
> Find the resource image for this project at
> http://aviary.com/artists/gettingstartED/creations/chapter_7_project_2_resource.

1. Import an image from which to sample color. Launch Toucan, and click the Color Wheel title bar, which minimizes that section of the interface. Then, click the Image Picker bar to open its interface.

   Next, click the Import Image button [icon] to open the Resource Browser (see Figure 7-26). Locate the image you want to take color samples from, and import it into Toucan. A screen capture of the Aviary home page is used for this example. You can use Aviary's screen capture application Talon by typing `Aviary.com/` in front of the URL address of the page for which you want a screen capture. The address should look like this: `aviary.com/http://aviary.com/`. This takes a screen capture of the web page, and opens it into Falcon, Aviary's Markup editor. (See Chapter 8 for more information on Talon and Falcon.) You can then easily import the image directly into Toucan by clicking the Color Palette button at the top right of the application.

Figure 7-26. Close the Color Wheel panel and open the Image Picker for clarity.

2. Look around your imported image for colors you might want to sample. When hovering over the imported image, the cursor turns into an **Eye Dropper** tool. Any pixel that the tool is on is displayed in a large color swatch to the right of the image. Clicking the image samples the current color and pastes it into the current selected color well in the palette (see Figure 7-27). Start by sampling a few for the main colors in the image and selecting a new color well in the palette for each sample.

Figure 7-27. Use the Eye Dropper to pick colors from the image.

3. In areas where colors are varied or hard to select, such as a gradient of bitmap image, use the pixel width to simplify the image. This merges pixels and averages the color by the pixel width setting. A setting of 3 averages the color in a 3 x 3 pixel area. Set the pixel width to 7 and select colors at the edges of the gradients (see Figure 7-28). Add color wells to the palette if needed. Sample seven colors from this image; from the body of the page, sample a light gray base color (#fbfefe) and a darker gray shade color (#ededdf). From the header sky image, sample a light (#7fd5e8) and a dark blue (#188fec). Sample a light (#a4e072) and dark green (#61d040) from the menu bar. Finally, sample a dark gray (#4c4c4c) from the footer. The sampled color is, of course, different if you use a different image. The idea here is to get a few of the most prominent colors from the source image.

Figure 7-28. Use the pixel parameter to simplify the image.

4. When you have the colors you want sampled set in your palette, you need to save it. Clicking the **Save** button in the blue HTML bar at the top of the application opens the save options. You should use a name for the file that is easy for you to remember (see Figure 7-29). Again, you can also add a description and tags and set the file permissions at this stage.

Figure 7-29. Save the palette.

5. Use Raven with your imported palette to mock up a web page. Launch Raven, and accept the default 625 x 625 file dimension by clicking the **Create** button. Then, double-click the color selector box in the lower, left corner of the application, which opens the **Color Picker**. Next, click the double arrow button at the bottom of the Color Picker to open the **Toucan Palette browser**. In the text box, type the name of the palette of the sampled colors you created earlier (see Figure 7-30). After you find it, click the blue arrow to the left of the palette to paste it into the **Color Swatches** area. After colors are loaded as swatches, they are

there every time you open the **Color Picker**, so you have access to the colors during your session.

Figure 7-30. Import your palette into Raven.

6.   Now that you have your colors loaded into the **Color Picker**, you can use Raven's basic shapes to lay out the mockup. Use the Rectangle Shape tool ◼ with the **Corner width** and **Ellipse Height** values set to 0, and draw a rectangle around the Canvas. Fill this shape by setting it to the dark gray color you sampled earlier. Next, draw a smaller rectangle that extends horizontally across the Canvas, and fill it with the light base color for the body of the mock up. Remove the stroke by setting the type to **none** in the **Stroke tab** of the **Fill and Stroke panel**. Some of the dark gray color should show at the bottom making the footer of the mock up. Then, draw a third rectangle across the top quarter of the Canvas to make the header. Change this rectangle's fill type to gradient by clicking the **Linear Gradient Fill** button ◼ in the **Fill and Stroke panel**. The panel now has a gradient colorbar with two color stops. Double-click the left triangle color stop icon to open the **Color Picker**. Choose the light blue color, and click **OK** to set its color. Double-click the right color stop, and set its color to dark blue. Finally, set the direction of this gradient using the Gradient Transform tool ◼, and then drag the circular control handle so that the gradient transitions vertically from dark blue at the top to light blue at the bottom of the rectangle (see Figure 7-31).

469

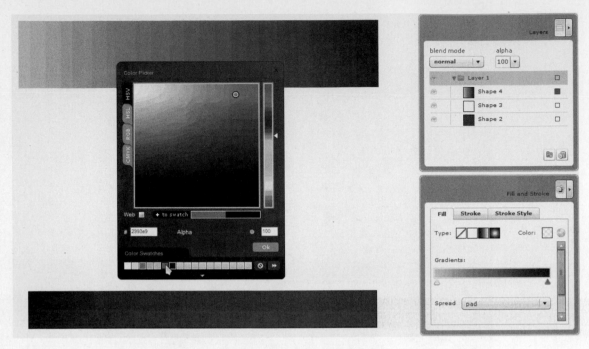

Figure 7-31. Lay out your interface using the basic shapes in Raven.

7. Create a green navigation bar for the mockup. Draw another rectangle below the blue header and extend it across the Canvas. This should be roughly the same height as the blue header. Set this rectangle to **a Linear Gradient Fill** of light green to dark green, and use the Gradient

Transform tool ⬛ to change the orientation of the gradient vertically with the dark green at the top and the light green at the bottom (see Figure 7-32).

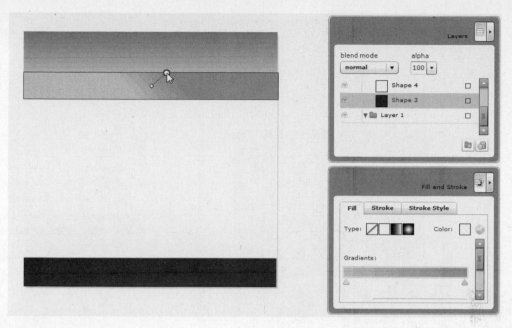

Figure 7-32. Draw the navigation bar.

8. Make the center section of the mockup. Select the Rectangle Shape tool again, but this time, set the **Corner Width** and **Ellipse Height** values to 10. Draw a rectangle in the center of the Canvas with the top extending half way over the green menu bar. You can use the Transform tool to position this new rectangle. Set the flll to **Linear Fill gradient** with the light gray base color fading to the dark gray shade color. Again, use the Gradient Transform tool to position the gradient and shorten it, positioning it near the top (see Figure 7-33). Next, add a **Stroke** to the outside of this rectangle, and set it to the light gray base color. Finally, set the Width of this **Stroke Style** to 5 to give a light border around the top of this rectangle.

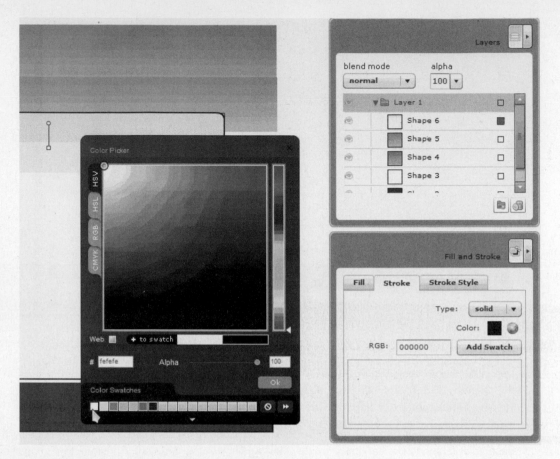

Figure 7-33. Draw a rounded rectangle for the display area of the mockup.

9. Now that you have the base features of the mockup laid out, you can start adding any bitmap elements to it. Use the `File ➤ Import` command to open the `Resource Browser` at the top of the application. Here, you can navigate to the bitmaps that you want to use in the mockup. If you want to use the bitmap from this example, use the search in the resource browser. First, uncheck the `Only your stuff` option, and then type `Chapter 7 Project 2` in the search box. This narrows the results. Find the resource and import it into the image. Use the Transform tool to scale and position the bitmap at the top of the mockup in the blue section. See Figure 7-34.

Figure 7-34. Import any decorations for the mockup.

10. Finally, add text for your menu options using the Text tool ⊞. Click the Canvas with the Text tool to set a text start point, and then type in your text. Use the Select and Move tool ▶ to scale and position the text at the top of the mockup in the green. While the text is still selected, set the color to the dark gray in the `Fill and Stroke panel (see Figure 7-35)`.

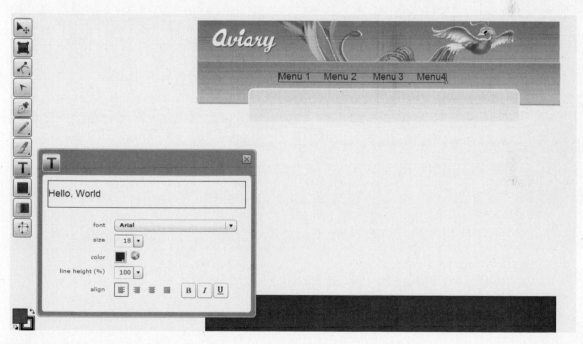

Figure 7-35. Add text with the Text tool.

Project Review

Knowing how to match colors is important when working with a client who has preset color schemes or when you want to maintain colors across several images. In this project, you learned how to import an image into Toucan by using either the resource browser or Talon. After the image was inside the application, you sampled colors and built a palette based off the colors of the images. You then used Raven to lay out a mockup of a web page using the colors sampled from the image. This enabled you to match colors and maintain a consistent color scheme throughout the project.

Chapter review

Toucan is a versatile and powerful color palette generator. It enables you to find, sample, arrange, and export color palettes. These palettes can be used in any of Aviary's graphic applications, imported via the Color Picker. In this chapter, you learned how to use the built-in color formulas to generate a cohesive color scheme. Toucan has the flexibility to fine tune any of the color selections using several different color spaces. Import images into the application and sample colors directly for the resource, making color matching a precise and simple process. In the next chapter, you become familiar with Talon and Falcon, Aviary's screen capture and markup applications respectively. You see how you can use Talon to gather resources from around the web, and use them in the other applications. You also learn to use Falcon to do simple edits and graphic overlays on your images, which is well suited for blog posts.

Chapter 8

Screen Capture and Markup with Talon and Falcon

Talon and Falcon are Aviary's screen capture and markup application, respectively. **Screen captures** are images taken directly from your computer screen; anything you see on your screen can be saved as a resource. Although **Markups** are simple graphic overlays used to highlight something, decorate an image, or make notes, they are designed to be quick and useful for simple tasks. This can all be done from your browser, so there is no longer a need to launch several different applications to post a quick image to your blog or grab a starting image for a creation.

Talon, Aviary's screen capture tool

Talon comes either as an add-on extension for the Firefox® browser, Google Chrome browser, or as a URL-based web page capture. Since extensions for Google Chrome are only available for the development release of the browser, it won't be explicitly covered in this book. However, most of its functionally will be the same as the Firefox® version. With the Firefox® extension, you have commands to launch all the Aviary applications and take screen captures, and you have a set of quick links to all your Aviary settings. If you are not running Firefox® or Google Chrome, you can access Talon's screen capture function by adding Aviary.com/ followed by the URL of the page you want to capture, and Talon captures the web page and opens it in Falcon. For example, to capture an image of Google's search page, type Aviary.com/http://www.google.com/ into your browser.

Find the Firefox® Talon add-on online at
https://addons.mozilla.org/en-US/firefox/addon/11587.
Find the Google Chrome Talon add-on online at
https://chrome.google.com/extensions/detail/ncgcgghbabbopfcpgcjpfffdgnbadegf.

Install Talon from the Mozilla add-on library; a link can be found in the sidebar or on `Your Dashboard` page at Aviary.com. Form the Mozilla add on page, click the green `Add to Firefox` button to download and install the Talon add-on. Your browser will need to restart for the effects to take effect. After your browser is open again, you notice an `Aviary` menu on the menu bar and an `Aviary` button on the Navigation toolbar. The Aviary menu gives you links to open any of Aviary's applications and various links to the site and settings.

Clicking the `Aviary` button enables you to take a screen capture. By default, Talon takes a "capture region on page" grab, which lets you `drag with your mouse to capture a specific region` of the page (see Figure 8-1). The area you choose is highlighted, and you are able to adjust your capture region with the control handle, save, or cancel (see Figure 8-2). You can change the setting to `Capture Visible Portion of Page` or `Capture Entire Page` from the Aviary menu.

Drag with your mouse to capture a region

Figure 8-1. The screen prompt when taking a capture of a region on the page

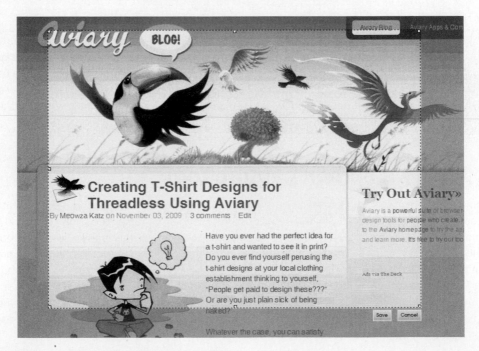

Figure 8-2. This is what a region capture looks like.

After you commit to a capture, you are asked where you want to save it (see Figure 8-3). You can **Edit it in Aviary.com**, which opens the capture in the application of your choosing. The default application can be set from the Aviary menu. The capture can be saved to your computer by clicking the **Save to Desktop** option. A **Copy to Clipboard** option places the capture on your computer's clipboard, so that you can paste it where you want. You can save it to your Aviary account with the **Host it at Aviary.com** option. Finally, if you want to discard the capture, you can just click the **Cancel** button.

Figure 8-3. Talon asks you, "**What you would like to do with this image?**"

The Talon add-on can take quick screen captures. You can specify to grab a portion of a web page, the visible region, or the entire page (see Figure 8-4). After Talon captures an image, you can edit it immediately with one of the applications, save to your computer, or add it to your Aviary account. Talon also has application launch buttons for quick access to graphic editor at Aviary.

After Talon is installed, you see a new menu option on the main toolbar and an Aviary dedicated capture button (see Figure 8–5). By default, this button lets you capture a Region on Page, clicking the arrow next to the button for different capture options. The following are the options for capturing an image with Talon.

- **Capture Region on Page**: Enables you to capture a certain area of the screen. See the Capture window for details.
- **Capture Visible Portion of Page**: Captures an image of just what is showing on the screen.
- **Capture Entire Page**: Captures an image of the entire page. Talon even captures areas that require scrolling to see.

Capture Region on Page	Capture Visible Portion of Page	Capture Entire Page

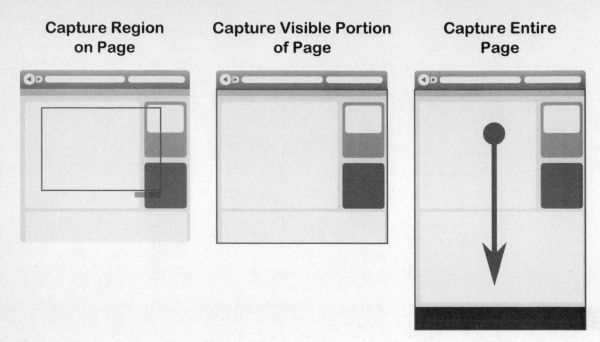

Figure 8-4. The different capture types.

There is a set of quick links to each of the graphic-editing applications; clicking any one of them opens the respective application even when Aviary.com is not open in the browser.

- `Aviary Home`: Opens Aviary's Home page in a new tab.
- `Aviary.com Dashboard`: Opens Your Dashboard in a new tab if logged in.
- `Aviary.com Settings`: Opens Your Profile and Account Settings in a new tab if logged in to Aviary.
- `Login/Logout`: Opens the Log In page if you are not currently logged in. Logs you out if you are logged in.
- `Aviary.com Firefox Extension Options`: Opens the Firefox® Extension Options, which includes default preferences for your Aviary toolbar button.
- `Clicking the Aviary toolbar item will`: Sets the default action when clicking the toolbar button (see Figure 8-5).

Figure 8-5. The screen capture button on the Firefox® toolbar

- **`Capture Region on Page`**: Enables you to capture a certain area of the screen. See the Capture window for details.
- **`Capture Visible Portion of Page`**: Captures an image of just what is showing on the screen.
- **`Capture Entire Page`**: Captures an image of the entire page. Talon even captures areas that require scrolling to see.
- **`Edit images with`**: Sets the default application that your captures open with.
- **`Aviary Image Editor`**: Capture opens in Phoenix.
- **`Aviary Color Editor`**: Capture opens in Toucan.
- **`Aviary Effects Editor`**: Capture opens in Peacock.
- **`Aviary Vector Editor`**: Capture opens in Raven.
- **`About Aviary.com`**: Opens Aviary's **`About Us`** page in a new tab.
- **`About Aviary.com Firefox Extension`**: Opens Talon's Tool Page.

Falcon

Falcon is Aviary's quick edit and markup editor (see Figure 8-6). This application enables you to make quick crops, resize images, and add simple graphic elements to images. You can save the results directly to your computer, host the file with Aviary, or import it into one of Aviary's other full-featured editors. You can use Falcon with screen captures from Talon, import you own image, grab an image from a web page, or even start an empty file.

Figure 8-6. Layout of Falcon's tools and commands

When you open Falcon, you see the imported or blank image in the center. On the left is the toolbar with several drawing and selection tools that let you perform various function to your image. The Picker tool lets you move, scale, and rotate any objects in the file. You can move the Canvas around in the application with the Pan tool ; this is helpful when you are zoomed in or working on a large image. Falcon has five tools that let you add graphic elements to your image. They range from circles, rectangles, lines, arrows, or drawn objects. These elements do not actually change any pixels in your image but in fact lay on top. This means that at any time you can select and manipulate these elements. With the Eyedropper tool , you can sample colors from your image. You can make notes on your image with the Text tool . The Crop tool lets you manually set the area to which you want to crop. Finally, the selection tools let you cut areas from your image making them free-floating elements. These tools let you do all the simple everyday graphic editing.

In the bottom left corner of the application are the **Crop**, **Resize**, and **Rotate & flip** functions (see Figure 8-7). Clicking any of the buttons opens the panel to reveal the respective function's parameters. The Crop function lets you crop or enlarge the Canvas using a width and height dimensions. You can resize your image to a specific size or scale proportionally. The **Rotate & flip** function lets you rotate your image either arbitrarily with the rotation slider or by 90-degree increments with the rotate buttons. The two flip buttons let you mirror your image vertically or horizontally.

Figure 8-7. The crop, resize, and rotation controls are accessible in the lower panel.

On the upper, right side of the application is the **Undo**, **Redo**, and **Restore** buttons (see Figure 8-8). The **Undo** and **Redo** buttons let you take a step forward or backward in the history of the actions performed in Falcon. The **Restore** function returns your image to its initial state when it was imported into the application. This function removes any graphics added, crops, and even scales.

Figure 8-8. The history controls let you move forward or backward through actions.

Under the restore button are the **Colors** and style selectors (see Figure 8-9). Clicking the large color square opens the Color Picker where you can set the current color and Alpha. You can even set the color with the hexadecimal color code. There are six predefined color swatches for quick color setting. Below the color selector are the style parameters. Each graphic element can have an outline and drop shadow styling. The size scales the graphic element, outline, and shadow together. The Outline and shadow can be turned off by unchecking their options in the menu.

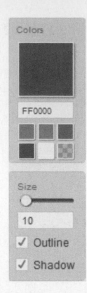

Figure 8-9. The color and style controls for the graphic elements in the file.

Further down are the zoom and navigation tools (see Figure 8-10). This lets you zoom into your image, which enables you to work on details. You can navigate around your zoomed image by dragging the white rectangle in the preview image. You can quickly reset the zoom to 100% by clicking the `magnifying`

`glass` button .

Figure 8-10. Zoom in and out of your image.

Finally, at the top are the file command buttons (see Figure 8-11). They enable you to export your image to one of Aviary's full-featured editors.

Figure 8-11. File commands give you quick access to saving and exporting your image.

482

Project 8.1—Quickly Crop and Resize one of Your Images

Falcon makes it quick and easy to crop, resize, and change the orientation of your photos. The application is under 90k, so it loads fast and is responsive. From the first glance, it might seem like Falcon is underpowered, lacking advanced features. However, you find that the speed at which you can perform everyday edits makes Falcon a staple in your graphic editor repertoire. Images can be captured, opened directly in the application, cropped, sized, manipulated, and saved before a desktop image editor even loads. Falcon is so fast and responsive that you turn to it all the time. In this project, you import an image for quick cropping (see Figure 8-12).

Figure 8-12. Make quick and simple adjustments to your photos.

1. Launch Falcon from one of the quick launch buttons on the sidebar of `Your Dashboard`, from the `Create` menu at the top of each page, or from the `Aviary` menu from the Talon add-on. The application presents you with a `New File` dialog where you can choose different options to load images. You can import an existing image from your computer, load one from a URL link, or open a blank file ready to draw onto. For this project, load an image from your computer; any image works for this project. Start by selecting the `Choose file from desktop` option, and click the `Browse` button (see Figure 8-13). Locate the image you want to adjust and click the `Get started` button to load it into Falcon. A standard image of a couple is used in this example.

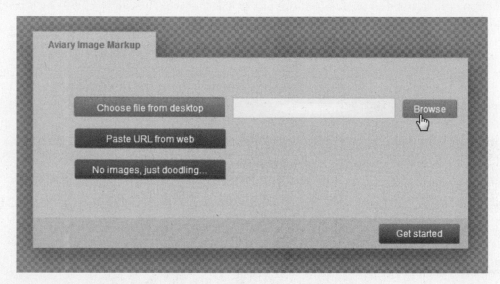

Figure 8-13. Click the Browse button to locate the image you want to adjust.

2. Rotate the image to add some drama. Click the `Rotate` button to slide open the Rotate Control panel. There are three main controls here: `Flip vertical`, `Flip horizontal`, and `Angle`. The `Flip vertical` and `Flip horizontal` control mirrors the image in the respective direction. The `Angle` controls give you several ways to rotate your image. The round slider control rotates the image to any angle from 1 to 360 degrees. The two buttons inside the slider rotate the image clockwise or counterclockwise in 90-degree increments. Finally, you can type an angle into the text to set the rotation to a specific angle. Rotate your image to give it some drama. In this example, the couple is straight up and down, but a rotation of 25 degrees makes them feel like they are going to topple over (see Figure 8-14), which imparts a feeling of excitement like something might happen or a sense of movement. Click the Apply button to commit the rotation to the image.

Figure 8-14. Rotate your image to add excitement.

3. When you crop, resize, or rotate your image, you are prompted to flatten your image. Note that this applies only to the dedicated controls and not the Crop tool. Flattening an image makes any element that you add permanent. Clicking `Yes` proceeds with the rotation (Figure 8-15). This means that you cannot use the Undo feature to go back and undo your rotation. However, you can always use the `Restore` function to reset the image to its initial state. At anytime while using Falcon, you can always return to your original image using the `Restore` command in the `History` panel.

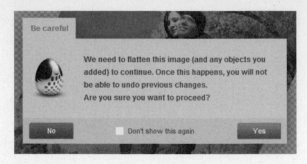

Figure 8-15. Falcon flattens the image after a crop resize and rotation.

4. Crop the image to remove the now empty space in the corners. Select the Crop tool  and drag out a rectangular crop area. The crop border is defined by a white rectangle with a darker center, eight control handles, and `Cancel` and `Apply` buttons. Dragging on any of the four-corner control handles resizes the crop area. Dragging on the side control handles resizes the crop area constrained to the horizontal or vertical axis. Size the crop area so that the now empty areas in the corners of the image are excluded from the crop and your subject is in the center (see Figure 8-16). After you are satisfied with the crop area, click the `Apply` button to crop the image to your desired specifications.

Figure 8-16. Use the crop tool to define the area you want to crop.

5. Resize the image if you want it to be close to the original dimensions. After cropping an image, it is smaller because you removed some of the image. You might need to resize it to return it to a size that is similar to the original. Open the resize function by clicking the button in the lower left of the application window. After open, drag the `Target width` slider to 1800 (Figure 8-17). Notice that both sliders move in unison. This is because the `Keep aspect ratio` option is checked and keeps the ratio of width and height the same in the resize process.

Figure 8-17. Resize your image if you want it back to its original size.

6. After you are done, you have several different choices. You can save the image to your computer by clicking the `Save to Desktop` button. This opens your computer's File Manager so that you can chose the save location on your computer for the image. If you want to save the image to your Aviary account so it will show up in your gallery, click the `Save & Host Online` button (see Figure 8-18). If you want to perform more advanced editing on your image, you can export the image to Phoenix, Aviary's image editor, by clicking the `Advanced Editor` button at the top. If you want to apply effects to the image, you can send it to Peacock, Aviary's effects editor, by clicking the `Image Effects` button. Finally, if you want to sample colors from the image, send it to Toucan, Aviary's color palette creator, by clicking the `Color palette` button.

487

Figure 8-18. Save your file when you are done.

Project review

Falcon, just as the name implies, is a fast and nimble application. It lets you make simple edits to your images without having to start up heavier applications. In this project, you saw how you can easily add excitement to an image with just a rotation and crop. Performing many basic actions to your images becomes light work for your online gallery, blog postings, and more. In the next project, you learn how you can use Talon and Falcon together to take notes about things you find online.

Project 8.2—Take a Screenshot of a Shopping Item and Make Annotations

Combined, Falcon and Talon can be useful when you want to take notes of any interesting items you find online. You can use these tools to make a visual scrapbook of items that interest you. There are several web-based note taking and scrapbooking style sites, but many limit your usages without a premium account. Aviary can fill that role without limits. In this project, you use Talon to grab an image from the web, import it into Falcon, and make notes about your find (see Figure 8-19).

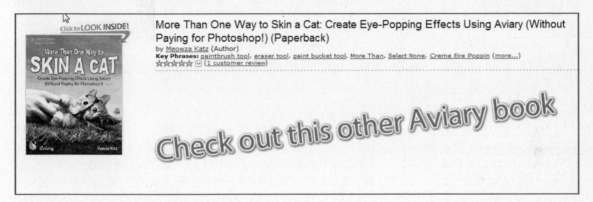

Figure 8-19. Create notes with Falcon and Talon.

1a. If you are running Firefox® as your web browser and have Aviary's Talon add-on installed (see the start of the chapter for notes on where to find the plug in), you can use the capture region function, which lets you set the area to be captured. However, if you are not using the Firefox® Talon add-on, skip to Step 1b. If you are using the Firefox® plug in, click the **Aviary** button in the toolbar. The screen darkens and you are prompted to **Drag with your mouse to capture a region**. Now, drag a rectangle around the area you would like to capture. The capture region is defined with a rectangle with eight control handles and **Save** and **Cancel** buttons. Dragging on any of the control handles resizes the capture area with the side control handles constraining the resize to the horizontal or vertical orientation (see Figure 8-20). After you're satisfied with the capture region, click the **Save** button, which brings up the save location dialog.

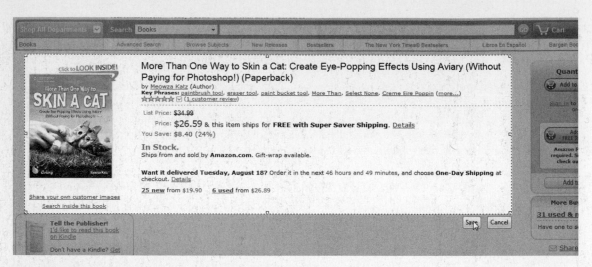

Figure 8-20. Using Talons Capture region option.

1a. (continued) You can save your screen capture to four different locations. The `Edit it in Aviary.com` option opens the capture directly in Falcon. `Save to Desktop` saves the capture to your computer. `Copy to Clipboard` places the capture on your computer clipboard, so that you can paste it into many different applications. Finally, you can also save it directly to your Aviary account with the `Host it at Aviary.com` option (see Figure 8-21). Select the `Edit it in Aviary.com` to open the capture in Falcon.

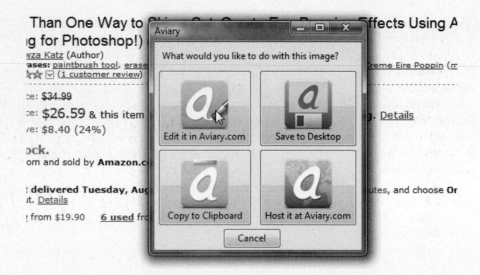

Figure 8-21. You can save a screen capture to several different locations.

1b. If you do not have Talon installed or aren't using the Firefox® web browser, you can take a screen capture of any web page just by adding Aviary.com/ in front of the web address. For example, you can take a screen capture of Peacock's tool page by taking the URL of the page, http://aviary.com/tools/peacock, and changing it to Aviary.com/http://aviary.com/tools/peacock. This opens the online version of Talon that captures the entire webpage. You have to wait 10 to 20 seconds for the application to complete the capture and open it in Falcon (see Figure 8-22).

The capture is of the entire page, so you must use the Crop tool ⬚ to remove the areas of the page you don't want. Drag the Crop tool around the area to keep and click the `Apply` button to perform the crop. Refer back to Figure 8-20 to see how this image needs to be cropped to match the image for this project.

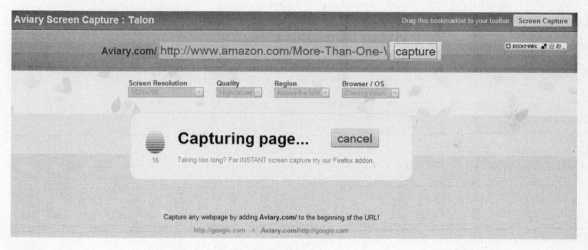

Figure 8-22. Use Aviary's Talon URL screen capture function.

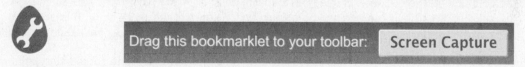

Figure 8-23. Add a bookmark to quickly take a Talon Screen capture.

You can easily add a button to your bookmarks that lets you take Talon screen captures. Go to http://aviary.com/launch/talon. This is the main Talon capture page. At the top right of this page, you see a button that says Screen Capture (see Figure 8-23). Drag this button to your bookmark toolbar or bookmark folder. This has not been tested in every browser but should work with most modern ones. Now, when you visit a site that you want to take a capture of, you can click that bookmark and the URL is formatted to take a screen capture of that page.

2. Select the **Eyedropper** tool and click the background color of your image. In this example, it turns out that the background is white. With the background color sampled, select the **Brush** tool and set the **Size** to 50, making the brush big enough to cover more area. Now, paint over any section of the capture that you want removed (see Figure 8-24). In this example, the extraneous information in the center of the image is painted out. You might need to change the **Size** of the brush to get into tight areas.

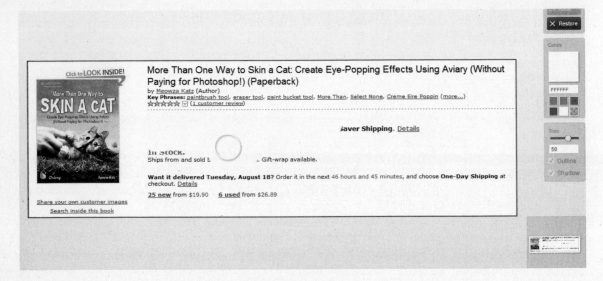

Figure 8-24. Use the brush tool to clean up an image.

3. With the image cleaned up, you can add your notes to the image. Start by setting the color to red so that it stands out on your image. Depending on your image, you might want to change the color so it can be read against the background. Then, set the **Size** to 6. This sets the amount of Outline and Shadow around your text. These two effects can be turned off by unchecking each option. Select the **Text** tool and click the Canvas to set the start point of your text. Now, type your text on your image, and don't worry if your text is not quite where you want it because you position it in the next step (see Figure 8-25).

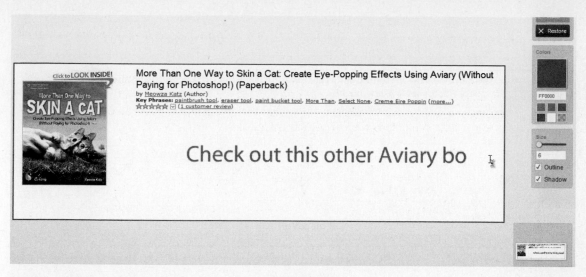

Figure 8-25. Use the Text tool to make notes on your image.

4. At this point, you can use the Picker tool 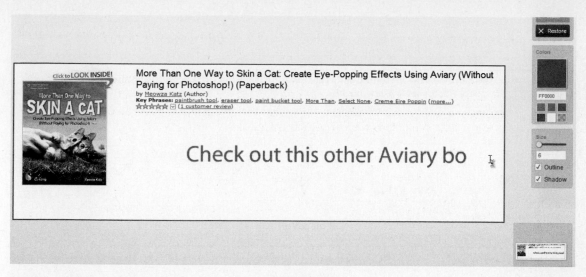 to scale and position the text element that you just added. With the Picker tool selected, click the text element and a rectangle is drawn around the text. This rectangle has scale control handles around it and a rotation handle above it. Clicking and dragging the text element lets you position it anywhere on your Canvas. Center the text in the blank area of the image. Dragging any of the corner scaling control handles lets you resize the text element, while dragging any of the side control handles lets you resize it while constraining vertically or horizontally. Next, you can rotate the text by dragging on the rotation handle. Rotate the text slightly to add a little emphasis to it (see Figure 8-26). After you are satisfied with the results, click the **Save & Host Online** button to save the image to your Aviary account.

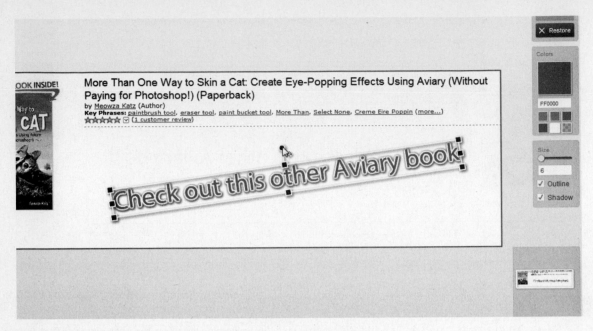

Figure 8-26. Use the Picker tool to position elements in your file.

5. If you want to share your find with one of your friends, go to the image's creation page. On the right sidebar of the page is a set of buttons. Click the **Send to friends** button ⬛ **Send to friends** . This opens a dialog that enables you to email this creation to your friends and let them know about your cool find (see Figure 8-27). In the To textbox, insert the username of the friend you want to send the image to. Add any notes in the personal message. The user receives an email with a link to the creation.

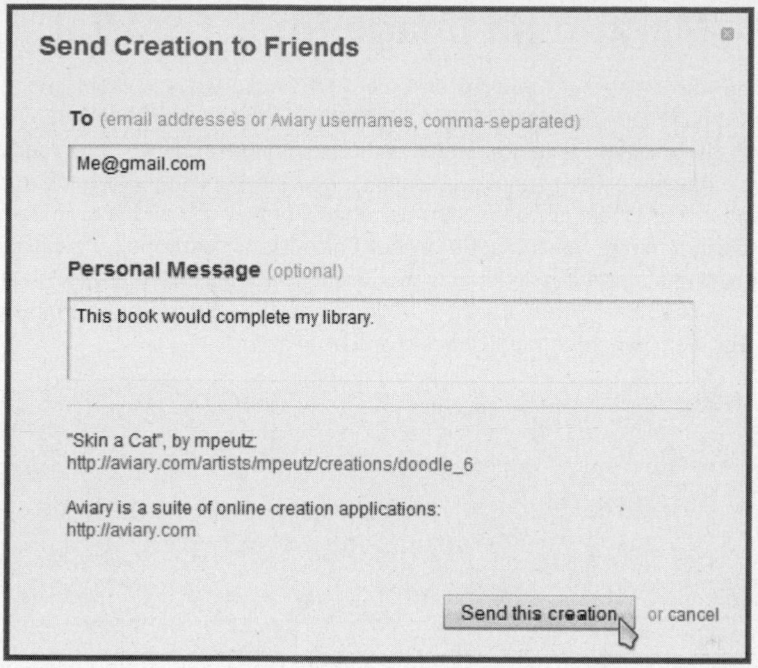

Figure 8-27. Use the Send Creation to Friends feature to inform your friends of your find.

Project review

Combining the power of Talon and Falcon gives you easy-to-use tools for capturing, annotating, and organizing images from around the web. Talon lets you capture images with the Firefox® add-on or as URL-based capture application. After Talon captures your image, it opens in Falcon, which lets you make alterations. Using the text tool, you are able to make any notes on your image. Finally, you can share your find with your friends with the built-in Send to friend option. In the next project, you add markups and notes to an image so that you can post it in a tutorial or blog post.

Project 8.3—Markup an Image for a Tutorial

The rise of blogging has created a need for an easy and simple ways to post images in these online articles. There have been many applications that filled that role but had to be installed on your computer. This meant that there are always extra steps capturing images online, downloading them to your computer, opening a graphic editor to make alterations, and then uploading it back to the web. With the release of Talon and Falcon, there is no longer a disconnect of the web and your images. These two give you the tools to quickly prepare your images online. Falcon is an extremely useful tool for highlighting areas of images, pointing out features in images that might not be apparent at first glance. This is perfect for showing areas that need attention in tutorials or blog posts (see Figure 8-28). In this project, you make an image for a tutorial about where to paint shading and highlights.

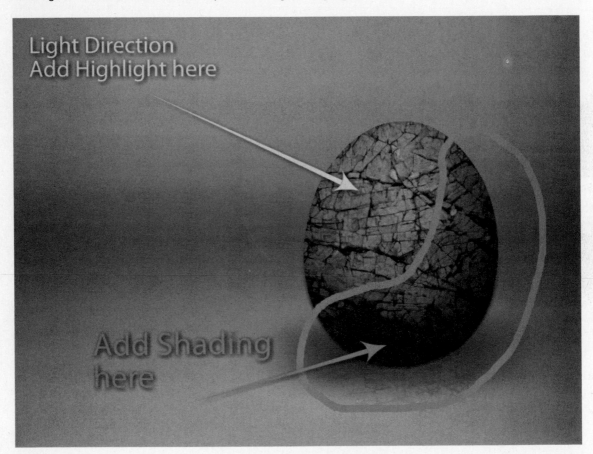

Figure 8-28. Point out areas that need attention with Falcon's Markup tools

1. Capture your image. You might find yourself working on a creation in one of Aviary's applications that you want to point out to other users, use in a tutorial, or post to your blog. This is usually the case when you have questions about a technique or you are writing a tutorial for others. If you are running Firefox® with the Talon extension installed, you can access the screen capture function by right-clicking the blue HTML save bar at the top of the application. This opens the browser's context menu where there is an option to use Talon. Select the **Take Screenshot** ➤ **Capture Visible Portion of Page**, which takes a screenshot of the entire application (see Figure 8-29). You are prompted to choose a destination for your capture. Select the **Edit it in Aviary** option to open it in Falcon. If you do not have Talon installed, you have to save a version of your image and open that in Falcon.

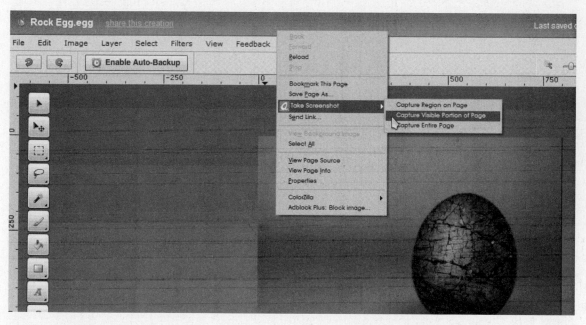

Figure 8-29. Right-clicking in your browser gives you access to your Talon Screen Capture.

2. Now that your image is in Falcon, use the Crop tool ⌗ to crop out any details that aren't pertinent to what you are pointing out in your image. Drag the crop rectangle around the area that you want to keep in your image, adjusting the crop selection with the control handles (see Figure 8-30). After you are satisfied with the area, click **Apply** to perform the crop function. The reason you captured the whole image and then cropped it in Falcon instead of just capturing a region is that you can easily undo any crop by using Falcon's Restore function. If you just capture a region and later realize that you missed an important detail, you have to go back to the original file and take another capture, which can be time consuming.

Figure 8-30. Crop out any extraneous details in the image.

3. Set a bright contrasting color for your first set of markups. You can do this by clicking the large color square in the **Colors** sidebar. This opens Falcon's Color Picker where you can choose a bright yellow color (#ffe100) (see Figure 8-31). Falcon doesn't use Aviary's full-featured Color Picker; instead it opts for a simplified chooser to keep the application running fast and responsive. Finally, in the **Size** sidebar, set the size to 8, and uncheck the **Outline** option to turn off the white halo around mark-up elements.

Figure 8-31. Select a contrasting color for your mark-ups.

4. Now use the Arrow tool [image]. Click where you want the base of the arrow to start and drag out to set the end point of the arrow. In this example, the light direction is coming from the upper, left, so the intent is to point out the area on the object that needs highlights painted on. Start by clicking in the upper, left and drag right and down to end in the area where the highlight should go (see Figure 8-32).

Figure 8-32. Use the Arrow tool to point out the highlight area in the image.

5. Select the Text tool **T** , and click near the base of the arrow to set the start point for the text. Type your annotation for the detail the arrow is pointing out. In this case, this is the light direction and where the highlight needs to be painted (see Figure 8-33). If needed, use the Picker tool to scale and position the two markup elements, so it is clear what is needed for the image.

Figure 8-33. Use the Text tool to add annotations to your image.

6. Draw a shape to point out the area that requires shadows painted on. Start by selecting a bright blue color. Again, click the color square to open the Falcon Color Picker to set the blue color (#008aed). This contrasts the other yellow markup elements to show that they require different actions. Next, select the Brush tool , and draw a shape around the lower and back half of the egg shape (see Figure 8-34). This highlights where the shadow needs to be added to the image.

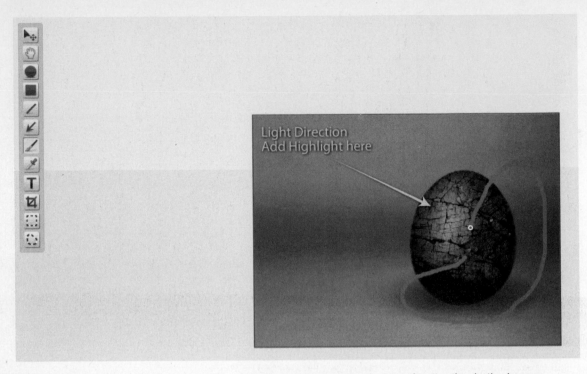

Figure 8-34. Use the Paint brush tool to highlight a separate area that needs attention in the image.

7. Now add your annotations with the Text tool ⊤ in the same blue color. Make a note on the image with the text tool that directs you to add shading to the area you just highlighted with the Paintbrush tool. This lets the viewer of the tutorial know that this information belongs to the area you highlighted in the previous step. You can add one last arrow to tie the two elements together and point out the actions that need to be performed. See Figure 8-35. Finally, use the Picker tool ⧉ to scale and position the last elements. When you are satisfied with the results, you can save the image to your Aviary account by clicking the **Save & Host Online** button.

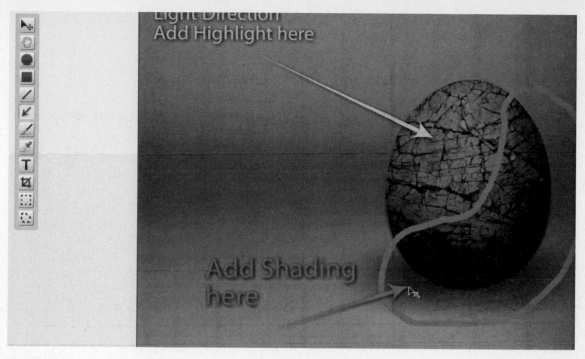

Figure 8-35. Add annotations and an arrow to finish the tutorial image.

Project review

Falcon gives you the tools to mark up your images, which helps you to convey concepts, draw attention to specific areas, or add notes to images. This is well suited to tutorials; you can easily point out areas that need attention, which is more direct than writing out the process. The markup tools are simple yet versatile enough for most tasks. Arrows can be used to pin point things in an image, whereas the brush tool can point to a broader area. This project is just a taste of what can be done with the application. It is recommended that you experiment with the other markup elements. You might be surprised how much you can accomplish with them.

Chapter review

Talon and Falcon might seem like small tools next to the powerhouses Phoenix, Raven, and Peacock. However, this is not the case. You will find that their functions become indispensable. Even users who aren't going to Aviary to make creations find that Talon gives them tools to gather, store, and organize images from around the web. The Firefox® add-on also gives you additional tools integrating your browser with the Aviary site. You can launch the various applications, links to the site, and even logout/login to your account. Aviary is never out of arms reach with the Talon add-on installed. Falcon was designed from the ground up to be small, fast, and responsive. Just clocking in around 90k, it loads quickly even on the slowest computers. It has the essential tools to markup, crop, resize, and rotate your images. Markup elements are the overlain shapes such as arrows, rectangles, and even text that you can use to annotate, draw attention to an area, or alter images. Talon and Falcon speed up your image capture and editing workflow. In the next chapter, you explore application switching. Aviary's applications are designed to work together to give you access to Raven's path tools in Phoenix, Phoenix's images manipulation in Peacock, or any other combination you can come up with. Combined, these applications become the only graphic editor you ever need.

Chapter 9

Application Switching

Application switching is a powerful feature that can extend your image creation and manipulation options. Aviary's applications are designed to be quick and simple to use; thus, many advanced features have been omitted to keep the applications nimble. To offset this smaller feature set compared to the more expensive desktop applications, Aviary has added easy application switching. For instance, if you are working on an image in Phoenix and find that you need the precision of Raven's vectors to create a mask, instead of going through the time-consuming process of saving the Phoenix file, launching Raven, making the vector paths, saving, reopening, and importing it into Phoenix, you can just switch applications. Application switching is a feature that lets you pass resources between applications without having to actually leave, close, or save the original file. You can create, edit, and see updates of resources from separate Aviary applications while still having the original file open. This extends to each application well beyond its native feature set and gives you more power to create with and speed up your workflow.

Application switching in Phoenix

Peacock and Raven files can be imported, exported, or created from Phoenix. This lets you tap into the power of these applications for use in your Phoenix creations. You can use Raven to create precise vector masks, graphic elements, or imported Encapsulated Post Script (EPS) files. Access Peacock's vast array of effects by creating and editing Peacock layers or by using **a Custom Filter** Blackbox. Multiply your creation power and speed up your workflow by using Aviary's application-switching capability.

In the previous projects in the book, the resources you imported into Phoenix have been normal bitmaps. These bitmaps are flat images and give you access only to what you can see. However, with Aviary's application switching, when you import files made in Phoenix, Raven, or Peacock, you have access to their layers, paths, and effects. Furthermore, they remain editable in their native applications and can be manipulated while still working on the original Phoenix file. To add a Raven or Peacock layer into your file, use the **Import Resource** command from the **File** menu to load a previously saved file from the Aviary Library. This gives you access to a vast library of public files on the site.

Note that when an editable resource from another application is imported into Phoenix, the layer has an egg badge (see Figure 9-1). This badge denotes the application that the resource was made with and that it is still editable. This is what is known as a smart layer. At any time, you can open one of these resources by double-clicking the smart layer. This opens the resource in its native application in a new browser window. This means that a Raven file is opened with all its vector paths ready to be edited. Peacock files open and give you access to all the effect hubs, which let you manipulate effect parameters and effect chains. Finally, Phoenix files open with the files layers still intact. Switching focus back to the original application, any changes made to the resource in the new window reflects those updates. This gives you the ability to preview the resource in the original file and lets you make any necessary adjustments.

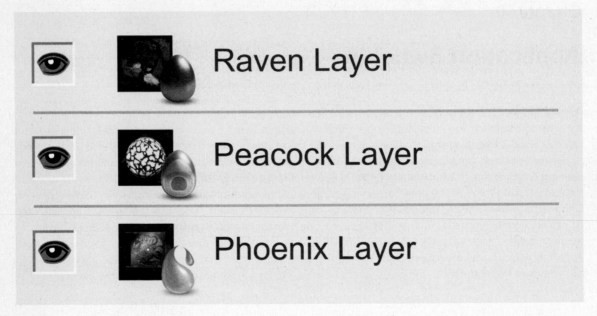

Figure 9-1. Resources that have been created in Aviary applications have a corresponding application badge.

This does not only apply to previously constructed files that you import; you can create a blank smart layer. From the Options menu in Phoenix's **Layers** panel, there are options to create a **New Peacock layer**, **New Phoenix layer**, or **New Raven layer** (see Figure 9-2). These layers react just like the imported smart layers; double-clicking the layer opens it in the application in a new browser window where you can create resources from scratch.

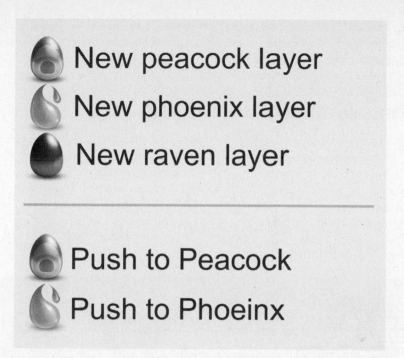

Figure 9-2. The Options menu in the Layers panel has functions for application switching.

Finally, if you have a layer that is a regular Phoenix bitmap layer, maybe one you have painted or a resource you have altered, you can push it to Peacock or Phoenix. Select the layer and use the `Push to Peacock` or `Push to Phoenix` command in the `Options` menu in Phoenix's Layers panel (see Figure 9-2). This opens the respective application in a new browser window and imports the layer that was "pushed" as a resource. You can then treat it as a Smart layer.

When you finish manipulating the resource in the new application and want to commit it to the original file, you have two options. First, you can save the edited resource as a new file by clicking the `Save As` button at the top right of the application (see Figure 9-3). This saves the image you manipulated in the new applications. You have to name it, and it ends up in your images. The new application automatically closes, and the edited resource is imported into the original Phoenix file. The resource has an application badge and remains editable like any other smart layer. The second option is to use the `Close and preserve changes` button at the top right of the new applications. This option closes the new application, imports the edited resource to the original application, and converts it to a regular bitmap layer. It doesn't have an application badge and it is flattened. The flattened image no longer contains editable layers, effects, or paths.

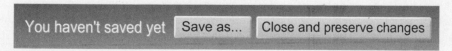

Figure 9-3. Controls for application switching

Finally, if at any time you are in the new application window and want to discard any changes that you have made, just close the window. Because you didn't commit anything to the original file, the smart layer is restored to its original state.

Application switching in Peacock

Application switching in Peacock is essentially the same as in Phoenix; it just has a different process for handling the application resources. While in Peacock, if you import a resource from Aviary's Library that was made in Phoenix, Raven, or Peacock, it is still editable in its native application. Like in Phoenix, any application resource has an application badge attached. You can examine your resource in Peacock by sliding open the **Resources** sidebar (see Figure 9-4.) From the **Resources** sidebar, you can drag the resource to the workspace and add it to your Peacock file, or open in its native application in a new browser window. Just select the resource in the sidebar and click the `Edit in [Phoenix/Raven/Peacock]` button.

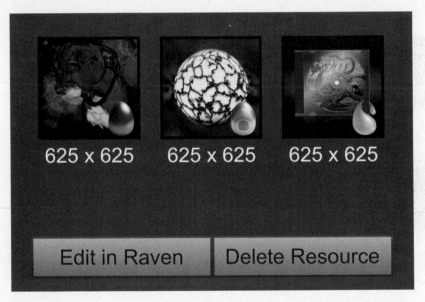

Figure 9-4. Resources that have been created in Aviary applications have a corresponding application badge.

If you find that you need the functions of a different application when working on your Peacock file, you can use application switching to create a new application resource. In the **Resources** sidebar, a dropdown menu lets you `Import a Resource`, which imports a normal bitmap resource, or you can create a `New [Phoenix/Raven/Peacock] Resource` by choosing which application you want to use (see Figure 9-5). This opens the chosen application with a black file so you can use the application tools to create your resource.

Figure 9-5. Choose the application you want to open and in which you want to make the resource.

After you are finish editing your resource in the new application, you can use the **Save as** button to save the resource; you add it to your image library and inject it into the original appllcation. Or, use the **Close and preserve changes** option to inject the resource in your original file as a normal bitmap resource (see Figure 9-3). Just like Phoenix, while editing the file in the other window, the resource also updates in Peacock whenever you switch the focus of the two windows. Consequently, you do not need to save or commit your file until you are absolutely satisfied with the results.

Project 9.1—Use Raven to Create a Vector Mask for Phoenix

Phoenix has many selection tools to separate objects in images, but the precision Raven's vectors can give you finer control over this process. Trying to separate a foreground and background in an image where there are similar colors can be tedious using Phoenix's native selection tools, but it can be quick and painless using Raven's vector paths (see Figure 9-6). Aviary's application switching makes this process of creating a vector-based selection mask for your image seamless. Your workflow is not interrupted, and it almost seems as if you are working in a single application. In this project, you learn how to perform application switching and tap into Raven's path tools for use in a Phoenix file. This process is referred to as creating a selection mask because it isn't a true mask but is instead an object used to aid selection.

Figure 9-6. This is the final image you will create in this project.

Key features used in this project

- Application switching between Phoenix and Raven
- Create Bézier and Lines tool
- Selection tools
- Paint Brush tool

> The file for this project can be found online at
> http://aviary.com/artists/gettingstartED/creations/chapter_9_project_1.

1. Import the image you are going to mask. Open a new file in Phoenix and import your image. Make sure that you size the Canvas to the same dimensions as your image. This automatically happens if you use the **Load Existing File** option to import your image. Otherwise, you have to follow the next steps. Use the **File ➤ Import File option**, locate your image to import from the **Resource Browser,** and click the **Import Image** button. Select the **Resize Canvas** option if it comes up while importing. Next, while pressing Shift, click the thumbnail of the imported image in the **Layers** panel, which selects all the pixels in the image. Finally, use the **Image ➤ Crop Selection** command to remove any extra Canvas area. The image used in this example is perfect for the Raven selection masking technique because the color on the right side of the front pear blends in with the second and is difficult to select using Phoenix's native selection tools (see Figure 9-7). Finally, name the layers in your file, as follows: Pear for the imported image and Background for the blank layer.

Figure 9-7. This resource has a similar foreground color and background, so it is hard to separate.

2. Prepare Raven to make the layer selection mask. Unfortunately, there is no Push to Raven function yet; however, the plan is to include it in a future update. Making the Raven vector mask takes a few extra steps than if you were planning to work in Peacock or a second Phoenix file. Start by creating a new smart layer. From the Layers panel **Options** menu, select the **New Raven layer** option, which creates a new layer above the imported Image. Smart layers are layers that can be edited only in one of Aviary's other applications. You can

511

tell if a layer is editable in another application if it has an application icon badge on the layer's thumbnail. In this case, a small Raven icon 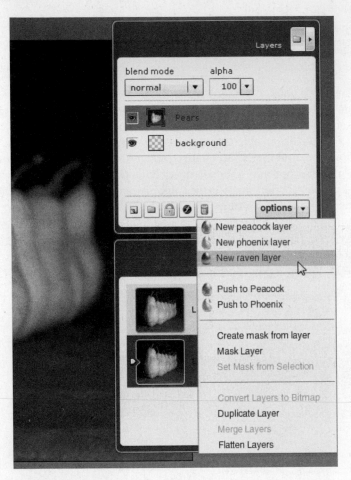 is on the layer (see Figure 9-8). Finally, name this layer Mask.

Figure 9-8. Create a New Raven Layer.

3. Smart layers maintain their native properties, so if you double-click a Peacock layer, it opens the layer in Peacock with all the hubs, and any editing that is done there is updated in Phoenix. Double-click this layer to open it in Raven, which is launched in a new window (see Figure 9-9).

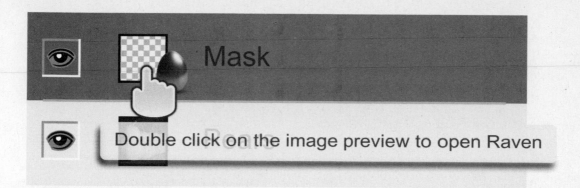

Figure 9-9. Smart layers have application badges on them.

4. When Raven opens, you need to set the file size to the same dimensions as your original Phoenix file. An easy way to find out the size is to use the **Image ➤ Image Resize** command in Phoenix. The **Resize image** dialog box opens with the **Width** and **Height** parameters set to the current dimensions of the file. Transfer these numbers to the corresponding parameters in the Raven file (see Figure 9-10).

Figure 9-10. Set the start size of your Raven file.

5. For reference, you need to import the same image as in Step 1. In the future, there will be an option to have the resource automatically imported from Phoenix, but for now you have to do it manually. Use the **File ➤ Import File** command to open the resource browser to import the image (see Figure 9-11).

513

Figure 9-11. Import the same image into Raven.

6. With the image imported into Raven, create your selection mask. Select the Bézier and lines tool 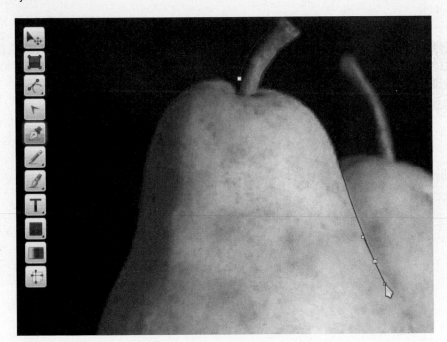, and then draw a path around the object you want to separate; in this case, it is the pear (see Figure 9-12). At this stage, you don't have to get the path perfect because you can adjust it later. For more information about using the Bézier and Line tools, see Chapter 4, Project 1.

Figure 9-12. Use the Bézier and Lines tool to draw a path around the shape.

7. After you finish your rough path around the object, set the fill to **none** by clicking the **No Fill** button in the **Fill and Stroke** panel. Next, set the Stroke to a contrasting color to make it easier to see. Then, select the Edit Paths by Nodes tool and adjust the anchor points and control handles to correct any errors in the path (see Figure 9-13). The intent is to

create a path that is just slightly inside the edge of the object you are separating. You don't want it to be directly on the edge because you run the chance that some of the background is included in the selection mask and ruin the effect. By making this path smaller than the object, you do not have to manually clean up the object later, which defeats the purpose of creating a selection mask in Raven.

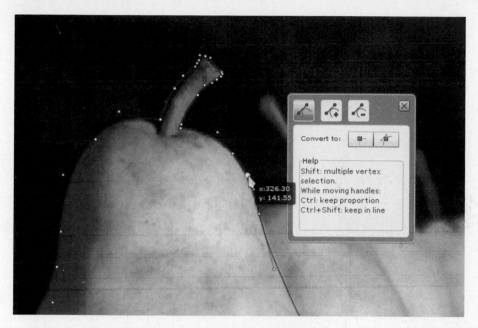

Figure 9-13. Fine-tune your path with the Edit Paths by Nodes tool.

8. After you are satisfied with the path, change the fill back to a solid color ☐ in the Fill and Stroke panels **Fill** tab. Then, switch to the **Stroke** tab, and remove the stroke by setting its **Type** to None. Then, delete the reference image that you had imported because you already have a copy in the Phoenix file by selecting it in Raven's Layers panel and clicking the **Delete** button at the bottom of the panel (see Figure 9-14).

Figure 9-14. Remove the reference image before switching back to Phoenix.

9. You can check your progress by bringing the Phoenix application to the front. Any change you made in Raven is updated soon after Phoenix gains focus so you can see how the Raven file looks when it is imported. You are going to see the Raven shape lying on the first pear. You want just a small piece of this pear to show at the edges so you don't get any of the background in the select mask. When you are satisfied and ready to commit it to Phoenix, click the `Close and preserve changes` button in the upper right corner of Raven, which exports the object into Phoenix and close the application (see Figure 9-15).

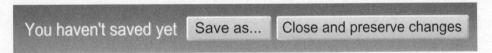

Figure 9-15. Switch back to Phoenix.

There are three options for how a file is handled in application switching. These options are available only in the application that was launched from a smart layer.

- **`Save as`**: Saves the file as an .egg file and shows up in your creations; the result is exported to the original .egg file.

- **`Close and preserve changes`**: Converts the file to a bitmap and does not save it as an extra file. The resulting bitmap is exported into the original .egg file.

- **`Discard`**: If you want to discard the changes, just close the new window and the old version is restored.

10. With the Raven object now in Phoenix, hold Shift down and click its thumbnail in the **`Layers`** panel to select all of its pixels. Then use the **`Selection ➤ Invert Selection`** to select everything but the Raven object (see Figure 9-16). Next, select the layer that contains the imported image and press the Delete button on your keyboard or use the **`Edit ➤ Delete`** command, which both remove everything but the area under the Raven object. Now, you can delete the layer with the Raven object because it is no longer needed. Although this process is not as fast as using the Eraser tool in Phoenix, it gives you better control over the separation of the object, and the edge is crisper, which gives a more professional look.

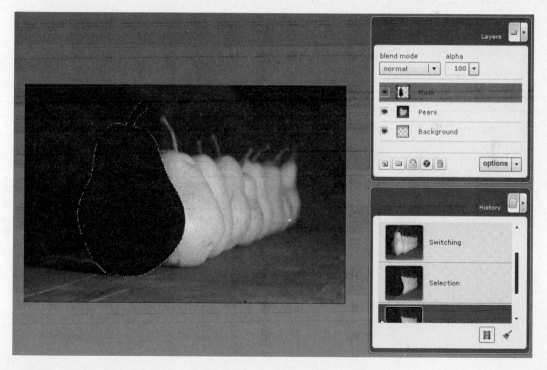

Figure 9-16. Use the Raven object to separate the part of the image you want.

11. Next, import the image you want to use as a background. If the image is bigger than the current Canvas, use the `Resize Canvas` feature so that nothing is clipped (see Figure 9-17). This resource is added as the top layer, so you need to arrange the layer stacking order so that the object that you just separated, the pear in this example, is at the top. Name the newly imported layer Kid.

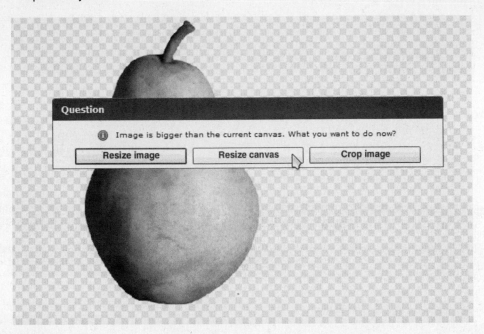

Figure 9-17. Import the background image and resize the Canvas as needed.

12. Position the pear in the boy's arms. Now, use the Transformation tool to scale position and rotate the object so that it fits with the background. To make this process easier, lower the layer's Alpha to 60. This helps you see how it relates to the background image. In this example, the idea is to position and scale the pear so that it looks like the boy is holding it instead of the ball. As you can see, the light on the boy is coming from the upper, left but the light on the pear is coming from the upper, right. You need to mirror the pear horizontally. This can be done with the Transform tool by dragging one of the left or right control handles on the transformation box through and beyond the opposite side. This flips the image of the pear so that it appears that the light is coming from the upper, left like the boy (see Figure 9-18).

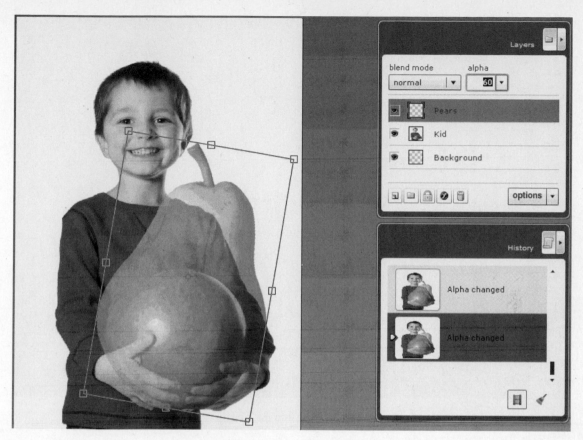

Figure 9-18. Position your object on the background.

13. Remove some of the pear so that it appears as if the boy is holding it. With the object still at a lower Alpha so that you can see the underlying image, use the Eraser tool 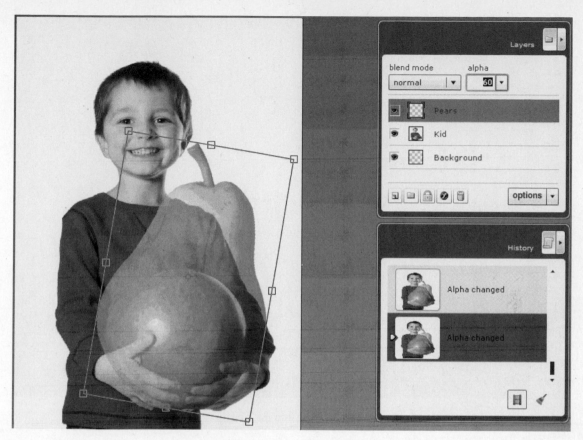 to remove any area of the background that you want to appear above the object. In this example, the boy's hands need to appear as though they are wrapping around the pear, so you need to erase parts of the pear that are covering his hands. With the Eraser tool, set the **Hardness** level between 60 and 80 to soften the edges of the erased area (see Figure 9-19). You probably need to adjust the **Size** of the tool according to the need, using a smaller eraser to erase minute details.

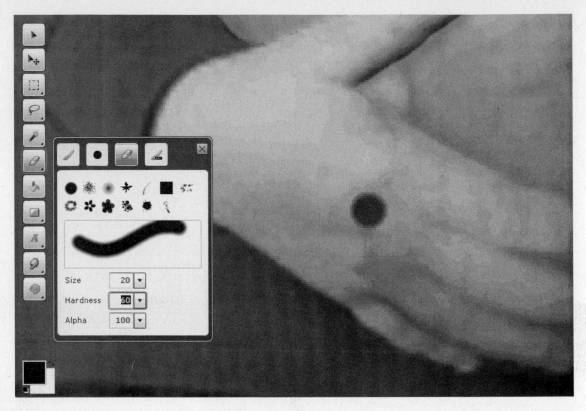

Figure 9-19. Use the Eraser Tool to place the object into the background.

14. Paint some shading on the boy. Create a new layer and place it between the background image, the boy, and the pear object, and name the layer shadow 1. Using the Paintbrush Tool

with **Alpha** set between 10–30 and **Hardness** set at 0, paint in any cast shadows from the object that might fall onto the background (see Figure 9-20). In this case, the pear casts a shadow on the boy, and because the layer is in between the pear and the boy, the shadow does not show up on the pear. If you find that the shadow is too dark, you can adjust the shadow layer's **Alpha** in the **Layers** panel without disrupting the rest of the image.

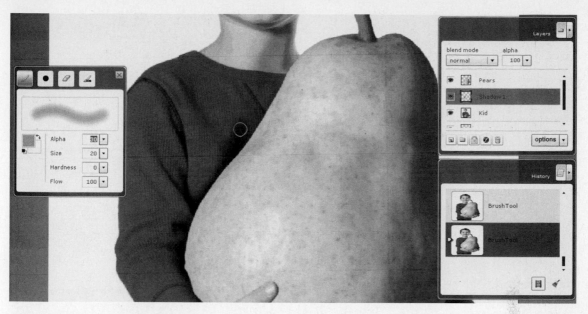

Figure 9-20. Add shading to help merge the object and the background.

15. Next, add shading to the pear. Again, select all the pear object pixels by pressing the Shift key and clicking its thumbnail in the **Layers** panel. Next, create a new layer and make sure it is above all others, naming it Shadow 2. Take the Paintbrush tool and paint in a shadow that is on the object itself (see Figure 9-21). Experiment with changing the color of the shadow to darker hues of the original object where the shadow is placed, because most are not pure black. In this example, the shadow color is set to brown, which was sampled from a dark area on the pear with the Eye Dropper tool . Add more layers and shadows as needed to give the illusion that the object and background are occupying the same space. Don't forget that you can add Layer filters for fine-tuning blurs, adding glows, or adding drop shadows.

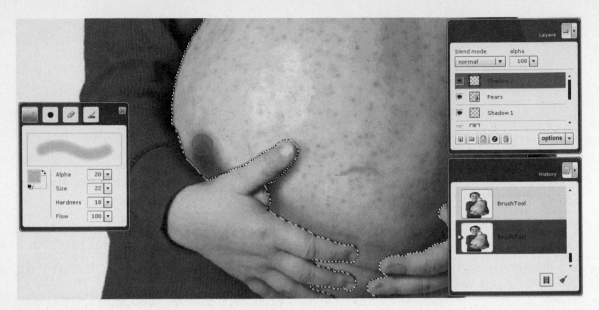

Figure 9-21. Create shadows and highlights on the object.

Project review

In this project, you saw how to use application switching to seamlessly utilize the unique assets of two applications at once. You created a vector mask in Raven to cut out the pear shape, and then used this mask instantly in Phoenix to cut out the pear. From there, it was a simple matter of adding the correct shading and highlights to merge the pear into the scene. In the next project, you see how you can use application switching to give Peacock text elements.

Project 9.2—Use Phoenix to Create Text Elements in Peacock

Peacock is an incredible application for creating web elements, with its nondestructive effects, powerful blending hub, and robust pattern generation. It can create stunning web elements. However, in all its power, it has no way to generate text elements. This is where application switching and Phoenix come in to save the day. In this project, you construct a button that can be used as a button on a website or other user interface. This button is styled to fit with a Web 2.0 type of interface. This consists of large colorful elements with smooth gradients or stripes. It must have easy to read graphics (see Figure 9-22). You switch applications to create and position the text for the button in Phoenix, and use Peacock's vast array of effects to construct the button itself (see Figure 9-23).

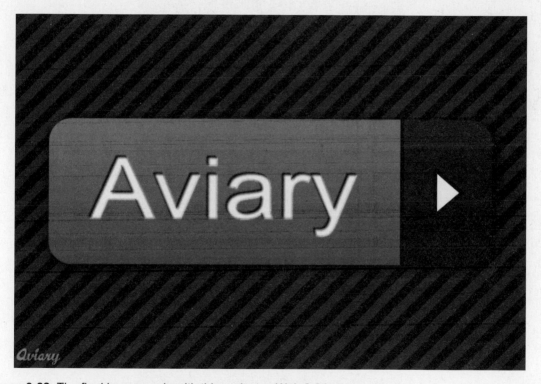

Figure 9-22. The final image made with this project, a Web 2.0 button

Key features used in this project

- Application switching between Peacock and Phoenix
- Gradient hub
- Masker hub
- Text tool

The file for this project can be found online at
http://aviary.com/artists/gettingstartED/creations/chapter_9_project_2.

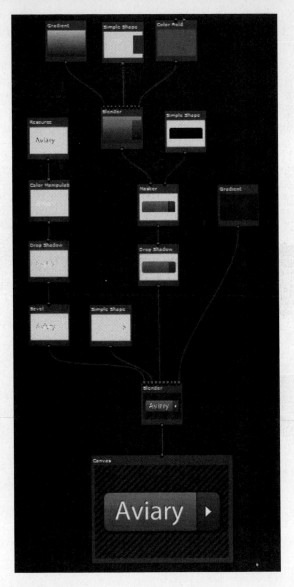

Figure 9-23. The hub layout for this file

1. Start a new Peacock file, but before you start adding any hubs, set the Canvas dimensions. Because you are making a button, the Canvas needs to be resized so that it more closely reflects the dimensions of the button. Set the **Width** of the Canvas in the **Properties** panel

to 800 and the **Height** to 550 (see Figure 9-24). This wider Canvas is closer to the dimensions of the button you are creating and is a better use of the Canvas space.

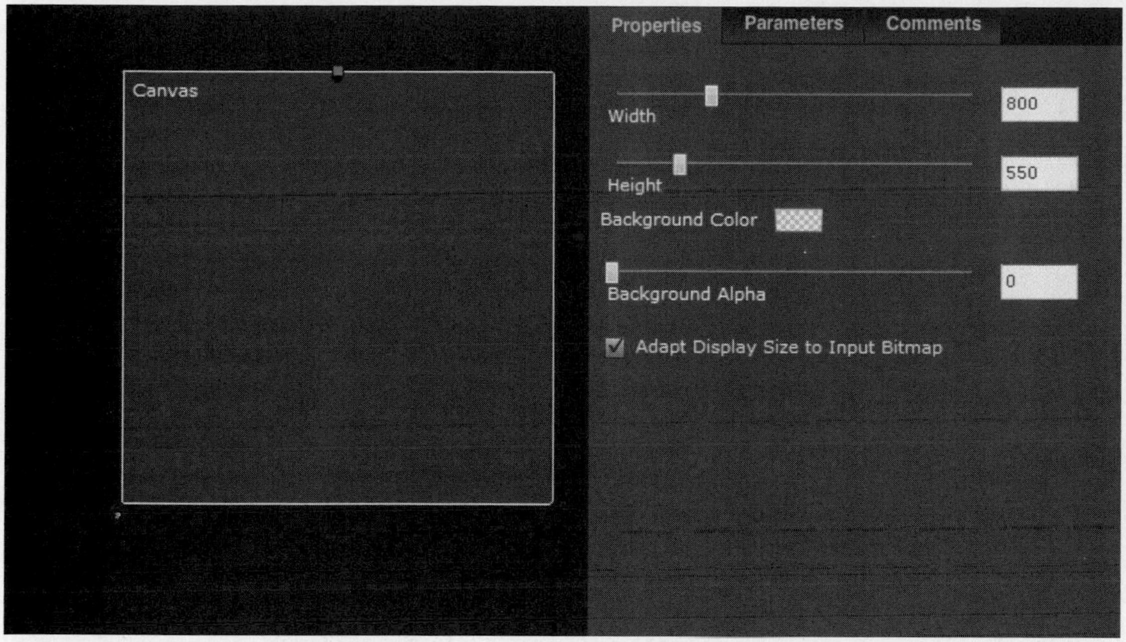

Figure 9-24. Set the Canvas dimension to be wider and shorter than the default.

2. Drag a Simple Shape hub from the **Generators** tab; it automatically connects to the Canvas hub because it is the first hub introduced into the file. You want this button to have round corners so it fits with the Web 2.0 style, but there is no direct option to round the corners of the shapes. The best way to create rounded edges is to use a wide stroke around the shape; the wider the stroke, the rounder the corners. Start by setting the **Stroke Width** of the shape to 70. Because the **Stroke Joint Type** is set to **Round**, the stroke produces smooth corners on the shape. Finally, set the **Horizontal Scale** to 160 and the **Vertical Scale** to 40, which sizes the shape to fit the space. Make sure that the **Proportional Lock** checkbox to the right of the scale sliders is unchecked, so that you are able to move the slider independently (see Figure 9-25).

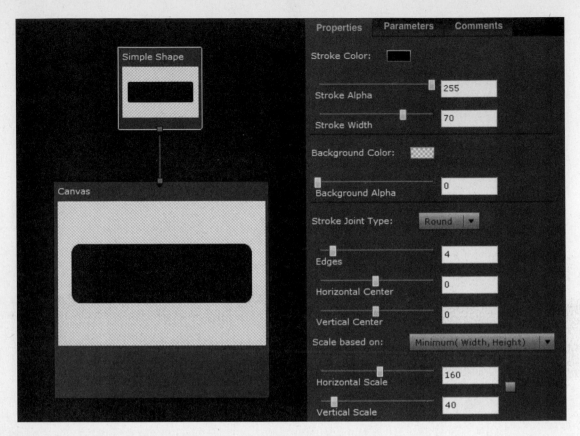

Figure 9-25. Create a rounded rectangle for the Base button shape.

3. Give your button some color with a masked color field. Add a Masker hub from the **Controllers** sidebar between the Simple Shape and Canvas hubs. Leave the **Properties** of the Masker to their default settings. Next, drag a Color Field hub from the **Generators** sidebar, and connect it to the first Input pin on the Masker. Set the **Color** in the **Color Field Properties** to a bright blue (#0075ff). See Figure 9-26. This is the main color of the button, but you can change this to any color you would like to match your color scheme.

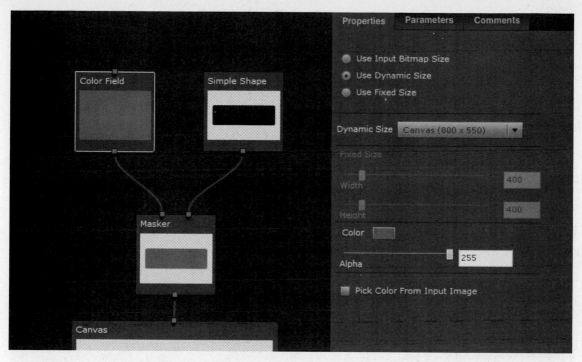

Figure 9-26. Add a Color Field hub and a `Masker` to clip it to the button shape.

4. Use a Simple shape to give your button a second tone. Drag a Blender hub from the `Controllers` sidebar, and connect it between the Color Field hub and the Masker. Adjust the connection so that the Color Field is connected to the last Input pin on the Blender. Next, add a Simple Shape hub to one of the middle Input pins on the Blender. Set the Simple Shape's `Color` to dark gray, `Stroke Width` to 6, and `Horizontal Center` to 50, which offsets the new shape to the right and creates a second color on the button (Figure 9-27).

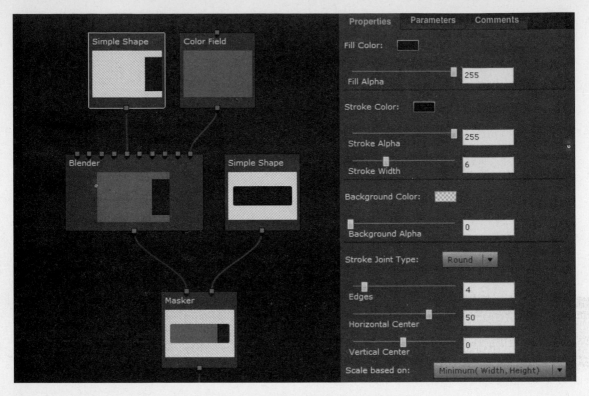

Figure 9-27. Add another Simple Shape with a Blender to divide the button.

5. Create a smooth gradient to your button with an overlay. Drag a Gradient hub from the **Generators** sidebar, and connect it to the Blender hub's first Input pin. Set the **Rotation** parameter for this hub to 90 so that it is a vertical gradient. Next, select the Blender hub, and set this new layer's **Blend Mode** to **Overlay**, which gives the button a slight gradation of value that is lighter at the top and darker at the bottom (see Figure 9-28).

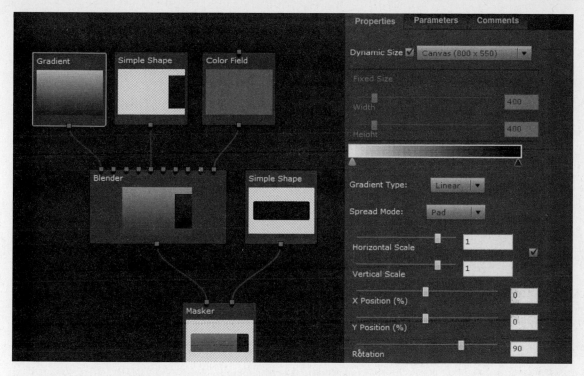

Figure 9-28. Add a Gradient hub to give the button some depth.

6. Give your button some depth with a shadow. Drag a Drop Shadow hub from the **Effects** sidebar, and connect it between the Masker and the Blender hubs. Set the **Horizontal Blur** and **Vertical Blur Radius** to 24, to give a soft shadow under the button (see Figure 9-29). This sets it off from the background.

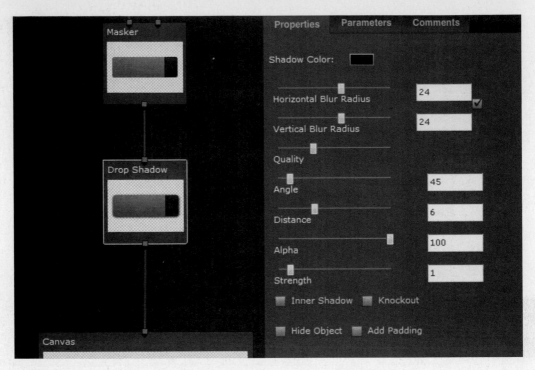

Figure 9-29. Add a Drop Shadow to set the button off of the background.

7. Add a Blender to your file so that you can combine a label and background for your button. Drag a Blender hub from the **Controllers** sidebar, and connect it between the Drop Shadow and Canvas hubs. Move the connection from the Drop shadow to a middle Input pin on the Blender hub (see Figure 9-30).

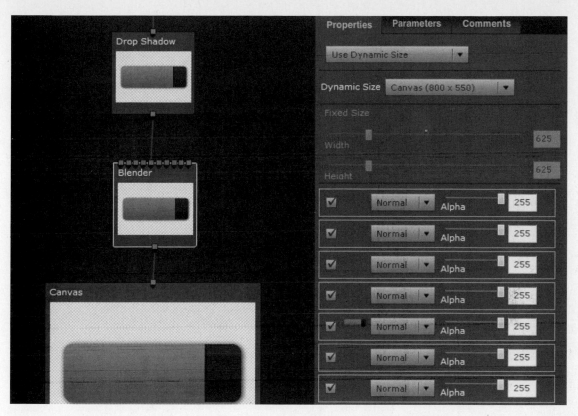

Figure 9-30. Add a second Blender to the file so you can combine the label and button.

8. Now switch to Phoenix to make the text label for the button. Drag a Resource hub from the **Generators** sidebar, and connect it to the first Input pin on the new Blender hub. Next, open the **Resources** sidebar, select **New Phoenix Resource** from the dropdown menu, and click the **OK** button. This opens Phoenix in a new window and starts the application with the same

Canvas dimension as the Peacock file. After the application is loaded, select the Text tool and click the Canvas to set the start point of your text. Set the font that you want for your button, the color to gray, and the size to around 288. Type the text you want on your button. In

this case, use the word Aviary for the label. Using the Move tool, roughly position the text where you think it should appear on the button (see Figure 9-31). Bring Peacock back to the top, do not close Phoenix at this time, and open the **Resources** sidebar. The image you just created in Phoenix now shows up as a Resource. Drag the new Resource hub, and connect it to the first Input pin on the first Blender hub.

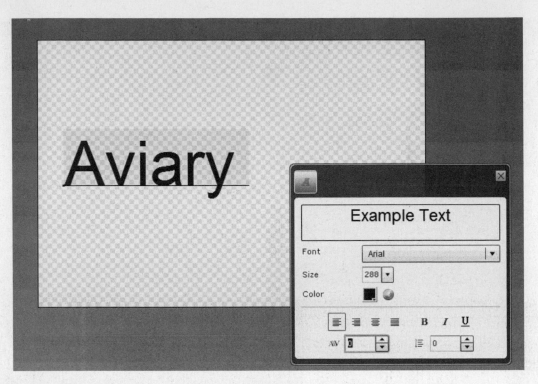

Figure 9-31. Switch to Phoenix to set the text for the button.

9. Check the position of the Phoenix text resource on the button. If it needs to be adjusted, just switch back to Phoenix, change its position, and switch back to Peacock. Any changes you make in Phoenix are updated in Peacock, which makes it easy to align objects (see Figure 9-32). After you are satisfied with the placement, set the `color` of the text to white, and click the `Close and Preserve changes` button in the top, right of Phoenix. This closes Phoenix and commits the file as a resource in Peacock.

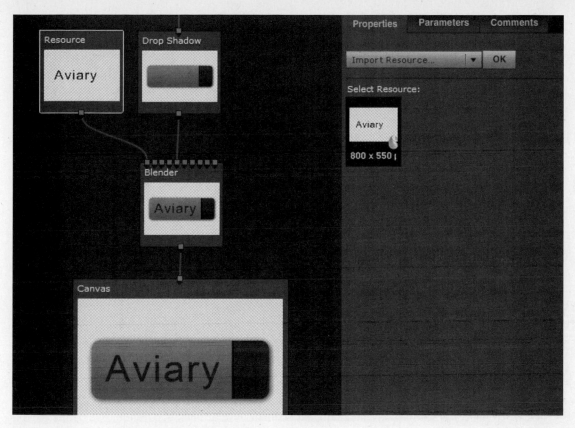

Figure 9-32. Adjust the position of the Phoenix resource.

10. Inset the text into the button. Drag a Drop Shadow hub from the **Effects** sidebar, and connect it between the Resource and the Blender hubs. Enable the **Inner Shadow** option, which gives the illusion of the text inset into the button. Set the **Horizontal Blur Radius** and **Vertical Blur Radius** to 4 and the **Distance** parameter to 2 to tighten up the shadow (see Figure 9-33).

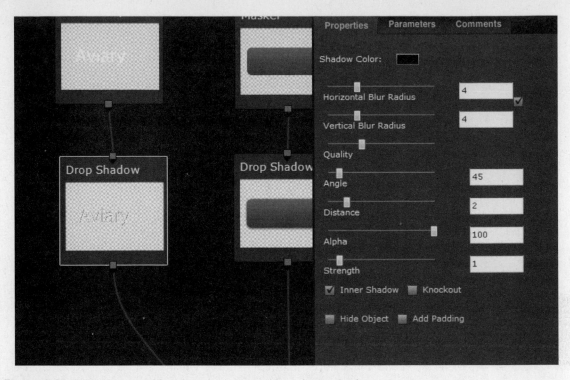

Figure 9-33. Inset the text object into the button with an inner shadow.

11. Create a chiseled effect around the text element. Add a Bevel hub from the `Effects` sidebar, and connect it between the second Drop Shadow and the first Blender hubs. Set the `Type` to `Outer Bevel`, `Horizontal Blur Radius` and `Vertical Blur Radius` to 2, `Angle` to 225, and the `Distance` to 2 (see Figure 9-34). This gives a thin highlight around the text, which gives the impression of light reflecting off the edges of the inset text.

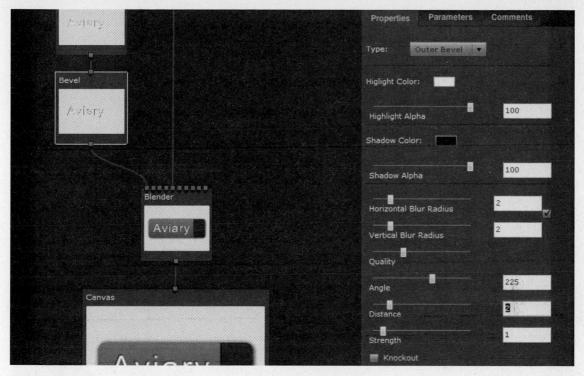

Figure 9-34. Use an outer Bevel to give some contour to the inset text.

12. Make an arrow on the right side of the button. Add a Simple Shape hub from the `Generators` sidebar to the second or third Input pin on the first Blender hub, and make sure that it is connected above the base button shape. Set the `Fill Color` of the shape to white, and set the `Stroke Color` to black with a `Stroke Width` of 3. Change the `Edges` parameter to 6, making the shape a triangle. Size the shape by setting the `Horizontal Scale` to 10 and the `Vertical Scale` to 15. Finally, set the `Shape Rotation` to -165 and the `Horizontal Center` to 34; this points the shape to the right and centers it on the gray part of the button (see Figure 9-35).

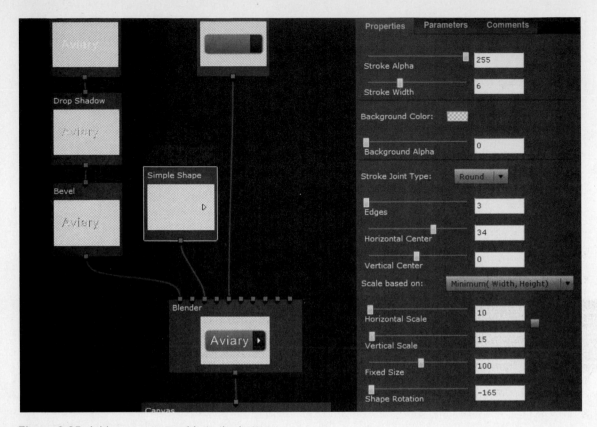

Figure 9-35. Add an arrow graphic to the button.

13. Add a background to your button. This is an optional step because you do not want a background for the button when you use it in an interface. However, adding a background is good for preview purposes. Drag a Gradient hub from the **Generators** sidebar, and connect it to the last Input pin on the Blender just above the Canvas. Start by setting the two colors in the Gradient to dark gray (#333333) fading into a slightly darker gray (#121212). Drag the two color stops so they are both in the center of the colorbar, and set the **Spread Mode** to **Repeat**. Finally, set the **Horizontal Scale** and **Vertical Scale** to 0.035 and the **Rotation** parameter to 45; this produces a striped pattern for the background of the button (see Figure 9-36).

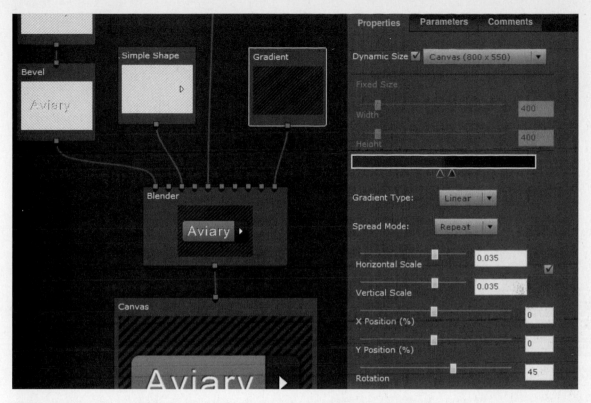

Figure 9-36. You can add a background to your button for preview purposes.

Project review

Application switching lets Peacock, Phoenix, and Raven share their tools. This fills in any lack of feature in any given application. Peacock might have vast power to create effects but it has no way to generate text, and Phoenix's effect and filters are pretty limited. However, these two applications can lend their features to the other giving you the best of both. You learned in this project how to perform application switching from inside Peacock. Using Phoenix's text tool is flexible because the resource is updated when changing focus of the applications. You easily created a text element, positioned it on the button, and added it to your file, which gives you a tool that was not offered in Peacock. In the next project, you are introduced to Blackboxed files. These dynamic effect files can be used to automate a process, quickly reuse complex effects, be used as custom filters, and more.

Blackboxes and custom filters

A Blackbox is an object that is viewed in terms of its input, output, and transforming ability without any knowledge of its internal workings. As by definition, the Blackboxed Peacock file's inner workings are hidden. You can think of a Blackbox as a machine; you deposit a resource at the top. Then, as it passes through the machine actions are performed that alter the resource, and at the end, the manipulated resource is output below. This means you can perform the same action on many different resources by feeding them through the Blackbox machine. However, like many things, one size does not fit all. This is where User Interface (UI) Elements play their role. UI Elements are user-interface objects that essentially reach into a Blackbox file and allow you to change parameters in the machine (see Figure 9-37). Peacock uses Blackboxes to group a set of hubs into one so it can be reused repeatedly. This is similar to Photoshop's actions or Gimp's scripts; it is a set of predefined actions and effects that are performed automatically. This streamlines some tedious processes that you might set up repeatedly. Create one Blackboxed file to reuse these commands with constant results. Phoenix can also tap into the power of Blackboxes and use them as custom filters. Soon you will be able to use these Blackbox files anywhere. Because these files are a self-contained set of effects, they are great to share. Any user can use public Blackbox files to enhance images. This enables users who might not understand how to use Peacock tap into the powerful application. Aviary is developing, a standalone Blackbox application. Look for it to be added to the Aviary suite in the near future.

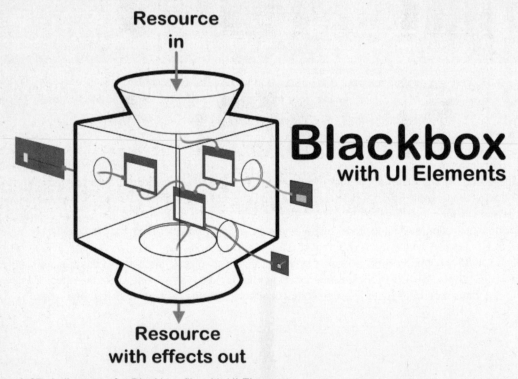

Figure 9-37. A diagram of a Blackbox file with UI Elements

Blackbox files are automatically defined in Aviary if they contain one or more of the following objects. These Blackbox files are imported from a dedicated `Blackbox Browser`. To open the `Blackbox Browser` in Peacock, open the Blackboxes sidebar, and select the `Import Blackbox` from the dropdown menu. In Phoenix, use the `Filters` ➤ `Import Custom Filter` to open the `Blackbox Browser`.

- `Dynamic Resource`: Creates a file with one or more dynamic resources in it. When it is imported as a Blackbox file, each (dynamic resource) shows up as an Input pin.
- `Dynamic Output`: Creates a file with one or more dynamic outputs in it. When it is imported as a Blackbox file, each (dynamic output) shows up as an Output pin.
- `UI Elements`: Creates a file with one or more UI Elements in it. When it is imported as a Blackbox file, each slider, checkbox, or Color Picker shows up as control in the Properties panel for that Blackbox.

Project 9.3—Build a Blackbox File and Use It as a Custom Filter in Phoenix

Blackboxes can range from simple actions such as adding a preset bevel to complex object-generating templates. However complex the Blackbox, you soon become aware of the time it saves you when you want to reuse Peacock effects for other images or even share an effect with other users. In this project, you construct a simple Blackbox file that produces a snow effect. This effect alters the color of the input image and adds a flurry of snowflakes over the top. You even use UI Elements to give you control over the amount of snow that is added to the image. After this Blackbox is constructed, you learn how to use it as a custom filter in Phoenix (see Figure 9-38). You explore how you can build reusable and controllable filters with Peacock.

Figure 9-38. The final image created with a Blackbox custom filter in Phoenix

Key features used in this project

- Blackbox creation
- UI Elements
- Custom filters

> *The file for this project can be found online at*
> *http://aviary.com/artists/gettingstartED/creations/chapter_9_project_3.*
>
> *Image resource for this project can be found online at*
> *http://aviary.com/artists/gettingstartED/creations/chapter_9_project_3_custom_*
> *filter.*

1. Start by opening a new Peacock file, and dragging a Dynamic Resource hub from the **Generators** sidebar onto the workspace. This hub automatically connects to the Canvas hub because it is the first hub introduced to the file. The Dynamic Resource hub's default state output a small Peacock icon; this is just a placeholder (see Figure 9-39). When the Blackbox file is imported into Phoenix as a custom filter, the layer that the filter is performed on takes the place of the Dynamic Resource. Because the inner workings of a Blackbox file are hidden, it is good practice to label any dynamic hubs so that others who use the filter know what each one does. Change the **Label** parameter to "Input image."

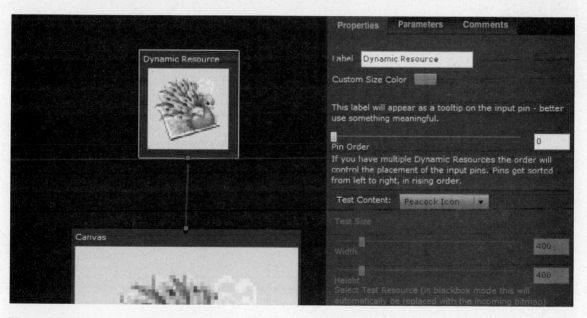

Figure 9-39. A Dynamic Resource automatically defines a Blackbox file.

Figure 9-40. The Dynamic Resource is a place holder for inputs in Blackbox files.

The Dynamic Resource hub is a placeholder for an input resource utilized in Blackboxed files or custom filters (see Figure 9-40). Its default output is a 64 x 64 peacock icon, but it can be changed to a set dimension or bitmap resource. This resource is replaced with the input image or layer when the Blackbox file or a custom filter is used.

- **Label**: This title displays when hovering over a pin on the Blackboxed file when it is imported into another file.
- **Custom Size Color**: Sets the highlight color of a hub when it uses the dynamic resource size.
- **Pin Order**: Sets the order in which the Input pins appear on the hub.
- **Test Content**: The image that the Dynamic hub outputs while building the Blackbox file. After the file is put into actual use, this is replaced by the image that is fed into the Blackbox or custom filters.
  - **Peacock Icon**: Uses the Peacock application icon at 64 x 64 pixel size.
  - **Checkerboard**: Uses a black and white checkerboard pattern. You can set the output dimensions with the **Size** parameters.
  - **Resource**: Uses any loaded resource. Choose from available resources in the selection area directly below this parameter.
- **Size**: Sets the size of the dynamic resources height and width. It is available only when using the checkerboard source.
- **Select Area**: All available resources are displayed here. If a resource is used as test content, choose it from here.

2. The input to be used with this Blackbox can be any dimension. This can cause problems if the hubs in a Blackbox are at several different dimensions. You need to have the Blackbox adjust its size according to the image used as the input. Because most hubs' sizes are based on the dimension of the Canvas, link the Height and Width parameters of the Dynamic Resources and Canvas hubs. This can be done by exposing these parameters. In the **Dynamic Resources Properties** panel, switch from the **Properties** tab to the **Parameters** tab. You see a list of all the parameters assigned to the hub. Checking the **In** box next to a parameter adds an Input pin that accepts a setting from an outside source. Checking the **Out** box adds an Output pin that pushes the parameter setting to another hub. These parameter pins are added on the

left and right sides of the hub and can be connected only to other parameters pins. Check the **Out** boxes for the **Resource Width** and **Resource Height** in the Dynamic Resource's **Parameters**. Note that there are two new Output pins on the right side of the hub (see Figure 9-41). These push the **Height** and **Width** parameters to another hub.

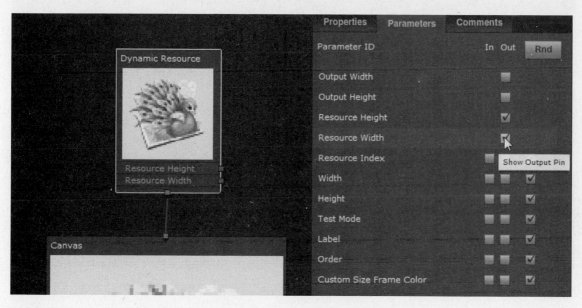

Figure 9-41. Expose parameters to pass information between hubs.

3. Next, select the Canvas hub and open the **Parameters** tab. Check the **Canvas Width** and **Canvas Height** parameters in the **In** column to add the two Input pins. Next, drag a connection line from the **Canvas Width** parameter pin to the **Resource Width** parameter pin on the Dynamic resource. Then, connect the two height parameters in the same way (see Figure 9-42). Now, the Canvas automatically matches the size of the resource that is used in the Blackbox file. Any width or height of input dimensions of the image is pushed as the Width and Height setting of the Canvas. A thing to be aware of when constructing Blackbox files is that they can get overly complicated quickly from the added Input pins, Output pins, and connector lines. Take your time and you should not have problems.

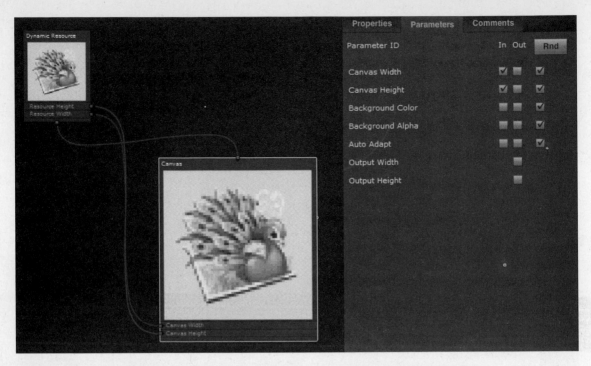

Figure 9-42. Linking the width and height parameters to the Dynamic Resource hub.

4. Give your snow-producing Blackbox a color tone with a Color Manipulation hub. Drag a Color Manipulation hub from the **Effects** sidebar, and connect it in between the Dynamic Resource and the Canvas hubs. Because you want to give the image the feeling of being out in the snow, this brightens reduces contrast and gives a slight blue tint to the image, all which can be achieved with the Color Manipulation hub. Set the **Saturation** to 0.5, the **Contrast** to 0.05, and increase the **Brightness** to 75. Finally, set the **Tint** color to a bright blue and set the **Tint** slider to 0.25. You can see the setting in a tooltip while setting this parameter (see Figure 9-43).

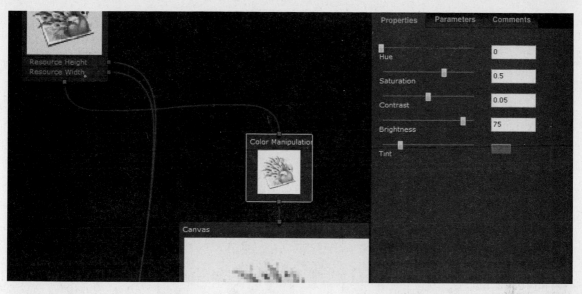

Figure 9-43. Add a Color Manipulation hub to give the resource an overall cooler tone.

5. Use a Perlin Noise hub to create the base for the snowflakes. Add a Blender hub from the **Controllers** sidebar between the Color Manipulation and the Canvas hubs. Adjust the connection so that the Color Manipulation hub is connected to the last Input pin on the Blender. Drag a Perlin Noise hub from the **Generators** sidebar, and connect it to the first Input pin on the Blender hub. Reduce the **Horizontal Scale** and **Vertical Scale** to 0.02 (see Figure 9-44). This looks like the regular noise due to the small size of the Dynamic Resource. It is at 64 x 64. Don't worry about the small size because the input image used with this `file` is larger, and the effect scales to accommodate the larger dimension.

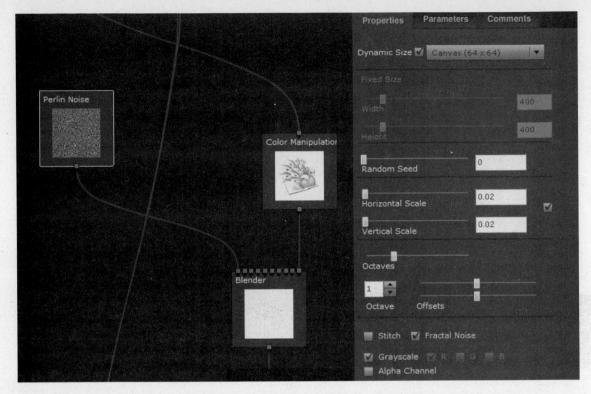

Figure 9-44. Add Blender and Perlin Noise hubs as a base for the snow effect.

6. Refine the snowflakes with a Threshold effect. Drag a Threshold hub from the **Effects** sidebar and connect it between the Perlin Noise and Blender hubs. For now, set the **Threshold** level to 150; you add a UI Element to control this parameter later (see Figure 9-45). Select the Blender hub, and change this layer's Blend Mode to **Add**, which lets only the white elements from the Threshold show.

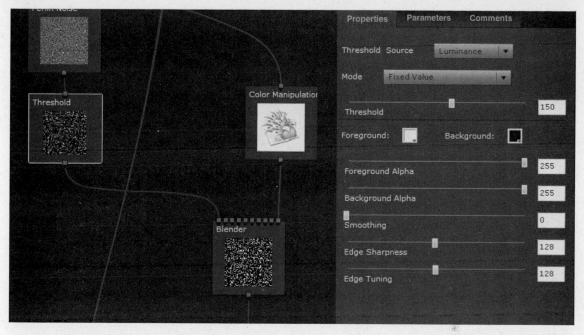

Figure 9-45. Use a Threshold hub to refine the snowflakes.

7. Give your snowflakes some motion. Drag out a Motion Blur hub from the **Effects** sidebar, and connect it between the Threshold and Blender hubs. Set the **Angle** parameter to 60 and the **Blur Amount** to 10. This makes the snowflakes look as if they are falling (see Figure 9-46).

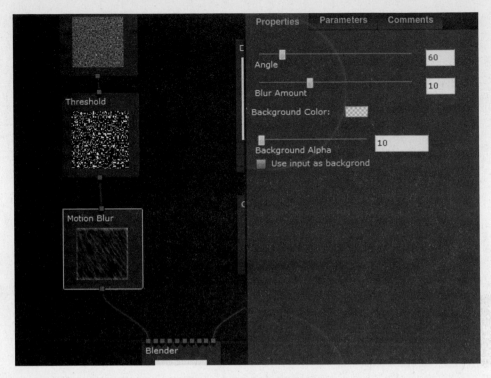

Figure 9-46. Add a Motion Blur to give the snow some movement.

8. You might want to change the amount of snow that is produced with this Blackbox file, which can be done with a UI Element. **UI Elements** are `Controllers` that can be linked to the Properties of hubs. Some of these Controllers are presented to the user in Blackboxed files, and others perform adjustment functions on them. Slider, Checkbox, Number List, and Random Number produce controls for the user of the Blackbox to interact with, whereas the other hubs modify the parameters produced by these controls. Add controls to the `Threshold` parameter. Select the Threshold hub, open the `Parameters` tab, and check the `Threshold` parameter in the `In` column, which adds a new Input pin on the hub (Figure 9-47).

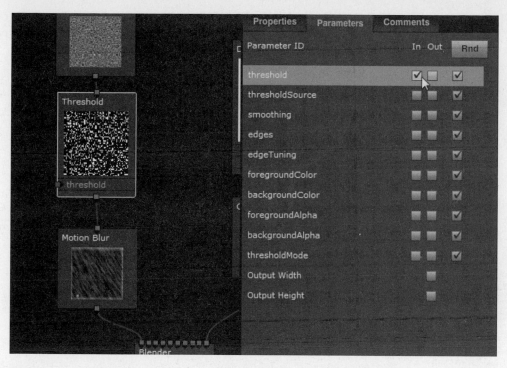

Figure 9-47. Add a UI Element to dynamically adjust parameters in a Blackbox file.

9. Use a Slider hub to give the Blackbox user control of the threshold parameter. Drag a Slider hub from the **UI Element** sidebar. Connect the Value Output pin on the Slider to the **Threshold** parameter pin on the Threshold hub, which transfers the control of the **Threshold** parameter to the slider. In the Slider **Properties** panel, set the **Label** to **Snow Amount** so that others know what this slider does. Set the **Minimum Value** parameter to 150 and the **Maximum Value** to 200, which sets the **Threshold** parameter range that the user is allowed to set. Set the start value of the slider by setting the **Value** parameter to 150. Finally, set the **Decimals** parameter to 0 because the **Threshold** parameter uses only whole integers and ignores any decimals (see Figure 9-48).

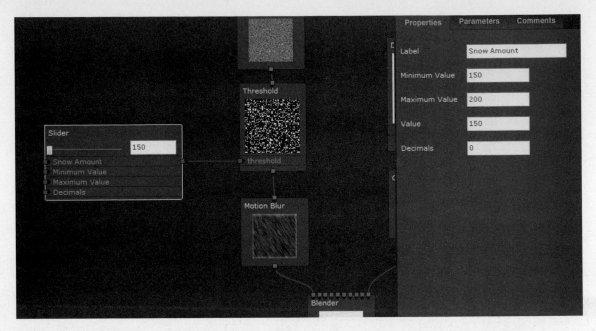

Figure 9-48. A Slider hub in the file produces a slider control in the Blackbox file or custom filter.

10. Save the file like any other file. Aviary automatically categorizes this file as a Blackbox, because it contains a Dynamic Resource and Slider hubs. It is good practice to add a description and tags to make it easier to find and to know what it does (see Figure 9-49). You are done with the Blackbox and can close Peacock now.

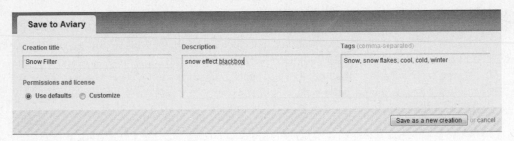

Figure 9-49. Save the file normally.

11. Use the Blackbox you just created as a **custom filter**. Start a new Phoenix file, and use the **File ➤ Import File** command to import an image to use with the snow effect Blackbox you just made. After this image is loaded into the file, adjust the Canvas so that it is the same dimensions as the image. To load the Blackbox file into Phoenix, use the **Filters ➤ Import Custom Filter** command, which opens the Blackbox browser (see Figure 9-50).

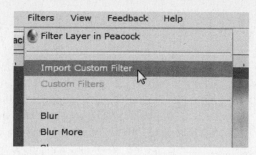

Figure 9-50. Use the `Import Custom Filter` command to load a Blackbox file.

12. Locate the Blackbox file you just made in the browser window. If you just made the file, it might not show up right away and can take up to 30 minutes to be added to this list. Also, if your Blackbox file permission is set to private, you must check the `Search only my library` option for it to show (see Figure 9-51). After you have selected the Blackbox, click the `OK` button to load it into Phoenix.

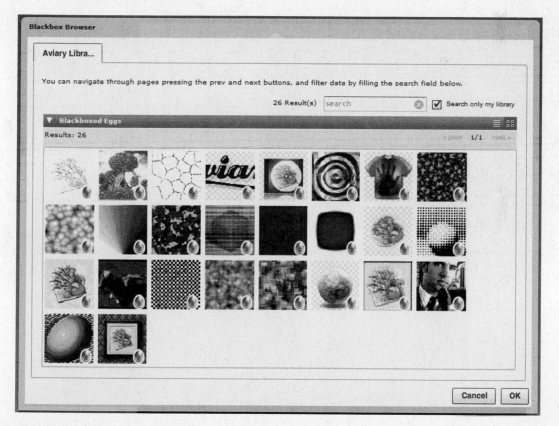

Figure 9-51. The Blackbox browser shows only Blackbox files.

13. Apply the snow **custom filter**. After the Blackbox is loaded into Phoenix, it opens the filter's window. This displays a preview of the filter and any parameter controls. For this file, you had a Slider attached to the threshold parameter, so it shows in the **Properties** section. Set it to 180, which gives a heavy snow effect to the image (Figure 9-52). You can play with other settings to see the range this effect produces. When you are satisfied with the results of the filter, click the **Apply** button to close the Filter window and apply the resulting image as a new layer to the Phoenix file. If at any time you want to apply this Blackbox filter to another layer in your file, you can find it under the **Filters ➤ Custom Filters** command (see Figure 9-53). Now you can easily apply this snow custom filter to any image you want.

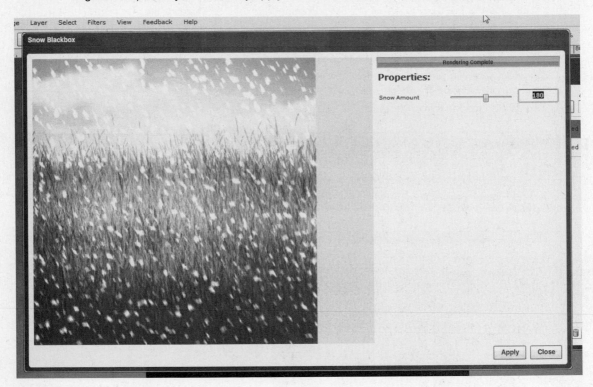

Figure 9-52. The Filter window lets you see a preview and set the parameters of the Blackbox.

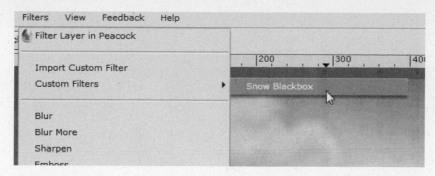

Figure 9-53. Access the filter at any time from the Filter menu.

Project review

Blackboxes are useful, self-contained effect files. They can take extra time to construct due to the extra pins and connectors; however, they save time when you want to reuse effects for many images. In this project, you got your first taste of Blackboxes. You learned how to expose parameters in hubs and link them to share information. UI Elements can be used to give you control over your Blackbox when applying the file to an image. This project barely scratched the surface of what a Blackbox can do. It is a complicated system, and it might take several attempts to get used to making them. However, after you know how to build them, they can help you in your other projects and enhance your image creation.

Chapter review

Aviary's applications are not just a group of graphic tools; they are more than their parts. These applications are closely integrated and enable you to share features between the tools. Application switching keeps you from interrupting your workflow. While working on an image in Phoenix, you can quickly switch to Raven and tap into its vector tools or jump to Peacock and add complex effects. Through this chapter, you learned about Phoenix's smart layers, which enable you to create an application-specific layer. These smart layers remain editable in their native applications. It is like nesting the power of the other applications in Phoenix itself. You then looked at how you can use application resources in Peacock. Just as in Phoenix's smart layers, these resources can be edited in another application. They are also updated after Peacock regains focus, making it easy to match the resource to the original file. Finally, you were introduced to Peacock's Blackbox system. These Blackbox files enable you tap into, reuse, and share Peacock effects. Now that you have been acquainted with Aviary's Graphic applications, you learn how you can extend your experience. In the next chapter, you see what other tools the Aviary.com site has to offer. You set up **Your Profile**, add feeds to **Your Dashboard**, and connect with other artists in the **Forum**. The site is almost an application in itself, helping to display, organize, and promote your artwork.

Chapter 10

Getting to Know Aviary.com

Aviary has more to offer than just launching applications for creating and editing images. The site is set up to exhibit your creations, give you notifications of changes, help you connect and collaborate with other artists, and much more. In this the final chapter, you learn how to maximize your experience using the Aviary site. You also learn how to set up an Avatar; a graphical representation of you on the site. You learn how to adjust your email notifications about almost any change to your creations, comments, activities, and more. You also personalize the Dashboard, your landing page for Aviary. Finally, you learn about how to participate in the large community of artists by using and exploring the forums.

Project 10.1—Setting Up Your Online Persona and Preferences

Now that you have created some images with Aviary, you can customize your experience to show off those images, go back to work on ones you've saved, or make derivatives. The first step to make Aviary work the way you want it to is to customize your profile settings.

Key concepts used in this project

- Changing your avatar
- Setting email notifications
- Assigning default permission and license settings

1. Go to your Profile page. From the Dashboard, click the egg image in the top right corner. This is your avatar and can used to represent you on the site. It is currently set to the default image, the egg (see Figure 10-1). Whenever you click it, you will be directed to Your Profile page. Or, you can access your profile using the **You ➤ Profile & Account Settings**. Here, you can set many options that pertain to your online persona on Aviary. There are three tabs at the top of the page: **Edit Your Profile**, **Notification Settings**, and **Permissions & License**.

Figure 10-1. Access your profile settings by clicking your avatar.

2. In the main area of your profile page, you can set personal information about yourself and you can specify who can view that information (see Figure 10-2). It is a good idea to write information about yourself in the **Your public bio** section. This is displayed on your personal page and introduces others to you. If you want, you can add you real name, birthday, gender, and home town to provide more information about yourself. Click the **Submit Your Updates** to save any changes to your profile. You can also set links to other sites. Others who want to know more about you can follow those links to a blog, your Twitter page, or even a social networking profile. Type the name you want to display on your page in the first textbox and in the second textbox, add the link. Add more links by clicking the **Add a new link** button. You can, of course, keep this information private if you choose. You must click the **Submit Your Links** button for the links to be saved.

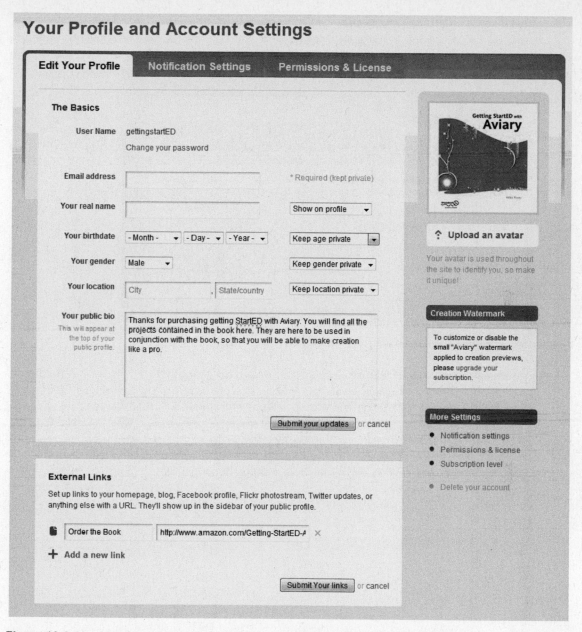

Figure 10-2. Your Profile page is where you set your Avatar and biographical information.

3. It is easy to customize your avatar with a graphic that will represent you on the site. Your avatar is an image that the site uses to represent you. Your creations, comments, feeds, and messages will have your avatar attached to them, so others can easily indentify your activity. Click the `Upload an avatar` button on the right and a dialog box that will let you access files on your computer displays

(see Figure 10-3). Click the **Browse** button, navigate to an appropriate avatar image, click **Open**, and then click **Upload** to make the image your avatar. The image you use should be over 175 pixels wide and high. It is automatically sized and cropped to a square shape. If you are using a large image, the subject should be in the center or it might be cropped from the image.

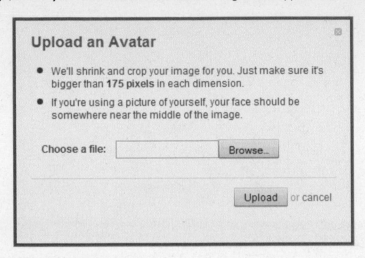

Figure 10-3. The Avatar upload dialog

4. Users with a **Pro** account can also control their watermark image or even remove it. A watermark is a small image that displays on all your images to show where the image comes from and to keep others from appropriating your image without your permission. Clicking the **Use custom watermark** option from the **Creation Watermark** dropdown menu opens the Upload dialog, where you can load your custom watermark (see Figure 10-4). Remember to keep the size small so that it doesn't cover too much of your image, as Aviary will not resize the watermark to fit specific dimensions. A good dimension for a watermark should be less than 75 pixels in either direction, and it is good to reduce the Alpha to 50%. This lets the watermark show but not be too obtrusive.

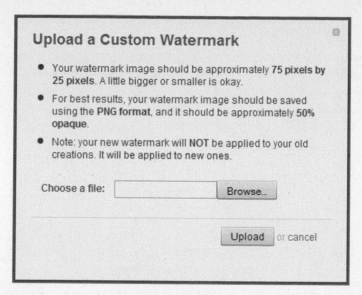

Figure 10-4. You can upload your own watermark if you have a `Pro` account.

5. To tell Aviary how and what you want email notifications for, you use the notification settings. Switch to the `Notification Setting` tab (see Figure 10-5). You can set up several different email notifications from this page. These notifications are sent to the email that you used during the setup process. You can get emails whenever another user marks as favorite or comments on any one of your creations. You can also set it so that you get an email notification when a derivative of one of your works is created, that is, when someone has built upon one of your public images. You can receive a notification when someone replies to one of your comments, a forum thread, or when someone sends you a private message. Finally, you can opt in to receive Aviary's weekly and monthly newsletter. You can set up any different combination of notifications to suit your needs. By default, you are sent all the email notifications except for the weekly and monthly newsletters.

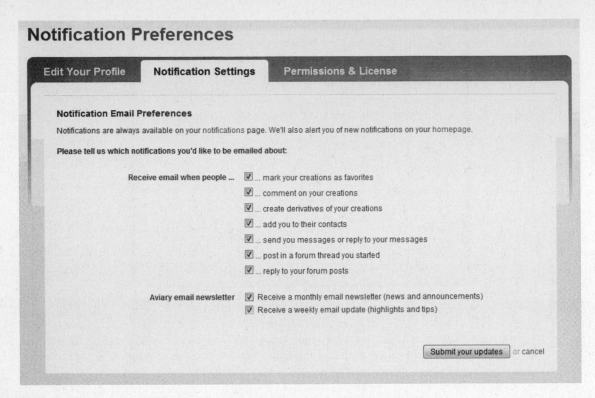

Figure 10-5. You can choose what notification, if any, you would like to receive.

6. Switch to the `Permissions & License` tab. This is where you set up your default viewing and editing permission on uploaded files and where you set up your default license on your creations (see Figure 10-6). All creations in Aviary can be set so certain people can have access to view or edit them. If you have a `Pro` member subscription, you can set permissions on an individual image, but here you can set up the default setting that is applied to your uploaded creations. These can even be set up to allow only certain contact groups from your contact list to access your files. There are three different levels of licenses that give usage rights for your images outside of the Aviary site. **Copyright** means no one outside of Aviary can use your work in any capacity without first obtaining your permission. **Creative Commons Attribution** means anyone outside of Aviary can use your work in any capacity without asking, provided they credit you and link back to your work. **Creative Commons Attribution-NonCommercial** means anyone outside of Aviary can use your work in a noncommercial capacity without asking, provided they credit you and link back to your work. You can set permissions for individual images during the saving process or on the individual creation's page. Furthermore, Aviary can use any of your images for advertising purposes and other users may make derivatives of your creations. For further information, review the Terms of Use at http://aviary.com/terms, or, for more information on Creative Commons licenses, visit http://creativecommons.org/about/licenses/.

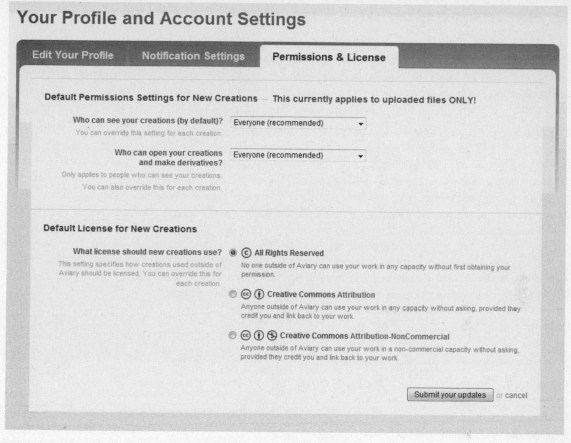

Figure 10-6. Set the default permission for your uploaded creations.

Project review

Aviary enables you to customize your experience on the site. You learned how to personalize your graphical representation your avatar, so others can easily recognize your comments, posts, creations, or messages. Combining any number of e-mail notifications can give you a customized way to follow many different actions on the site. Finally, you set the default permission and license settings for your images so you can control who can access and use them.

The Dashboard, your control panel to Aviary

When you sign into the Aviary site, you are greeted with `Your Dashboard`. The Dashboard is the control panel for Aviary. Here, you can get an overview of the site with feeds that enable you to keep track of your creations and other creations, groups, and activities. You can also launch the applications, get personal message notifications, and navigate to other pages on the site. This is your personal hub to all that Aviary has to offer.

The green bar at the top of the Dashboard page is your quick access to the inner workings of Aviary (see Figure 10-7). It is on almost every page of Aviary, so you can navigate around the site easily. The `You` menu gives you access to your profile, creations, favorites, and messages. The `Create` menu gives you buttons to launch all the applications and upload any image directly to the site. The `Contacts` menu lets you manage and explore your contacts and groups. The `Discover Creations` menu takes you to the Aviary gallery to see all the creations made with the applications. The `Tutorial` menu takes you to professional quality tutorials for the applications. The `Help` menu gives you more information about the site, applications, and lets you contact the staff directly. The `Forum` menu takes you to the community area of the site. The `Blog` menu takes you directly to the Aviary Blog where you can keep updated about application development. Finally, as you have seen, the avatar image gives you access to your profile, whereas the message icon notifies you when you have a personal message.

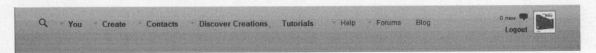

Figure 10-7. The navigation bar at the top of all the pages at Aviary enables you to move around the site.

On the right side of the page is another set of useful commands. There are quick launchers for all the applications and for uploading images. If you use Firefox, there is a direct link to install the **Talon** extension so you can launch the applications even when you are away from the site. Next are the advanced features for finding your friends, editing your profile, and setting a watermark. Below that are usage stats; this displays how much time you have spent in each of the applications.

In the center of the page is the Dashboard. Here, you can customize what information is seen by adding different feeds or modules (see Figure 10-8). At the top of this page is a greeting that lets you know that you're signed into the site and below that is the most resent blog posting. Clicking the title of the blog post takes you directly to it, whereas clicking the left and right arrows cycles through older posts. The area below is where any feeds that you have set up are shown. A **feed** is a dynamically generated information panel that updates frequently changing information. You can set several different types of feeds that provide information. There is an image feed showing thumbnails of the five most recent creations that meet the criteria you set for it. The list feed makes a list of eight of the most recent creations or activities for which the feed is set. Finally, there is a graph feed that shows a line graph illustrating the amount of creations or activity for the feeds setting.

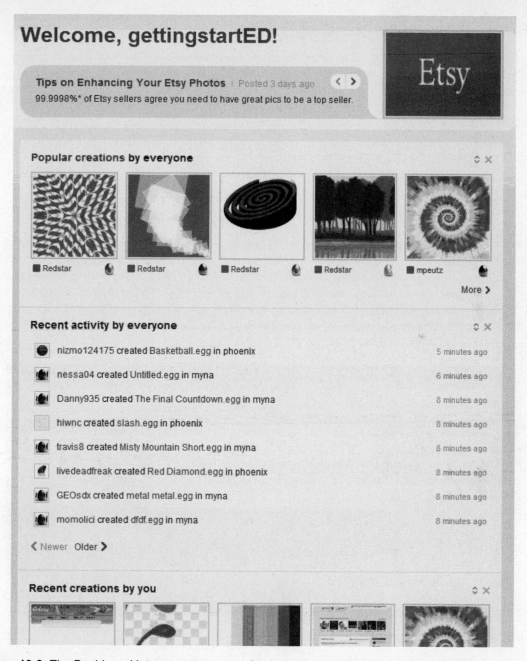

Figure 10-8. The Dashboard lets you set up many feeds to keep updated about site activities.

Project 10.2—Setting Up Feeds on Your Dashboard

The `Your Dashboard` is your best friend on Aviary. It gives you a quick overview of your creations and activities. In this project, you learn how to add new feeds, arrange them, and how to get the most out of `Your Dashboard`. These feeds can be set to give you a personalized view of Aviary. You can set the feeds to follow your friend's creations and activity. You can use feeds to monitor your groups or forum posts. You can even set up feeds to give you feedback on only your creations.

Key concepts used in this project

- Adding feeds
- Organizing feeds
- Removing feeds

1. First, you will remove unused feeds. Aviary automatically sets up seven feeds on `Your Dashboard` when you sign up. Most of these are useful, I but every feed that you have on `Your Dashboard` takes a little time to load and update. If you have eight or more feeds, you might see some slowdown of the page because it loads all the information. To remove a feed, click the red x icon in the upper right of each one; this removes the feed after a confirmation of the removal (see Figure 10-9). For this example, it is assumed that all the feeds have been removed for the Dashboard. You can leave ones that you find useful so you don't have to add them back later.

Figure 10-9. You have to confirm the removal of a feed.

2. You can add any number for feeds to the Dashboard. At the bottom of the dashboard, there is the `Add a new feed` button **+ Add a new feed** . This opens a dialog box that enables you to set three different types of feeds (see Figure 10-10).

What would you like to keep track of?

○ Recent creations [▾] by you [▾]

○ 30-day chart of views [▾] on all of your creations [▾]

○ Creations that match the search keywords: [   ]

[Add your feed]   or cancel

Figure 10-10. Feed setting dialog

3. Start by adding a feed that shows you all the new creations that have been made in Aviary (see Figure 10-11). Select the first radio button on the top option. In the next dropdown menu, leave it at its default setting of `Recent creations`. The other settings let you select `Recent Creations`, `Recent Activity`, or `Most Popular Creations`. This option sets what information is used in the feed. The `Recent creations` option creates an image feed showing five thumbnails of the information set by the second menu. The `Recent activity` creates a list feed showing comments, creations, and favorites based on the information set in the second menu. Finally, the `Most Popular` creations create an image feed filtering the popular creations based on the information set in the send menu. As implied previously, the second menu filters that information even more. You can set this to filter information `by you`, `by a specific contact`, `by a contact list`, `by all your contacts`, `in a specific group`, `in all your groups`, or `by everyone`. In the next dropdown menu, set it to the last setting of `by everyone`, so you can follow everyone's creations. Finally, confirm the addition of the feed by clicking the `Add your feed` button. You should see your new module added to `Your Dashboard` and displaying the five most recently created images in Aviary by all users.

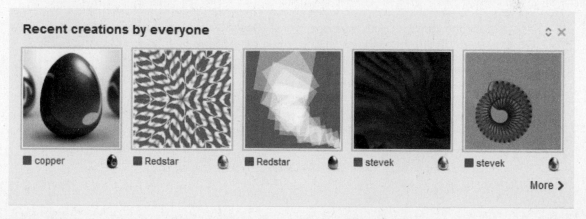

Recent creations by everyone ↕ ✕

■ copper   ■ Redstar   ■ Redstar   ■ stevek   ■ stevek

More ›

Figure 10-11. An image feed showing the most recent creations by everyone

4. Next, add a feed that shows a list of all the activities on your creations (see Figure 10-12). An activity can be any of the following: `created`, `uploaded`, `commented on`, or `gave a star to`. Again, click the `Add a new feed` button and select the first option; however, this time set the first dropdown to `recent activity` and the second to `on your creations`. Now, when you add this module to the Dashboard, you see a list of the last eight actions on your creations, including who performed the action and when they happened.

Recent activity on your items	⇕ ✕
☛ Redstar commented on Pin.png	1 day ago
☛ Redstar gave a star to Pin.png	1 day ago
◎ eXtc68 commented on Chapter 7 project 1.egg	3 days ago
⌒ you created Chapter 7 Project 2 Resource.egg in phoenix	3 days ago
⌒ you uploaded Peacock Header image.png	3 days ago
▬ you created Chapter 7 Project 2.egg in raven	3 days ago
▮ you created Chapter 7 Project 2 Color.egg in toucan	3 days ago
▬ you created Chapter 7 project 1.egg in peacock	3 days ago
‹ Newer Older ›	

Figure 10-12. A list feed showing activity on your creations

5. Add a chart to see how many other users view your creations (see Figure 10-13). This time, when you click the `Add a new feed`, select the second option. Leave the first and second dropdowns as is with `views` and `All your creations`. When you add this feed, you see a chart that displays all the views on your creations over the last 30 days. You can set the chart to show `Views`, `Favorites`, or `Comments` on `all your creations` or on `a specific creation`.

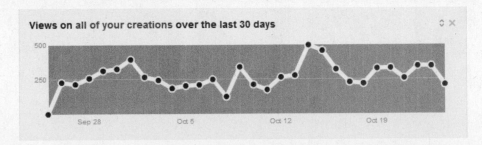

Figure 10-13. Monitor actions on your creations over the last month with the graph feed.

6.   Add an image feed based on a keyword (see Figure 10-14). If you want to keep track of images that follow a theme, you can set a keyword. Again, click the **Add a new feed button**, and this time select the third option, **Creations that match the search keywords**. In the textbox, type in the keywords that you want this feed to filter and separate them by a comma (,). For this example, use the keywords "Blue, Earth." When you add this feed, it produces an image grid of the 12 most recent images that fit with you keywords.

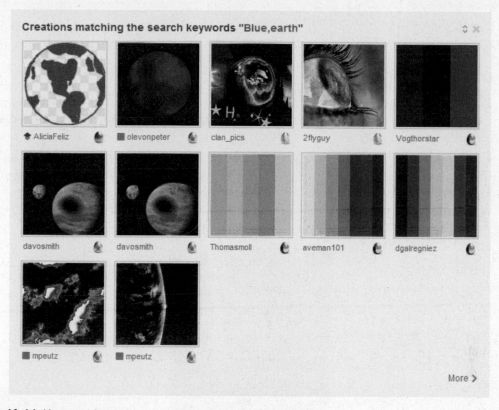

Figure 10-14. Keyword feeds let you follow images that fall into a theme.

7.   Now that you have a few feeds on **Your Dashboard**, you have better control of your surroundings at Aviary. You can change the order of these modules by dragging the double arrow icon. Moving them up or down automatically arranges the other feeds. You can add as many modules as you want, but each one takes time to update, so it is best to add only the most useful.

Project review

Your Dashboard is your landing area for Aviary, and adding feeds to it is easy and customizes your experience. Feeds filter, sort, and display information that follow criteria that you set. In this project, you learned that you can quickly modify the feeds by removing them, adding new feeds, and changing the order. After you have Your Dashboard set up, you can follow almost any activity that is performed on the site. In the next section, you see that you and each of your creations have a page at Aviary. These pages give you information and control over your creations.

Your profile page

Every user on Aviary has a personal profile page that shows their creations, biography, activities, and more. You can navigate to this profile page to manage your images. Other users can also go to this page to find more about you and your creations.

To get to your page, hover over the You menu in the navigation bar to open the dropdown, and select the Your Profile option (see Figure 10-15). Just clicking the You menu directs you to the Dashboard page. On Your Profile page, you should see your name and biography at the top of the page, a large version of your avatar, and various stats and links about you on the right sidebar. Finally, in the middle there is a content area with several tabs.

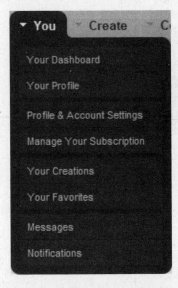

Figure 10-15. The You dropdown menu contains links to your Profile, Creations, and Settings.

At the top of Your Profile page, you see your username letting you know that this is your page. To the right of this is your subscription level. There are currently four different subscription levels; each has its own badge and functionality. The free subscription is a fledgling, the Pro subscription is the paid subscription with full functionality, and the green subscription is included with the Aviary book *More than One Way to Skin a Cat*. If you are a student, you can request a student subscription at a reduced price. It might take some time for your request to be completed because the staff reviews each application. There is a fifth level, but it is reserved for staff members. Below this is where your biography is displayed. This is the biographical information you set up when you edit your settings. In the top, right corner is your lifetime star count (see Figure 10-16).

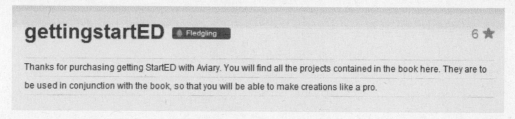

Figure 10-16. The top of `Your Profile` page.

Down the right side of `Your Profile` page are additional commands, statistics, and links (see Figure 10-17). Under you avatar is a link to edit your profile, which takes you to the page where you can set or change your biography, email address, links, and more. There is also a button to add a feed for your creations. Every artist has one of these links so if you come across an artist whose work you would like to follow, you can click this button on page to automatically add an image feed to `Your Dashboard`. Under that is a list of statistics about your activity on the site. Next is the area where your personal link is displayed. These are the links you set up while editing your profile. Then there are two links to add either creations or an activity RSS feed. This sends any new creations or activity to your feed reader such as Google reader Feedly or any other RSS reader. Finally, at the bottom is a link to flag this user. If you feel a user is inappropriate, you can send the user's profile to staff members so they can review and take action as necessary.

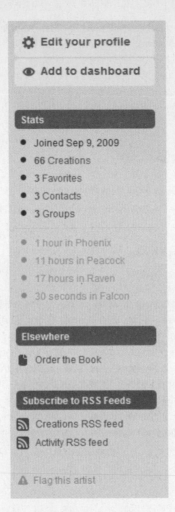

Figure 10-17. Find additional information about you in the sidebar.

The `Activity` tab shows thumbnails of your seven most recent creations (see Figure 10-18). Underneath that is a list of the most recent activities by you and the most recent activities performed on your creations. Like the Dashboard, this is a place where you can get an overview of what is going on in Aviary concerning you and your creations.

Figure 10-18. The `Activity` tab shows the actions you've made on the site or actions others have made on your creations.

The `Creations` tab shows a dozen thumbnails of your most recent creations (see Figure 10-19). You can sort and search with the dropdown menus at the top of this tab. Each one of your creations has its own page; you can go to that page by clicking the thumbnail image or the title.

Figure 10-19. From the `Creations` tab, you can view and manage all your creations.

The **Favorite** tab displays all the creations you have given a star (see Figure 10-20). You can give stars to any of the creations you come across on Aviary by clicking the star icon on the creation's page. Stars are a good way to save other's creations that you want to find later, and this gives the creator of that image a notification that someone liked his image. When someone stars your image, it is displayed next to that image and a total star count can be found at the top of the Your Artist page. After enough people have given a star to an image, it is promoted to the **Popular Creations** page. With even more stars, an image can get added to the **Hall of Fame** page. Both of these pages can be found by going to **Discover Creations ➤ Popular Creations**, and then selecting **Discover Creations ➤ Hall of Fame** from the green menu bar.

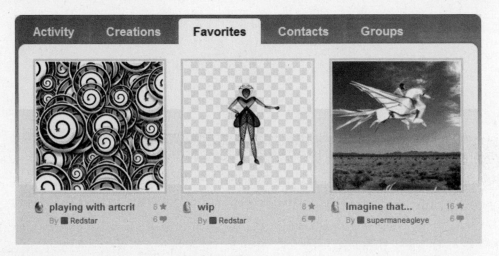

Figure 10-20. Shows images that you have given stars

The **Contacts** tab displays all your contacts or people who call you a contact (see Figure 10-21). Contacts are other users whose creations you want to keep track of or users you want to grant special permissions. You can see all your contacts' creations by choosing the option in the dropdown at the top. You can make anyone a contact by going to her **Profile** page and clicking the **Add to Contacts** button.

Figure 10-21. Find your contacts' images in the **Contacts** tab.

The `Groups` tab displays the Groups to which you have subscribed (see Figure 10-22). Groups provide a great way for you to set up little communities for work or play. Groups are essentially self-contained forums where you can gather users that want to focus on a common project, theme, or interest. They can be set to `public` with any user joining, or `private`, which requires an invitation to join and is not shown in the forum. Each group gets its own pool of creations, a discussion forum, and options for easy moderation. You can't start a group if you are at the free fledgling subscription level.

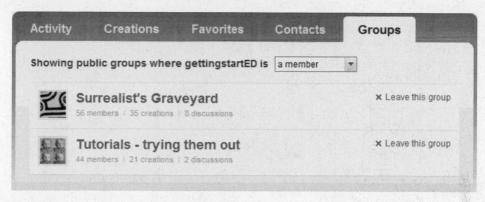

Figure 10-22. Keep track of your Group subscriptions.

Individual creation page

The individual creation page is where you can manage a creation. Clicking the thumbnail of any of your creations brings up its page. On the page, you can open It In any of Aviary's applications, manage the license, and delete and view stats and comments on the creation. The Page consists of a large preview of the image with five tabs for tracking information underneath, comments below that, and a sidebar with extra commands (see Figure 10-23).

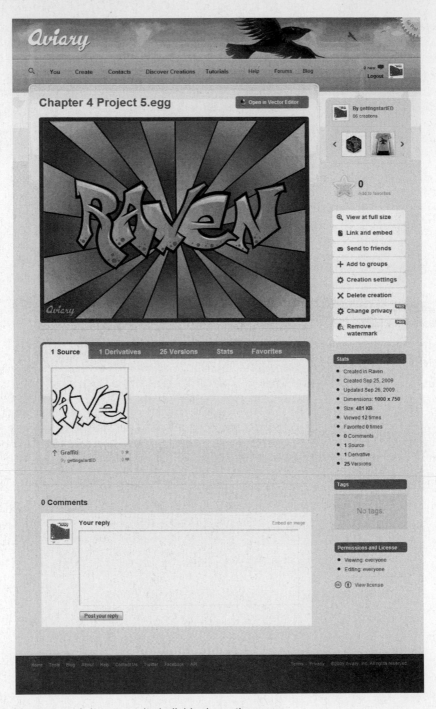

Figure 10-23. Manage each image on its individual creation page.

The creation is displayed in the main area of the page with its title above it. You can open the creation in the editor it was made with by clicking the `Open in` [application] button above the preview (see Figure 10-24). Alternately, if you hover over this button, you get a dropdown menu giving you the option to import the creation into a different Aviary application. If you have permission, you can open other users' files as well. Images that you do not have permission to open have a gray locked icon instead of the open button. If someone uses your file in their work, the work shows up as a derivative on the creations page.

Figure 10-24. The Open in button enables you to import the image into other Aviary applications.

The sidebar holds a lot of good information about the creation and commands for managing it. At the top is the creator of the image with that person's total creation count. Under this is a creations preview scroll bar where you can see the image made before and after this creation and scroll through a timeline of them. Next are the stars or `Favorite` button (see Figure 10-25). When you give a creation a star, you are given the opportunity to share it on various sites. Clicking the star a second time removes the star that you gave if you change your mind. After a creation has received a certain amount of stars over a period of time, it is added to the popular page. You can explore all the popular creations at `Discover Creations ➤ Popular Creations`.

Figure 10-25. Give creations stars to let the creator know that you liked it and to make it easy to find later.

Next, in the sidebar are several commands that perform various creation-specific functions (see Figure 10-26). These commands are different for different subscription levels. `View at full size` opens the creation in a blank page with no scaling reduction. There is a command for the `Pro` level subscriber that removes the watermark in the full-size view. The `Link and embed` command opens a dialog with code for linking the page, embedding in forum, posting in HTML, and even embedding a launcher to open the creation in the application. `Send to friends` opens a preformatted email that has links to the creation and a short message. `Add to groups` pushes the image to any group to which you belong. Creation settings let you edit the title, description, tags, permission, and license for the creation. Finally, you can use the `Delete creation` to remove the creation from your profile. However, if anyone has used the creation in their work as a derivative, they will still have a copy of it.

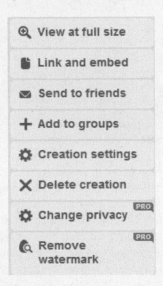

Figure 10-26. Sidebar commands for fledglings

In the Stats section, you can find when the creation was made or updated, its dimensions, how many sources were used in its construction, and more (see Figure 10-27). Tags that you add to your image are displayed in the tag section. Tags are used in the search functions, and it is good to add a few descriptive words to help find the image. Clicking any of these tags performs a search with that tag as the keyword. Finally, at the bottom of the sidebar are the license restrictions and permission levels for the creation.

Figure 10-27. Stats, tags, and license for the creation can be found in the sidebar.

Tracking information tabs

The tabbed section under the preview is where you find tracking information about this creation. Because Aviary allows other users to open and modify creations, it has a robust tracking system. This system logs and tracks who has used the creation in their works and which sources were used in a file, even if it has been altered beyond recognition. There is also a version history so at any time you can open a previously saved version of the file.

The first and default is the `Sources` tab (see Figure 10-28). It displays all the sources used to create the image. This means that any bitmaps or other files that were used to make this image are displayed here. It also shows who created the resource. Clicking them takes you to a creation page.

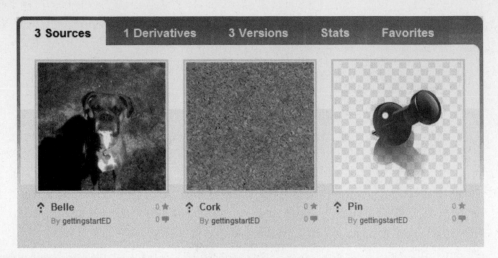

Figure 10-28. Outside resources used in the creation of an image show up in the `Sources` tab.

The `Derivatives` tab is where the images that used this file in one form or another are displayed (see Figure 10-29). This is an easy way to track who and how others use your work.

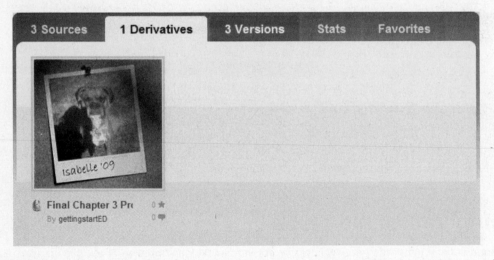

Figure 10-29. You can see what other artists have done with your work under the `Derivatives` tab.

The `Versions` tab displays all saved versions of the file (see Figure 10-30). Use this feature to open past iterations of a creation. Imagine, for example, you accidentally saved and closed a file before you realized it was wrong, or the power went out and you lost your work. You can just open a previous version and work from there.

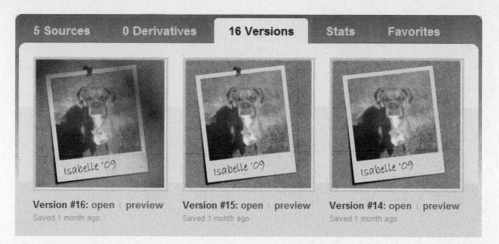

Figure 10-30. The `Versions` tab gives you access to older versions of the file.

The `Stats` tab displays a graph of views or comments on this creation by day and amount (see Figure 10-31). This is helpful to see how popular your image is in the community for the last 30 days.

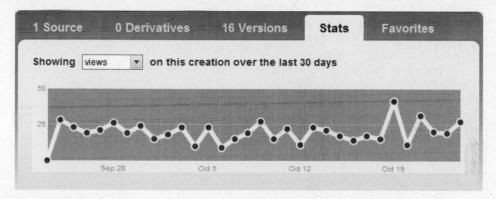

Figure 10-31. The `Stats` tab displays a graph of views or comments on the creation.

The `Favorites` tab shows all the users who gave this particular creation a star (see Figure 10-32). You can track which users liked this creation and even visit their profiles by clicking their avatar.

Figure 10-32. The `Favorites` tab show who gave the creation a star.

You and any other user can leave a message concerning the image in the area below the Tracking tabs in the Comment area (see Figure 10-33). Here, other users might make a statement about how cool your image is or ask questions about how you made it. You can reply to those comments if you choose. Type in your comment or response in the area provided and click the `Post your reply` button to commit the comment. If you update your creation after it has been commented on, the update shows up in the comments so that you will know which version of the image received which comment. If you have comment notifications set up, you receive a notification email when anyone comments on one of your creations.

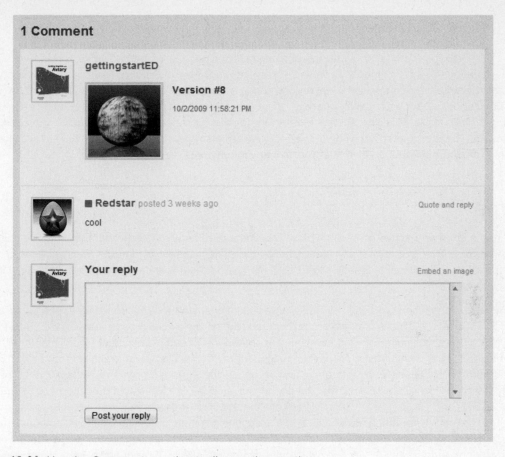

Figure 10-33. Use the Comments section to discuss the creation.

Profile and creation page review

At Aviary, every user gets a personal `Profile` page. Here you can manage virtually every aspect of your experience on the site. In this section, you explored the `Your Profile` page, looking at the various commands that you can perform regarding your creations and profile. The `Creations` tab lets you explore all the work you have made at Aviary ordered by most recent creations showing up first. In the `Favorites` tab, you can see all the images you ever gave a start to, which lets you find images later. The `Contacts` and `Groups` tabs let you see who you call a contact and what groups you belong to. The individual creations page lets you perform various actions and edits to the creation. It also helps you keep track of `sources`, `derivatives`, `versions`, `stats,` and who gave the creation a `star`. In the next section, you see how you can extend Aviary by using contacts, joining groups, participating in the community forum, and where to find help and tutorials.

Extending Aviary

By now you probably have seen all the graphic applications at Aviary and you have learned what to do with the creations you have made. However, Aviary has more to offer. From the beginning, Aviary was meant to be a learning and open site. Anyone can open another user's file to see how it was made. Users can organize into `groups` to collaborate and share ideas. If you have questions, the large and friendly community of artists is willing to answer them in the `forum` or by chat. You can set up `contact` lists, which makes it easy to keep up with your friends. Aviary also has an extensive `tutorial` section and user-generated `documentation` to help you with any rough spots.

Forums

Aviary has a large and active community of artists, and a great way to interact with them is to participate in the `Forum`. The `Forum` is an area where users can leave comments, ask questions, post suggestions, and start conversations. The `Forum` is split into several categories pertaining to different applications or themes.

The `Forum` is place where you can ask and answer questions, start friendly challenges, and connect with others. The threads or groups of posts are laid out as a list on the `Forums` page (see Figure 10-34). Each thread has a title and a category, and the user who started the thread is indicated. Under the Latest Reply column is the time and who posted the last comment in the thread. There is a green egg icon that displays the total number of comments in a thread. Clicking any of the threads opens that discussion so that you can read through and comment in the thread. In the sidebar are links to the different `discussion categories,` and clicking any of them filters the threads in that category. The category is the general theme that the forum thread follows. There is a category for each of the applications, announcements, collaborations, challenges, and more. You can even just see the threads from the groups to which you belong. Under that is a Search function, which you can use to search for a specific word or phrase in any of the comments. At the top, right is the `Start Discussion` button so you can start a new thread. Finally, you can subscribe to an RSS feed with any changes in the forum for your feed reader of choice.

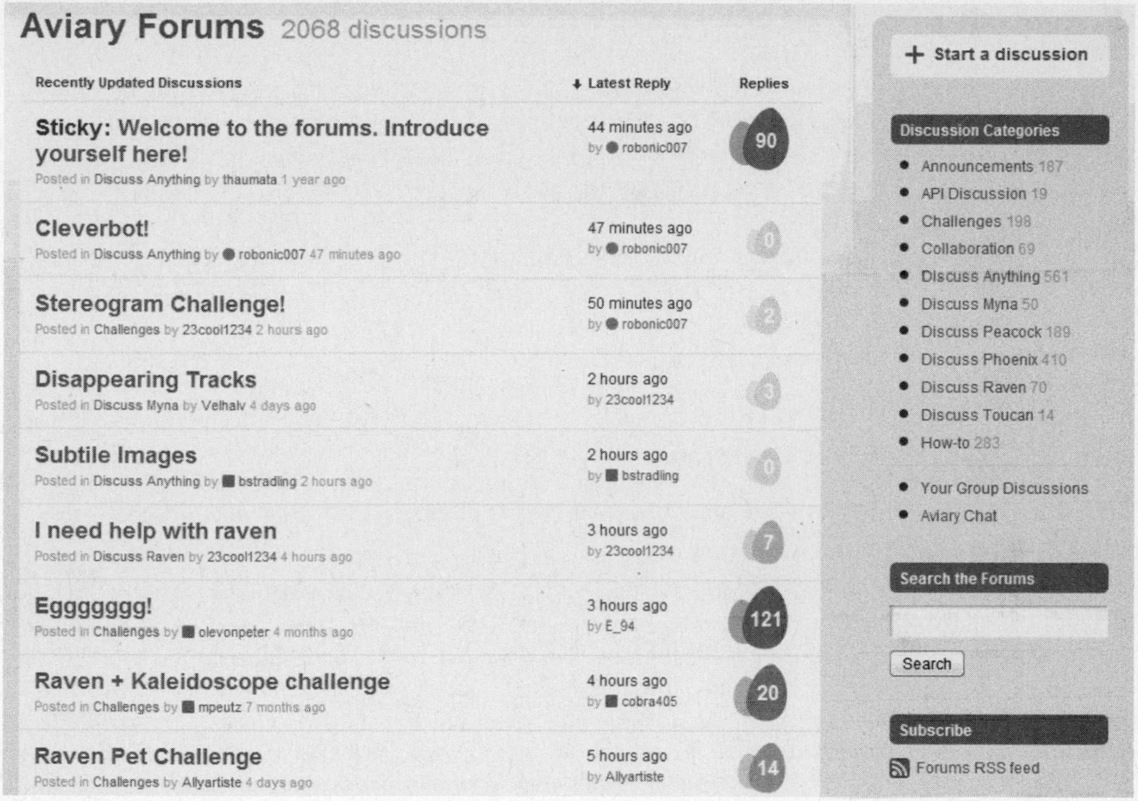

Figure 10-34. The Aviary forums are used to connect with other artists.

Groups

Groups are like private forums for specific discussions. Groups have their own forum threads and galleries. There are two levels of groups: **public** where anyone can join and participate, and **private**, where you must get an invitation from a moderator of the group to join. You can browse the public groups from the `Contacts` menu (see Figure 10-35).

Groups are a great way to organize a few users to collaborate, discuss a common theme, or collect images. Any user can join a public group, whereas you must have an invitation to join a private group. Only Pro subscription level users are allowed to start a new group. The user who starts a group is the moderator and has extra control over the group. A moderator can give others moderator rights, send invitations to others, manage members for the groups, change settings, and upload a group avatar. As a member of a group, you are able to start discussions, add a desktop feed to follow the discussions, or even leave the group. Discussions from the groups you belong to show up in the forum. These discussions have the group avatar attached so you can easily identify them from a regular forum discussion. You can also add any of your images to a group's image pool by using the `Add to Group` button on the individual creation page.

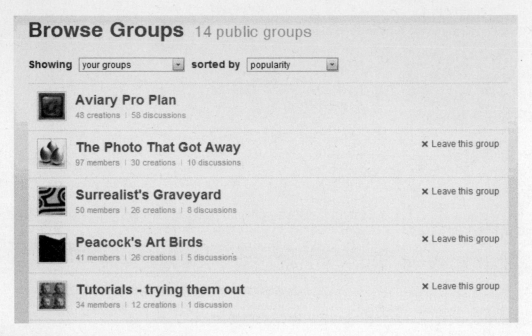

Figure 10-35. Browse the public groups.

Contacts

Using `Contacts` is a great way to keep track of other users' activities and creations. On any user's profile page, there is an `Add to contacts` button located under the user's avatar. Clicking this button adds this user to your contacts. This is a one-way action; the user will be notified that you added them as a contact and in return, the user might add you to her contacts.

You can do many things with your contacts. You can set up dashboard feeds to follow all, a list of, or a single contact's creations or actions. You can see all your contact's creations by selecting the `contacts creations` option from the dropdown menu in the `Contacts` tab on Your `Profile` page. You can even set view and editing permissions for all your contacts, contacts on a list, and a single contact. You can manage these contacts with the `Contacts Manager` by selecting the `Organize Your Contacts` link from the `Contacts` tab (see Figure 10-36). In the `Contacts Manager` page, you can set up different lists of contacts so that you can give groups of contacts access to your creations. To make a contact list, click the `New contact list` and name this list. Next, check the box next to each contact you want to add to this list. Finally, click the `Add to contact list` in the right sidebar and select the list to add these contacts. A contact can belong to several different lists. You can customize these lists to allow you to have complex control over who can access and view your creations.

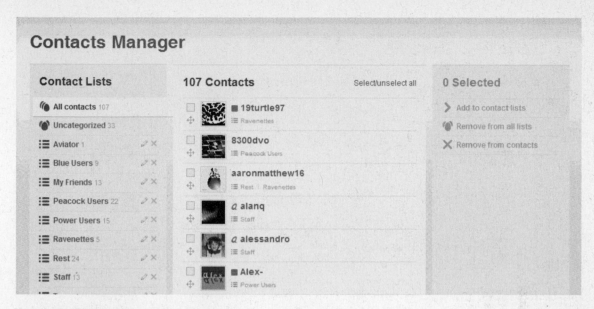

Figure 10-36. Manage contacts lists.

Tutorials, help, and documentation

Aviary has more than 70 professional tutorials with more being added every day. These are informative, and it is highly recommended that you refer to them. The `Aviary Tutorials` are separated by application and difficulty (see Figure 10-37). You can view them either as individual steps or as a single page.

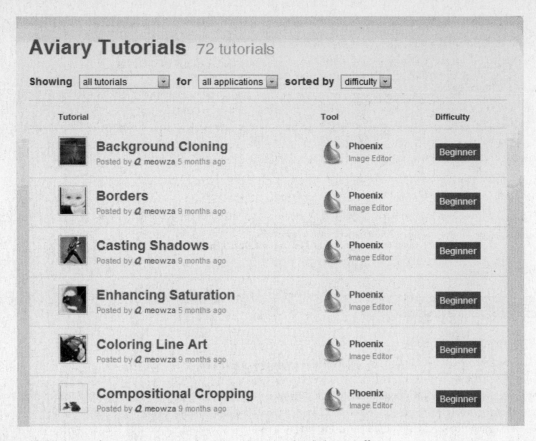

Figure 10-37. Learn from some great tutorials written by the Aviary staff.

On the `Help` page of the site, you can find a lot of useful information (see Figure 10-38). You can use the `Contact Us` feature to send a direct message to the staff. You should contact them if you find a bug, have a great suggestion for improving the site, find an abusive user, or just want to give general feedback. The staff is friendly and wants any help that makes the site and tools better. You can find an `FAQ` (or frequently asked questions) that answers basic questions about the site. Finally, you can find information about the subscription levels and pricing.

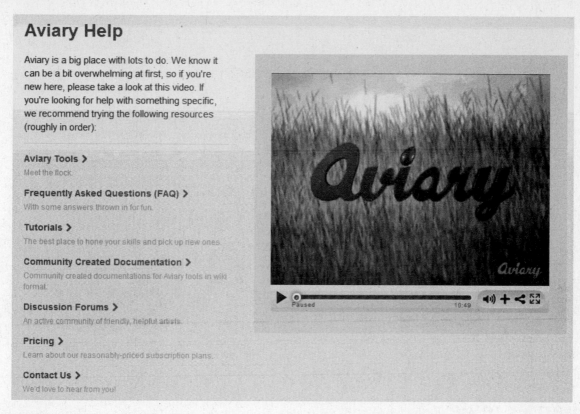

Aviary Help

Aviary is a big place with lots to do. We know it
can be a bit overwhelming at first, so if you're
new here, please take a look at this video. If
you're looking for help with something specific,
we recommend trying the following resources
(roughly in order):

Aviary Tools >
Meet the flock.

Frequently Asked Questions (FAQ) >
With some answers thrown in for fun.

Tutorials >
The best place to hone your skills and pick up new ones.

Community Created Documentation >
Community created documentations for Aviary tools in wiki
format.

Discussion Forums >
An active community of friendly, helpful artists.

Pricing >
Learn about our reasonably-priced subscription plans.

Contact Us >
We'd love to hear from you!

Figure 10-38. The Help page gives you access to many useful features at Aviary.

A good resource for getting to know the applications is the `Community Created Documentation`. It is
a basic manual for the applications and is written by the users (see Figure 10-39). It gives you a brief
overview of the application and explanations of each tool or hub. You should use them as references when
you have questions about how a tool or function works.

Figure 10-39. The `Community Created Documentation` is a great reference resource.

Chapter review

Aviary has an impressive suite of graphic editors, but the site is what ties everything together. Aviary lets you display, share, and collaborate on your images. You saw how you can set up your profile and your avatar to let other users get to know you. There was a project teaching you how to customize Your Dashboard with different feeds, making the site work the way you like. You explored your personal and individual creation page and learned about the vast information at your fingertips. The site also lets you extend your experience by giving you access to the large artist community with the forums, groups, and contacts. Finally, the Help page has many useful resources for new and experienced users.

Conclusion

Aviary and its applications is a liberating service. It gives everyone the opportunity to create, edit, and explore graphics, without the heavy cost of many similar desktop applications. The motto, is "Creation on the Fly," and it is well suited to what Aviary represents. The service is hosted online so you do not need to have any special software or operating system to create images, which gives you the freedom to create almost anywhere on almost every computer. You first worked with Phoenix, Aviary's image manipulator. With the projects, you saw how you can edit and modify resources into high-quality images. Adjusting colors and fixing blemishes lets you enhance your images. Then, you worked with Raven, Aviary's vector editor. Raven gave you the tools to create professional quality designs, logos, icons, and more. You became familiar with the Bezier and Line tool, which is the heart and soul for creating vector paths. You used the powerful Trace feature to convert bitmaps into vector images. There isn't anything quite like it available as an online service. Peacock, Aviary's effects editor, might arguably be the most powerful application in the suite. You learned about the hub and connection workflow that enables you to build complex and varied effect chains. You saw how you can create various textures that can be used in other applications, even outside of Aviary. Next, you worked with Toucan, the color palette editor at Aviary. You created color palettes using the color formula or sampled from an image and used them in other applications. Talon, Aviary's Firefox and Falcon, the Markup editor, are useful tools to round out the suite. You used Talon to capture resources from around the Web. You then used Falcon's speed to make quick notes and edits. Aviary's applications are powerful on their own but when used with application switching, it rivals most desktop editors. You learned how to switch in and out of different applications giving you the ability to use almost every tool Aviary offers. Finally, you learned about the features the Aviary site itself had to offer. From sharing and collaborating to building upon others' work, the site is more than a collection of tools. This book has only scratched the surface of what can be done with the Aviary suite of tools. It is now up to you to explore, experiment, and grow by building off the basic techniques. You have the tools to create on the fly; now get out there and create.

Appendix A

Examples of the Various Blend Modes

Blend Modes are used throughout Aviary's applications to combine two separate layers. Each mode follows a formula for determining how one layer is affected by another. Blend Modes can affect Alphas, brightness values, and hues. Knowing what each Blend Mode does will enable you to create better images and effects. This appendix gives examples of each of the currently available Blend Modes. The chapter is split into Blend Modes used in Phoenix and Raven and the advanced Blend Modes used in Peacock.

Blend Modes for Phoenix and Raven

Phoenix and Raven use the same Blend Modes, and for the most part, those Blend Modes have the same results. To show the results of each Blend Mode, these examples use a simple image of a circle being overlapped by a square. In all the examples, the circle in the lower layer is referred to as the **Base layer**, whereas the square in the upper layer is referred to as the **Blending layer**.

In the Normal Blend Mode (see Figure A-1), the layers maintain their own native properties and are not blended together. The upper layer covers the lower layer.

Figure A-1. The Normal Blend Mode

The Add Blend Mode adds the color values of the Base layer with the Blending layer (see Figure A-2). Any area with a maximum value is displayed as white. This greatly intensifies the lighter areas.

Figure A-2. The Add Blend Mode

The Alpha Blend Mode masks the Base layer by the Alpha in the Blending layer (see Figure A-3). This Blend Mode hides the Blending layer only in Phoenix and Raven.

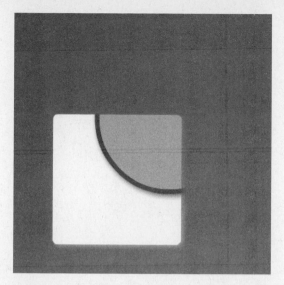

Figure A-3. The Alpha Blend Mode

The Darken Blend Mode uses multiple Blend Modes on areas where the Blending layer is lighter than the Base layer (see Figure A-4). This gives an overall darkness to the lightest areas of the Base layer.

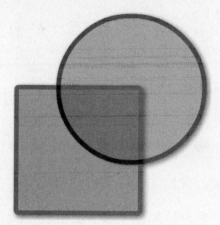

Figure A-4. The Darken Blend Mode

The Difference Blend Mode inverts the colors in the Blending layer and subtracts the results from the Base layer (see Figure A-5). If both layers are the same, the result will be black. This Blend Mode shows any differences in similar layers and is useful to align two of the same layers.

Figure A-5. The Difference Blend Mode

The Erase Blend Mode masks the Base layer by the invert of the Alpha in the Blending layer (see Figure A-6). This Blend Mode hides only the Blending layer in Phoenix and Raven.

Figure A-6. The Erase Blend Mode

The Hardlight Blend Mode combines both the Screen and Multiply Blend Modes (see Figure A-7). The overall effect intensifies colors in the Blending layer; darker areas get darker, and lighter areas get lighter. The 50% values are not affected.

Figure A-7. The Hardlight Blend Mode

The Invert Blend Mode inverts colors in the Base layer that is covered by the Blending layer (see Figure A-8). The transparent areas in the Base layer are displayed as black.

Figure A-8. The Normal Blend Mode

The Lighten Blend Mode uses Screen Blend Mode on areas where the Blending layer is darker than the Base layer (see Figure A-9). This gives an overall lightening to the darkest areas of the Base layer.

Figure A-9. The Lighten Blend Mode

The Layer Blend Mode currently produces the same effect as the Normal Blend Mode (see Figure A-10). This Blend Mode will change in the future to give it added usability.

Figure A-10. The Layer Blend Mode

The Multiply Blend Mode multiples the Base layer and the Blending layer colors (see Figure A-11). White areas in the Blending layer turn transparent, and only the darker colors appear. Because this Blend Mode removes the white areas from the Blending layer, it is useful for quickly cutting out white backgrounds from images. You can think of this Blend Mode as the opposite of Screen.

Figure A-11. The Multiply Blend Mode

The Overlay Blend Mode combines both Screen and Multiply Blend Modes such as Hardlight (see Figure A-12). However, Overlay preserves the color in the Base layer and gives a more subtle blend than Hardlight. The overall effect intensifies colors in the Blending layer; darker areas get darker, and lighter areas get lighter. The mid range values are not affected.

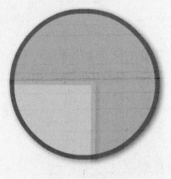

Figure A-12. The Overlay Blend Mode

The Screen Blend Mode divides the Base layer and Blending layer colors (see Figure A-13). Black areas in the Blending layer become transparent, and lighter areas get lighter. You can think of this Blend Mode as the opposite of Multiply.

Figure A-13. The Screen Blend Mode

The Subtract Blend Mode subtracts the Blending layer from the Base layer (see Figure A-14). Any resulting negative values are displayed as black.

Figure A-14. The Subtract Blend Mode

Peacock Blend Modes

The Normal, Add, Alpha, Darken, Difference, Hardlight, Lighten, Multiply, Overlay, Screen, and Subtract Blend Modes are also used in Peacock. However, it also has a few advanced modes in the Blender hub. These advanced Blend Modes are more complicated, and take more time to render.

The Linear Blend Mode takes averages the brightness of the Blending layer and the brightness of the Base layer and uses that information as the brightness information for the Base layer (see Figure A-15). Any 100% transparent areas in the Blending layer produce black in the image.

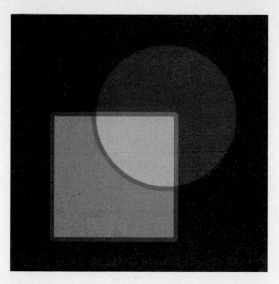

Figure A-15. The Linear Blend Mode

The Hue Blend Mode changes the hue of the Base layer to the hue of the Blending layer (see Figure A-16). Any transparent areas change the Base layer's hue to red.

Figure A-16. The Hue Blend Mode

The Saturation Blend Mode uses the saturation of the Blending layer to set the saturation in the Base layer (see Figure A-17). Any pure transparent areas in the Blending layer will turn the pixels in the Base layer red.

Figure A-17. The Saturation Blend Mode

The Brightness Blend Mode takes the brightness of the Blending layer and uses that information as a Multiply blended overlay (see Figure A-18). This Blend Mode changes any areas that are transparent to black.

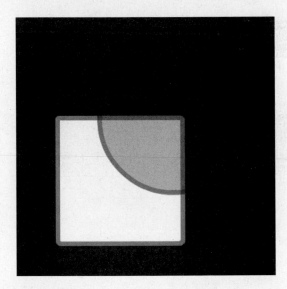

Figure A-18. The Brightness Blend Mode

The Layover Blend Mode is an exaggerated version of the Overlay Blend Mode (see Figure A-19). This Blend Mode produces more contrast between the two layers than the Overlay Blend Mode.

Figure A-19. The Layover Blend Mode

The Lighter Cover Blend Mode takes the lighter value from either the Blending or Base layers and covers the other layer (see Figure A-20).

Figure A-20. The Lighter Cover Blend Mode

The Darker Cover Blending Mode takes the darker value from either the Blending or Base layers and covers the other layer (see Figure A-21).

Figure A-21. The Darker Cover Blend Mode

Wrap, XOR, AND, and OR Blend Modes convert the color values of each pixel in the Blending layer and Base layer to a string of numbers; they then perform a mathematical function on them. The resulting numbers are converted back into a color value to produce the Blend Mode output. These methods can produce abstract and unpredictable results, and the more variety and detail in the original layers, the more abstract the result. Following are examples of the Wrap (see Figure A-22), XOR (see Figure A-23), AND (see Figure A-24), and OR (see Figure A-25).

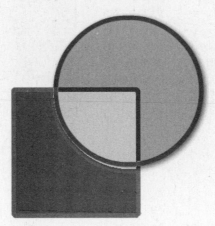

Figure A-22. The Wrap Blend Mode

Figure A-23. The XOR Blend Mode

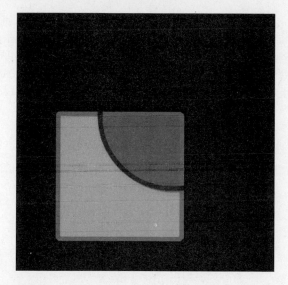

Figure A-24. The AND Blend Mode

Figure A-25. The OR Blend Mode

Blend Modes are an indispensable tool in almost every layer-based graphic editor. They can be difficult to predict; the Blend Mode that works great in one image can give you an undesirable result in another. It is recommended that you try several different Blend Modes while building your image to see which works the best. Experiment, explore, and play with this powerful tool because the more you use it, the easier it is to understand.

Appendix B

The Color Picker Tool

The **Color Picker** is a versatile multifunction tool used to choose colors. Raven, Phoenix, and Peacock use the same color picker (see Figure B-1). Falcon uses its own simple color picker to keep the application quick, and Toucan is essentially a color picker itself. The Color Picker pops up when you need to choose a color.

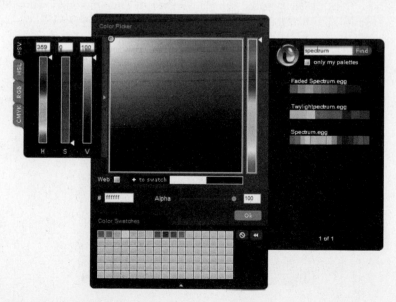

Figure B-1. The Color Picker dialog with all the fly-out panels open

Whenever you need to choose a color in Phoenix, Raven, or Peacock, the applications open the color picker tool (see Figure B-2). The Color Picker pops up, enabling you to pick colors, import Toucan color palettes, and save swatches.

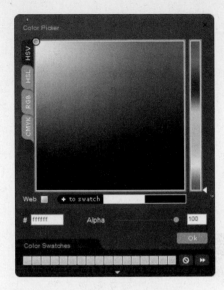

Figure B-2. Initially, the Color Picker's fly-out panels are hidden.

In the center of the Color Picker is an area where you can choose the brightness and saturation of the color (see Figure B-3). The small circle is the sample point and is centered on the currently selected color. Clicking and dragging this circle lets you change the current color.

Figure B-3. The color choosing area

To the right of the color chooser area in the center is the hue slider (see Figure B-4). This looks like a vertical gradient colorbar with a single color stop. This slider changes the hue or color of the center color chooser area.

Figure B-4. The hue slider changes the main color in the color chooser area.

The current selected color shows up in the color display box below the color chooser area (see Figure B-5). This box also shows the previously selected color from the last time the Color Picker was used. The two colors are displayed side by side, which makes it easy to compare them. To the left of this box is the + to swatch button. Pressing this button saves the currently selected color to the swatch area at the bottom of the Color Picker (see Figure B-14).

Figure B-5. The color display box shows the current and previously selected colors.

The transparency of the current color is set with the Alpha slider (see Figure B-6). You can also type a number in the text box to set a specific Alpha value between 0–100.

Figure B-6. The Alpha slider controls the transparency of the current color.

Hexadecimal color codes can be input in the # box (see Figure B-7). These are color codes used in HTML, CSS, and more. Many of the projects in this book are referenced in hexadecimal, and you can input those values in this textbox to get the same color.

Figure B-7. Hexadecimal color codes can be input into the Color Picker.

Enabling the Web option constrains the colors in the picker to Web-safe colors (see Figure B-8). Web-safe colors are a predefined set of colors that will display the same way on different platforms and browsers. This is useful for designing images that will be used as web resources and must have consistent colors across many different platforms.

Figure B-8. The Web option constrains the colors to Web-safe only.

When you are satisfied with your color selection, commit to your file with the Ok button (see Figure B-9). The Color Picker window closes and your color selection shows up in your file. To cancel your color selection and close the Color Picker window, click the X in the top right corner.

Figure B-9. The Ok button commits your color selection to the file and closes the Color Picker.

Clicking one of the tabs on the left opens the color sliders (see Figure B-10). Each tab controls a different color space. To close the color sliders fly-out, click the gray bar with the arrow to the right. These sliders act the same as the one in Toucan. See Chapter 7 for more information on color spaces and color sliders. Following are the four available color spaces that can be accessed from the slider fly-out:

1. **HSV** = Hue, Saturation, Value
2. **HSL** = Hue, Saturation, Lightness
3. **RGB** = Red, Green, Blue
4. **CMYK** = Cyan, Magenta, Yellow, Key (or Black)

Colors can be adjusted with the sliders or by typing in specific values in the textboxes.

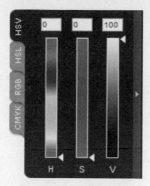

Figure B-10. For more accurate color selection, you can use the color sliders.

Toucan color palettes can be imported into the Color Picker to be used throughout your creation (see Figure B-11). Open or close the palette loader by clicking the double arrow button (see Figure B-12). Locate palettes by inputting search terms in the search box and pressing the Find button. Enabling the only my palettes option constrains the search to only Toucan palettes that you have made. After the desired palette is found, load it into the Color Swatches panel by clicking the arrow icon next to it (see Figure B-13). All the colors in the palette are loaded as a swatch and are available every time the color picker tool Is loaded in the session (see Figure B-14).

Figure B-11. The Toucan palette importer loads color palettes into the Color Picker.

Figure B-12. The double arrow button opens and closes the Toucan palette importer fly-out.

Figure B-13. The arrow button loads the currently selected palette into the Colors Pickers swatch area.

Swatches are saved color samples. The Color Picker displays all the saved swatches each time they are opened. The color picker's Color Swatches panel can save over 100 colors. Add color swatches by dragging a color to the Color Swatches panel, clicking the + to swatch button (see Figure B-5), or loading from the Toucan palette importer (see Figure B-11).

Figure B-14. Color swatches save many sampled colors for use throughout your file.

All swatches can be removed from the swatch area by clicking the Clear button.

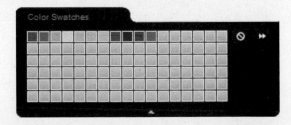

Figure B-15. Clear all the colors from the swatch area with this Clear button.

The Color Picker is a powerful color-choosing tool that is available in Phoenix, Raven, and Peacock. You can even think of it as Toucan lite. The Color Picker lets you select colors and set Alphas several different ways: adjusting sliders, sampling from an image, hexadecimal color codes, and more. You can also import color palettes from Aviary's full feature color-picking application Toucan and use these palettes to unify your images' color schemes. Your color choices are virtually limitless with this handy tool.

Index

Z

You Need the Companion eBook

Your purchase of this book entitles you to buy the companion PDF-version eBook for only $10. Take the weightless companion with you anywhere.

We believe this Apress title will prove so indispensable that you'll want to carry it with you everywhere, which is why we are offering the companion eBook (in PDF format) for $10 to customers who purchase this book now. Convenient and fully searchable, the PDF version of any content-rich, page-heavy Apress book makes a valuable addition to your programming library. You can easily find and copy code—or perform examples by quickly toggling between instructions and the application. Even simultaneously tackling a donut, diet soda, and complex code becomes simplified with hands-free eBooks!

Once you purchase your book, getting the $10 companion eBook is simple:

1. Visit **www.apress.com/promo/tendollars/**.

2. Complete a basic registration form to receive a randomly generated question about this title.

3. Answer the question correctly in 60 seconds, and you will receive a promotional code to redeem for the $10.00 eBook.

233 Spring Street, New York, NY 10013

Offer valid through 4/10.